CliffsNotes®

Praxis I®: PPST® with CD-ROM

4TH EDITION

by

Jerry Bobrow, Ph.D.

Contributing authors:

Ed Kohn, M.S.

Joy Mondragon-Gilmore, M.S.

Jean Eggenschwiler, M.A.

WILEY

Wiley Publishing, Inc.

About the Author

Jerry Bobrow, PhD, was a national authority in the field of test preparation. As founder of Bobrow Test Preparation Services, he administered test preparation programs at over 25 California institutions for more than 30 years. Dr. Bobrow authored over 30 national best-selling test preparation books, and his books and programs have assisted more than 2 million test-takers. Each year, the faculty at Bobrow Test Preparation Services lectures to thousands of students on preparing for graduate, college, and teacher credentialing exams.

Publisher's Acknowledgments

Editorial
Project Editor: Greg Tubach

Project Editor: Christina Stambaugh

Production
Proofreaders: Melissa D. Buddendeck, John Greenough, Lindsay Littrell

Graphics: Nikki Gately, Ronald G. Terry

Wiley Publishing Inc. Composition Services

CliffsNotes® Praxis I®: PPST® with CD-ROM, 4th Edition

Published by:

Wiley Publishing, Inc.

111 River Street

Hoboken, NJ 07030-5774

www.wiley.com

Published by Wiley, Hoboken, NJ

Published simultaneously in Canada

ISBN: 978-0-470-45455-8

Library of Congress Control Number: 2009933754

Printed in the United States of America

10 9 8 7 6 5 4 3 2

For general information on our other products and services or to obtain technical support please contact our Customer Care Department within the U.S. at (877) 762-2974, outside the U.S. at (317) 572-3993 or fax (317) 572-4002.

Wiley also publishes its books in a variety of electronic formats. Some content that appears in print may not be available in electronic books. For more information about Wiley products, please visit our web site at www.wiley.com.

Dedication

This book is dedicated to the memory of Dr. Jerry Bobrow, award-winning author and educator who assisted thousands of prospective teachers in reaching career goals. Dr. Bobrow died prior to the publication of this book after a two-year battle with cancer. His life-long commitment to helping others seek advancement through higher education continues with *CliffsNotes Praxis I: PPST.* Dr. Bobrow recognized that all people have unique abilities, and believed that one's highest potential is achieved through learning. Born in Rome, Italy, he is survived by his wife, Susan of 33 years, his children Jennifer, Adam, and Jonathan, and his parents Abram and Julia Bobrow, both Holocaust survivors.

Acknowledgments

This book would not be possible without the collaborated efforts of a team of professional educators and administrators at school districts throughout California. Sincere thanks and appreciation are extended to Michele Spence, formerly of CliffsNotes, Inc., for reviewing the original manuscript; to Linnea Fredrickson and Melinda Masson for proofreading the revised edition; and to Christina Stambaugh of Wiley Publishing for her dedication and careful attention to editing details during the production process.

Table of Contents

PART I: INTRODUCTION

PART II: ANALYSIS OF EXAM AREAS

PART IV: SELECTIVE REVIEW OF GRAMMAR AND USAGE

PART V: FOUR FULL-LENGTH PRACTICE TESTS

Preface

We know that achieving a high score on the PPST is important to you, and thorough preparation is the key to doing your best! This guide is designed to provide you with the information necessary for a comprehensive and successful preparation while reintroducing you to some basic skills and knowledge that you may not have used in many years. To help increase your understanding of the test, we have included a complete analysis of exam areas and question types, instructional problem-solving explanations, up-to-date examples, and extensive practice in **four full-length practice tests.**

In keeping with the fine tradition of CliffsNotes, this material was carefully researched and developed by leading test preparation experts and instructors. The strategies and time-saving techniques have been tested and evaluated in test preparation programs presently being used at many colleges and universities.

To make it easy to follow, this guide is organized into five different parts:

Part I: Introduction—general description of the paper-based and computer-based exams, recent format of the exams, questions commonly asked basic overall strategies, and a tutorial for the computer-based exam.

Part II: Analysis of Exam Areas—focuses on ability tested, basic skills necessary, directions, analysis, suggested approaches with samples, and additional tips.

Part III: Mathematics Review—brief, but intensive, review in the basics of arithmetic, algebra, and intuitive geometry, with diagnostic tests in each area. Important terminology is also included.

Part IV: Selective Review of Grammar and Usage—concise review focusing on avoiding some of the most common grammar and usage errors.

Part V: Four Full-Length Practice Tests—three complete, full-length practice tests with answers and in-depth explanations geared toward the paper-based exam and one full-length computer-based practice test with answers and in-depth explanations.

This guide is not meant to substitute for comprehensive courses, but if you follow the Study Guide Checklist on the next page and study regularly, you will get the best PPST preparation possible.

Study Guide Checklist

❑ 1. Read the PPST information materials available at the Testing Office, Counseling Center, or Credential Preparation Office at your undergraduate institution.

❑ 2. Become familiar with the paper-based and computer-based test formats (page 4).

❑ 3. Read the general description and "Questions Commonly Asked about the PPST," (pages 5–6).

❑ 4. Learn the techniques of two successful overall approaches (pages 7–10).

❑ 5. Carefully read Part II, "Analysis of Exam Areas," (pages 15–90).

❑ 6. Review mathematical terminology (pages 93–100).

❑ 7. Take the "Arithmetic Diagnostic Test," (page 101); check your answers and review the appropriate areas in the "Arithmetic Review" (pages 103–119).

❑ 8. Take the "Algebra Diagnostic Test," (page 121); check your answers and review the appropriate areas in the "Algebra Review" (pages 122–128).

❑ 9. Take the "Geometry Diagnostic Test," (pages 129–131); check your answers and review the appropriate areas in the "Geometry Review" (pages 134–148).

❑ 10. Study Part IV, "Selective Review of Grammar and Usage" (pages 149–164).

❑ 11. Strictly observing time allotments, take Practice Test 1 (pages 169–199).

❑ 12. Check your answers and analyze your Practice Test 1 results (pages 200–201).

❑ 13. Fill out the tally sheet for questions missed to pinpoint your mistakes (page 201).

❑ 14. Study **all** the answers and explanations for Practice Test 1 (pages 205–214).

❑ 15. Have a friend or English instructor read and evaluate your essay using the "Essay checklist" (page 203).

❑ 16. Review weak areas as necessary.

❑ 17. Strictly observing time allotments, take Practice Test 2 (pages 217–249).

❑ 18. Check your answers and analyze your Practice Test 2 results (pages 250–251).

❑ 19. Fill out the tally sheet for questions missed to pinpoint your mistakes (page 251).

❑ 20. Study **all** the answers and explanations for Practice Test 2 (pages 255–265).

❑ 21. Have a friend or English instructor read and evaluate your essay using the "Essay checklist" (page 253).

❑ 22. Strictly observing time allotments, take Practice Test 3 (pages 269–301).

❑ 23. Check your answers and analyze your Practice Test 3 results (pages 302–303).

❑ 24. Fill out the tally sheet for questions missed to pinpoint your mistakes (page 303).

❑ 25. Study **all** the answers and explanations for Practice Test 3 (pages 307–317).

❏ 26. Have a friend or English instructor read and evaluate your essay using the "Essay checklist" (page 305).

❏ 27. Strictly observing time allotments, take Practice Test 4 (pages 321–361).

❏ 28. Check your answers and analyze your Practice Test 4 results (pages 362–363).

❏ 29. Fill out the tally sheet for questions missed to pinpoint your mistakes (page 363).

❏ 30. Study **all** the answers and explanations for Practice Test 4 (pages 367–388).

❏ 31. Have a friend or English instructor read and evaluate your essay using the "Essay checklist" (page 365).

❏ 32. Review weak areas as necessary.

❏ 33. Review Part II, "Analysis of Exam Areas" (pages 15–90).

❏ 34. Carefully read "Final Preparations: The Final Touches" (page 389).

PART I

INTRODUCTION

Introduction to the PPST
Pre-Professional Skills Test

The Pre-Professional Skills Test (PPST) measures your proficiency in basic academic abilities consisting of reading, mathematics, and writing. The PPST is required by most university departments of education for admission to teacher preparation programs, and many state departments of education require the PPST before teacher licensure and certification are issued. The successful passing of the PPST varies from state to state. You should contact your local state department of teacher certification to learn more about required standards.

The format of the exam is multiple-choice along with one written essay, and you have the choice to take either a paper-based version or a computer-based version.

Pre-Professional Skills Test

The PPST is composed of three multiple-choice tests and one essay:

The Reading Test. This multiple-choice test requires your ability to read, comprehend, and evaluate passages or statements and answer questions based upon the content of these passages. The reading passages are taken from a wide range of subject areas, but no prior knowledge of the topic is necessary to answer the questions. All questions are based upon the content of the passage provided.

The Mathematics Test. This multiple-choice test requires a cumulative understanding of math basics from problem solving to quantitative reasoning. Knowledge should include basic math from elementary school to at least one year of high school and possibly one year of college.

The Writing Test. This test is divided into two sections. Part A is a multiple-choice section and contains questions related to English usage and sentence correction. This section requires your ability to detect and correct errors in standard written English. Part B requires your ability to plan and write a well-organized essay on an assigned topic.

		Minutes		Approximate Number of Questions	
	Test	Paper-Based	Computer-Based	Paper-Based	Computer-Based
Reading	I. Literal Comprehension	27	35	18	21
	II. Critical and Inferential Comprehension	33	40	22	25
	Totals	**60 minutes**	**75 minutes**	**40 questions**	**46 questions**
Mathematics	I. Number and Operations	20	24	13	15
	II. Algebra	12	15	8	9
	III. Geometry and Measurement	13	16	9	10
	IV. Data Analysis and Probability	15	20	10	12
	Totals	**60 minutes**	**75 minutes**	**40 questions**	**46 questions**
Writing	I. Grammatical Relationships	10	13	13	15
	II. Structural Relationships	11	14	14	16
	III. Word Choice and Mechanics	9	11	11	13
	IV. Essay	30	30	1	1
	Total: Multiple Choice	**30 minutes**	**38 minutes**	**38 questions**	**44 questions**
	Total: Essay	**30 minutes**	**30 minutes**	**1 essay**	**1 essay**

Format of the Tests

Paper-Based Test	Computer-Based Test
Total Time: 180 minutes	Total Time*: 218 minutes
Total Questions: 118 questions plus 1 essay	Total Questions: 136 questions plus 1 essay

*Suggested time. The test may contain some experimental questions, which will not count toward your score. Note: Format and scoring are subject to change.

Questions Commonly Asked about the PPST

Q: Who administers the PPST?

A: Educational Testing Service (ETS) prepares and scores the PPST, but unless otherwise specified, institutions and agencies that plan to use the tests arrange for the administration with ETS. For further information regarding test administration, contact PPST Program, Educational Testing Service, Box 6051, Princeton, NJ 08541-6051 or call (609) 771-7395, www.ets.org/praxis.

Q: Is the PPST part of the Praxis Series?

A: Yes. ETS has grouped a number of its beginning teacher tests under the title "The Praxis Series." Praxis I includes the PPST tests of reading, writing, and mathematics skills that all teachers need. Praxis II includes exams on the specific subjects prospective teachers will actually teach. Praxis III includes tests that evaluate classroom teaching performance.

Q: How long is the PPST?

A: The computer-based PPST is approximately 3 hours and 45 minutes; however, you should allow at least 4.5 hours for this version of the test since there are computer tutorials and a verification process to collect your background information. The actual testing time for the paper-based PPST is approximately 3 hours if you take the entire test in one day.

Q: How is the PPST scored?

A: Both the PPST paper-based and computer-based tests are scored on a scale ranging from 150 to 190. Separate scores are reported for each test. The Reading Test and the Mathematics Test are scored solely on the number of items answered correctly. The Writing Test score is a composite score adjusted to give approximately equal weight to the number right on the multiple-choice section and the essay score. Since each state determines passing standards, it is important to check the passing score required for certification in your state.

Q: How is the PPST score used?

A: The PPST may be used for selection, admission, evaluation, and certification in conjunction with other relevant information. Because each institution or agency may set its own minimum standards and requirements, you should contact the appropriate institution, district, department, or agency to find out if you must take the test and to learn the required standards.

Q: How long does it take to receive my score?

A: It will take approximately four weeks for you to receive your score results if you take the paper-based test. Unofficial results for the computer-based test are available immediately on the day of your test for the multiple-choice results; but your official test report, including the written essay portion of the PPST, will be sent to you by mail approximately two weeks after your test date.

Q: Should I take the PPST by paper-and-pencil or by computer?

A: There are several factors to consider when deciding if you should take the PPST as the traditional paper-based version or as the computer-based version. Since both versions have the same level of difficulty, what matters most is that you are at ease with the method of test administration. For more information about the advantages of computer-based testing, read our section on "Taking the Computer-Based PPST" on page 11.

Q: When and where is the PPST *paper-based* test administered, and how do I register?

A: The paper-based version of the PPST is administered at locations throughout each state. You will need to list your first-choice and alternative-choice locations on your registration form. To register for the PPST, find a testing site, or obtain information about registration fees, check the PPST registration bulletin available from your local university department of education or contact ETS via www.ets.org/praxis to register online. Once you submit a registration form to ETS, you will receive an admission ticket to take with you the day of the test.

Q: When and where is the PPST *computer-based* test administered, and how do I register?

A: The computer-based administration of the PPST is made by appointment through Prometric Candidate Services at (800) 853-6773. Walk-in appointments are available on a "space-available basis only." There are over 300 test locations in the United States. You cannot take a computer-based test more than six times within one calendar year, and you may not take the computer-based test more than one time per calendar month.

Q: Are there any special arrangements for taking the PPST?

A: There are some special arrangements available for people with disabilities. Call or write to ETS long before your test date to inquire about special arrangements at www.ets.org/disability.

Q: What materials should I bring to the PPST?

A: Bring positive photo-bearing identification and a watch. If taking the paper-based test, you should also bring three or four sharpened No. 2 pencils and a good eraser. You may *not* bring scratch paper, calculators (including watch calculators), books, compasses, rulers, papers of any kind, or recording or photographic devices.

Q: How should I prepare for the PPST?

A: Understanding and practicing test-taking strategies will help a great deal. Subject matter review in arithmetic, simple algebra, plane geometry, and measurement, as well as in English grammar, usage, and punctuation is also very valuable.

Q: Should I guess on the PPST?

A: Yes. Since there is no penalty for wrong answers, guess if you have to. If possible, first try to eliminate some of the choices to increase your chances of guessing the correct answer. But don't leave any questions unanswered.

Q: Where can I get more information?

A: For more information, write to Educational Testing Service, The Praxis Series, P. O. Box 6051, Princeton, NJ 08541-6051 or visit www.ets.org/praxis.

Getting Started: Five Steps to Success on the PPST

1. **Awareness** – Become familiar with the test format, test directions, test material, and scoring by visiting the PPST Website at www.ets.org/praxis.

2. **Basic Skills** – Review the basic abilities required for success on the test in reading, mathematics, and writing in Part II, "Analysis of Exam Areas." Know what to expect on the exam. This will help you to determine your strengths and weaknesses so that you can develop a study plan unique to your individual needs.

3. **Question Types** – Become familiar with the question types of each area on the test outlined in Part II, "Analysis of Exam Areas," so that you can practice different versions of the same question type.

4. **Strategies and Techniques** – Practice using the strategies outlined in the next section of this book and decide what works best for you. Remember that if it takes you longer to recall a strategy than to solve the problem, it's probably not a good strategy for you to adopt. The goal in offering strategies is for you to be able to work easily, quickly, and efficiently. Remember not to get stuck on any one question. Taking time to answer the most difficult question on the test correctly, but losing valuable test time, won't get you the score you deserve. And most importantly, remember to answer every question, even if you answer with an educated guess. There is no penalty for wrong answers, so it is to your advantage to answer all questions.

5. **Practice** – In addition to the sample practice problems in Part II, "Analysis of Exam Areas," this book offers you four complete practice tests. Practice, practice, practice, practice is the key to your success on the PPST.

Taking the PPST: Two Successful Overall Approaches

The PPST is offered in paper-based and computer-based formats. Although the test question types are identical in both versions, there are a few considerations to think about when using general test-taking strategies. This section will present overall test-taking approaches to help you prepare for success. Keep in mind that there is no right or wrong way to answer questions, but there are general strategies that can help you get your bes-possible score. Following, we identify strategies that are applicable to each format of the test.

The "Plus-Minus" system

Paper-based strategy

Many who take the PPST don't get their best-possible score because they spend too much time on difficult questions, leaving insufficient time to answer the easy questions. Don't let this happen to you. Since every question within each section is worth the same amount, use the following system.

1. Answer easy questions immediately.

2. **Solvable (+):** When you come to a question that seems solvable but appears too time consuming, mark a large plus sign (+) next to that question in your test booklet and make an educated guess answer on your answer sheet. Then move on to the next question.

3. **Difficult (−):** When you come to a question that seems "impossible" to answer, mark a large minus sign (−) next to it on the test booklet. Then mark a "guess" answer on your answer sheet and move on to the next question.

   Since your time allotment is about a minute per question or less, a "time-consuming" question is a question that you estimate will take you more than several minutes to answer. But don't waste time deciding whether a question is a "+" or a "−." Act quickly, as the intent of this strategy is, in fact, to save you valuable time. After you've worked all the easy questions, your booklet should look something like this:

   1.

   + 2.

   3.

   − 4.

   + 5.

   etc.

4. After answering all the questions you immediately can in that section (the easy ones), go back and work on your "+" questions. Change your "guess" on your answer sheet, if necessary, for those questions you are now able to answer.

5. If you finish your "+" questions and still have time left,

   (a) you can attempt those "−" questions—the ones that you considered "impossible." Sometimes a question later in that section will "trigger" your memory and you'll be able to go back and answer one of the earlier "impossible" questions.

   or

   (b) you can not bother with those "impossible" questions. Rather, spend your time reviewing your work to be sure you didn't make any careless mistakes on the questions you thought were easy to answer.

Remember: You don't have to erase the pluses and minuses you made on your question book-let. And be sure to fill in all your answer spaces—if necessary, with a guess. As there is no penalty for wrong answers, it makes no sense to leave an answer space blank. And, of course, remember that you may work in only one section of the test at a time.

Computer-based strategy

The abovementioned plus-minus system can be used with the computerized test as well. By using scratch paper (or dry erase board) provided by the test administrators, you can quickly identify two types of questions: solvable (+) and very difficult (–).

- **Solvable (+):** This type of question is too time consuming, but you know you can solve it.
- **Difficult (–):** This type of question appears to be "impossible to solve." This is a question that you should come back to only if you have answered easy problems first. **Don't spend too much valuable test time deciding whether a question is solvable or not. Since you have about one minute to answer each question, you must act quickly.** Follow these steps:

   1. Answer easy questions immediately.

   2. Use a sheet of paper to list those questions that may be solvable, but will require more time.

   3. Draw two columns on a sheet of paper. Label the top of column one with a plus symbol "+" and the top of column two with a minus symbol "–."

   4. The computer-based test allows you to move forward and backward, from question to question. Before you proceed, mark the problem on your computer screen by clicking on the "mark tool." Note that there are two boxes on the computer screen that help you to easily identify unanswered questions. One box you can click on at any time is labeled "GO TO QUESTION ," and the other is labeled "RETURN TO WHERE I WAS." Take advantage of these tools to help you maneuver through the test.

   5. Quickly write down the problem number with any notes to help trigger your memory.

   6. After you have solved all problems in the "+" column, attempt to solve those impos-sible problems. If you cannot solve difficult problems, pick one letter answer choice (A, B, C, D, or E) and use that letter on the remaining questions. Spend no more than a few minutes to mark all difficult problems that are left unanswered. Remember that there is no penalty for wrong answers, and statistically, your chances are better if you pick one letter and use it on all unanswered questions.

   7. Work on one section at a time. Do not proceed to the next section without answering all questions within your section. DO NOT EXIT THE TEST UNTIL YOU HAVE ANSWERED ALL QUESTIONS. Once you exit, you cannot return.

Your scratch paper should look like this:

+	–
3. B or E	6. not ~~D~~ or ~~E~~
11. A, not ~~B~~	14. A?
15. C?	
17. not ~~D~~	

The elimination strategy

Paper-based strategy

Take advantage of being allowed to mark in your testing booklet. As you eliminate an answer choice from consideration, make sure to *mark it out in your question booklet* as follows:

(~~A~~)

?(B)

(~~C~~)

(~~D~~)

?(E)

Notice that some choices are marked with question marks, signifying that they may be possible answers. This technique will help you avoid reconsidering those choices you have already eliminated. It will also help you narrow down your possible answers.

Again, these marks you make on your testing booklet do not need to be erased.

Computer-based strategy

ETS recommends that you try to eliminate as many of the answer choices as possible, and then make an educated guess. On the computer-based exam you may find it helpful to quickly write on your scratch paper the letters of the answer choices you wish to eliminate so you don't keep reconsidering them. Your scratch paper should look like the example above.

Taking the Computer-Based PPST

The computer-based PPST is offered at many locations throughout the United States. Like the paper-based exam, the computer-based exam contains questions that test your knowledge in reading, mathematics, and writing. All of the material covered in this book—subject matter reviews, the practice test questions and explanations, and the essay practice problems—will help prepare you for the computer-based test, as well as the paper-based test. You will notice that the format of Practice Test 4 simulates the computer-based PPST and includes extra practice problems and instructions related to computerized testing. Here are some of the benefits of taking the PPST computer-based test:

- There are numerous test dates available since appointments can be scheduled throughout the week (the paper-based test is administered about five or six times per year on specified dates).

- There is same-day testing, which means that you can sometimes test on the same day that you make the appointment.

- Even though there are more questions, you are given a little extra time on the computer-based exam, and are allowed time to practice using a tutorial program.

- Your unofficial scores are available immediately after the test (except the written portion).

- Your answers are recorded electronically, which can often reduce the chance of human error in posting your written responses.

Computer-based tutorial

Immediately before taking the computer-based test, you will be led through a tutorial in order to show you how to read and answer the questions for each section on the PPST. You do not need advanced computer skills to take the computer-based exam. Basic computer skills are sufficient to operate the mouse, keyboard, and word processor. The types of questions given on the test are used in the tutorial. Remember that you are allowed enough time to work through a tutorial, so take advantage of this excellent opportunity to learn more about what you will encounter on the test.

Computer screen layout

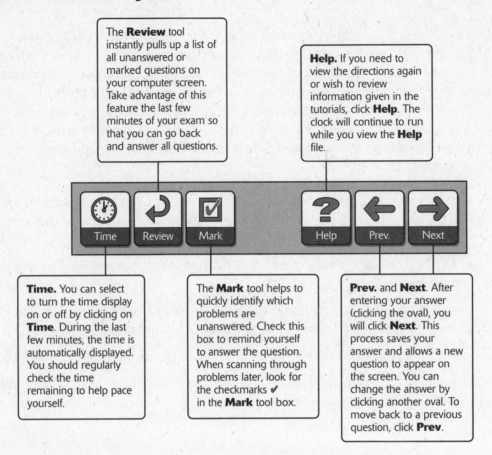

The **Review** tool instantly pulls up a list of all unanswered or marked questions on your computer screen. Take advantage of this feature the last few minutes of your exam so that you can go back and answer all questions.

Help. If you need to view the directions again or wish to review information given in the tutorials, click **Help**. The clock will continue to run while you view the **Help** file.

Time. You can select to turn the time display on or off by clicking on **Time**. During the last few minutes, the time is automatically displayed. You should regularly check the time remaining to help pace yourself.

The **Mark** tool helps to quickly identify which problems are unanswered. Check this box to remind yourself to answer the question. When scanning through problems later, look for the checkmarks ✔ in the **Mark** tool box.

Prev. and **Next**. After entering your answer (clicking the oval), you will click **Next**. This process saves your answer and allows a new question to appear on the screen. You can change the answer by clicking another oval. To move back to a previous question, click **Prev**.

Sample review of answered and unanswered questions

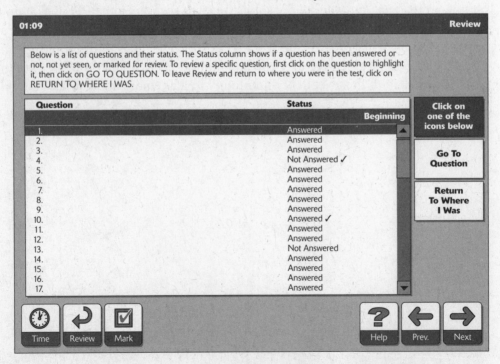

Sample reading passage

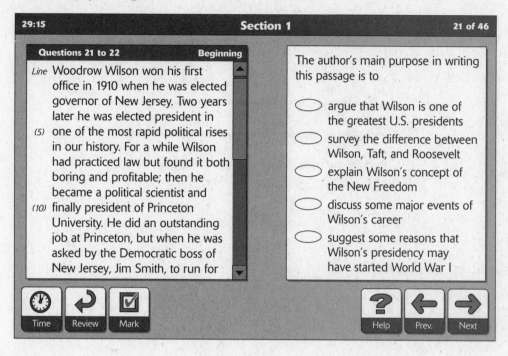

Sample math question

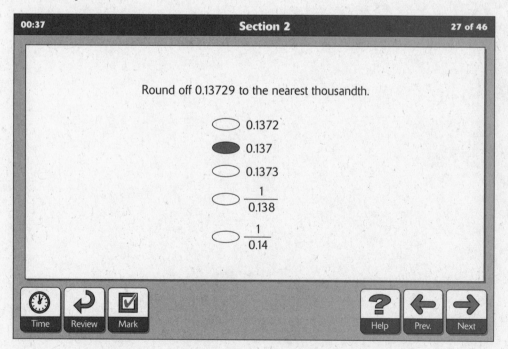

Sample writing question

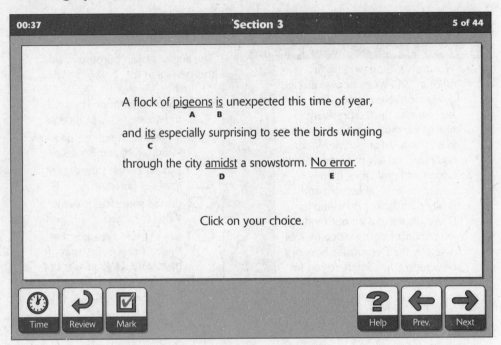

PART II

ANALYSIS OF EXAM AREAS

This section is designed to introduce you to each area of the PPST by carefully reviewing

1. Ability tested

2. Basic skills necessary

3. Directions

4. Analysis of directions

5. Suggested approach with samples

This section emphasizes important test-taking techniques and strategies and how to apply them to a variety of problem types. Sample essays are also included in this section as a guideline to assist students in evaluating their own essays and to point out some of the common errors in essay writing.

Introduction to the Reading Test

The Reading Test consists of passages of approximately 200 words, shorter passages of approximately 100 words, and short statements of one or more sentences. Each passage or statement is followed by questions based on its content.

Reading Test Format

Paper-based: 60 minutes and 40 multiple-choice questions
Computer-based: 75 minutes and 46 multiple-choice questions

The test is composed of the following content areas and approximate number of questions.

Literal Comprehension (directly stated content)

Paper-based: 18 questions
Computer-based: 21 questions

These are straightforward questions used to determine if you comprehend the passage and its direct meaning. The four types of literal comprehension questions will assess your ability to identify:

- the main idea or primary purpose of the passage

- the supporting ideas or specific details of the passage

- the organization of the passage

- the meaning of words or phrases used in the passage

Critical and Inferential Comprehension (non-directly stated content)

Paper-based: 22 questions
Computer-based: 25 questions

These are questions requiring you to read "beneath the surface" and understand deeper meanings that are directly implied by the passage. The three types of critical and inferential comprehension questions will assess your ability to evaluate:

- the argument's strengths or weaknesses, the relevance of its evidence, or whether the ideas presented are fact or opinion

- implications, inferences, or assumptions of the passage, or the author's underlying attitude

- generalizations or conclusions that can be drawn to apply to or predict new situations

Ability Tested

This section tests your ability to understand the content of the passage and any of the following: its main idea, supporting ideas, or specific details; the author's purpose, assumptions, or tone; the strengths and weaknesses of the author's argument; inferences drawn from the passage; the relationship of the passage to its intended audience; supporting evidence in the passage; and so forth.

Although the reading passages are from a broad spectrum of general-interest topics (i.e., journals and magazines), no outside knowledge of the topic is necessary to answer the questions. All questions can be answered on the basis of what is *stated* or *implied* in the passage.

Basic Skills Necessary

Understanding, interpreting, and analyzing passages are the important skills for this section. The technique of *actively* reading and marking a passage is also helpful.

Directions

A question or number of questions follow each of the statements or passages in this section. Using only the *stated* or *implied* information given in the statement or passage, answer the question or questions by choosing the *best* answer from among the five choices given.

Analysis of Directions

1. Answer all the questions for one passage before moving on to the next one. If you don't know the answer, take an educated guess or skip it.

2. Use only the information given or implied in a passage. Do not consider outside information, even if it seems more accurate than the given information.

3. Use your time wisely! You have about 1.5 minutes to answer each question (the allotment is slightly longer for the computer-based test). This includes the time required to mark and read the passages. If you're stuck on a question, mark it and move on. There is no penalty for guessing because your score is based upon the number of correct responses and does not count the number of incorrect responses. Therefore, if you're uncertain about your answer choice, mark the question and come back later to make an educated guess.

Suggested Strategies with Sample Passages

Two strategies that will improve your reading comprehension are *prereading the questions* and *marking the passage*. Computer-based examinees can write down key words or phrases on scratch paper. Readers who become comfortable using these strategies tend to score higher on reading tests than readers who do not use these strategies.

Active Prereading

The technique of *active reading* is an important skill in understanding the text of a passage. As you become actively engaged and purposeful in your reading, you are in control of the test reading experience. This can be accomplished by marking, highlighting, underlining, and circling important words and phrases in the passage (computer-based test-takers can use scratch paper). The skill of gathering information by using active reading will help you to quickly identify and visually focus on the main ideas of the passage and the questions, but it should be concise so that it will not interfere with your valuable allotted testing time.

Paper-based

Readers who become comfortable using prereading strategies tend to score higher on reading tests than readers who do not use this strategy. Before reading the passage, read the question or questions that follow it. Do not read the multiple-choice answer choices at this time. Underline or circle the operative phrase in each question—that is, what you are being asked to answer.

Computer-based

When taking the test by computer, you can preread questions by using the **NEXT** and **PREV** buttons while taking notes. You will see a passage on the screen, and a question with five answer choices will appear. For the first question only, do not read the passage first; *read the question on the right side of the screen first,* and write down one or two key words. Writing down one or two words helps you immediately remember the operative phrase for the question.

Don't try to memorize everything from the passage. Read the passage while focusing on the author's main point, primary purpose, or common themes. Briefly write down key words or phrases, along with the line number, on scratch paper to help trigger your memory for upcoming questions. Each passage contains numbered lines for reference to help you easily refer back to details of the passage. The entire passage may not fit on the screen, so make sure that you're comfortable with scrolling down and up the screen. Remember that you can move forward to the next question and back to a previous question by clicking the buttons marked **NEXT** and **PREV.**

In the example below, circle or underline the key words or phrases.

> The author's argument in favor of freedom of speech may be summarized in which of the following ways?
>
> **A.** If every speaker is not free, no speaker is.
>
> **B.** Speech makes us different from animals.
>
> **C.** As we think, so we speak.
>
> **D.** The Bill of Rights ensures free speech.
>
> **E.** Lunatic speeches are not free speeches.

In this example, the operative phrase is "author's argument . . . may be summarized (how?)." So you might underline or write down the words "author's argument" and "may be summarized." Thus, prereading allows you to focus on and clarify exactly what you're being asked to answer.

Marking the passage

For paper-based examinees, after prereading the questions, read and mark the passage. Computer-based examinees can write down key words or phrases on scratch paper. Underline or circle those spots that contain information relevant to the questions you've read as well as other important ideas and details. However, don't overmark. A few marked phrases per paragraph help those ideas stand out.

A short sample passage

   *By the time a child starts school, he has mastered the major task of understanding the basic rules of grammar. He has managed to accomplish this remarkable feat in such a short time by experimenting with and generalizing the rules all by himself. Each child, in effect, rediscovers language <u>in the first few years of his life.</u>

(5)   *When it comes to vocabulary growth, it is a <u>different story</u>. Unlike grammar, the chief means through which vocabulary is learned is memorization. *<u>Some people have a hard time learning and remembering new words.</u>

*Indicates portions of the passage that refer directly to a question you've skimmed. Also marked are main points and key terms.

Understand what is given

> **1.** A <u>child</u> has <u>mastered</u> many <u>rules of grammar</u> by about the <u>age</u> of
>
> **A.** 3
>
> **B.** 5
>
> **C.** 8
>
> **D.** 10
>
> **E.** 18

The first sentence of the passage contains several words from this question, so it is likely to contain the correct answer. "By the time a child starts school" (line 1) tells us that the answer is age 5. The correct answer is **B.**

Eliminate and mark out choices that are incorrect

> **2.** Although vocabulary growth involves memorization and grammar learning doesn't, we may conclude that <u>both vocabulary and grammar make use of</u>
>
> **A.** memorization
>
> **B.** study skills
>
> **C.** words
>
> **D.** children
>
> **E.** teachers

You should mark out or write down choices **A, D,** and **E.** (Computer test-takers should have scratch paper that looks like this: 2-A̸, D̸, E̸.) The question asks you to simply use your common sense. **A** is incorrect; it contradicts both the passage and the question itself. **D** and **E** make no sense. **B** is a possibility, but **C** is better because grammar learning in young children does not necessarily involve study skills but does necessarily involve words. The correct answer is **C.**

Understand what is implied in the passage

> **3.** The last sentence in the passage implies that
>
>   **A.** some people have no trouble learning and remembering new words
>
>   **B.** some people have a hard time remembering new words
>
>   **C.** grammar does not involve remembering words
>
>   **D.** old words are not often remembered
>
>   **E.** learning and remembering are kinds of growth

Implies tells us that the answer is something suggested but not explicitly stated in the passage. **B** is explicitly stated in the passage, so it may be eliminated. But it implies its opposite: If *some* people have a hard time, then it must be true that *some* people don't. **C, D,** and **E** are altogether apart from the meaning of the last sentence. The correct answer is **A.**

Another short sample passage

     St. Augustine was a contemporary of Jerome. After an early life of pleasure, he became interested in a philosophical religion called Manichaeism, a derivative of a Persian religion, in which the <u>forces of good</u> constantly struggle with those of <u>evil</u>. Augustine was eventually converted to Christianity by St. Ambrose of Milan. Augustine's *Confessions* was
(5) an autobiography that served <u>as an inspiration</u> to countless thousands who believed that virtue would ultimately win.

Make sure that your answer is well-supported by the information in the passage

> **4.** St. Augustine's conversion to Christianity was probably influenced by
>
>   **A.** his confessional leanings
>
>   **B.** his contemporaries
>
>   **C.** the inadequacy of a Persian religion to address Western moral problems
>
>   **D.** his earlier interest in the dilemma of retaining virtue
>
>   **E.** the ravages of a life of pleasure

Having skimmed this question, you may have marked the portion of the passage that mentions Augustine's conversion and paid attention to the events (influences) leading to it. **A** requires speculating beyond the facts in the paragraph; there is also no evidence in the passage to support **C** or **E**. **B** is too vague and general to be the best answer. **D** points toward Augustine's earlier interest in Manichaeism, and the last sentence suggests that Augustine's interest in retaining virtue continued through his Christian doctrine. The correct answer is **D.**

Understand meaning, style, tone, and point of view of the passage

> **5.** From the information in the passage, we must conclude that <u>Augustine was a</u>
>
>   **A.** fair-weather optimist
>
>   **B.** cockeyed optimist
>
>   **C.** hardworking optimist
>
>   **D.** failed optimist
>
>   **E.** glib optimist

Skimming *this* question is not very helpful; it does not point specifically to any information in the passage. Questions of this sort usually assess your overall understanding of the meaning, style, tone, or point of view of the passage. In this case, you should recognize that Augustine is a serious person; therefore, more lighthearted terms like *fair-weather* (**A**), *cockeyed* (**B**), and *glib* (**E**) are probably inappropriate. **D** contradicts Augustine's success as an "inspiration to countless thousands." **C** corresponds with his ongoing, hopeful struggle to retain virtue in the world. The correct answer is **C**.

Know where to look for information

> **6.** Judging from the <u>reaction of</u> thousands <u>to Augustine's *Confessions*</u>, we may conclude that much of his <u>world at that time was</u> in a state of
>
>   **A.** opulence
>
>   **B.** misery
>
>   **C.** equanimity
>
>   **D.** reformation
>
>   **E.** sanctification

Having skimmed this question, you may have marked the last sentence of the passage as the place to look for the answer. That Augustine's readers were inspired may imply that they *required inspiration*. **A, C,** and **E** must therefore be eliminated because they are positive terms. **D** is not necessarily a negative term and so is probably not the best answer. The correct answer is **B**.

A longer passage

Woodrow Wilson won his first office in 1910 when he was elected governor of New Jersey. Two years later, he was elected president in one of the most rapid political rises in our history. For a while, Wilson had practiced law but found it both boring and unprofitable; then he became a political scientist and finally president of Princeton University. He
(5)   did an outstanding job at Princeton, but when he was asked by the Democratic boss of New Jersey, Jim Smith, to run for governor, Wilson readily accepted because his position at Princeton was becoming untenable.

Until 1910, Wilson seemed to be a conservative Democrat in the Grover Cleveland tradition. He had denounced Bryan in 1896 and had voted for the National Democratic candidate who supported gold. In fact, when the Democratic machine first pushed Wilson's
(10) nomination in 1912, the young New Jersey progressives wanted no part of him. Wilson later assured them that he would champion the progressive cause, and so they decided to work for his election. It is easy to accuse Wilson of political expediency, but it is entirely possible that by 1912 he had changed his views as had countless other Americans. While governor of New Jersey, he carried out his election pledges by enacting an impressive list of reforms.
(15)

Wilson secured the Democratic nomination on the 46th ballot. In the campaign, Wilson emerged as the middle-of-the-road candidate—between the conservative William H. Taft and the more radical Theodore Roosevelt. Wilson called his program "the New Freedom," which he said was the restoration of free competition as it had existed before the growth of the trusts.
(20) In contrast, Theodore Roosevelt was advocating a "New Nationalism," which seemed to call for massive federal intervention in the economic life of the nation. Wilson felt that the trusts should be destroyed, but he made a distinction between a trust and legitimately successful big business. Theodore Roosevelt, on the other hand, accepted the trusts as inevitable but said that government should regulate them by establishing a new regulatory agency.

Always look for the main point of the passage

> **7.** The author's main purpose in writing this passage is to
>
> **A.**   argue that Wilson is one of the great U.S. presidents
>
> **B.**   survey the difference between Wilson, Taft, and Roosevelt
>
> **C.**   explain Wilson's concept of the New Freedom
>
> **D.**   discuss some major events of Wilson's career
>
> **E.**   suggest reasons that Wilson's presidency may have started World War I

There are many ways to ask about the main point of a passage. What is the main idea? What is the best title? What is the author's purpose? Choices **A** and **E** are irrelevant to the information in the passage, and choices **B** and **C** mention secondary purposes rather than the primary one. The correct answer is **D**.

Be aware of information not directly stated in the passage

> **8.** The author implies which of the following about New Jersey progressives?
>
>   **A.** They did not support Wilson after he was governor.
>
>   **B.** They were not conservative Democrats.
>
>   **C.** They were more interested in political expediency than in political causes or reforms.
>
>   **D.** Along with Wilson, they were supporters of Bryan in 1896.
>
>   **E.** They particularly admired Wilson's experience as president of Princeton University.

Some information is not directly stated in the passage but can be gleaned by reading between the lines. Implied information can be valuable in answering some questions. In the second paragraph, Wilson's decision to champion the progressive cause after 1912 is contrasted with his earlier career, when he seemed to be a conservative Democrat. Thus, one may conclude that the progressives, whom Wilson finally joined, were not conservative Democrats as was Wilson earlier in his career. Choices **A** and **D** contradict information in the paragraph, while choices **C** and **E** are not suggested by any information given in the passage. The correct answer is **B**.

Watch for important conclusions or information that supports a conclusion

> **9.** The passage supports which of the following conclusions about the progress of Wilson's political career?
>
>   **A.** Few politicians have progressed so rapidly toward the attainment of higher office.
>
>   **B.** Failures late in his career caused him to be regarded as a president who regressed instead of progressed.
>
>   **C.** Wilson encountered little opposition after he determined to seek the presidency.
>
>   **D.** The League of Nations marked the end of Wilson's reputation as a strong leader.
>
>   **E.** Wilson's political allies were Bryan and Taft.

Choice **A** is explicitly supported by the second sentence in the first paragraph, which states that Wilson was "elected president in one of the most rapid political rises in our history." The correct answer is **A**.

Understand the meaning and possible reason for using certain words or phrases

> **10.** In the statement "Wilson readily accepted because his position at Princeton was becoming untenable" (lines 6–7), the meaning of "untenable" is probably which of the following?
>
>   **A.** Unlikely to last for years
>
>   **B.** Filled with considerably less tension
>
>   **C.** Difficult to maintain or continue
>
>   **D.** Filled with achievements that would appeal to voters
>
>   **E.** Something he did not have a tenacious desire to continue

On any reading comprehension test, be alert to the positive and negative connotations of words and phrases in each passage as well as in the questions themselves. In the case of *untenable,* the prefix *un-* suggests that the word has a negative connotation. The context in which the word occurs does as well. Wilson *left* his position at Princeton; therefore, we may conclude that the position was somehow unappealing. Only two of the answer choices, **C** and **E,** provide a negative definition. Although choice **E** may attract your attention because *tenacious* looks similar to *tenable,* choice **C** is the conventional definition of *untenable.* The correct answer is **C.**

Eliminate those choices that are not supported by the passage

> **11.** According to the passage, which of the following was probably true about the presidential campaign of 1912?
>
>   **A.** Woodrow Wilson won the election by an overwhelming majority.
>
>   **B.** The inexperience of Theodore Roosevelt accounted for his radical position.
>
>   **C.** Wilson was unable to attract two-thirds of the votes but won anyway.
>
>   **D.** There were three nominated candidates for the presidency.
>
>   **E.** Wilson's New Freedom did not represent Democratic interests.

Your answer choice must be supported by information either stated or implied in the passage. Choices **A, B,** and **C** contain information that is not addressed in the passage. We may eliminate them as irrelevant. Choice **E** contradicts the fact that Wilson was a Democratic candidate. The discussion of Taft and Roosevelt as the candidates who finally ran against Wilson for the presidency supports choice **D.** The correct answer is **D.**

General Procedure for Answering Reading Comprehension Questions

1. **Skim the questions.** Underline, write down, or circle the word or phrase that stands out in each question. *Don't* read the answer choices.

2. **Read and mark the passage.** Pay special attention to information relevant to the questions you've skimmed. Computer-based examinees, write down key words or phrases on scratch paper.

3. **Answer the questions.** Base your answers on *only the material given in the passage.* Assume that the information in each passage is accurate. The questions test your understanding of the passage alone; they do *not* test the historical background of the passage, the biography of the author, or previous familiarity with the work from which the passage is taken.

Five Key Questions for Understanding and Interpreting What You Read

Main idea

What is the main idea of the passage? After reading any passage, try summarizing it in a brief sentence. To practice this very important skill, read the editorials in your local paper each day and *write* a brief sentence summarizing each one.

Details

What details support the main idea? Usually such details are facts, statistics, experiences, and so on, that strengthen your understanding of and agreement with the main idea.

Purpose

What is the purpose of the passage? Ask yourself what the author is trying to accomplish. The four general purposes are (1) to narrate (tell a story), (2) to describe, (3) to inform, and (4) to persuade.

Style and tone

Are the style and tone of the passage objective or subjective? In other words, is the author presenting things *factually* or from a *personal point of view*? If an author is subjective, you might want to pin down the nature of the subjectivity. Ask yourself, is the author optimistic? pessimistic? angry? humorous? serious?

Difficult or unusual vocabulary

What are the difficult or unusual words in the passage? Readers who do not mark or write down words that are difficult or used in an unusual way in a passage often forget that the words occurred at all and have difficulty locating them if this becomes necessary. By calling your attention to difficult or unusual words, you increase your chances of defining them by understanding their meaning in context.

A PATTERNED PLAN OF ATTACK
Reading Comprehension

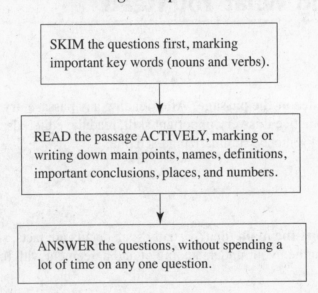

SKIM the questions first, marking important key words (nouns and verbs).

READ the passage ACTIVELY, marking or writing down main points, names, definitions, important conclusions, places, and numbers.

ANSWER the questions, without spending a lot of time on any one question.

Introduction to the Mathematics Test

The Mathematics Test consists of questions that are selected from different areas of mathematics including arithmetic, elementary algebra, basic geometry, measurement, and graph and chart reading. The use of calculators is prohibited, but complex computation is not required. Most of the terms used are general, commonly encountered mathematical expressions (for instance, area, perimeter, integer, and prime number).

Mathematics Test Format

Paper-based: 60 minutes and 40 multiple-choice questions
Computer-based: 75 minutes and 46 multiple-choice questions

Ability Tested

This part of the exam tests your ability to use your cumulative knowledge of mathematics and your reasoning ability. Computation is minimal; you are not required to have memorized any specific formulas or equations.

The test is composed of the following content areas and *approximate* percentages.

Category	Paper-Based	Computer-Based	Approximate Percentage
Number and Operations	13	15	32.5%
Algebra	8	9	20%
Geometry and Measurement	9	10	22.5%
Data Analysis and Probability	10	12	25%
Total Questions	40	46	

Number and Operations: ordering numbers (whole numbers, fractions, decimals), equivalence, place value, properties of numbers (i.e., commutative, associative, and distributive) and their operations (i.e., addition, subtraction, multiplication, and division), computation, estimation, ratio, proportion, percentage, and showing knowledge of number reasoning (logical connectives, deductive reasoning, and generalization).

Algebra: solving simple equations and inequalities, predicting outcomes, algorithmic thinking, recognizing patterns in data (i.e., direct and inverse), algebraic representations and relationships between symbolic expressions and graphs, and algebraic reasoning.

Geometry and Measurement: geometric properties (i.e., 2-D shapes, Pythagorean theorem, congruence, and similarity), symmetry, *x*- and *y*-coordinates, geometric reasoning, measurement systems (i.e., metric system, conversion, basic units of measure, and graduated scale), solving measurement problems (linear, area, volume, formula, rates of measures, visual comparisons, scaling, proportional reasoning), and using a nonstandard unit.

Data Analysis and Probability: data interpretation (i.e., bar graphs, line graphs, pie charts, pictographs, tables, stem-and-leaf plots, scatterplots, schedules, and Venn diagrams); data representation (i.e., data sets); comparing, predicting, or drawing conclusions about trends and inferences; determining mean, mode, median, and range; and probability.

Directions

Each of the questions or incomplete statements below is followed by five suggested answers or completions. Select the best answer or completion of the five choices given and fill in the corresponding lettered space (computer-based test-takers, click on the oval to fill in your identified choice).

Analysis of Directions

1. Paper-based examinees have 60 minutes to do 40 problems, and computer-based examinees have 75 minutes to do 46 problems; this averages to just over one minute per problem. Keep that in mind as you attack each problem. Even if you know you can work a problem but that it will take you far longer than one minute, you should skip it and return to it later if you have time. Remember, you want to do all the easy, quick problems first before spending valuable time on the others. Computer-based examinees, remember to work within this section only, answering all math questions before proceeding to another section.

2. There is no penalty for guessing, so you should not leave any blanks. If you don't know the answer to a problem but you can size it up to get a general range for your answer, you may be able to eliminate one or more of the answer choices. This procedure will increase your odds of guessing the correct answer. But even if you can't eliminate any of the choices, take a guess because there is no penalty for wrong answers.

3. Above all for paper-based examinees, be sure that your answers on your answer sheet correspond to the proper numbers on your question sheet. Placing one answer in the incorrect number on the answer sheet could possibly shift *all* your answers to incorrect spots. Be careful to avoid this problem!

4. Remember that the use of a calculator is prohibited.

Suggested Approach with Samples

Here are a number of approaches that can be helpful in attacking many types of mathematics problems. Of course, these strategies won't work on all the problems, but if you become familiar with them, you'll find they'll be helpful in answering quite a few questions.

Mark key words

Circling or underlining key words in each question is an effective test-taking technique. Many times you may be misled because you may overlook a key word in a problem. By circling, underlining, or writing down these key words, you'll help yourself focus on what you are being asked to find. Remember, you are allowed to mark and write on your testing booklet, and you are given scratch paper for notes and computation. Take advantage of this opportunity.

---

1. In the following number, which digit is in the thousandths place?

$$6574.12398$$

- **A.** 2
- **B.** 3
- **C.** 5
- **D.** 7
- **E.** 9

The key word here is *thousandths*. By marking it, you will be paying closer attention to it. This is the kind of question which, under time pressure and testing pressure, may often be misread. It may be easily misread as *thousands* place. Your marking the important words can minimize the possibility of misreading. Your completed question might look like this after you mark or note the important words or terms. The correct answer is **B.**

---

1. In the following number, which <u>digit</u> is in the <u>thousandths</u> place?

$$6574.12\underline{3}98$$

- **A.** 2
- **B.** <u>3</u>
- **C.** 5
- **D.** 7
- **E.** 9

Here are a few more examples.

---

2. If 3 yards of ribbon cost $2.97, what is the price per foot?

    A. $0.33

    B. $0.99

    C. $2.94

    D. $3.00

    E. $8.91

The key word here is *foot*. Dividing $2.97 by 3 will tell you only the price per *yard*. Notice that $0.99 is one of the choices, **B.** You must still divide by 3 (since there are 3 feet per yard) to find the cost per foot. $0.99 divided by 3 is $0.33. Therefore, it would be very helpful to mark or note the words *price per foot* in the problem. The correct answer is **A.**

---

3. If $3x + 1 = 16$, what is the value of $x - 4$?

    A. 19

    B. 16

    C. 5

    D. 1

    E. −1

The key here is *what is the value of* $x - 4$. Therefore, circle $x - 4$. Note that solving the original equation will tell only the value of x.

$$3x + 1 = 16$$
$$\frac{-1 \quad -1}{\frac{3x}{3}} = \frac{15}{3}$$
$$x = 5$$

Here again, notice that 5 is one of the choices, **C.** But the question asks for the value of $x - 4$, not just x. To continue, replace x with 5 and solve.

$$x - 4 = ?$$
$$5 - 4 = 1$$

The correct answer is **D.**

---

4. Together a sweet roll and a cup of coffee cost \$2.75. The sweet roll costs \$0.75 more than the coffee. What is the cost of the sweet roll?

    A. \$0.75

    B. \$1.00

    C. \$1.75

    D. \$2.00

    E. \$2.75

The key words here are *cost of the sweet roll*, so mark or note those words. Solving this algebraically,

x = coffee

$x + 0.75$ = sweet roll (costs \$0.75 more than the coffee)

Together they cost \$2.75

$$(x + 0.75) + x = 2.75$$
$$2x + 0.75 = 2.75$$
$$2x = 2.00$$
$$x = 1.00$$

Therefore, the cost of the coffee is \$1.00, and the cost of the sweet roll is \$1.75.

Notice that \$1.00 is one of the choices, **B.** Since $x = 1.00$, then $x + 0.75 = 1.75$. Therefore, the sweet roll costs \$1.75. *Always answer the question that is being asked.* Circling, underlining, or writing the key word or words will help you do that. The correct answer is **C.**

Pull out information

Pulling information out of the wording of a word problem can make the problem more workable and give you additional insight into the problem. Pull out the given facts and identify which of those facts will help you work the problem. Not all facts will always be needed.

---

5. Bill is 10 years older than his sister. If Bill was 25 years of age in 1993, in what year could he have been born?

    A. 1958   **B.** 1963   **C.** 1968   **D.** 1973   **E.** 1978

The key words here are *in what year* and *could he have been born*. Thus, the solution is simple: $1993 - 25 = 1968$. Notice that you should pull out the information *25 years of age* and *in 1993*. The fact about Bill's age in comparison to his sister's age is not needed, however, and is not pulled out. The correct answer is **C.**

6. John is 18 years old. He works for his father for $\frac{3}{4}$ of the year, and he works for his brother for the rest of the year. What is the ratio of the time John spends working for his brother to the time he spends working for his father per year?

    A. $\frac{1}{4}$

    B. $\frac{1}{3}$

    C. $\frac{3}{4}$

    D. $\frac{4}{3}$

    E. $\frac{4}{1}$

The key word *rest* points to the answer.

$$1 - \frac{3}{4} =$$

$$\frac{4}{4} - \frac{3}{4} = \frac{1}{4} \text{ (the part of the year John works for his brother)}$$

Also, a key idea is the way in which the ratio is written. The problem becomes that of finding the ratio of $\frac{1}{4}$ to $\frac{3}{4}$

$$\frac{\frac{1}{4}}{\frac{3}{4}} = \frac{1}{4} \div \frac{3}{4} = \frac{1}{{}_1 4} \times \frac{4^1}{3} = \frac{1}{3}$$

Note that John's age is not needed to solve the problem. The correct answer is **B**.

Sometimes, you may not have sufficient information to solve the problem. For example,

7. A woman purchased several books at $15 each plus one more for $12. What was the average price of each book?

    A. $12

    B. $13

    C. $14

    D. $15

    E. There is not enough information to tell.

To calculate an average, you must have the total amount and then divide by the number of items. The difficulty here, however, is that *several books at $15* does not specify exactly *how many* books were purchased at $15 each. Does *several* mean two? Or does it mean three? *Several* is not a precise mathematical term. Therefore, there is not enough information to pull out to calculate an average. The correct answer is **E**.

Plug in numbers

When a problem involving variables (unknowns, or letters) seems difficult and confusing, simply replace those variables with numbers. Usually, problems using numbers are easier to understand. Simple numbers will make the arithmetic easier for you to do. Be sure to make logical substitutions. Use a positive number, a negative number, or zero when applicable to get the full picture.

---

8. If x is a positive integer in the equation $2x = y$, then y must be

   A. a positive even integer

   B. a negative even integer

   C. zero

   D. a positive odd integer

   E. a negative odd integer

At first glance, this problem appears quite complex. But let's plug in some numbers and see what happens. For instance, first plug in 1 (the simplest positive integer) for x.

$$2x = y$$
$$2(1) = y$$
$$2 = y$$

Now try 2.

$$2x = y$$
$$2(2) = y$$
$$4 = y$$

Try it again. No matter what positive integer is plugged in for x, y will always be positive and even. Therefore, the correct answer is **A**.

---

9. If a, b, and c are all positive whole numbers greater than 1 such that $a < b < c$, which of the following is the largest quantity?

   A. $a(b + c)$

   B. $ab + c$

   C. $ac + b$

   D. They are all equal.

   E. The largest quantity cannot be determined.

Substitute 2, 3, and 4 for *a, b,* and *c,* respectively.

$$a(b+c)= \qquad ab+c= \qquad ac+b=$$
$$2(3+4)= \qquad 2(3)+4= \qquad 2(4)+3=$$
$$2(7)=14 \qquad 6+4=10 \qquad 8+3=11$$

Since 2, 3, and 4 meet the conditions stated in the problem and choice **A** produces the largest numerical value, it will consistently be the largest quantity. Therefore, $a(b+c)$ is the correct answer, **A.**

Work from the answers

At times, the solution to a problem will be obvious to you. At other times, it may be helpful to work from the answers. If a direct approach is not obvious, try working from the answers. This technique is even more efficient when some of the answer choices are easily eliminated.

---

10. Barney can mow the lawn in 5 hours, and Rachel can mow the lawn in 4 hours. How long will it take them to mow the lawn together?

    A.   8 hours

    B.   5 hours

    C. $4\frac{1}{2}$ hours

    D.   4 hours

    E. $2\frac{2}{9}$ hours

You may never have worked a problem like this, or perhaps you have worked one but don't remember the procedure required to find the answer. In that case, try working from the answers. Since Rachel can mow the lawn in 4 hours by herself, it will take less than 4 hours if Barney helps her. Therefore, choices **A, B, C,** and **D** are not reasonable. Thus, the correct answer—by working from the answers and eliminating the incorrect ones—is **E.**

---

11. Find the counting number that is less than 15 and when divided by 3 has a remainder of 1, but when divided by 4 has a remainder of 2.

    A.   5

    B.   8

    C.   10

    D.   12

    E.   13

By working from the answers, you can eliminate wrong answer choices. For instance, **B** and **D** can be immediately eliminated because they are divisible by 4, leaving no remainder. Choices **A** and **E** can also be eliminated because they leave a remainder of 1 when divided by 4. Therefore, 10 leaves a remainder of 1 when divided by 3 and a remainder of 2 when divided by 4. The correct answer is **C**.

Approximate

If a problem involves number calculations that seem tedious and time consuming, round off or approximate the numbers. Replace the given numbers with whole numbers that are easier to work with. Find the answer choice that is closest to your approximated answer.

---

12. The value for $(0.889 \times 55) / 9.97$ to the nearest tenth is

    A. 49.1

    B. 17.7

    C. 4.9

    D. 4.63

    E. 0.5

Before starting any computations, take a glance at the answers to see how far apart they are. Notice that the only close answers are **C** and **D,** but **D** is not a possible choice, since it is to the nearest hundredth, not tenth. Now, make some quick approximations, $0.889 \approx 1$ and $9.97 \approx 10$, leaving the problem in this form.

$$\frac{1 \times 55}{10} = \frac{55}{10} = 5.5$$

Notice that choices **A** and **E** are not reasonable. The closest answer is **C;** therefore, it is the correct answer.

---

13. The value of $\sqrt{7194/187}$ is approximately

    A. 6

    B. 9

    C. 18

    D. 35

    E. 72

Round off both numbers to the hundreds place. The problem then becomes $\sqrt{\dfrac{7200}{200}}$.

This is much easier to work. By dividing, the problem now becomes $\sqrt{36}$. The closest answer choice is the exact value of choice **A**.

Make comparisons

At times, questions will require you to compare the sizes of several decimals or of several fractions. If decimals are being compared, make sure that the numbers being compared have the same number of digits. (Remember, zeros to the far right of a decimal point can be inserted or eliminated without changing the value of the number.)

---

14. Put these in order from smallest to largest: $0.6, 0.16, 0.66\frac{2}{3}, 0.58$

    A. $0.6, 0.16, 0.66\frac{2}{3}, 0.58$

    B. $0.58, 0.16, 0.6, 0.66\frac{2}{3}$

    C. $0.16, 0.58, 0.6, 0.66\frac{2}{3}$

    D. $0.66\frac{2}{3}, 0.6, 0.58, 0.16$

    E. $0.58, 0.6, 0.66\frac{2}{3}, 0.16$

Rewrite 0.6 as 0.60. Therefore, all of the decimals now have the same number of digits: $0.60, 0.16, 0.66\frac{2}{3}, 0.58$. Treating these as though the decimal point were not there (this can be done only when all the numbers have the same number of digits to the right of the decimal), the order is as follows: $0.16, 0.58, 0.60, 0.66\frac{2}{3}$. Remember to mark *smallest to largest* in the question. The correct answer is **C**.

---

15. Put these in order from smallest to largest: $\frac{5}{8}, \frac{3}{4}, \frac{2}{3}$

    A. $\frac{2}{3}, \frac{3}{4}, \frac{5}{8}$

    B. $\frac{2}{3}, \frac{5}{8}, \frac{3}{4}$

    C. $\frac{5}{8}, \frac{2}{3}, \frac{3}{4}$

    D. $\frac{3}{4}, \frac{5}{8}, \frac{2}{3}$

    E. $\frac{3}{4}, \frac{2}{3}, \frac{5}{8}$

Using common denominators, $\frac{5}{8} = \frac{15}{24}, \frac{3}{4} = \frac{18}{24}$, and $\frac{2}{3} = \frac{16}{24}$. Therefore, the order becomes $\frac{5}{8}, \frac{2}{3}, \frac{3}{4}$.

Using decimal equivalents, $\frac{5}{8} = 0.625, \frac{3}{4} = 0.75$ or 0.750, and $\frac{2}{3} = 0.66\frac{2}{3}$ or $0.666\frac{2}{3}$. The order again becomes $\frac{5}{8}, \frac{2}{3}, \frac{3}{4}$. The correct answer is **C**.

16. Which of the following values is least?

    A. $\frac{3}{8}$

    B. 38

    C. 0.38

    D. $\frac{8}{3}$

    E. 38%

The least value is choice **A.** Choices **C** and **E** are equal, and choices **B** and **D** are each more than 1. The fraction $\frac{3}{8}$ can be changed into a decimal by dividing 3 by 8, which gives 0.375, which is just a little less than choices **C** and **E.** The correct answer is **A.**

17. On a number line, all of the following fractions lie between $\frac{7}{8}$ and $\frac{19}{20}$ EXCEPT

    A. $\frac{8}{9}$

    B. $\frac{9}{10}$

    C. $\frac{10}{11}$

    D. $\frac{15}{16}$

    E. $\frac{9}{8}$

Before you get bogged down analyzing each of the first few choices, notice that the last choice, **E,** has a numerator larger than the denominator. This means that it is greater than 1, which would mean it does not lie between $\frac{7}{8}$ and $\frac{19}{20}$, each of which are less than one. The correct answer is **E.**

Mark diagrams

When a figure is included with the problem, mark or draw the given facts on the diagram. Marking or drawing in this way will help you visualize all the facts that have been given.

---

18. If each square in the figure has a side of length 1, what is the perimeter?

    A. 8

    B. 12

    C. 14

    D. 16

    E. 20

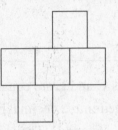

Mark or draw the known facts.

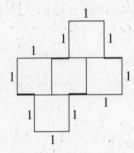

You now have a calculation for the perimeter: 10 *plus* the darkened parts. Now, look carefully at the top two darkened parts. They will add up to 1. (Notice how the top square may slide over to illustrate this fact.)

The same is true for the bottom darkened parts. They will add up to 1. Thus, the total perimeter is 10 + 2, or 12.

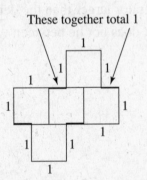

These together total 1

All the squares are identical in size, so to check your work, move the top and bottom squares to form the figure on the right:

Each side has a length of 1, the perimeter becomes 12 groups of 1, or 12. The correct answer is **B.**

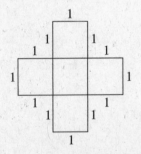

19. The perimeter of the isosceles triangle shown at right is 42".
The two equal sides are each three times as long as the third side.
What are the lengths of each side?

A. 21, 21, 21

B. 6, 6, 18

C. 18, 21, 3

D. 18, 18, 6

E. 4, 19, 19

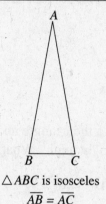

$\triangle ABC$ is isosceles
$\overline{AB} = \overline{AC}$

Mark the equal sides
of the diagram.

$\overline{AB}$ and $\overline{AC}$ are each
three times as long as $\overline{BC}$.

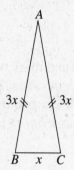

The equation for perimeter is

$$3x + 3x + x = 42$$
$$7x = 42$$
$$x = 6$$

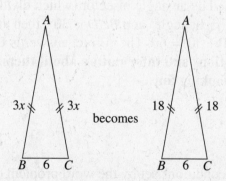

becomes

Note: This problem can also be solved by eliminating the wrong answers. Choices **A** and **B** do not have a perimeter of 42". **C** is not an isosceles triangle since it does not have two sides of equal length. **E** does not have long sides that are three times the short side. The correct answer is **D**.

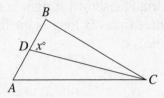

20. In the triangle above, *CD* is an angle bisector, angle *ACD* is 30°, and angle *ABC* is a right angle. What is the measurement of angle *x* in degrees?

    A.   30°

    B.   45°

    C.   60°

    D.   75°

    E.   180°

You should read the problem and mark or draw as follows. In the triangle above, *CD* is an angle bisector (*stop and mark in the drawing*), angle *ACD* is 30° (*stop and mark in the drawing*), and angle *ABC* is a right angle (*stop and mark in the drawing*). What is the measurement of angle *x* in degrees? (*Stop and mark in or circle what you are looking for in the drawing.*)

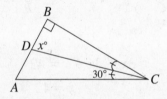

Now, with the drawing marked in, it is evident that, since angle *ACD* is 30°, angle *BCD* is also 30° because they are both formed by an angle bisector (which divides an angle into two equal parts). Since angle *ABC* is 90° (right angle) and *BCD* is 30°, then angle *x* is 60° because there are 180° in a triangle, 180 − (90 + 30) = 60. The correct answer is **C. Always mark or draw in diagrams as you read descriptions and information about them. Marking and drawing should include what you are looking for.**

Draw diagrams

Drawing diagrams to meet the conditions set by the word problem can often make the problem easier to work. Being able to "see" the facts is more helpful than just reading the words.

21. If all sides of a square are doubled, the area of that square

    A. is doubled

    B. is tripled

    C. is multiplied by 4

    D. remains the same

    E. Not enough information is provided.

One way to solve this problem is to draw a square, double all its sides, and then compare the two areas.

Your first diagram:

Doubling every side,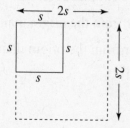

Notice that the total area of the new square will now be four times the original square. The correct answer is **C.**

22. A hiking team begins at camp and hikes 5 miles north, then 8 miles west, then 6 miles south, then 9 miles east. In what direction must they now travel in order to return to camp?

    A. North

    B. Northeast

    C. Northwest

    D. West

    E. They already are at camp.

For this question, your diagram would look something like this.

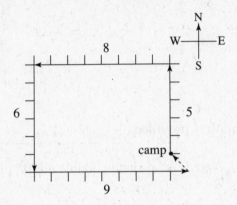

Thus, they must travel northwest to return to camp. Note that in this case it is important to draw your diagram very accurately. The correct answer is **C.**

---

23. If points $P(1,1)$ and $Q(1,0)$ lie on the same coordinate graph, which must be true?

   I. P and Q are equidistant from the origin.

   II. P is farther from the origin than P is from Q.

   III. Q is farther from the origin than Q is from P.

   A. I only

   B. II only

   C. III only

   D. I and II only

   E. I and III only

First draw the coordinate graph and then plot the points as follows:

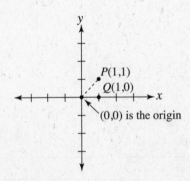

Only II is true. P is farther from the origin than P is from Q. The correct answer is **B.**

Try possibilities in probability problems

Some questions will involve probability and possible combinations. If you don't know a formal method, try some possibilities. Set up what could happen. But set up only as much as you need to.

---

24. What is the probability of throwing two dice in one toss so that they total 11?

    A. $\dfrac{1}{6}$

    B. $\dfrac{1}{11}$

    C. $\dfrac{1}{18}$

    D. $\dfrac{1}{20}$

    E. $\dfrac{1}{36}$

You should simply list all the possible combinations resulting in 11 (5 + 6 and 6 + 5) and realize that the total possibilities are 36 (6 × 6). Thus the probability equals

$$\frac{possibilities\ totaling\ 11}{total\ possibilities} = \frac{2}{36} = \frac{1}{18}$$

The correct answer is **C**.

---

25. What is the probability of tossing a penny twice so that both times it lands heads up?

    A. $\dfrac{1}{8}$

    B. $\dfrac{1}{4}$

    C. $\dfrac{1}{3}$

    D. $\dfrac{1}{2}$

    E. $\dfrac{2}{3}$

The probability of throwing a head in one throw is

$$\frac{chances\ of\ a\ head}{total\ chances\ (1\ head + 1\ tail)} = \frac{1}{2}$$

Since you're trying to throw a head *twice*, multiply the probability for the first toss $\left(\frac{1}{2}\right)$ times the probability for the second toss $\left(again\ \frac{1}{2}\right)$. Thus, $\frac{1}{2} \times \frac{1}{2} = \frac{1}{4}$, and $\frac{1}{4}$ is the probability of throwing heads twice in two tosses. The correct answer is **B**.

Another way of approaching this problem is to look at the total number of possible outcomes:

	First Toss	Second Toss
1.	H	H
2.	H	T
3.	T	H
4.	T	T

There are four different possible outcomes. There is only one way to throw two heads in two tosses. Thus, the probability of tossing two heads in two tosses is 1 out of 4 total outcomes, or $\frac{1}{4}$.

26. How many combinations are possible if a person has 4 sports jackets, 5 shirts, and 3 pairs of slacks?

   A.   4
   B.   5
   C.   12
   D.   60
   E.   120

Since each of the 4 sports jackets may be worn with 5 different shirts, there are 20 possible combinations. These may be worn with each of the 3 pairs of slacks for a total of 60 possible combinations. Stated simply, $5 \times 4 \times 3 = 60$ possible combinations. The correct answer is **D.**

Interpret special symbols

In some problems, you may be given special symbols that you are unfamiliar with. Don't let these special symbols alarm you. They typically represent an operation or combination of operations that you are familiar with. Look for the definition of the special symbol or how it is used.

27. If $\odot$ is a binary operation such that $a \odot b$ is defined as $\frac{a^2 - b^2}{a^2 + b^2}$, then what is the value of $3 \odot 2$?

   A. $-\frac{5}{13}$
   B. $\frac{1}{13}$
   C. $\frac{1}{5}$
   D. $\frac{5}{13}$
   E.   1

The value of $a \odot b =$

$$\frac{a^2 - b^2}{a^2 + b^2}$$

Simply replacing a with 3 and b with 2 gives

$$\frac{3^2 - 2^2}{3^2 + 2^2} = \frac{9 - 4}{9 + 4} = \frac{5}{13}$$

The correct answer is **D.**

Determine the method in procedure problems

Some problems may not ask you to solve and find a correct numerical answer. Rather, you may be asked *how to work* the problem.

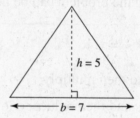

28. To find the area of the figure above, a student could use which formula(s)?

   I.   Area = base times height

   II. Area = $\frac{1}{2}$ times base times height

  III. Area = one side squared

  A. I only

  B. II only

  C. III only

  D. I and II only

  E. I and III only

Notice that it is not necessary to use any of the numerical values given in the diagram. You are simply to identify how the problem can be worked. In such cases, don't bother working the problem; it's a waste of time. The correct answer is **B,** II only.

29. 51×6 could be quickly mentally calculated by

    A. $50 \times 6 + 1$

    B. $51 + 51 + 51 + 51 + 51 + 51$

    C. $(50 \times 6) + (1 \times 6)$

    D. $(50 \times 6) + \dfrac{1}{6}$

    E. adding fifty-one sixes

The quickest method of calculating 51×6 is to first multiply 50×6 (resulting in 300), then multiply 1×6 (resulting in 6), and then add the two answers together ($300 + 6 = 306$). Answer choices **B** and **E** will give the correct answer as well (306), but neither is the best way to *quickly* calculate the answer. The correct answer is **C.**

Sometimes, however, actually working the problem can be helpful, as in the following example.

30. The fastest method to solve $\dfrac{7}{48} \times \dfrac{6}{7} =$ is to

    A. invert the second fraction and then multiply

    B. multiply each column across and then reduce to lowest terms

    C. find the common denominator and then multiply across

    D. divide 7 into numerator and denominator, divide 6 into numerator and denominator, and then multiply across

    E. reduce the first fraction to lowest terms and then multiply across

In this problem, the way to determine the fastest procedure may be to actually work the problem as you would if you were working toward an answer. Then see if that procedure is listed among the choices. You should then compare it to the other methods listed. Is one of the other *correct* methods faster than the one you used? If so, select the fastest.

These types of problems are not constructed to test your knowledge of *obscure* tricks in solving mathematical equations. Rather, they test your knowledge of common procedures used in standard mathematical equations. Thus, the fastest way to solve this problem would be to first divide 7 into the numerator and denominator.

$$\frac{\overset{1}{7}}{48} \times \frac{6}{\underset{1}{7}}$$

Then, divide 6 into the numerator and denominator.

$$\frac{\overset{1}{7}}{\underset{8}{48}} \times \frac{\overset{1}{6}}{\underset{1}{7}}$$

Then, multiply across.

$$\frac{\overset{1}{7}}{\underset{8}{48}} \times \frac{\overset{1}{6}}{\underset{1}{7}} = \frac{1}{8}$$

The correct answer is **D.**

Interpret data—graphs, charts, and tables

Certain problems will be based on graphs, charts, or tables. You will need to be able to read and interpret the data on each graph, chart, or table as well as do some arithmetic with this data.

Spend a few moments to understand the title of each graph, chart, or table as well as what the numbers are representing. Carefully review the coordinate labels in the graphs and the row and column headings in the charts or tables.

- Identify numbers and facts given on the graph, chart, or table and determine what amount those numbers represent.

- There are three main types of charts and tables. The basic ones focus on information given in rows and columns.

- The amounts in decimal or fractional form on a circle graph always total one whole. The amounts in percentage form on a circle graph always total 100%.

- The amounts written as money or in numerical form on a circle graph always add to the total amount being referred to.

- Be sure to thoroughly read a paragraph under a graph if there is one and to interpret a legend if one is included.

- On bar or line graphs, it is sometimes helpful to use the edge of your answer sheet as a straightedge so that you can line up points on the graph with their numerical values on the graph scale. Also, look for trends such as increases, decreases, sudden low points, or sudden high points.

Questions 31, 32, and 33 refer to the following circle graph (pie chart).

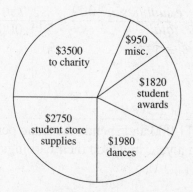

How the Kettle School Distributed
Its Fundraising Earnings

(2009 fundraising earnings totaled $11,000)

---

31. The amount of money given to charity in 2009 was approximately what percent of the total amount earned?

    A. 18%

    B. 34%

    C. 45%

    D. 50%

    E. 82%

Set up a simple ratio.

$$\frac{money\ to\ charity}{total} = \frac{\$3,500}{\$11,000} \approx \frac{1}{3} = 33\frac{1}{3}\%$$

The correct answer is **B.**

---

32. The previous year, 2008, the Kettle School spent 40% of its earnings on student store supplies. This percentage exceeds the 2009 figure by how much?

    A.   0%

    B.   10%

    C.   15%

    D.   30%

    E.   85%

$$\frac{student\ store\ supplies\ in\ 2009}{total} = \frac{\$2,750}{\$11,000} = 25\%$$

$$40\% - 25\% = 15\%$$

The correct answer is **C.**

---

33. If the Kettle School raised $11,000 and spends the same percentage on dances every year, how much will they spend in a year in which their earnings are $15,000?

    A. $270

    B. $2,700

    C. $4,000

    D. $11,000

    E. $15,000

The correct answer is **B.**

$$\text{In } 2009, \frac{\$1,980}{\$11,000} = 18\%$$

$$\text{So } 18\% \text{ of } \$15,000 = \$2,700$$

Questions 34, 35, and 36 refer to the following circle graph (pie chart).

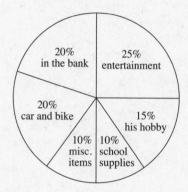

How John Spends His Weekly Paycheck

---

34. If John receives $1000 per paycheck, how much money does he put in the bank?

   A. $20

   B. $200

   C. $350

   D. $800

   E. $1000

20% of $1000 = 0.2(1000) = $200.00. The correct answer is **B.**

---

35. John spends more than twice as much on _____ as he does on school supplies.

   A.   car and bike

   B.   his hobby

   C.   entertainment

   D.   miscellaneous items

   E.   It cannot be determined from the information given.

School supplies are 10%. The only amount more than twice 10% (or 20%) is 25% (entertainment). The correct answer is **C.**

36. The ratio of the amount of money John spends on his hobby to the amount he puts in the bank is

  A. $\frac{1}{6}$

  B. $\frac{1}{2}$

  C. $\frac{2}{3}$

  D. $\frac{3}{4}$

  E. $\frac{5}{8}$

The correct answer is **D.** Set up the ratio.

$$\frac{amount\ to\ hobby}{amount\ to\ bank} = \frac{15}{20} = \frac{3}{4}$$

Questions 37, 38, and 39 refer to the following bar graph.

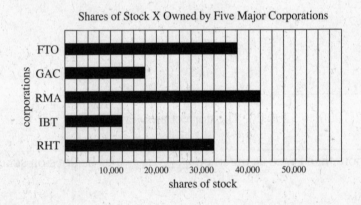

37. The number of shares owned by RHT exceeds the number of shares owned by GAC by

  A. 10,000

  B. 15,000

  C. 17,500

  D. 20,000

  E. 32,500

The correct answer is **B.**

$$\begin{array}{r} 32,500 \text{ RHT} \\ -\ 17,500 \text{ GAC} \\ \hline 15,000 \end{array}$$

38. The number of shares of stock owned by IBT is approximately what percent of that owned by FTO?

    A. 18%

    B. 25%

    C. 33%

    D. 42%

    E. 50%

The correct answer is **C.** 12,500 is what percent of 37,500?

$$\frac{12,500}{37,500} = \frac{1}{3} \approx 33\%$$

39. The number of shares of stock owned by RMA exceeds which other corporations' by more than 20,000?

    A. GAC and IBT

    B. FTO and RHT

    C. GAC and FTO

    D. IBT and FTO

    E. IBT and RHT

$$
\begin{array}{r}
42,500 \text{ RMA} \\
-\ 17,500 \text{ GAC} \\
\hline
25,000 \\
42,500 \text{ RMA} \\
-\ 12,500 \text{ IBT} \\
\hline
30,000
\end{array}
$$

The correct answer is **A.**

Questions 40, 41, and 42 are based on the following graph.

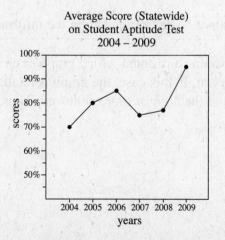

Average Score (Statewide) on Student Aptitude Test 2004 – 2009

40. Between which two years was the greatest rise in average test scores?

    A. 2004 and 2005

    B. 2005 and 2006

    C. 2006 and 2007

    D. 2007 and 2008

    E. 2008 and 2009

The most efficient way to compute greatest rise is to locate the *steepest* upward slope on the chart. Note that the steepest climb is between 2008 and 2009. Therefore, choice **E** indicates the greatest rise in average test scores. The correct answer is **E.**

41. In which year was the average score approximately 85%?

    A. 2004

    B. 2005

    C. 2006

    D. 2007

    E. 2008

According to the graph, the average test score was approximately 85% in 2006. In cases such as this, when you must read the graph for a precise measurement, it may be helpful to use your answer sheet as a straightedge to more accurately compare points with the grid marks along the side. The correct answer is **C.**

42. Approximately what was the highest score achieved statewide on the test?

    A. 80%

    B. 85%

    C. 90%

    D. 97%

    E. The highest score cannot be determined from the information in the graph.

The first thing you should do when confronted with a graph or chart is read its title to understand what the graph is telling you. In this case, the graph is relating information about *average scores*. It tells you nothing about the *highest* score achieved. Thus, the correct answer is **E.**

Question 43 refers to the following table.

Month	Expenses
January	$121,343
February	101,229
March	380,112
April	91,228
May	499,889
June	9,112

43. A product-development division of a corporation allocated the expenses shown in the above chart for the first half of the fiscal year. Approximately how many thousands of dollars were allocated for expenses in that half year?

A.   800

B.   1,000

C.   1,200

D.   1,400

E.   1,600

Since the problem asks for an answer in terms of thousands of dollars, drop the last three digits when estimating.

Month	Expenses
January	$121
February	101
March	380
April	91
May	499
June	9

You can now add the numbers exactly or round them off first to make the addition easier.

Month	Expenses
January	$120
February	100
March	380
April	90
May	500
June	10
	$1,180

$1,180 is closest to 1,200. The correct answer is **C**.

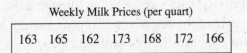

Weekly Milk Prices (per quart)

163   165   162   173   168   172   166

44. The range of a set of numbers is the difference between the two most extreme values, and it is found by subtracting the lowest value from the highest value. Listed above are the weekly prices of milk during the course of two months. What is the range of weekly milk prices?

    A. 3

    B. 9

    C. 10

    D. 11

    E. 12

The highest price in the set is 173. The lowest price is 162. Therefore, the range is $173 - 162 = 11$. The correct answer is **D**.

Questions 45 and 46 refer to the following table.

Average Expenditures for Monthly Housing Expenses					
Metropolitan Area	Mortgage Payment	Property Tax	Hazard Insurance	Utility Cost	Total Monthly Expenses
Large					
Chicago	$2291	$1064	$314	$160	$3829
Houston	$2292	$1048	$326	$174	$3840
Los Angeles	$2403	$1099	$315	$150	$3967
New York	$2291	$1111	$325	$170	$3897
San Francisco	$2445	$1099	$320	$150	$4014
Washington D.C.	$2388	$1085	$314	$191	$3978
All U.S. metropolitan areas with populations of 1.5 million or more	$2299	$1070	$313	$160	$3842
All of the United States	$2273	$1054	$313	$160	$3800

45. Which city's total monthly expenses were closest to the total monthly expenses for areas with populations of 1.5 million or more?

 A. Chicago

 B. Houston

 C. New York

 D. Los Angeles

 E. Washington

First, you must determine the total monthly expenses for all U.S. cities with a population of 1.5 million or more. The last column of the next to the last line shows that the number is $3842 per month. The column at the left shows the cities, and the last column shows their total monthly expenses. Second, you must determine which city's total monthly expenses are closest to the $3842 monthly figure. The correct answer is Houston, which has a total monthly expense of $3840. The correct answer is **B.**

46. You could conclude which of the following statements from information presented in the table?

    A. Los Angeles residents have larger incomes than residents in New York.

    B. The median mortgage payment in Los Angeles is lower than that in Washington.

    C. Housing dollars would stretch further in smaller cities.

    D. Hazard insurance is higher as the total monthly expenses increase.

    E. It costs more for monthly expenses in Washington, San Francisco, and New York than anywhere else in the country.

To answer this question, you must draw a conclusion from information presented in the table. The information in choice **A** cannot be determined from the data in the table. (Don't choose as an answer information that is not presented in a table, even if the statement might be based on accepted fact.) You can quickly eliminate choice **B** because the mortgage payment table shows that the Los Angeles average is $2403, while the Washington average is $2388. You can see that choice **D** is false by looking at the Houston hazard insurance ($326), the highest in the chart, and Houston's total monthly expenses ($3840), one of the lowest in the chart. Choice **E** is false because Los Angeles has the third highest total monthly expenses ($3967).

Notice that the monthly expense column is not in rank order—lowest to highest. **C** can be supported by data presented in the table. Notice that all cities with populations of 1.5 million or more have a total monthly expense figure of $3842. "All of the United States" (the United States considered as a whole) has a total monthly expense of $3800. This means that many small cities reduced the $3842 total monthly figure. So you can conclude that housing dollars would stretch further in smaller cities. The correct answer is **C**.

One special type of chart is a flow chart. Following the flow of information is the key to understanding and using this special kind of chart.

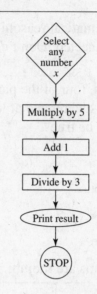

47. If the number chosen, x, is equal to 7, what result will be printed in the flow chart above?

    A. 6

    B. 8

    C. 10

    D. 12

    E. 15

If x is 7, then the steps in the flow chart are as follows:

$$7 \text{ multiplied by } 5 = 35$$

$$35 \text{ plus } 1 = 36$$

$$36 \text{ divided by } 3 = 12$$

So the printed result is 12. The correct answer is **D**.

Focus on the words of formal mathematical reasoning problems

Some questions will contain formal mathematical reasoning. Be sure to focus on the words used, their meaning, and how they are connected. Don't complicate the problem.

---

48. In a drawing with five parallelograms, four of the parallelograms are rectangles and one is a rhombus. If the rhombus is not a square, and at least two of the rectangles are squares, which of the following must be true?

    A. No rhombus is a parallelogram.

    B. Exactly one rectangle is a rhombus.

    C. No rectangles are parallelograms.

    D. Each parallelogram is a rectangle.

    E. At least three of the parallelograms are rhombi.

Since each square is a rhombus, and at least two of the rectangles are squared, then at least three of the parallelograms are rhombi. Use elimination as a tool to help you recognize the correct answer. **A** is false because every rhombus is a parallelogram. **B** is false because at least two of the rectangles are squares; therefore, at least two of the rectangles are rhombi. **C** is false because all rectangles are parallelograms. **D** is false because only four of the five parallelograms are rectangles, and the one that is a rhombus is not a square and therefore not a rectangle. The correct answer is **E**.

> Games are played only by children.
> All children have brown eyes.

---

49. Which of the following conclusions is true if the above statements are true?

    A. Games are not played by children.

    B. Children with brown eyes don't play games.

    C. All brown-eyed people play games.

    D. Children with brown eyes are the only ones who play games.

    E. No games are not played by adults.

Since all children have brown eyes, and games are played only by children, then it can be concluded that children with brown eyes are the only ones who play games. The correct answer is **D**.

> All cats have tails. Some cats are furry. Chico is a cat.

50. If the statements above are true, which of the following statements is true based on the information given?

    A. Some furry animals don't have tails.

    B. Chico has a tail but no fur.

    C. Cats without tails must be furry.

    D. Chico has a tail but doesn't have to be furry.

    E. Chico has fur but doesn't have to have a tail.

Since all cats have tails, and Chico is a cat, then Chico must have a tail. Since some cats are furry, Chico doesn't have to be furry. The correct answer is **D**.

Tips for Working Math Problems

1. Read the question carefully, circling, underlining, and writing down what you are looking for.

2. Pull out important information.

3. Draw, sketch, or mark in diagrams or on scratch paper.

4. If you know a simple method or formula, work the problem out as simply and quickly as possible.

5. If you don't know a simple method or formula,

    (a) try eliminating some unreasonable choices.

    (b) work from the answers or substitute in numbers if appropriate.

    (c) try approximating to clarify thinking and simplify work.

6. Always make sure that your answer is reasonable.

A PATTERNED PLAN OF ATTACK
Mathematics

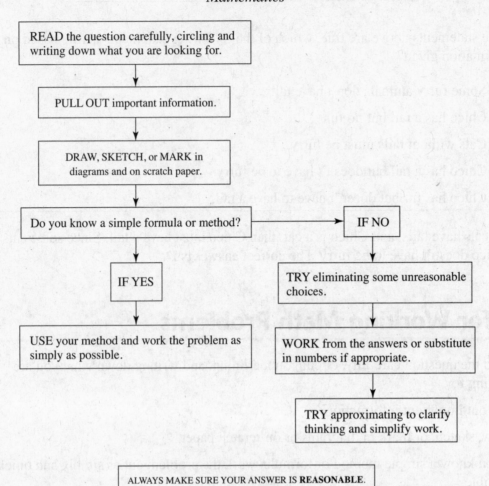

READ the question carefully, circling and writing down what you are looking for.

↓

PULL OUT important information.

↓

DRAW, SKETCH, or MARK in diagrams and on scratch paper.

↓

Do you know a simple formula or method? → IF NO

IF YES (from "Do you know a simple formula or method?")

IF NO → TRY eliminating some unreasonable choices.

USE your method and work the problem as simply as possible.

WORK from the answers or substitute in numbers if appropriate.

↓

TRY approximating to clarify thinking and simplify work.

ALWAYS MAKE SURE YOUR ANSWER IS **REASONABLE**.

Introduction to the Writing Test Multiple-Choice Section

Paper-based: 30 minutes and 38 multiple-choice questions
Computer-based: 38 minutes and 44 multiple-choice questions

Multiple-Choice Writing Test Format

The PPST Writing Test contains two parts in multiple choice and one part in essay writing. This section will review the multiple-choice format, which is composed of two parts—Part A: **English usage** and Part B: **sentence correction**—with the following content areas and approximate percentages:

Grammatical Relationships (noun, pronoun, verb, adjective, and adverb errors)	17%
Structural Relationships (coordination, subordination, comparison, and parallelism errors)	19%
Word Choice and Mechanics (word choice, idiom, mechanics errors)	14%

Part A – English Usage

Ability tested

This section tests your ability to recognize errors in standard written English.

Basic skills necessary

Knowledge of some basic grammar is essential in this section. Review the rules of correctness that have been emphasized in your high school and college English classes.

Directions

Some of the following sentences are correct. Others contain problems in grammar, usage, idiom, diction, punctuation, and capitalization in standard written English.

If there is an error, it will be underlined and lettered. Find the one underlined part that must be changed to make the sentence correct and choose the corresponding letter on your answer sheet. No sentence has more than one error. Mark **E** if the sentence contains no error.

Analysis of directions

1. You are looking for errors in standard written English, the kind of English used in most textbooks. Do not evaluate a sentence in terms of the spoken English we all use.

2. When deciding whether an underlined portion is correct or not, assume that *all other parts of the sentence are correct.*

Suggested approach with samples

Focus on the verbs

First focus on the verb or verbs. A verb is a word that expresses a state of being, event, or action. It is an important part of the sentence since it reveals something about the subject.

> **1.** <u>Here</u> on the table <u>is</u> an <u>apple</u> and <u>three pears</u>. <u>No error</u>
>   A   B   C   D   E

Focus on the verb (*is*) and ask yourself what the subject is. In this sentence, the subject (*an apple and three pears*) follows the verb. Since the subject is plural, the verb must be plural—*are* instead of *is*. The correct answer is **B**.

Check the verb tenses

Another type of verb error occurs when the verb tenses (past, present, future) are inconsistent. If there are two verbs in the sentence, make sure that the verb tense of each is in agreement.

> **2.** He walked <u>for</u> miles <u>and</u> finally <u>sees</u> a <u>sign</u> of civilization. <u>No error</u>
>   A   B   C   D   E

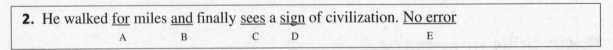

Walked describes the past; *sees* describes the present. *Sees* must be changed to *saw* so that the whole sentence describes the past. But remember, on this section of the test you don't have to actually make the corrections, and you don't have to know the precise term that describes a given error. You need only recognize the error. Therefore, learning what the errors "look like" is more efficient preparation than memorizing grammatical terminology. The correct answer is **C**.

Look for pronoun errors

Watch for incorrect pronoun references. There are many types of pronouns, but pay close attention to personal subjective pronoun errors (*I, you, he, she, it, they*) and personal objective pronoun errors (*me, you, him, her, it, them*). Other common errors are found in possessive pronouns used as adjectives (*my, your, his, her, its, their*) and pronoun-antecedent agreement errors when the pronoun does not match the noun it is replacing. The following example illustrates this type of pronoun error.

> **3.** We rewarded the workers <u>whom</u>, according <u>to</u> the manager, <u>had done</u> the most
>   A   B   C
>
>   <u>imaginative</u> job. <u>No error</u>
>   D   E

To test between *who* and *whom*, try replacing *whom* with either *him* or *them:* "them . . . had done the most imaginative job." To test whether *who* is correct instead, try substituting *he* or *they:* "they . . . had done the most imaginative job." Remember, if *him* or *them* fits when substituted, *whom* is correct. If *he* or *they* fits when substituted, *who* is correct. The correct answer is **A.**

Check the adjectives and adverbs

A common error is using an adjective when an adverb is required or vice versa. An adjective is a word that describes or modifies a noun or a pronoun. An adverb is a word that describes or modifies a verb, an adjective, or another adverb.

> **4.** The mechanic <u>repaired</u> <u>my</u> engine and <u>installed</u> a new clutch <u>very quick</u>. <u>No error</u>
>   A   B   C   D   E

Adjectives describe things (nouns and pronouns), and adverbs describe actions (verbs). In this case, actions are being described (*repaired* and *installed* are verbs), so the word that describes those actions should be an adverb, *quickly* instead of *quick*. As you might notice, adverbs often end with *–ly*. The correct use of the adjective *quick* in a sentence occurs in this example: "The quick work of the mechanic pleased me very much." In this case, a thing is being described (*work*), so an adjective is appropriate. The correct answer is **D.**

Notice parallelism

Parallelism is matching grammar structure within a sentence. The following sentence contains an example of faulty parallelism.

> **5.** He <u>liked</u> <u>swimming</u>, <u>weight lifting</u>, and <u>to run</u>. <u>No error</u>
>   A   B   C   D   E

To run is incorrect. It should end with *–ing* to match the structure of the other words (*swimming* and *lifting*). The correct answer is **D.**

Consider idioms

The following sentence contains an error in idiom.

> **6.** The young man <u>had been</u> <u>addicted of</u> drugs <u>ever since</u> his <u>thirteenth</u> birthday. <u>No error</u>
>   A   B   C   D   E

The correct idiom is *addicted to,* not *addicted of.* The correct answer is **B.**

Watch for dangling elements

A dangling element (modifier) affects the meaning of a sentence by implying something that does not actually appear in the sentence. Sentences with dangling elements often appear illogical and cause the reader to become confused about the author's intended meaning.

> **7.** <u>Stumbling around</u>, the light switch <u>was</u> <u>nowhere</u> <u>to be</u> found. <u>No error</u>
>   A   B   C   D   E

The sentence seems to say that the light switch is *stumbling around.* In order to change this absurd and humorous meaning, you would need to insert *I realized that* or similar wording so the sentence now reads, "Stumbling around, I realized that . . . " Otherwise, *stumbling around* dangles, not referring clearly to any other element in the sentence. The correct answer is **A.**

Pay attention to comparisons

A sentence may contain a comparison error.

> **8.** After <u>deliberating</u> <u>for</u> hours, the judges could not decide <u>who</u> was the <u>greatest</u> of the two
>   A   B   C   D
>
> boxers. <u>No error</u>
>   E

When only two things are being compared, in this case two boxers, *-er* words (*greater, taller, more beautiful*) should be used; *-est* words like *greatest* are used only when more than two things are being compared. "He was the greatest contender in the history of boxing." The correct answer is **D.**

Notice capitalization and punctuation

A sentence may contain an error of capitalization or punctuation.

> **9.** We have invested over ten thousand dollars in <u>C</u>anadian postage stamps<u>,</u> English china<u>;</u>
>   A   B   C
>
> and <u>F</u>rench wines. <u>No error</u>
>   D   E

The capital letters here are correct, but the semicolon should be a comma in a series. The correct answer is **C.**

Practice in English Usage

Questions

1. Some <u>symphonic arrangements</u> of the
A
Beatles tunes <u>sound</u> more <u>melodiously</u>
B$$C
than the original Beatles <u>band versions</u>.
D
<u>No error</u>
E

2. The scientist <u>reported</u> his latest
A
laboratory findings <u>as to</u> the
B
<u>biochemical and physiological</u> causes
C
of alcohol <u>addiction</u>. <u>No error</u>
DE

3. Black Americans <u>were legally</u>
A
<u>enfranchised</u> by ratification of the
A
Fourteenth and Fifteenth <u>Amendments</u>
B
<u>and by subsequent</u> acts of <u>Congress, but</u>
B$$C
<u>enforcement</u> of their voting rights
C
<u>has remained</u> a continuing struggle.
D
<u>No error</u>
E

4. <u>Of the twelve teachers</u>, Mr. Feingold
A
was the <u>more widely</u> respected because
B
of <u>his reputation</u> for fairness and
C
consistency <u>in grading</u> his students.
D
<u>No error</u>
E

5. After discussing the <u>depleted</u> treasury
A
with <u>Mr. Taylor</u>, John felt that
B
<u>he should have been</u> the one to head
C
the committee's fundraising drive
<u>in November, 2008</u>. <u>No error</u>
D$$E

6. The rookie first <u>baseman, who</u> was
A
a better player than most of the
veterans, could <u>throw, catch</u>, and hit
B
<u>more consistent</u> than any player
C
<u>with twice</u> the years of experience.
D
<u>No error</u>
E

7. "<u>Who</u> cares whether poor people
A
<u>can take</u> care of themselves or
B
<u>not?" asked</u> the rich old <u>woman while</u>
C$$D
munching her caviar dreamily. <u>No error</u>
E

8. Hoping <u>to reserve</u> a room at an
A
inexpensive <u>hotel Bill</u> phoned many
B
lodgings before he <u>concluded that</u>
C
cheap accommodations <u>were</u>
D
impossible to find. <u>No error</u>
E

67

9. The Venus'-flytrap, a <u>well-known</u>
A
carnivorous plant <u>that eats animals,</u>
B
<u>responds</u> almost <u>instantaneously</u> to an
C D
entering insect. <u>No error</u>
E

10. The <u>drama's</u> charm might be seen as
A
<u>being comprised of</u> these elements<u>:</u> an
B C
extraordinary leading <u>lady, an</u>
D
exceptionally vivid rendering by all
players of the author's intent, and an
exquisite set design. <u>No error</u>
E

11. A major task of the reader of
instructional materials in science <u>is</u> to
A
understand a <u>host</u> of details in <u>their</u>
B C
textbook that <u>lead</u> up to generalizations
D
or abstractions. <u>No error</u>
E

12. "It is a matter of <u>principal,"</u> he
A
<u>said, "and</u> I will not be <u>dissuaded from</u>
B C
the task <u>at hand."</u> <u>No error</u>
D E

13. With tears in their <u>eyes, the</u> mourners,
A
<u>including the widow of the late John T.</u>
B
<u>Smith,</u> <u>filed by</u> the <u>grave and</u> then
B C D
returned to their cars for the long
journey home. <u>No error</u>
E

14. <u>Unable</u> to keep a secret, he <u>announced</u>
A B
the <u>stupidity of his friend</u> to <u>each and</u>
C D
<u>every member</u> of the class. <u>No error</u>
D E

15. <u>Either he meant to arrive at the business</u>
A
<u>meeting</u> in time for the <u>chairman's</u>
A B
opening statement or the sales
manager's report<u>;</u> in any case<u>,</u> he
C D
missed both. <u>No error</u>
E

Answers

1. **C.** *Melodious,* the adjective, is correct here to modify *tunes. Sound* is used here in the same sense as *seem,* rather than in the sense of *the bell sounded,* meaning *made a sound.* Linking verbs of this kind may be followed by an adjective but not by an adverb.

2. **B.** *About* or *regarding* or *concerning* would be correct. *As to* is nonstandard usage.

3. **E.** The sentence contains no error. The comma after *Congress* correctly separates the two complete sentences.

4. **B.** *Most widely* is the correct comparative form in this sentence because Mr. Feingold is being compared with several teachers. Were he being compared with only one other, *more* would be correct.

5. C. While the verb form *should have been* is correct, referring to an event in the past, it is unclear to whom the pronoun *he* refers—Mr. Taylor or John. There are several methods that might be used to correct the ambiguity. For example, *him* could be substituted for Mr. Taylor and Mr. Taylor for *he* (if that is what is meant). Or a complete rewrite might be called for. *John was convinced that he should have been the one to head the committee's fundraising drive in November, 2008, especially after discussing the matter with Mr. Taylor.*

6. C. *More consistently,* the comparative adverb, is correct, modifying the verbs *throw, catch,* and *hit.*

7. E. There is no error here. The question mark is correctly placed. It applies only to the part of the sentence in quotation marks.

8. B. A comma is needed after *hotel* to separate the introductory descriptive phrase from the rest of the sentence.

9. B. *That eats animals* is redundant, repeating the meaning of *carnivorous,* and should be omitted. The words *well* and *known* are correctly joined by the hyphen when used as a modifier preceding the noun.

10. B. *Being comprised of* is incorrect. It should be *comprising.* The word comprise means to be composed of. Thus, *being comprised of* would translate to *being composed of of.* The colon **C** correctly introduces the series.

11. C. *Their* should be singular because it refers to *reader,* which is singular. *His or her* would be correct. To avoid the *his or her* construction, the sentence might be rewritten using the plural *readers;* however, that is not given as an option.

12. A. *Principal* is either a noun meaning the administrator of a school or an adjective meaning main or primary. What is required here is the noun *principle,* meaning a fundamental law or doctrine. The use of quotation marks and commas is correct throughout.

13. B. *Late* means dead and *widow* is the name for a woman whose husband has died. Using both words is repetitious. All other underlined portions are correct. The comma after *eyes* is correct to separate the introductory phrase from the rest of the sentence; *filed by* is acceptable idiom; and there is no need for punctuation separating the compound predicate *filed and returned.*

14. D. *Each and every* is both a cliché and unnecessary repetition. Either *each* or *every* is correct but not both.

15. A. There is confusion in meaning because of the placement of the word *either.* As the sentence stands, the reader expects a parallel structure to *to arrive,* and there is none. *He meant to arrive at the business meeting in time for either the chairman's opening statement or the sales manager's report* would be clearer, providing the parallel *statement or . . . report* closer to *either.*

A PATTERNED PLAN OF ATTACK
English Usage

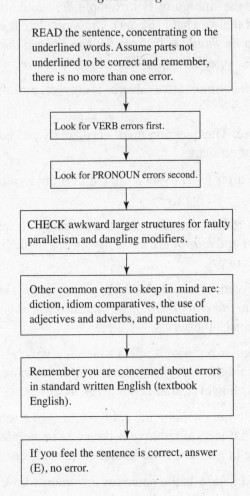

READ the sentence, concentrating on the underlined words. Assume parts not underlined to be correct and remember, there is no more than one error.

Look for VERB errors first.

Look for PRONOUN errors second.

CHECK awkward larger structures for faulty parallelism and dangling modifiers.

Other common errors to keep in mind are: diction, idiom comparatives, the use of adjectives and adverbs, and punctuation.

Remember you are concerned about errors in standard written English (textbook English).

If you feel the sentence is correct, answer (E), no error.

Part B – Sentence Correction

Ability tested

This section tests your knowledge of correct and effective English expression.

Basic skills necessary

Knowledge of basic rules of grammar, language, and usage is essential in this section.

Directions

Some part of each sentence below is underlined; sometimes the whole sentence is underlined. Five choices for rephrasing the underlined part follow each sentence. The first choice **A** repeats the original, and the other four choices are different. If choice **A** seems better than the alternatives, choose answer **A**; if not, select one of the other choices.

For each sentence, consider the requirements of standard written English. Your choice should be a correct, concise, and effective expression, not awkward or ambiguous. Focus on grammar, word choice, sentence construction, and punctuation. If a choice changes the meaning of the original sentence, do not select it.

Analysis of directions

1. Several alternatives to an underlined portion may be correct. You are to pick the best (most clear and exact) one.

2. Remember that in sentence-correction questions, there may be *more* than one kind of error in the sentence.

3. Any alternative that changes the *meaning* of the sentence should not be chosen, no matter how clear or correct it is.

Suggested approach with samples

Focus on the verbs

As with the usage questions, begin with a careful study of the verb or verbs.

---

1. The trunk containing <u>costumes, makeup, and props were left</u> at the stage entrance of the theater.

    A. costumes, makeup, and props were left

    B. costumes, makeup, and props were all left

    C. costumes, makeup, and props was left

    D. costumes, makeup, and props to be left

    E. costumes, makeup, and props left

The verb is *were*. Since the subject is singular (*trunk*), the verb must be singular—*was* instead of *were*. Don't assume that the subject immediately precedes the verb. In this case, the subject and verb are some distance apart. The correct answer is **C.**

Check the verb tenses

Look carefully at the verb tenses (past, present, future). If there are two or more verbs in the sentence, make sure the verb tense of each is appropriate.

---

2. He <u>read the recipe carefully, follows</u> directions, and used expensive ingredients, but the cake was inedible.

   A. read the recipe carefully, follows

   B. had read the recipe carefully, follows

   C. reads the recipe carefully, followed

   D. reads the recipe carefully, follows

   E. read the recipe carefully, followed

All three verbs in the first part should be in the same tense. Since *used* is in the past tense and cannot be changed, **E** is the correct choice, since it uses two past tenses (*read, followed*). The correct answer is **E**.

Notice parallelism

Another common error is faulty parallelism. Look for a series of items separated by commas and make sure each item has the same *form*.

---

3. <u>To strive, to seek, to find, and not yielding</u> are the heroic goals of Ulysses in Tennyson's famous poem.

   A. To strive, to seek, to find, and not yielding

   B. To strive, to seek, to find, and to yield

   C. To strive, to seek, to find, and not to yield

   D. To strive, to seek, to find, and yet to yield

   E. Striving, seeking, finding, and yielding

Not yielding is incorrect. It should have the "to ___" form of the other items. **B, D,** and **E** are correct, but they change the meaning of the sentence. The correct answer is **C**.

Check the adjectives and adverbs

Adjective or adverb misuse constitutes another type of error.

---

4. <u>The tired mechanic, happily to be finished with a hard day's work</u>, closed the hood over the newly tuned engine.

    A. The tired mechanic, happily to be finished with a hard day's work

    B. Happily, the tired mechanic being finished with a hard day's work

    C. Tired but happy with a hard day's work being done, the mechanic

    D. The tired mechanic, happy to be finished with a hard day's work

    E. With the pleasant fatigue of a job well done, the mechanic

---

Happily is used here to describe a person, the mechanic. The correct part of speech for describing a person or thing is an adjective, *happy*. The correct choice is grammatically correct, logical, economical, and clear without unnecessarily changing the intended meaning of the original sentence. The correct answer is **D.**

Consider idioms

Sometimes a sentence contains an error in idiom—that is, it employs a word or phrase that is incorrect simply because it has not been established as standard usage. Such errors just don't "sound right."

---

5. <u>After waiting on the arrival of a washer repairman for hours</u>, the customer resigned himself to using the laundromat.

    A. After waiting on the arrival of a washer repairman for hours

    B. With no arrival of a washer repairman for hours

    C. After hours of waiting for the arrival of a washer repairman

    D. Waiting after hours for the arrival of a washer repairman

    E. In the face of hours of waiting for a washer repairman

---

Waiting on is not idiomatic in this context, although a waiter may *wait on* a table. Here, the correct expression is *waiting for*. Choices **C, D,** and **E** employ this construction, but **D** and **E** significantly obscure and change the intended meaning of the original sentence. The correct answer is **C.**

Watch for dangling elements

A type of error that affects a whole phrase rather than just one word is a dangling element, or misplaced modifier.

---

6. <u>Looking through the lens of a camera,</u> Mount Rushmore seemed much smaller and farther away than it had only seconds before.

   A. Looking through the lens of a camera

   B. With camera in hand

   C. Through the effects of the lens of a camera she looks through

   D. When she looked through the camera lens

   E. Against the camera

The sentence seems to say that Mount Rushmore is looking through the camera lens. Choice **D** makes it clear that a person is looking through the lens and does so without the excessive wordiness of choice **C**. The correct answer is **D**.

Pay attention to comparisons

A sentence may contain a comparison error.

---

7. She wished that her career could be <u>as glamorous as the other women</u> but was not willing to work as hard as they had.

   A. as glamorous as the other women

   B. as glamorous as the other women's careers

   C. with the glamour of other women

   D. more glamorous than the careers of the other women

   E. glamorous

Here, two very different *incomparable* things are being compared. *Her career* is being compared to the *other women*. Choice **B**, the most clear, complete, and sensible construction, compares *her career* to *the other women's careers*. The correct answer is **B**.

Summary

Generally, watch out for pronouns, verbs, and awkward larger structures (illustrated by errors like faulty parallelism). Other possible errors that have not been explained above are fully explained in the answer sections following the practice tests. Remember that, unlike these examples, the sentences on the test may contain more than one kind of error.

Practice in Sentence Correction

Questions

1. Many professional-football fans feel Peyton Manning is <u>the best quarterback when compared to</u> Tom Brady.

   A. the best quarterback when compared to

   B. a better quarterback than

   C. one of the best quarterbacks when compared to

   D. the best quarterback that compared to

   E. the best quarterback compared to

2. Many college freshmen with poor writing skills <u>are liable from making careless grammar and punctuation errors</u>, but many writing instructors try to teach them to be more self-corrective.

   A. are liable from making careless grammar and punctuation errors

   B. are liable from making careless grammar and punctuation mistakes

   C. are liable to make careless grammar and punctuation errors

   D. are careless and liable to make grammar and punctuation errors

   E. are liable for making careless grammar and punctuation errors

3. The mayor, in addition to the city council members, <u>are contemplating the rezoning</u> of a hundred acres of undeveloped land within the city limits.

   A. are contemplating the rezoning

   B. are contemplating rezoning

   C. is contemplating over the rezoning

   D. is contemplating the rezoning

   E. all contemplate over the rezoning

4. Because of the accident <u>his insurance policy was canceled, his friends alienated, and his car abandoned</u>.

   A. his insurance policy was canceled, his friends alienated, and his car abandoned

   B. his insurance policy canceled, friends alienated, and car abandoned

   C. he canceled his insurance policy, alienated his friends, and abandoned his car

   D. his insurance policy was canceled, his friends were alienated, and his car was abandoned

   E. his insurance policy, his friends, and his car were canceled, alienated, and abandoned respectively

5. The ability to understand written English improves as <u>the skills of oral language increases</u>.

   A. the skills of oral language increases

   B. oral language increases

   C. oral language increase

   D. the skills of oral language increase

   E. the skills improve oral language

6. <u>To function well in the business world, requires that one be willing to spend long hours preparing materials for effective visual presentations.</u>

   A. To function well in the business world, requires that one be willing to spend long hours preparing materials for effective visual presentations.

   B. To function good in the business world requires that one be willing to spend long hours preparing materials for effective visual presentations.

   C. To function well in the business world, requires that one be willing to spend long hours preparing materials for affective visual presentations.

   D. To function well in the business world, requires that one be willing and able to spend long hours preparing materials for effective visual presentations.

   E. To function well in the business world requires that one be willing to spend long hours preparing materials for effective visual presentations.

7. Taking an occasional respite between chapters or assignments is more desirable <u>than a long, continuous period of study</u>.

   A. than a long, continuous period of study

   B. than a period of long, continuous study

   C. than a long period of continuous study

   D. than studying for a long, continuous period

   E. than a study period long and continuous

8. The small seagoing craft was washed against the rocks <u>while the captain struggled to turn the wheel, and the craft foundered</u> with all on board.

   A. while the captain struggled to turn the wheel, and the craft foundered

   B. while the captain struggled to turn the wheel and the craft floundered

   C. , while the captain struggled to turn the wheel and the craft foundered

   D. because the captain struggled to turn the wheel, and the craft foundered

   E. while the captain struggled to turn the wheel: and the craft foundered

9. Secularization of schools during the Renaissance is evidenced by school curricula that focused on the individual's place in society, de-emphasizing religious matters and <u>became more interested in affairs of this world</u>.

   A. became more interested in affairs of this world

   B. had become more interested in affairs of this world

   C. became interested more in worldly affairs

   D. becoming more interested in affairs of this world

   E. interest in worldly affairs

10. After many years of saving, worrying, and <u>studying, she took great pride in being the first in her family to graduate college</u>.

   A. studying, she took great pride in being the first in her family to graduate college

   B. studying, she took great pride in being the first in her family to graduate from college

   C. study, she took great pride in being the first in her family to graduate from college

   D. studying, he or she took great pride in being the first family member to graduate college

   E. study, she took great pride in being the first in her family to be graduated from college

11. Rolling the ball down the hill, <u>the toddler did not see the bicycle and narrowly escaped being struck by it's front wheel</u>.

   A. the toddler did not see the bicycle and narrowly escaped being struck by it's front wheel

   B. the toddler did not see the bicycle and narrowly escaped being struck by it's front wheels

   C. the toddler did not see the bicycle and narrowly escaped being struck by its front wheel

   D. the bicycle was not seen by the toddler, and he narrowly escaped being struck by its front wheel

   E. the toddler did not see the bicycle and narrowly escaped being stricken by it's front wheel

12. We trust your judgment implicitly, knowing that <u>whoever you choose will do a fine job</u>.

   A. whoever you choose will do a fine job

   B. you will choose whoever will do a fine job

   C. whomever you choose will do a fine job

   D. you will choose whomever will do a fine job

   E. a fine job will be done by whomever you choose

13. <u>After having won first place in the regional finals</u>, the talented twelve-year-old girl began working out for the national gymnastics competition.

   A. After having won first place in the regional finals

   B. Having won first place in the regional finals

   C. To win first place in the regional finals

   D. Soon after having won first place in the regional finals

   E. After the regional finals

14. <u>The board feels strongly that at this point in time there is no proven need</u> for a new gymnasium floor or a repaved track.

   A. The board feels strongly that at this point in time there is no proven need

   B. The board feels strong that at this point in time there is no proven need

   C. The board says strongly, that at this point in time there is no proven need

   D. The board feels strongly that at present there is no proven need

   E. There is a strong feeling that at this point in time there is no proved need

15. <u>Less rainfall means less traffic accidents</u> according to several experts on highway safety.

   A. Less rainfall means less traffic accidents

   B. A lack of rainfall means less traffic accidents

   C. Less rainfall means the least traffic accidents

   D. Less rainfall means fewer traffic accidents

   E. Fewer rainfalls means less traffic accidents

Answers

1. **B.** When you compare two items, *better* is correct. Choice **B** correctly words the comparison of the two quarterbacks. In addition, choice **B,** by deleting *when compared to,* is concise and less wordy.

2. **C.** *Liable from* is idiomatically incorrect. Choice **C** corrects the error with *liable to,* meaning having a tendency to. Choice **D** changes the original meaning, and **E** suggests a legal meaning with *liable for,* a meaning not implied by the context of the original sentence.

3. **D.** There is a subject-verb error here, which is corrected by choice **D.** *Contemplating over* in choices **C** and **E** is idiomatically wrong. Phrases beginning with constructions such as *in addition to, as well as,* and *along with* affect the number of neither the subject nor the verb.

4. **D.** The difficulty with the original sentence is that the verb *was* is being made to function with three separate elements: insurance policy, friends, and car. One can say *insurance policy was* and *car was* but not *friends was.* Choice **D** corrects the problem by using the proper form of the verb with each element. Choice **B** suggests that the *policy, friends,* and *car* are acting, which the original sentence does not suggest. Choice **C** suggests that *he* is acting, again something not suggested in the original. While choice **E** retains the intent of the original, it is extremely wordy and awkward.

5. **D.** *Skills,* a plural noun, requires a plural verb, *increase.* Choices **B** and **E** change the meaning of the original sentence, and **C** has another subject-verb error.

6. **E.** The phrase *to function well in the business world* acts as the subject of this sentence and, as such, should not be separated from its verb, *requires,* by a comma. Choice **B** removes the comma but introduces an error in using the adjective *good* rather than the adverb *well.* Choice **C** both retains the comma and introduces an error in using *affective* instead of *effective.* Choice **D** retains the comma and introduces a cliché in *willing and able.*

7. **D.** You cannot compare *taking . . . respite* and a *period of study.* Choice **D** correctly words the comparison so that the sentence compares *taking* and *studying.*

8. **A.** The sentence is correct as given. Choice **B** uses the word *floundered* (meaning *to move awkwardly*) for *foundered* (which in nautical terms means *to sink*) and removes the necessary comma separating the two complete sentences. Choice **C** adds a comma before *while,* changing its meaning from *at the same time* to the meaning of the conjunction *but* or *and* and drops the necessary comma. Choice **D** introduces a cause-and-effect relationship that the original does not suggest, and **E** improperly uses a colon.

9. **D.** The original sentence lacks parallel structure. Choice **D** corrects this error by using *becoming,* a verb form that is parallel with *de-emphasizing.*

10. **B.** The correct idiom is *graduate from college,* not *graduate college.* Choices **C** and **E** both introduce an error in parallelism in that they substitute *study* for *studying.* *Study* is not parallel to *saving* and *worrying.* While the phrase *to be graduated from college* in choice **E** is accepted in informal English, it is not preferred in standard written English. There is no reason to add *he or she* as in choice **D,** because the original sentence is speaking of a specific individual.

11. **C.** *Its* is the possessive form. *It's* is the contraction for *it is.* Choice **B** retains the original error and adds another, the plural *wheels,* which would be inappropriate in speaking of a bicycle. Choice **D** introduces a misplaced modifier and suggests that the bicycle was rolling the ball down the hill. Choice **E** incorrectly uses *stricken* (which most commonly means *afflicted*) and also retains the original apostrophe error.

12. **C.** This is a pronoun error. *Whoever* should be changed to *whomever.* Choices **D** and **E** change the original sentence unnecessarily and slightly alter its meaning.

13. **B.** *After* is unnecessarily repetitious; it may be eliminated without damaging the clarity or meaning of the original sentence. Choices **C, D,** and **E** either change the meaning of the original or leave out necessary information.

14. **D.** *At this point in time* is clichéd and awkward. It should be replaced with a direct and concise form such as *at present* or *now.* All other choices retain the cliché. In addition, choice **B** incorrectly uses the adjective *strong* rather than the adverb *strongly;* choice **C** changes the original meaning by inserting *says* in place of *feels* and introduces an error by using a comma before *that;* choice **E** leaves out necessary information and unnecessarily changes *proven* to *proved* (both *proven need* and *proved need* are correct).

15. **D.** *Fewer* is used correctly to refer to items that are countable, and *less* is used correctly to refer to items that are not countable. In this sentence, *less* belongs with *rainfall* and *fewer* belongs with *accidents.*

A PATTERNED PLAN OF ATTACK
Sentence Correction

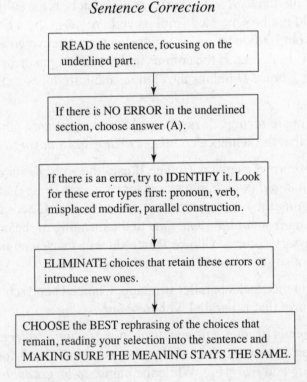

READ the sentence, focusing on the underlined part.

↓

If there is NO ERROR in the underlined section, choose answer (A).

↓

If there is an error, try to IDENTIFY it. Look for these error types first: pronoun, verb, misplaced modifier, parallel construction.

↓

ELIMINATE choices that retain these errors or introduce new ones.

↓

CHOOSE the BEST rephrasing of the choices that remain, reading your selection into the sentence and MAKING SURE THE MEANING STAYS THE SAME.

Introduction to the Writing Test
Essay Section

The essay section for both the paper-based and computer-based Writing Test is 30 minutes in length and contains one essay question. You are asked to draw upon your personal experiences and observations for information, examples, and generalizations to be used in your writing. The essay question generates a raw score that ranges from 2 to 12. (This raw score is the sum of the scores of two readers who each assign a score of 1 to 6.)

Ability Tested

The essay section of the exam tests your ability to read a topic carefully, to organize your ideas before you write, and to write with clarity and precision.

Basic Skills Necessary

This section requires a basic college-level writing background. Papers are scored on the writer's ability to achieve the following: organization and the logical development of ideas with supporting evidence of specific examples; understanding of the essay's intended audience (for example, a speech urging members of a city council to vote a certain way); comprehension of the assigned task; skillful use of language; and correctness of mechanics, usage, and paragraphing.

Directions

In this section, you will have 30 minutes to plan and write one essay on the topic given. You may use the paper provided to plan your essay before you begin writing. You should plan your time wisely. Read the topic carefully to make sure that you are properly addressing the issue or situation. **You must write on the given topic. An essay on another topic will not be acceptable.**

The essay question is designed to give you an opportunity to write clearly and effectively. Use specific examples whenever appropriate to aid in supporting your ideas. Keep in mind that the quality of your writing is much more important than the length of your essay.

Paper-based

Your essay is to be written in the space provided. There is a section for planning and outlining your essay. Your writing should be neat and legible. Because you have only a limited amount of space in which to write, please do **not** skip lines, do **not** write excessively large, and do **not** leave wide margins.

Computer-based

The computer screen appears split horizontally. The top part of the screen will show your essay topic. Type your essay on the lower half of the computer screen.

Analysis of Directions

1. On the essay part of the PPST, you will have 30 minutes to write on one assigned topic. You will have space for prewriting notes to help you organize your thoughts. (These notes will *not* be read by the persons grading your exam.)

2. It is recommended that you use this space to organize your thoughts. Paper-based examinees double-check to determine how much space you have in which to write your essay. At present, the test provides two blank sides of lined 8½" by 11" paper.

General Tips for Writing the Essay

1. Read the topic twice—three times if necessary—before writing. Circle, underline, or write down key words to help you focus on the assigned task.

2. Use a form of "prewriting" *before* you begin writing your actual essay. Prewriting may consist of outlining, brainstorming, clustering, or another variation. Spend about five minutes doing this "organizing" before you start writing. A poorly written essay is often the result of inadequate planning.

3. Don't let spelling slow down your writing. Keep the flow of your writing going; then come back later to correct spelling errors.

4. Try to leave several minutes at the end to reread and edit/correct your essay. At this time, don't make extensive changes. Simply correct spelling errors and other minor flaws.

5. For paper-based examinees, don't write excessively large. Don't leave wide margins. Don't skip any lines.

6. Double-check your time allotment and the amount of space you have in which to write your essay.

7. Computer-based examinees have three editing tools to help with changes and revisions. These tools are *cut, paste,* and *undo.*

Sample Essay Topic and Prewriting Methods

Topic

Teachers can play an important part in our lives. Choose one particular teacher you had during your school years and discuss one of his or her personal qualities which contributed to that teacher's impact on you.

Prewriting Methods

Clustering

Use clustering as a way of organizing your thoughts before you write. After you choose the "subject" (in this case, person) for your essay, write it down on the prewriting area and draw a circle around it.

For a few moments, think of a few possible "personal qualities which contributed to that teacher's impact on you." Write them down and connect them to the central subject cluster.

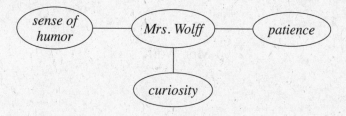

Now, from these qualities, select the one you can best develop into an essay. That is, choose the circle that you can support with *specific examples*.

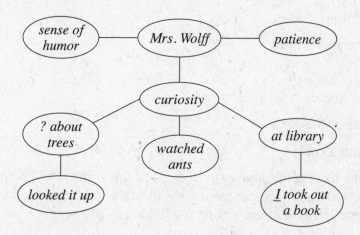

If you find that you can't come up with enough specific examples for the quality you initially chose, then choose another. You don't want to spend a great deal of time in clustering, however, just enough to give you a basic plan of how to write your essay. You can then number the parts of the cluster to give an order to your thoughts.

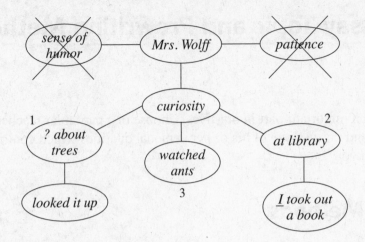

You don't have to use all of the elements of your cluster. (In fact, you'll be ignoring those headings for which you don't have support.) Clustering provides a way to put all of your thoughts down on paper before you write so that you can quickly see the structure of the whole paper.

Outlining

Another way of prewriting is outlining. A simple outline for this essay could go something like this.

Mrs. Wolff

  I. Sense of humor

 II. Patience

III. Curiosity

      A. Didn't know about trees

         1. Looked it up

         2. We were also excited

      B. Watched ants

      C. Saw her at library

         1. She studies Napoleon

         2. I took out a book

Organizing an outline like the one above (it need not be this formal) will help you write a well-structured, well-planned essay. You can readily see that constructing a good essay from the outline above would be much easier than writing it without any planning.

Whichever way you prewrite—cluster, outline, or another method—the important thing is that you think and plan before you actually begin to write the essay.

Essay Samples

Here's the topic again and the finished essay, first written well and then poorly. Both essays are evaluated (comments run alongside each paragraph). Analyze each essay's strengths and weaknesses.

Topic

Teachers can play an important part in our lives. Choose one particular teacher you had during your school years and discuss one of his or her personal qualities which contributed to that teacher's impact on you.

Well-written essay

Mrs. Wolff was my third-grade teacher more than ten years ago in upstate New York. Little did I know it then, but through one of her personal qualities—her curiosity— Mrs. Wolff helped to instill in me an enthusiasm for learning which I still have to this day.

Orienting reader to subject

Mrs. Wolff had an enormous curiosity. In whatever we were studying, Mrs. Wolff wanted to find out "why?" Once when we were learning about trees, a student asked her a question she couldn't answer: Is the bark on a tree dead? Mrs. Wolff thought for a few seconds and then responded that she didn't know. But rather than move on to another question, Mrs. Wolff moved instead to the class encyclopedia and began searching. When she found the answer and read it aloud to the class, the excitement of her discovery was contagious. And this happened many, many times throughout the school year.

Restating topic in thesis sentence

Vivid specific details to support generalization

"Impact" of event noted

One Saturday my mother asked me to go to the town library to return some books. Whom did I see there but Mrs. Wolff, eagerly reading from a pile of books stacked in front of her. I said hello and asked what she was doing. Mrs. Wolff told me about the French history class she was taking at night and proceeded to describe what she was

Another example with more specific details

learning. Her enthusiasm for Napoleon kept me riveted for over an hour, until the library closed, but not before Mrs. Wolff encouraged me to take out a book for myself about Napoleon.

Clear statement of significance of event

Another time I saw Mrs. Wolff lying on the lawn, face down. I thought she was hurt. But then I soon discovered that she had been watching an ant colony which had fascinated her for over an hour!

Another specific supporting detail

Mrs. Wolff's regard for her own education couldn't help but spread to her students. By her example, I came to love learning and to this day embrace it enthusiastically.

Summary sentence reinforcing overall point

Weak essay

Mrs. Wolff was a great teacher. She was good at helping us learn things and helping us like learning. The factor why she had an impact on me was that she loved learning so much, she would always keep on trying to find things out if she didn't know them. Like whenever she didn't have an answer for something. Instead of forgetting it, she would always try to find it out. If you asked her a question or something, and she didn't know, then she would go and find it out. Or if she wanted to know something she would always try to look it up.

Incorrect restatement of topic

Sentence fragment
Vague reference, no specific example

So Mrs. Wolff helped me to like learning because I could watch her and see what she did, and then pretty soon I started to like learning. And so even now I like learning a lot because it's fun and because you found out a lot of things that you wouldn't ordinarily know which sometimes might come in handy.

Again, lack of specific detail

Off-topic conclusion

Mrs. Wolff is also a great swimmer. I have seen her at the beach many times and she just loves to swim. My father told me that Mrs. Wolff was once an Olympic swimmer

Irrelevant point

Off topic

and, in fact, that she won a medal in the Olympics but she has never showed it to us, so I can't be sure.

So, in conclusion, Mrs. Wolff was a great teacher and made a big impact on me because of her liking to learn things so much that soon I began to like to learn things a lot too.

Summary statement adds nothing new

In general, the response is disunified, lacks relevant and specific details, lacks planning and organization, and displays several mechanical errors.

Remember, a well-written essay will be on the assigned topic, address each of the points in the given topic, use supporting examples with detail, and be well organized, showing unity, coherence, and logical progression. It should be written in correct standard written English.

Essay Scoring Guide

The following guide should give you some indication of the reader's basis for scoring your paper. It should also assist you in evaluating or having someone else evaluate your practice essays.

Score 6

Score 6 for an essay that demonstrates a high degree of competency in writing while keeping minor errors to a minimum. This essay is well organized and well developed, using appropriate supporting examples and details. The essay uses language that is mature and varied and shows unity, coherence, and logical progression.

Score 5

Score 5 for an essay that demonstrates competence in writing, although it may have minor errors. As in an essay scoring 6, this essay is well organized and well developed, using appropriate supporting examples and details. (It may have fewer examples and details than a 6 paper.) The essay uses some variety in language and again shows unity, coherence, and logical progression. A 5 paper may not be as fluent as a 6 paper.

Score 4

Score 4 for an essay that demonstrates competence in writing, although it may have occasional errors. This essay is adequately organized and developed, using some supporting examples and details. The essay may contain some writing errors that are not serious and is fairly fluent.

Score 3

Score 3 for an essay that demonstrates some competence in writing but is clearly flawed. This essay is inadequately organized and lacks proper development. Supporting examples and detail are minimal. There is little or no variety in sentence structure, and there are obvious errors in mechanics and usage.

Score 2

Score 2 for an essay that demonstrates incompetence in writing. This essay is disorganized, with little or no development, and lacks examples and detail. Serious errors in mechanics, usage, or sentence structure are evident.

Score 1

Score 1 for an essay that demonstrates incompetence in writing. This essay is poorly organized, showing no development or logical progression. It contains many serious errors in writing.

Score 0

Score 0 for an essay that is off topic.

Practice Essay Topics

Here are topics you may use for practice. Allow 30 minutes to plan and write each essay. Give yourself about a half page to organize your notes. Then, upon completion of each essay, evaluate (or have a friend evaluate) your writing using the criteria just mentioned and the checklist (page 90). Note: On the actual paper-based exam, space will be provided under the topic where you can do all scratch work before writing your essay. Computer-based examinees will be provided with scratch paper or a dry-erase board.

Topic 1

Suppose that the oldest building in your home town is to be torn down. In the space provided, write an essay in which you make a case to preserve the structure from demolition.

Topic 2

Choose a controversial film, novel, or play to which objections have been or might be raised. In the space provided, write an essay in which you argue either for or against exposing senior high school students to the work you have selected.

Topic 3

Many childhood experiences leave lifelong impressions on people. In the space provided, write an essay in which you describe a childhood experience and the effect it had on your life.

Topic 4

A local college is attempting to improve the college experience for its students by responding to suggestions for changes. If you could change one thing about the college experience in order to make it better, what would it be? Your answer may be based on your own experience or on the experience of others.

Topic 5

It is often said that we learn more from our mistakes than from our successes. Whether or not this is true, mistakes can play an important part in our lives. Think of a mistake you may have at one time made. In the space provided, write an essay discussing this mistake and its effect on you.

Topic 6

In the space provided, write an essay describing an event that was special to you as a high school or college student. Explain why you remember it and what effect, if any, that it had on your life.

Topic 7

Certain places bring back both good and bad memories. Recall a place from your childhood that brings back both good and bad memories for you. In the space provided, write an essay describing the place and the memories.

Topic 8

Is there a national holiday that you especially like or dislike? In the space provided, write an essay in which you choose one holiday and explain why you do or do not like it.

Topic 9

Of all the inventions of the last fifty years, which one do you think has the greatest importance in your life now? Write an essay in the space provided in which you select one invention and explain your choice.

Essay Checklist

Use this checklist to evaluate your essay.

Diagnosis/prescription for timed writing exercise

A good essay will:

❑ Address the assignment

Be well focused

❑ Be well organized

Have smooth transitions between paragraphs

Be coherent, unified

❑ Be well developed

Contain specific examples to support points

❑ Be grammatically sound (only minor flaws)

Use correct sentence structure

Use correct punctuation

Use standard written English

❑ Use language skillfully

Use a variety of sentence types

Use a variety of words

❑ Be legible

Have clear handwriting

Be neat

PART III

MATHEMATICS REVIEW

The following pages are designed to give you an intensive review of the basic skills used on the PPST Mathematics Test. Arithmetic, algebra, geometry, axioms, properties of numbers, terms, and simple statistics are covered. Before you begin the diagnostic review tests, it would be wise to become familiar with basic mathematics terminology, formulas, and general mathematical information, a review of which begins on the following page. Then proceed to the arithmetic diagnostic test, which you should take to spot your weak areas. Then use the arithmetic review that follows to strengthen those areas.

After reviewing the arithmetic, take the algebra diagnostic test and once again use the review that follows to strengthen your weak areas. Next, take the geometry diagnostic test and carefully read the complete geometry review.

Even if you are strong in arithmetic, algebra, and geometry, you may wish to skim the topic headings in each area to refresh your memory of important concepts. If you are weak in math, you should read through the complete review. Note, however, that recent PPSTs have emphasized arithmetic more than they have algebra and geometry. Therefore, you should spend the major portion of your review time on sharpening your arithmetic skills and knowledge of terms and concepts.

Symbols, Terminology, Formulas, and General Mathematical Information

Common Math Symbols and Terms

Symbol references:

$=$ *is equal to*

$\neq$ *is not equal to*

$>$ *is greater than*

$<$ *is less than*

$\approx$ *is approximately equal to*

$\geq$ *is greater than or equal to*

$\leq$ *is less than or equal to*

$\parallel$ *is parallel to*

$\perp$ *is perpendicular to*

Groups of numbers

Natural Numbers (counting numbers): 1, 2, 3, 4 ... (the numbers you would ***naturally*** count by). The number 0 is not a natural number.

Whole Numbers: 0, 1, 2, 3, 4 ... (the natural numbers together with 0).

Integers: ... –3, –2, –1, 0, 1, 2, 3 ... (all the whole numbers together with their opposites).

Rational Numbers: All values that can be expressed in the form $\frac{a}{b}$, where a and b are integers and $b \neq 0$ or when expressed in decimal form the expression either terminates or has a repeating pattern.

Examples:

$4\frac{1}{2} = \frac{9}{2}$, therefore $4\frac{1}{2}$ is a rational number

0.3 is a terminating decimal; therefore 0.3 is a rational number

0.134343434 ... is a repeating decimal; therefore 0.134343434 ... is a rational number

Irrational Numbers: Any value that exists but is not rational.

Examples:

π The decimal name for *pi* starts out 3.14159265 ... The decimal name for *pi* does not terminate, nor does it have a repeating pattern.

$\sqrt{2}$ The decimal name for the square root of 2 starts out 1.41421356 ... The decimal name for the square root of 2 does not terminate, nor does it have a repeating pattern.

Real Numbers: All the rational and irrational numbers.

Prime Number: A natural number greater than 1 and that is divisible only by 1 and itself. (An alternate definition is a natural number that has exactly two different divisors.) The first seven prime numbers are 2, 3, 5, 7, 11, 13, and 17.

Composite Number: A natural number greater than 1 that is not a prime number. (An alternate definition is a natural number that has at least three different divisors.) The first seven composite numbers are 4, 6, 8, 9, 10, 12, and 14.

Square Numbers: The results of taking numbers and raising them to the second power (squaring them). An alternate definition is the result when numbers are multiplied by themselves.

Examples:

$(-3)^2 = 9$, therefore 9 is a square number

$(0)^2 = 0$, therefore 0 is a square number, but is not a positive square number.

The first seven positive square numbers are 1, 4, 9, 16, 25, 36, and 49.

Cube Numbers: The results of taking numbers and raising them to the third power (cubing them).

Examples:

$(-3)^3 = -27$, therefore -27 is a cube number

$(0)^3 = 0$, therefore 0 is a cube number

The first seven positive cube numbers are 1, 8, 27, 64, 125, 216, and 343.

Important Equivalents

$\frac{1}{100} = 0.01 = 1\%$

$\frac{1}{10} = 0.1 = 10\%$

$\frac{1}{5} = \frac{2}{10} = 0.2 = 0.20 = 20\%$

$\frac{3}{10} = 0.3 = 0.30 = 30\%$

$\frac{2}{5} = \frac{4}{10} = 0.4 = 0.40 = 40\%$

$\frac{1}{2} = \frac{5}{10} = 0.5 = 0.50 = 50\%$

$\frac{3}{5} = \frac{6}{10} = 0.6 = 0.60 = 60\%$

$\frac{7}{10} = 0.7 = 0.70 = 70\%$

$\frac{4}{5} = \frac{8}{10} = 0.8 = 0.80 = 80\%$

$\frac{9}{10} = 0.9 = 0.90 = 90\%$

$\frac{1}{4} = \frac{25}{100} = 0.25 = 25\%$

$\frac{3}{4} = \frac{75}{100} = 0.75 = 75\%$

$\frac{1}{3} = 0.33\frac{1}{3} = 33\frac{1}{3}\%$

$\frac{2}{3} = 0.66\frac{2}{3} = 66\frac{2}{3}\%$

$\frac{1}{8} = 0.125 = 0.12\frac{1}{2} = 12\frac{1}{2}\%$

$\frac{3}{8} = 0.375 = 0.37\frac{1}{2} = 37\frac{1}{2}\%$

$\frac{5}{8} = 0.625 = 0.62\frac{1}{2} = 62\frac{1}{2}\%$

$\frac{7}{8} = 0.875 = 0.87\frac{1}{2} = 87\frac{1}{2}\%$

$\frac{1}{6} = 0.16\frac{2}{3} = 16\frac{2}{3}\%$

$\frac{5}{6} = 0.83\frac{1}{3} = 83\frac{1}{3}\%$

$1 = 1.00 = 100\%$

$2 = 2.00 = 200\%$

$3\frac{1}{2} = 3.5 = 3.50 = 350\%$

Math Formulas

Shape	Illustration	Perimeter	Area
Square		$P = 4a$	$A = a^2$
Rectangle		$P = 2b + 2h$ or $P = 2(b + h)$	$A = bh$
Parallelogram		$P = 2a + 2b$ or $P = 2(a + b)$	$A = bh$
Triangle		$P = a + b + c$	$A = \dfrac{bh}{2}$
Rhombus		$P = 4a$	$A = ah$
Trapezoid		$P = b_1 + b_2 + x + y$	$A = \dfrac{h(b_1 + b_2)}{2}$
Circle		Circumference: $C = \pi d$ or $C = 2\pi r$	$A = \pi r^2$

Shape	Illustration	Pythagorean theorem:
Right Triangle		$a^2 + b^2 = c^2$ The sum of the squares of the legs of a right triangle equals the square of the hypotenuse.

Measures

Customary system, or English system

Length

12 inches (in) = 1 foot (ft)

3 feet = 1 yard (yd)

36 inches = 1 yard

1,760 yards = 1 mile (mi)

5,280 feet = 1 mile

Area

144 square inches (sq in) = 1 square foot (sq ft)

9 square feet = 1 square yard (sq yd)

Weight

16 ounces (oz) = 1 pound (lb)

2,000 pounds = 1 ton (T)

Capacity

2 cups = 1 pint (pt)

2 pints = 1 quart (qt)

4 quarts = 1 gallon (gal)

4 pecks = 1 bushel

Time

365 days = 1 year

52 weeks = 1 year

10 years = 1 decade

100 years = 1 century

Metric system, or the International system of units

The following prefixes are used in the metric system:

basic unit (meter, liter, gram)

$$\text{milli} = \frac{1}{1,000}$$

$$\text{centi} = \frac{1}{100}$$

$$\text{deci} = \frac{1}{10}$$

deca = 10

hecto = 100

kilo = 1000

Weight (gram)	
kilogram (kg)	1,000 grams
hectogram (hg)	100 grams
decagram (dag)	10 grams
gram (g)	**1 gram**
decigram (dg)	0.1 gram
centigram (cg)	0.01 gram
milligram (mg)	0.001 gram
1,000 kilograms = 1 metric ton	

Length (meter)	
kilometer (km)	1,000 meters
hectometer (hm)	100 meters
decameter (dam)	10 meters
meter (m)	**1 meter**
decimeter (dm)	0.1 meter
centimeter (cm)	0.01 meter
millimeter (mm)	0.001 meter

Volume (liter)	
kiloliter (kl or kL)	1,000 liters
hectoliter (hl or hL)	100 liters
decaliter (dal or daL)	10 liters
liter (l or L)	**1 liter**
deciliter (dl or dL)	0.1 liter
centiliter (cl or cL)	0.01 liter
milliliter (ml or mL)	0.001 liter

Math Words and Phrases

Words that signal an operation:

Addition	Subtraction	Multiplication	Division
Sum	Difference	Product	Quotient
Plus	Minus	Times	Ratio
Is increased by	Is decreased by	Of (Example: $\frac{2}{3}$ of 15 is what?)	Is a part of (Example: 3 is what part of 15?)
More than (Example: 3 more than 7 is what?)	Less than (Example: 3 fewer than 7 is what?)	At (Example: 3 at 5 cents cost how much?)	Goes into (Example: 4 goes into 28 how many times?)

Mathematical Properties and Basic Statistics

Some properties (axioms) of addition and multiplication

Commutative property

The order in which addition or multiplication is done does not affect the answer.

Commutative property for addition

$$2 + 3 = 3 + 2$$
$$5 = 5$$

Commutative property for multiplication

$$(2)(3) = (3)(2)$$
$$6 = 6$$

In general,

$$a + b = b + a \qquad\qquad ab = ba$$

Subtraction does not have the commutative property.

Notice that $3 - 2 \neq 2 - 3$
($3 - 2 = 1$, but $2 - 3 = -1$)

Division does not have the commutative property.

Notice that $10 \div 2 \neq 2 \div 10$

$\left(10 \div 2 = 5,\ \text{but}\ 2 \div 10 = \frac{2}{10}\ \text{or}\ \frac{1}{5}\right)$

Associative property

The grouping, without changing the order, does not affect the answer.

Associative property for addition

$$8 + (4 + 2) = (8 + 4) + 2$$
$$8 + 6 = 12 + 2$$
$$14 = 14$$

Associative property for multiplication

$$8 \times (4 \times 2) = (8 \times 4) \times 2$$
$$8 \times (8) = 32 \times 2$$
$$64 = 64$$

In general,

$$a + (b + c) = (a + b) + c \qquad\qquad a(bc) = (ab)c$$

Subtraction does not have the associative property.

Notice $8 - (4 - 2) \neq (8 - 4) - 2$
$$8 - 2 \neq 4 - 2$$
$$6 \neq 2$$

Division does not have the associative property.

Notice $8 \div (4 \div 2) \neq (8 \div 4) \div 2$
$$8 \div 2 \neq 2 \div 2$$
$$4 \neq 1$$

Distributive property

Multiplication outside parentheses distributing over either addition or subtraction inside parentheses does not affect the answer.

$$7(3 + 9) = 7(3) + 7(9)$$
$$7(12) = 21 + 63$$
$$84 = 84$$

In general, $a(b + c) = ab + ac$

$$5(12 - 3) = 5(12) - 5(3)$$
$$5(9) = 60 - 15$$
$$45 = 45$$

In general, $a(b - c) = ab - ac$

Note: You *cannot* use the distributive property with only one operation.

$$3(4 \times 5) \neq 3(4) \times 3(5)$$
$$3(20) \neq 12 \times 15$$
$$60 \neq 180$$

Special properties of 0 and 1

An *identity number* is a value that when added to another number or multiplied with another number does not change the value of that number.

The *identity number for addition* is 0. Any number added to 0 gives that number.

$$0 + 3 = 3 + 0 = 3$$
$$0 + a = a + 0 = a$$

$0 + 3 = 3$ is an example of using the additive identity.

The *identity number for multiplication* is 1. Any number multiplied by 1 gives that number.

$$1(3) = 3(1) = 3$$
$$1(a) = a(1) = a$$

$1(3) = 3$ is an example of using the multiplicative identity.

Inverses

The *additive inverse of a number (also known as the opposite of the number)* is a value that when added to any number equals 0. Any number added with its additive inverse equals zero.

Since $7 + (-7) = 0$, 7 is the additive inverse of -7 and -7 is the additive inverse of 7.

The *additive inverse of a = −a* for any number a, $a + (-a) = 0$

$7 + (-7) = 0$ is an example of using additive inverses.

The *multiplicative inverse of a number (also known as the reciprocal of the number)* is a value that when multiplied with any non-zero number equals 1. Any non-zero number multiplied with its multiplicative inverse equals 1.

Because $\frac{4}{5} \times \frac{5}{4} = 1$, we would say that $\frac{4}{5}$ is the multiplicative inverse of $\frac{5}{4}$ and $\frac{5}{4}$ is the multiplicative inverse of $\frac{4}{5}$.

The *multiplicative inverse of a ($a \neq 0$) is $\frac{1}{a}$* for any a ($a \neq 0$), $a \times \frac{1}{a} = 1$.

$\frac{4}{5} \times \frac{5}{4} = 1$ is an example of using multiplicative inverses.

Arithmetic

Arithmetic Diagnostic Test

Questions

1. $6 = \frac{?}{4}$

2. Change $5\frac{3}{4}$ to an improper fraction.

3. Change $\frac{32}{6}$ to a whole number or mixed number in lowest terms.

4. $\frac{2}{5} + \frac{3}{5} =$

5. $\frac{1}{3} + \frac{1}{4} + \frac{1}{2} =$

6. $1\frac{3}{8} + 2\frac{5}{6} =$

7. $\frac{7}{9} - \frac{5}{9} =$

8. $11 - \frac{2}{3} =$

9. $6\frac{1}{4} - 3\frac{3}{4} =$

10. $\frac{1}{6} \times \frac{1}{6} =$

11. $2\frac{3}{8} \times 1\frac{5}{6} =$

12. $\frac{1}{4} \div \frac{3}{2} =$

13. $2\frac{3}{7} \div 1\frac{1}{4} =$

14. $0.07 + 1.2 + 0.471 =$

15. $0.45 - 0.003 =$

16. $\$78.24 - \$31.68 =$

17. $0.5 \times 0.5 =$

18. $8.001 \times 2.3 =$

19. $0.7\overline{)0.147}$

20. $0.002\overline{)12}$

21. $\frac{1}{3}$ of $\$7.20$

22. Circle the larger number: 7.9 or 4.35

23. 39 out of 100 means _____.

24. Change 4% to a decimal.

25. 46% of 58 =

26. Change 0.009 to a percent.

27. Change 12.5% to a fraction.

28. Change $\frac{3}{8}$ to a percent.

29. Is 93 prime?

30. What is the percent increase of a rise in temperature from 80° to 100°?

31. Average 0, 8, and 10.

32. $8^2 =$

33. Approximate $\sqrt{30}$

Answers

1. 24

2. $\frac{23}{4}$

3. $5\frac{1}{3}$

4. $\frac{5}{5}$ or 1

5. $\frac{13}{12}$ or $1\frac{1}{12}$

6. $4\frac{5}{24}$

7. $\frac{2}{9}$

8. $10\frac{1}{3}$

9. $2\frac{2}{4}$ or $2\frac{1}{2}$

10. $\frac{1}{36}$

11. $\frac{209}{48}$ or $4\frac{17}{48}$

12. $\frac{1}{6}$

13. $\frac{68}{35}$ or $1\frac{33}{35}$

14. 1.741

15. 0.447

16. $46.56

17. 0.25

18. 18.4023

19. 0.21

20. 6,000

21. $2.40

22. 7.9

23. 39% or $\frac{39}{100}$

24. 0.04

25. 26.68

26. 0.9% or $\frac{9}{10}$%

27. $\frac{125}{1,000}$ or $\frac{1}{8}$

28. 37.5% or $37\frac{1}{2}$%

29. No

30. 25%

31. 6

32. 64

33. 5.5 or $5\frac{1}{2}$

Arithmetic Review

Rounding off

To **round off** any number,

1. Underline the place value to which you're rounding off.

2. Look to the immediate right (one place) of your underlined place value.

3. Identify the number (the one to the right). If it is 5 or higher, round your underlined place value up 1. If the number (the one to the right) is 4 or less, leave your underlined place value as it is and change all the other numbers to its right to zeros.

Round to the nearest thousands.

$$345,678 \text{ becomes } 346,000$$
$$928,499 \text{ becomes } 928,000$$

This works with decimals as well. Round to the nearest hundredth.

$$3.4678 \text{ becomes } 3.47$$

$$298,435.083 \text{ becomes } 298,435.08$$

Place value

Each position in any number has **place value.** For instance, in the number 485, 4 is in the hundreds place, 8 is in the tens place, and 5 is in the ones place. Thus, place value is as follows.

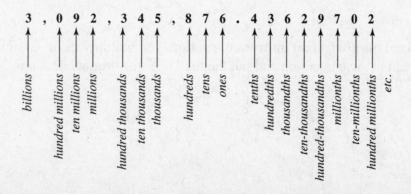

Fractions and mixed numbers

Fractions

Fractions consist of two numbers: a **numerator** (which is above the line) and a **denominator** (which is below the line).

$$\frac{1}{2} \begin{array}{l}\text{numerator}\\\text{denominator}\end{array} \quad \text{or} \quad \text{numerator } 1\!\!\Big/\!2 \text{ denominator}$$

The denominator lets us know the number of equal parts into which something is divided. The numerator tells us how many of these equal parts are contained in the fraction. Thus, if the fraction is $\frac{3}{5}$ of a pie, then the denominator 5 tells us that the pie has been divided into 5 equal parts, of which 3 (numerator) are in the fraction.

Sometimes it helps to think of the dividing line (in the middle of the fraction) as meaning *out of*. In other words, $\frac{3}{5}$ would also mean 3 *out of* 5 equal pieces from the whole pie.

Proper fractions and improper fractions

A fraction like $\frac{3}{5}$, where the numerator is smaller than the denominator, is less than 1. This kind of fraction is called a **proper fraction.**

But sometimes a fraction may be more than 1 or equal to 1 (when the numerator is larger than the denominator or the same as the denominator). Thus, $\frac{12}{7}$ is more than 1 and $\frac{8}{8}$ equals 1. These kinds of fractions are called **improper fractions.**

Mixed numbers

When a term contains both a whole number (such as 3, 8, 25, and so on) and a fraction (such as $\frac{1}{2}, \frac{1}{4}, \frac{3}{4}$, and so on), it is called a **mixed number.** For instance, $5\frac{1}{4}$ and $290\frac{3}{4}$ are both mixed numbers.

To **change an improper fraction to a mixed number,** you divide the denominator into the numerator.

$$\frac{18}{5} = 3\frac{3}{5} \qquad 5\overline{)18} \atop \underline{15} \atop 3$$

To **change a mixed number to an improper fraction,** you multiply the denominator times the whole number, add in the numerator, and put the total over the original denominator.

$$4\frac{1}{2} = \frac{9}{2} \qquad 2 \times 4 + 1 = 9$$

Reducing fractions

A fraction must be reduced to lowest terms, which is done by dividing both the numerator and denominator by the largest number that will divide evenly into both. For example, $\frac{14}{16}$ is reduced by dividing both terms by 2, thus giving us $\frac{7}{8}$. Likewise, $\frac{20}{25}$ is reduced to $\frac{4}{5}$ by dividing both numerator and denominator by 5.

Adding fractions

To **add fractions,** you must first change all denominators to their lowest common denominator (LCD)—the lowest number that can be divided evenly by all the denominators in the problem. When you have all the denominators the same, you may add fractions by simply adding the numerators (the denominator remains the same).

$$\frac{3}{8}=\frac{3}{8}$$
$$+\frac{1}{2}=\frac{4}{8} \leftarrow \left\{ \frac{1}{2} \text{ is changed to } \frac{4}{8} \right.$$
$$\frac{7}{8}$$

$$\frac{1}{4}=\frac{3}{12}$$
$$+\frac{1}{3}=\frac{4}{12} \left\{ \begin{array}{l} \text{change both} \\ \text{fractions to LCD of 12} \end{array} \right.$$
$$\frac{7}{12}$$

In the first example, we changed the $\frac{1}{2}$ to $\frac{4}{8}$ because 8 is the lowest common denominator, and then we added the numerators 3 and 4 to get $\frac{7}{8}$.

In the second example, we had to change both fractions to get the lowest common denominator of 12, and then we added the numerators to get $\frac{7}{12}$. Of course, if the denominators are already the same, just add the numerators.

$$\frac{6}{11}+\frac{3}{11}=\frac{9}{11}$$

Adding mixed numbers

To **add mixed numbers,** the same rule (find the LCD) applies, but make sure that you always add the whole numbers to get your final answer.

$$2\frac{1}{2}=2\frac{2}{4} \leftarrow \left\{ \frac{1}{2} \text{ is changed to } \frac{2}{4} \right.$$
$$+3\frac{1}{4}=3\frac{1}{4} \leftarrow \left\{ \text{remember to add the whole numbers} \right.$$
$$5\frac{3}{4}$$

Subtracting fractions

To **subtract fractions,** the same rule (find the LCD) applies, except that you subtract the numerators.

$$\frac{7}{8} = \frac{7}{8}$$
$$-\frac{1}{4} = \frac{2}{8}$$
$$\overline{\qquad \frac{5}{8}}$$

$$\frac{3}{4} = \frac{9}{12}$$
$$-\frac{1}{3} = \frac{4}{12}$$
$$\overline{\qquad \frac{5}{12}}$$

Subtracting mixed numbers

When you **subtract mixed numbers,** sometimes you may have to *borrow* from the whole number, just like you sometimes borrow from the next column when subtracting ordinary numbers.

$$6\,{5}\!\!\!/\,{1}^{11}$$
$$-129$$
$$\overline{522}$$

you borrowed 1
from the 10s
column

$$\not{4}\ ^{3}\not{1}\,^{\frac{7}{6}}\!\!\!\!/\,{6}$$
$$-2\frac{5}{6}$$
$$\overline{1\frac{2}{6} = 1\frac{1}{3}}$$

you borrowed 1 in
the form of $\frac{6}{6}$ from
the 1s column

To **subtract a mixed number from a whole number,** you have to borrow from the whole number.

$$6 = 5\frac{5}{5} \leftarrow \begin{cases} \text{borrow 1 in the form of} \\ \frac{5}{5} \text{ from the 6} \end{cases}$$

$$-3\frac{1}{5} = 3\frac{1}{5}$$
$$\overline{}$$
$$2\frac{4}{5} \leftarrow \begin{cases} \text{remember to subtract the} \\ \text{remaining whole numbers} \end{cases}$$

Multiplying fractions

To **multiply fractions,** simply multiply the numerators; then multiply the denominators. Reduce to lowest terms if necessary.

$$\frac{2}{3} \times \frac{5}{12} = \frac{10}{36} \qquad \text{reduce } \frac{10}{36} \text{ to } \frac{5}{18}$$

This answer had to be reduced as it wasn't in lowest terms.

Canceling when multiplying fractions: You could first have *canceled*. That would have eliminated the need to reduce your answer. To cancel, find a number that divides evenly into one numerator and one denominator. In this case, 2 will divide evenly into 2 in the numerator (it goes 1 time) and 12 in the denominator (it goes in 6 times).

$$\frac{\overset{1}{\cancel{2}}}{3} \times \frac{5}{\underset{6}{\cancel{12}}}$$

Now that you've canceled, you can multiply out as you did before.

$$\frac{\overset{1}{\cancel{2}}}{3} \times \frac{5}{\underset{6}{\cancel{12}}} = \frac{5}{18}$$

Remember, you may cancel only when *multiplying* fractions.

Multiplying mixed numbers

To **multiply mixed numbers,** first change any mixed number to an improper fraction. Then multiply as previously shown. To change mixed numbers to improper fractions,

1. Multiply the whole number by the denominator of the fraction.
2. Add this to the numerator of the fraction.
3. This is now your numerator.
4. The denominator remains the same.

$$3\frac{1}{3} \times 2\frac{1}{4} = \frac{10}{3} \times \frac{9}{4} = \frac{90}{12} = 7\frac{6}{12} = 7\frac{1}{2}$$

Then change the answer, if in improper fraction form, back to a mixed number and reduce if necessary.

Dividing fractions

To **divide fractions,** invert (turn upside down) the second fraction and multiply. Then reduce if necessary.

$$\frac{1}{6} \div \frac{1}{5} = \frac{1}{6} \times \frac{5}{1} = \frac{5}{6} \qquad \frac{1}{6} \div \frac{1}{3} = \frac{1}{6} \times \frac{3}{1} = \frac{3}{6} = \frac{1}{2}$$

Simplifying fractions

If either numerator or denominator consists of several numbers, these numbers must be combined into one number. Then reduce if necessary.

$$\frac{28+14}{26+17}=\frac{42}{43}$$

or

$$\frac{\frac{1}{4}+\frac{1}{2}}{\frac{1}{3}+\frac{1}{4}}=\frac{\frac{1}{4}+\frac{2}{4}}{\frac{4}{12}+\frac{3}{12}}=\frac{\frac{3}{4}}{\frac{7}{12}}=\frac{3}{4}\times\frac{12}{7}=\frac{36}{28}=\frac{9}{7}=1\frac{2}{7}$$

Decimals

Fractions may also be written in **decimal form** by using a symbol called a **decimal point.** All numbers to the left of the decimal point are whole numbers. All numbers to the right of the decimal point are fractions with denominators of only 10, 100, 1000, 10,000, and so on, as follows.

$$0.6=\frac{6}{10}=\frac{3}{5}$$
$$0.7=\frac{7}{10}$$
$$0.07=\frac{7}{100}$$
$$0.007=\frac{7}{1,000}$$
$$0.0007=\frac{7}{10,000}$$
$$0.00007=\frac{7}{100,000}$$
$$0.25=\frac{25}{100}=\frac{1}{4}$$

Adding and subtracting decimals

To **add or subtract decimals,** just line up the decimal points and then add or subtract in the same manner you would add or subtract regular numbers.

$$23.6+1.75+300.002=23.60$$
$$1.75$$
$$300.02$$
$$\overline{325.37}$$

Adding in zeros can make the problem easier to work.

$$23.600$$
$$1.750$$
$$\underline{300.002}$$
$$325.352$$

and

$$54.26 - 1.1 = 54.26$$
$$\underline{-\ 1.10}$$
$$53.16$$

and

$$78.9 - 37.43 = 78.\overset{8}{\cancel{9}}0$$
$$\underline{-\ 37.43}$$
$$41.47$$

Whole numbers can have decimal points to their right.

$$17 - 8.43 = 1\overset{6}{7}\overset{9}{\cancel{0}}0$$
$$\underline{-\ 8.43}$$
$$8.57$$

Multiplying decimals

To **multiply decimals,** just multiply as usual. Then count the total number of digits above the line that are to the right of all decimal points. Place your decimal point in your answer so there are the same number of digits to the right of it as there are above the line.

$$40.012 \quad \leftarrow 3 \text{ digits}$$ { total of 4 digits above the line that are to the right of the decimal point
$$\underline{\times \quad 3.1} \quad \leftarrow 1 \text{ digit}$$
$$40012$$

$$\underline{120036}$$
$$124.0372 \leftarrow 4 \text{ digits}$$ { decimal point placed so there is same number of digits to the right of the decimal point

Dividing decimals

Dividing decimals is the same as dividing other numbers, except that if the divisor (the number you're dividing by) has a decimal, move it to the right as many places as necessary until it is a whole number. Then move the decimal point in the dividend (the number being divided into) the same number of places. Sometimes you may have to add zeros to the dividend (the number inside the division sign).

$$1.25\overline{)5.} = 125\overline{)500.}^{\,4.}$$

or

$$0.002\overline{)26.} = 2\overline{)26000.}^{\,13000.}$$

Changing form

Changing decimals to percents

To **change decimals to percents,**

1. Move the decimal point two places to the right.

2. Insert a percent sign.

$$0.75 = 75\% \qquad 0.05 = 5\%$$

Changing percents to decimals

To **change percents to decimals,**

1. Eliminate the percent sign.

2. Move the decimal point two places to the left (sometimes adding zeros will be necessary).

$$75\% = 0.75 \qquad 5\% = 0.05$$

$$23\% = 0.23 \qquad 0.2\% = 0.002$$

Changing fractions to percents

To **change a fraction to a percent,**

1. Multiply by 100.

2. Insert a percent sign.

$$\frac{1}{2}: \quad \frac{1}{2} \times 100 = \frac{100}{2} = 50\%$$

$$\frac{2}{5}: \quad \frac{2}{5} \times 100 = \frac{200}{5} = 40\%$$

Changing percents to fractions

To **change percents to fractions,**

1. Divide the percent by 100.

2. Eliminate the percent sign.

3. Reduce if necessary.

$$60\% = \frac{60}{100} = \frac{3}{5} \qquad 13\% = \frac{13}{100}$$

Changing fractions to decimals

To **change a fraction to a decimal,** simply do what the operation says. In other words, $\frac{13}{20}$ means 13 divided by 20. So do just that (insert decimal points and zeros accordingly):

$$20\overline{)13.00}^{.65} = 0.65 \qquad \frac{5}{8} = 8\overline{)5.000}^{.625} = 0.625$$

Changing decimals to fractions

To **change a decimal to a fraction,**

1. Move the decimal point two places to the right.

2. Put that number over 100.

3. Reduce if necessary.

$$0.65 = \frac{65}{100} = \frac{13}{20}$$
$$0.05 = \frac{5}{100} = \frac{1}{20}$$
$$0.75 = \frac{75}{100} = \frac{3}{4}$$

Read it: 0.8

Write it: $\frac{8}{10}$

Reduce it: $\frac{4}{5}$

Percent

Finding percent of a number

To **determine percent of a number,** change the percent to a fraction or decimal (whichever is easier for you) and multiply. Remember, the word *of* means multiply.

What is 20% of 80?

$$\frac{20}{100} \times 80 = \frac{1600}{100} = 16$$

or

$$0.20 \times 80 = 16.00 = 16$$

What is 12% of 50?

$$\frac{12}{100} \times 50 = \frac{600}{100} = 6$$

or

$$0.12 \times 50 = 6.00 = 6$$

What is $\frac{1}{2}$% of 18?

$$\frac{\frac{1}{2}}{100} \times 18 = \frac{1}{200} \times 18 = \frac{18}{200} = \frac{9}{100}$$

or

$$0.005 \times 18 = 0.09$$

Other applications of percent

Turn the question word-for-word into an **equation.** For *what* substitute the letter *x;* for *is* substitute an *equal sign;* for *of* substitute a *multiplication sign.* Change percents to decimals or fractions, whichever you find easier. Then solve the equation.

18 is what percent of 90?

$$18 = x(90)$$
$$\frac{18}{90} = x$$
$$\frac{1}{5} = x$$
$$20\% = x$$

10 is 50% of what number?

$$10 = 0.50(x)$$
$$\frac{10}{0.50} = x$$
$$20 = x$$

What is 15% of 60?

$$x = \frac{15}{100} \times 60 = \frac{90}{10} = 9$$
or
$$0.15(60) = 9$$

Finding percentage increase or percentage decrease

To **find the percentage change** (increase or decrease), use this formula:

$$\frac{\text{change}}{\text{starting point}} \times 100 = \text{percentage change}$$

What is the percentage decrease of a $500 item on sale for $400?

Change: $500 - 400 = 100$

$$\frac{\text{change}}{\text{starting point}} \times 100 = \frac{100}{500} \times 100 = \frac{1}{5} \times 100 = 20\% \text{ decrease}$$

What is the percentage increase of Jon's salary if it went from $150 a week to $200 a week?

Change: $200 - 150 = 50$

$$\frac{\text{change}}{\text{starting point}} \times 100 = \frac{50}{150} \times \frac{1}{3} \times 100 = 33\frac{1}{3}\% \text{ increase}$$

Prime numbers

A **prime number** is a number that can be evenly divided by only itself and 1. For example, 19 is a prime number because it can be evenly divided only by 19 and 1, but 21 is not a prime number because 21 can be evenly divided by other numbers (3 and 7).

The only even prime number is 2; thereafter, any even number may be divided evenly by 2. Zero and 1 are *not* prime numbers. The first ten prime numbers are 2, 3, 5, 7, 11, 13, 17, 19, 23, and 29.

Mean, median, and mode

Arithmetic mean, or average

To find the **mean**, or average, of a group of numbers,

1. Add them.
2. Divide by the number of items you added.

What is the mean of 10, 20, 35, 40, and 45?

$$10 + 20 + 35 + 40 + 45 = 150$$
$$150 \div 5 = 30$$

The mean is 30.

What is the mean of 0, 12, 18, 20, 31, and 45?

$$0 + 12 + 18 + 20 + 31 + 45 = 126$$
$$126 \div 6 = 21$$

The mean is 21.

What is the mean of 25, 27, 27, and 27?

$$25 + 27 + 27 + 27 = 106$$
$$106 \div 4 = 26\frac{1}{2}$$

The mean is $26\frac{1}{2}$.

Median

A **median** is simply the middle number of a list of numbers after it has been written in order. (If the list contains an even number of items, average the two middle numbers to get the median.) For example, in the following list—3, 4, 6, 9, 21, 24, 56—the number 9 is the median.

Mode

The **mode** is simply the number most frequently listed in a group of numbers. In order to have a mode, at least one data value must be repeated. For example, in the following group—5, 9, 7, 3, 9, 4, 6, 9, 7, 9, 2—the mode is 9 because it appears more often than any other number.

Range

The **range** of a group of scores or numbers is calculated by subtracting the smallest from the largest.

Find the range of the scores 3, 2, 7, 9, 12. The range is $12 - 2 = 10$.

Squares and square roots

To **square a number** just multiply it by itself. For example, 6 squared (written 6^2) is 6×6 or 36. 36 is called a perfect square (the square of a whole number). Any exponent means multiply the number by itself that many times.

$$8^2 = 8 \times 8 = 64$$

$$5^3 = 5 \times 5 \times 5 = 125$$

Remember, $x^1 = x$ and $x^0 = 1$ when x is any number (other than 0).

Following is a list of **perfect squares.**

$1^2 = 1$	$5^2 = 25$	$9^2 = 81$
$2^2 = 4$	$6^2 = 36$	$10^2 = 100$
$3^2 = 9$	$7^2 = 49$	$11^2 = 121$
$4^2 = 16$	$8^2 = 64$	$12^2 = 144$ etc.

To find the **square root** of a number, you want to find some number that when multiplied by itself gives you the original number. In other words, to find the square root of 25, you want to find the number that when multiplied by itself gives you 25. The square root of 25, then, is 5. The symbol for square root is $\sqrt{}$. Following is a list of **perfect (whole number) square roots:**

$\sqrt{1} = 1$	$\sqrt{16} = 4$	$\sqrt{64} = 8$
$\sqrt{4} = 2$	$\sqrt{25} = 5$	$\sqrt{81} = 9$
$\sqrt{9} = 3$	$\sqrt{36} = 6$	$\sqrt{100} = 10$ etc.
	$\sqrt{49} = 7$	

Square roots of **nonperfect squares** can be approximated. Two approximations you may wish to remember are:

$$\sqrt{2} \approx 1.4$$

$$\sqrt{3} \approx 1.7$$

Square root rules

Two numbers multiplied under a radical (square root) sign equal the product of the two square roots.

$$\sqrt{(4)(25)} = \sqrt{4} \times \sqrt{25} = 2 \times 5 = 10 \text{ or } \sqrt{100} = 10$$

And likewise with division,

$$\sqrt{\frac{64}{4}} = \frac{\sqrt{64}}{\sqrt{4}} = \frac{8}{2} = 4 \text{ or } \sqrt{16} = 4$$

Addition and subtraction, however, are different. The numbers must be combined under the radical before any computation of square roots may be done.

$$\sqrt{10 + 6} = \sqrt{16} = 4 \ \left(\sqrt{10 + 6} \text{ does not equal } [\neq] \sqrt{10} + \sqrt{6} \right)$$

or

$$\sqrt{93 - 12} = \sqrt{81} = 9$$

Approximating square roots

To **find a square root which will not be a whole number,** you should approximate.

Approximate $\sqrt{57}$.

Because $\sqrt{57}$ is between $\sqrt{49}$ and $\sqrt{64}$, it will fall somewhere between 7 and 8. And because 57 is just about halfway between 49 and 64, $\sqrt{57}$ is therefore approximately $7\frac{1}{2}$.

Approximate $\sqrt{83}$.

$$\sqrt{81} < \sqrt{83} < \sqrt{100}$$
$$9 \qquad\qquad 10$$

Since $\sqrt{83}$ is slightly more than $\sqrt{81}$ (whose square root is 9), $\sqrt{83}$ is a little more than 9. Since 83 is only 2 steps up from the nearest perfect square (81) and 17 steps to the next perfect square (100), then 83 is $\frac{2}{19}$ of the way to 100.

$$\frac{2}{19} \approx \frac{2}{20} = \frac{1}{10} = 0.1$$

Therefore,
$$\sqrt{83} \approx 9.1$$

Simplifying square roots

To **simplify numbers under a radical (square root sign),**

1. Factor the number to two numbers, one (or more) of which is a perfect square.
2. Then take the square root of the perfect square(s).
3. Leave the other under the $\sqrt{}$.

Simplify $\sqrt{75}$.

$$\sqrt{75} = \sqrt{25 \times 3} = \sqrt{25} \times \sqrt{3} = 5\sqrt{3}$$

Simplify $\sqrt{200}$.

$$\sqrt{200} = \sqrt{100 \times 2} = \sqrt{100} \times \sqrt{2} = 10\sqrt{2}$$

Simplify $\sqrt{900}$.

$$\sqrt{900} = \sqrt{100 \times 9} = \sqrt{100} \times \sqrt{9} = 10 \times 3 = 30$$

Signed numbers (positive numbers and negative numbers)

On a **number line,** numbers to the right of 0 are positive. Numbers to the left of 0 are negative, as follows.

$$\text{etc.} \overset{}{\underset{-3 \quad -2 \quad -1 \quad 0 \quad +1 \quad +2 \quad +3}{\rule{5cm}{0.4pt}}} \text{etc.}$$

Given any two numbers on a number line, the one on the right is always larger, regardless of its sign (positive or negative).

Addition of signed numbers

When **adding two numbers with the same sign** (either both positive or both negative), add the numbers and keep the same sign.

$$
\begin{array}{r}
+5 \\
+\,+7 \\
\hline
+12
\end{array}
\qquad
\begin{array}{r}
-8 \\
+\,-3 \\
\hline
-11
\end{array}
$$

When **adding two numbers with different signs** (one positive and one negative), subtract the numbers and keep the sign from whichever number is farther from zero.

$$
\begin{array}{r}
+5 \\
+\,-7 \\
\hline
-2
\end{array}
\qquad
\begin{array}{r}
-59 \\
+\,+72 \\
\hline
+13
\end{array}
$$

Subtraction of signed numbers

To **subtract positive and/or negative numbers,** just change the sign of the number being subtracted and then add.

$$
\begin{array}{r}
+\ 12 \\
-\,+4 \\
\hline
\end{array}
\qquad
\begin{array}{r}
+\ 12 \\
-\,+4 \\
\hline
+8
\end{array}
$$

$$
\begin{array}{r}
-\ 14 \\
-\,-4 \\
\hline
\end{array}
\qquad
\begin{array}{r}
-\ 14 \\
+\,+4 \\
\hline
-10
\end{array}
$$

$$
\begin{array}{r}
-\ 19 \\
-\,+6 \\
\hline
\end{array}
\qquad
\begin{array}{r}
-\ 19 \\
+\,-6 \\
\hline
-25
\end{array}
$$

$$
\begin{array}{r}
+\ 20 \\
-\,-3 \\
\hline
\end{array}
\qquad
\begin{array}{r}
+\ 20 \\
+\,+3 \\
\hline
+23
\end{array}
$$

Multiplying and dividing signed numbers

To **multiply or divide signed numbers,** treat them just like regular numbers but remember this rule: An odd number of negative signs will produce a negative answer. An even number of negative signs will produce a positive answer.

$$(-3)(+8)(-5)(-1)(-2) = +240$$
$$(-3)(+8)(-1)(-2) = -48$$
$$\frac{-64}{-2} = +32$$
$$\frac{-64}{2} = -32$$

Parentheses

Parentheses are used to group numbers. Everything inside parentheses must be done before any other operations.

$$50(2+6) = 50(8) = 400$$

When a **parenthesis is preceded by a minus sign,** change the minus to a plus by changing all the signs in front of each term inside the parentheses. Then remove the parentheses.

$$6 - (-3 + a - 2b + c)$$
$$= 6 + (+3 - a + 2b - c)$$
$$= 6 + 3 - a + 2b - c$$
$$= 9 - a + 2b - c$$

Order of operations

There is an order in which the operations on numbers must be done so that everyone doing a problem involving several operations and parentheses will get the same results. The order of operations is:

1. **Parentheses:** Simplify (if possible) all expressions in parentheses

2. **Exponents:** Apply exponents to their appropriate bases (this may involve radicals if the exponent is a fraction)

3. **Multiplication or Division:** Do the multiplication or division in the order it appears as you read the problem left to right

4. **Addition or Subtraction:** Do the addition or subtraction in the order it appears as you read the problem left to right

For example:

$10 - 3 \times 6 + 10^2 + \underline{(6 + 12)} \div \underline{(4 - 7)}$ parentheses first

$10 - 3 \times 6 + \underline{10^2} + (18) \div (-3)$ exponents next

$10 - \underline{3 \times 6} + 100 + (18) \div (-3)$ multiplication or division in order from left to right

$10 - 18 + 100 + \underline{(18) \div (-3)}$ multiplication or division in order from left to right

$\underline{10 - 18} + 100 + (-6)$ addition or subtraction in order from left to right

$\underline{-8 + 100} + (-6)$ addition or subtraction in order from left to right

$\underline{92 + (-6)}$ addition or subtraction in order from left to right

86

Here is an easy way to remember the order of operations: **P**lease **E**xcuse **M**y **D**ear **A**unt **S**ally (parentheses, exponents, multiply or divide, add or subtract)—PEMDAS.

Algebra

Algebra Diagnostic Test

Questions

1. Solve for x: $x + 5 = 17$

2. Solve for x: $4x + 9 = 21$

3. Solve for x: $5x + 7 = 3x - 9$

4. Solve for x: $mx - n = y$

5. Solve for x: $\frac{r}{x} = \frac{s}{t}$

6. Solve for y: $\frac{3}{7} = \frac{y}{8}$

7. Evaluate: $3x^2 + 5y + 7$ if $x = -2$ and $y = 3$

8. Simplify: $8xy^2 + 3xy + 4xy^2 - 2xy =$

9. Simplify: $6x^2(4x^3y) =$

10. Simplify: $(5x + 2z) + (3x - 4z) =$

11. Simplify: $(4x + 7z) - (3x - 4z) =$

12. Factor: $ab + ac$

13. Solve for x: $2x + 3 \leq 11$

14. Solve for x: $3x + 4 \geq 5x - 8$

Answers

1. $x = 12$

2. $x = 3$

3. $x = -8$

4. $x = \dfrac{(y + n)}{m}$

5. $x = \dfrac{rt}{s}$

6. $y = \dfrac{24}{7}$ or $3\dfrac{3}{7}$

7. 34

8. $12xy^2 + xy$

9. $24x^5y$

10. $8x - 2z$

11. $x + 11z$

12. $a(b + c)$

13. $x \leq 4$

14. $x \leq 6$

Algebra Review

Equations

An **equation** is a relationship between numbers and/or symbols. It helps to remember that an equation is like a balance scale, with the equal sign (=) being the fulcrum, or center. Thus, if you do the *same thing to both sides* of the equal sign (say, add 5 to each side), the equation will still be balanced. To solve the equation $x - 5 = 23$, you must get x by itself on one side; therefore, add 5 to both sides.

$$
\begin{array}{rl}
x - 5 &= 23 \\
+5 \quad &+5 \\
\hline
x \quad &= 28
\end{array}
$$

In the same manner, you may subtract, multiply, or divide *both* sides of an equation by the same (nonzero) number, and the equation will not change. Sometimes you may have to use more than one step to solve for an unknown.

$$3x + 4 = 19$$

Subtract 4 from both sides to get the $3x$ by itself on one side:

$$\begin{array}{r} 3x + 4 = 19 \\ -4 \quad -4 \\ \hline 3x \quad\;\; = 15 \end{array}$$

Then divide both sides by 3 to get x:

$$\frac{3x}{3} = \frac{15}{3}$$
$$x = 5$$

Remember: Solving an equation is using **opposite operations,** until the letter is on a side by itself (for addition, subtract; for multiplication, divide; and so on).

Understood multiplying

When two or more letters, or a number and letters, are written next to each other, they are **understood to be multiplied.** Thus, $8x$ means 8 times x. Or ab means a times b. Or $18ab$ means 18 times a times b.

Parentheses also represent multiplication. Thus, $(a)b$ means a times b. A raised dot also means multiplication. Thus, $6 \cdot 5$ means 6 times 5.

Literal equations

Literal equations have no numbers, only symbols (letters).

$$\text{Solve for } Q: \quad QP - X = Y$$

First add X to both sides.

$$\begin{array}{r} QP - X = Y \\ +X +X \\ \hline QP \quad\;\; = Y + X \end{array}$$

Then divide both sides by P.

$$\frac{QP}{P} = \frac{Y + X}{P}$$

$$Q = \frac{Y + X}{P}$$

Again, opposite operations are used to isolate Q.

Cross multiplying

Solve for x: $\frac{b}{x} = \frac{p}{q}$

To solve this equation quickly, you **cross multiply.** To cross multiply,

1. Bring the denominators up next to the opposite side numerators.

2. Multiply.

$$\frac{b}{x} = \frac{p}{q}$$
$$bq = px$$

Then divide both sides by p to get x alone.

$$\frac{bq}{p} = \frac{px}{p}$$
$$\frac{bq}{p} = x \ \ or \ \ x = \frac{bq}{p}$$

Cross multiplying can be used only when the format is two fractions separated by an equal sign.

Proportions

A **proportion** is a statement that says that two expressions written in fraction form are equal to one another. Proportions are quickly solved using a **cross multiplying** technique.

Examples:

1. Solve for x:

   $$\frac{3}{x} = \frac{5}{7}$$

   Using the cross multiplying technique, you get

   $$5x = 21$$

   Dividing each side of the equation by 5, you get

   $$x = \frac{21}{5} \text{ or } 4\frac{1}{5}$$

   This problem could also have been presented in written form as "3 is to x as 5 is to 7; find the value of x."

2. Solve for x:

$$\frac{2x+3}{x-4} = \frac{5}{6}$$

Using the cross multiplying technique, you get $\qquad$ $6(2x+3) = 5(x-4)$

Distributing on each side of the equation, you get $\qquad$ $12x + 18 = 5x - 20$

Subtracting $5x$ from each side of the equation in order to get all the unknowns on one side of the equation, you get $\qquad$ $7x + 18 = -20$

Subtracting 18 from each side of the equation in order to get all the knowns on one side of the equation, you get $\qquad$ $7x = -38$

Dividing each side of the equation by 7, you get $\qquad$ $x = \frac{-38}{7}$ or $-5\frac{3}{7}$

3. Solve for x:

$$\frac{p}{q} = \frac{x}{y}$$

Using the cross multiplying technique, you get $\qquad$ $xq = py$

Dividing each side of the equation by q, you get $\qquad$ $x = \frac{py}{q}$

4. Triangle ABC is similar to triangle DEF with $AB = 6$, $BC = 9$, $AC = 12$, and $DE = 8$. Find the length of DF.

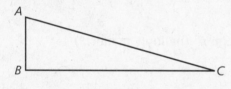 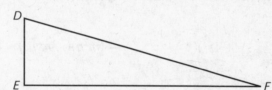

Similar triangles have corresponding sides, forming proportions. That is, since triangle ABC is similar to triangle DEF, then $\frac{AB}{DE} = \frac{BC}{EF} = \frac{AC}{DF}$, and therefore, $\frac{6}{8} = \frac{9}{EF} = \frac{12}{DF}$. Now use $\frac{6}{8} = \frac{12}{DF}$

$$6(DF) = 96$$

$$DF = 16$$

Evaluating expressions

To **evaluate an expression,** just insert the value for the unknowns and do the arithmetic.

Evaluate: $2x^2 + 3y + 6$ if $x = 2$ and $y = 9$

$$2(2^2) + 3(9) + 6$$
$$= 2(4) + 27 + 6$$
$$= 8 + 27 + 6$$
$$= 41$$

Monomials and polynomials

A monomial is an algebraic expression that consists of only one term. For instance, $9x$, $4a^2$, and $3mpxz^2$ are all monomials.

A **polynomial** consists of two or more terms; $x + y$, $y^2 - x^2$, and $x^2 + 3x + 5y^2$ are all polynomials.

Adding and subtracting monomials

To **add or subtract monomials,** follow the same rules as with regular signed numbers, provided that the *terms are alike*.

$$\begin{array}{r} 15x^2\,yz \\ -\,18x^2\,yz \\ \hline -\ \ 3x^2\,yz \end{array} \qquad 3x + 2x = 5x$$

Multiplying and dividing monomials

To **multiply monomials,** add the exponents of the same terms.

$$(x^3)(x^4) = x^7 \qquad -4(m^2n)(-3m^4n^3) = 12m^6n^4 \text{ (multiply numbers)}$$
$$(x^2y)(x^3y^2) = x^5y^3$$

To **divide monomials,** subtract the exponents of the like terms.

$$\frac{y^{15}}{y^4} = y^{11} \qquad \frac{x^5y^2}{x^3y} = x^2y \qquad \frac{36a^4b^6}{-9ab} = -\,4a^3b^5$$

Remember: x is the same as x^1.

Adding and subtracting polynomials

To add or subtract polynomials, just arrange like terms in columns and then add or subtract:

$$a^2 + \ ab + \ b^2$$
$$\underline{3a^2 + 4ab - 2b^2}$$
$$4a^2 + 5ab - \ b^2$$

Subtract:

$$\begin{array}{l} a^2 + b^2 \\ \underline{-\left(-2a^2 - b^2\right)} \end{array} \qquad \rightarrow \qquad \begin{array}{l} a^2 + \ b^2 \\ \underline{+2a^2 + \ b^2} \\ 3a^2 + 2b^2 \end{array}$$

Multiplying polynomials

To **multiply polynomials,** multiply each term in one polynomial by each term in the other polynomial. Then simplify if necessary.

$$(3x + a)(2x - 2a) =$$

$$\begin{array}{r} 2x - 2a \\ \underline{\times \ 3x + \ a} \\ + 2ax - 2a^2 \\ \underline{6x^2 - 6ax} \\ 6x^2 - 4ax - 2a^2 \end{array} \qquad \text{similar to} \qquad \begin{array}{r} 23 \\ \underline{\times 19} \\ 207 \\ \underline{23} \\ 437 \end{array}$$

Factoring

To **factor** means to find two or more quantities whose product equals the original quantity. To **factor out a common factor,**

1. Find the largest common monomial factor of each term.

2. Divide the original polynomial by this factor to obtain the second factor. The second factor will be a polynomial.

$$2y^3 - 6y = 2y\left(y^2 - 3\right)$$
$$x^5 - 4x^3 + x^2 = x^2\left(x^3 - 4x + 1\right)$$

To **factor the difference between two squares,**

1. Find the square root of the first term and the square root of the second term.

2. Express your answer as the product of the sum of the quantities from step 1 times the difference of those quantities.

$$x^2 - 144 = (x + 12)(x - 12)$$
$$a^2 - b^2 = (a + b)(a - b)$$

Inequalities

An **inequality** is a statement in which the relationships are not equal. Instead of using an equal sign (=) as in an equation, we use > (greater than) and < (less than) or ≥ (greater than or equal to) and ≤ (less than or equal to).

When working with inequalities, treat them exactly like equations, *except* if you multiply or divide both sides by a negative number, you must *reverse* the direction of the sign.

Solve for x: $2x + 4 > 6$

$$2x + 4 > 6$$

$$\underline{-4 - 4}$$

$$2x > 2$$

$$\frac{2x}{2} > \frac{2}{2}$$

$$x > 1$$

Solve for x: $-7x > 14$

$-7x > 14$ (divide both sides by –7 and reverse the sign)

$$\frac{-7}{-7} < \frac{14}{-7}$$

$$x < -2$$

Solve for x: $3x + 2 \geq 5x - 10$

$$-3x + 2 \geq -5x - 10$$

$$\underline{-5x - 2 -5x - 2} \text{(opposite operations of addition and subtraction;}$$

$$-2x \geq -12 \text{the sign direction stays the same)}$$

$$\frac{-2x}{-2} \leq \frac{-12}{-2} \text{(divide both sides by –2 and reverse the sign)}$$

$$x \leq 6$$

Geometry

Geometry Diagnostic Test

Questions

1. Name any angle of this triangle three different ways.

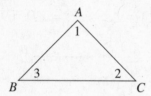

2. A(n) _____ angle measures less than 90 degrees.

3. A(n) _____ angle measures 90 degrees.

4. A(n) _____ angle measures more than 90 degrees.

5. A(n) _____ angle measures 180 degrees.

6. Two angles are complementary when their sum is _____.

7. Two angles are supplementary when their sum is _____.

8. In the diagram below, find the measures of $\angle a$, $\angle b$, and $\angle c$.

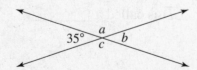

9. Lines that stay the same distance apart and never meet are called _____ lines.

10. Lines that meet to form 90 degree angles are called _____ lines.

11. A(n) _____ triangle has three equal sides. Therefore, each interior angle measures _____.

12. In the triangle below, $\overline{AC}$ must be shorter than _____ inches.

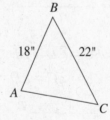

13. In the triangle above, which angle is smaller, $\angle A$ or $\angle C$?

14. What is the measure of $\angle ACD$ below?

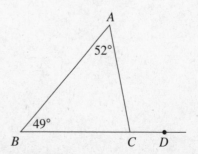

129

15. What is the length of $\overline{AC}$ below?

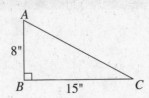

16. What is the length of $\overline{BC}$ below?

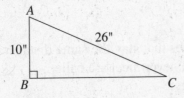

17. Name each of the following polygons.

A. $\overline{AB} = \overline{BC} = \overline{AC}$
$\angle A = \angle B = \angle C = 60°$

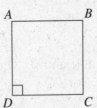

B. $\overline{AB} = \overline{BC} = \overline{CD} = \overline{AD}$
$\angle A = \angle B = \angle C = \angle D = 90°$

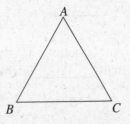

C. $\overline{AB} \| \overline{DC}$
$\overline{AB} = \overline{DC}$
$\overline{AD} \| \overline{BC}$
$\overline{AD} = \overline{BC}$
$\angle A = \angle C$

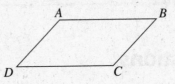

D. $\overline{AB} = \overline{DC}$
$\overline{AD} = \overline{BC}$
$\angle A = \angle B = \angle C = \angle D = 90°$

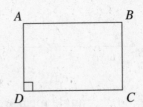

E. $\overline{AB} \| \overline{DC}$

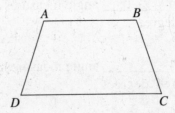

18. Fill in the blanks for circle R below.

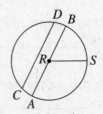

A. $\overline{RS}$ is called the _____.

B. $\overline{AB}$ is called the _____.

C. $\overline{CD}$ is called a _____.

19. Find the area and circumference for the circle below $\left(\pi \approx \frac{22}{7}\right)$.

   A. area =

   B. circumference =

20. Find the area and perimeter of the figure below.

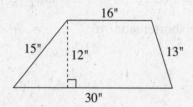

   A. area =

   B. perimeter =

21. Find the area and perimeter of the figure below (*ABCD* is a parallelogram).

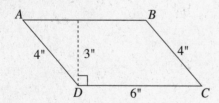

   A. area =

   B. perimeter =

22. Find the volume of the figure below if $V = \left(\pi r^2\right)h$ (use 3.14 for π).

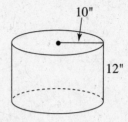

23. What is the surface area and volume of the cube below?

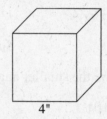

   A. surface area =

   B. volume =

Answers

   1. ∠1, ∠BAC, ∠CAB, ∠A

   ∠2, ∠ACB, ∠BCA, ∠C

   ∠3, ∠CBA, ∠ABC, ∠B

   2. acute

   3. right

4. obtuse

5. straight

6. 90°

7. 180°

8. $a = 145°$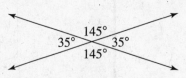

$b = 35°$

$c = 145°$

9. parallel

10. perpendicular

11. equilateral, 60°

12. 40 inches   Since $\overline{AB} + \overline{BC} = 40$ inches, then $\overline{AC} < \overline{AB} + \overline{BC}$ and $\overline{AC} < 40$.

13. $\angle C$ must be the smaller angle, since it is opposite the shorter side $\overline{AB}$.

14. $\angle ACD = 101°$

15. $\overline{AC} = 17$ inches

16. Since $\triangle ABC$ is a right triangle, use the Pythagorean theorem.

$$a^2 + b^2 = c^2$$
$$10^2 + b^2 = 26^2$$
$$100 + b^2 = 676$$
$$b^2 = 576$$
$$b = 24"$$

17. A. equilateral triangle

B. square

C. parallelogram

D. rectangle

E. trapezoid

18. A. radius

B. diameter

C. chord

19. A. area $= \pi r^2$

$$= \pi \left(7^2\right)$$
$$= \frac{22}{7}(7)(7)$$
$$= 154 \text{ square inches}$$

B. circumference $= \pi d$

$$= \pi (14") \left(d = 14" \text{ since } r = 7"\right)$$
$$= \frac{22}{7}(14)$$
$$= 22(2)$$
$$= 44 \text{ inches}$$

20. A. area $= \frac{1}{2}(a+b)h$

$$= \frac{1}{2}(16 + 30)12$$
$$= \frac{1}{2}(46)12$$
$$= 23(12)$$
$$= 276 \text{ square inches}$$

B. perimeter $= 16 + 13 + 30 + 15 = 74$ inches

21. A. area $= bh$

$$= 6(3)$$
$$= 18 \text{ square inches}$$

B. perimeter $= 6 + 4 + 6 + 4$

$$= 20 \text{ inches}$$

22. volume $= \left(\pi r^2\right)h$

$$= \left(\pi \cdot 10^2\right)(12)$$
$$= 3.14(100)(12)$$
$$= 314(12)$$
$$= 3,768 \text{ cubic inches}$$

23. A. All six surfaces have an area of 4×4, or 16 square inches, since each surface is a square. Therefore, $16(6) = 96$ square inches in the surface area.

B. Volume = side $\times$ side $\times$ side, or $4^3 = 64$ cubic inches.

Geometry Review

Plane geometry is the study of shapes and figures in two dimensions (the plane).

Solid geometry is the study of shapes and figures in three dimensions.

A **point** is the most fundamental idea in geometry. It is represented by a dot and named by a capital letter.

Lines

Straight lines

A **straight line** is determined by two points. It continues forever in both directions. A line consists of an infinite number of points. It is named by any two points on the line. The symbol $\leftrightarrow$ written on top of the two letters is used to denote that line.

This is line *AB*.

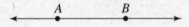

It is written $\overleftrightarrow{AB}$.

A line may also be named by one small letter. The symbol would not be used.

This is line *l*.

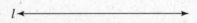

Line segments

A **line segment** is a piece of a line. A line segment has two endpoints. It is named by its two endpoints. The symbol — written on top of the two letters is used to denote that line segment.

This is line segment *CD*.

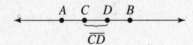

It is written $\overline{CD}$.

Note that it is a piece of $\overleftrightarrow{AB}$.

Rays

A **ray** has only one endpoint and continues forever in one direction. A ray can be thought of as a half-line. It is named by the letter of its endpoint and any other point on the ray. The symbol $\rightarrow$ written on top of the two letters is used to denote that ray.

This is ray *AB*.

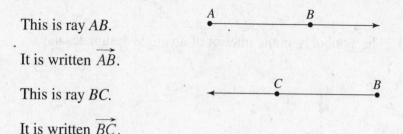

It is written $\overrightarrow{AB}$.

This is ray *BC*.

It is written $\overrightarrow{BC}$.

Note that the first letter is always the beginning point of the ray.

Angles

An **angle** is formed by two rays that start from the same point. That point is called the **vertex;** the rays are called the **sides** of the angle. An angle is measured in **degrees.** The degrees indicate the size of the angle, from one side to the other.

In the diagram, the angle is formed by rays $\overrightarrow{AB}$ and $\overrightarrow{AC}$. *A* is the vertex. $\overrightarrow{AB}$ and $\overrightarrow{AC}$ are the sides of the angle.

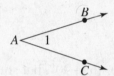

The symbol $\angle$ is used to denote an angle. An angle can be named in various ways.

1. By the letter of the vertex—therefore, the angle above could be named $\angle A$.

2. By the number (or small letter) in its interior—therefore, the angle above could be named $\angle 1$.

3. By the letters of the three points that form it—therefore, the angle above could be named $\angle BAC$, or $\angle CAB$. The center letter is always the letter of the vertex.

Types of angles

Adjacent angles

Adjacent angles are any angles that share a common side and a common vertex, but do not share any interior points.

In the diagram, $\angle 1$ and $\angle 2$ are adjacent angles.

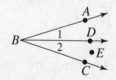

$\angle ABC$ and $\angle 2$ are not adjacent angles even though they share a vertex and a common side. They are not adjacent because they share some interior points. For example, these two angles have point *E* in both interiors.

Right angles

A **right angle** has a measure of 90°. The symbol ⌐ in the interior of an angle designates the fact that a right angle is formed.

In the diagram, ∠*ABC* is a right angle.

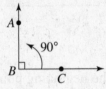

Acute angles

Any angle whose measure is less than 90° is called an **acute angle.**

In the diagram, ∠*b* is acute.

Obtuse angles

Any angle whose measure is larger than 90°, but smaller than 180°, is called an **obtuse angle.**

In the diagram, ∠4 is an obtuse angle.

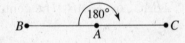

Straight angles

A **straight angle** has a measure of 180°.

In the diagram, ∠*BAC* is a straight angle (also called a line).

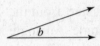

Complementary angles

Two angles whose sum is 90° are called **complementary angles.**

In the diagram, since ∠*ABC* is a right angle, ∠1 + ∠2 = 90°.

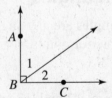

Therefore, ∠1 and ∠2 are complementary angles. If ∠2 = 35°, its complement ∠1, would be 90° − 35° = 55°.

Supplementary angles

Two angles whose sum is 180° are called **supplementary angles.** Two adjacent angles that form a straight line are supplementary.

In the diagram, since $\angle ABC$ is a straight angle, $\angle 3 + \angle 4 = 180°$.

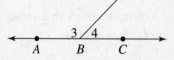

Therefore, $\angle 3$ and $\angle 4$ are supplementary angles. If $\angle 3 = 122°$, its supplement, $\angle 4$, would be $180° - 122° = 58°$.

Angle bisectors

A ray from the vertex of an angle that divides the angle into two equal pieces is called an **angle bisector.**

In the diagram, $\overrightarrow{AB}$ is the angle bisector of $\angle CAD$.

Therefore, $\angle 1 = \angle 2$.

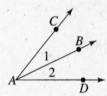

Vertical and adjacent angles

If two straight lines intersect, they do so at a point. Four angles are formed. Those angles opposite each other are called **vertical angles.** Those angles sharing a common side and a common vertex are, again, **adjacent angles.** Vertical angles are always equal.

In the diagram, line l and line m intersect at point Q. $\angle 1$, $\angle 2$, $\angle 3$, and $\angle 4$ are formed.

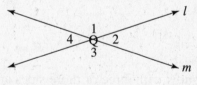

$\left.\begin{array}{l} \angle 1 \text{ and } \angle 3 \\ \angle 2 \text{ and } \angle 4 \end{array}\right\}$ are vertical angles

$\left.\begin{array}{l} \angle 1 \text{ and } \angle 2 \\ \angle 2 \text{ and } \angle 3 \\ \angle 3 \text{ and } \angle 4 \\ \angle 1 \text{ and } \angle 4 \end{array}\right\}$ are adjacent angles

Therefore, $\angle 1 = \angle 3$ and $\angle 2 = \angle 4$.

Types of lines

Intersecting lines

Two or more lines that cross each other at a point are called **intersecting lines.** That point is on each of those lines.

In the diagram, lines *l* and *m* intersect at *Q*.

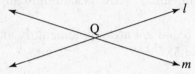

Perpendicular lines

Two lines that meet to form right angles (90°) are called **perpendicular lines.** The symbol ⊥ is used to denote perpendicular lines.

In the diagram, line *l* ⊥ line *m*.

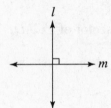

Parallel lines

Two or more lines that remain the same distance apart at all times are called **parallel lines.** Parallel lines never meet. The symbol ‖ is used to denote parallel lines.

In the diagram, *l* ‖ *m*.

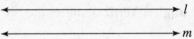

Polygons

Closed shapes or figures with three or more sides are called **polygons.** (*Poly-* means "many"; *-gon* means "sides"; thus, *polygon* means "many sides.")

Triangles

This section deals with those polygons having the fewest number of sides. A **triangle** is a three-sided polygon. It has three angles in its interior. The sum of these angles is *always* 180°. The symbol for triangle is △. A triangle is named by all three letters of its vertices.

This is △ *ABC*.

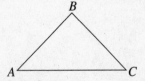

Types of triangles

1. A triangle having all three sides equal (meaning all three sides have the same length) is called an **equilateral triangle.**

2. A triangle having two sides equal is called an **isosceles triangle.**

3. A triangle having none of its sides equal is called a **scalene triangle.**

4. A triangle having a right (90°) angle in its interior is called a **right triangle.**

5. A triangle in which each of its angles is less than 90° is called an **acute triangle.**

6. A triangle in which one of its angles is more than 90° is called an **obtuse triangle.**

Facts about triangles

Every triangle can be drawn showing a **base** (bottom side) and a **height** (altitude). Every height is the **perpendicular** (forms right angles) segment from a vertex to its opposite side (the base).

In this diagram of $\triangle ABC$,
$\overline{BC}$ is the base, and
$\overline{AE}$ is the height. $\overline{AE} \perp \overline{BC}$.

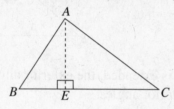

In this diagram, the base $\overline{BC}$ had to be extended in order to draw the height $\overline{AE}$.

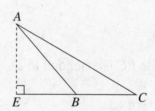

Every triangle has three **medians.** A median is the line segment drawn from a vertex to the midpoint of the opposite side.

In this diagram of $\triangle ABC$,
E is the midpoint of $\overline{BC}$.

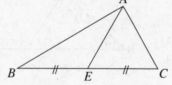

Therefore, $BE = EC$. $\overline{AE}$ is a median of $\triangle ABC$.

In an equilateral triangle, all three sides are equal, and all three angles are equal. If all three angles are equal and their sum is 180°, the following must be true:

$$x + x + x = 180°$$
$$3x = 180°$$
$$x = 60°$$

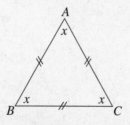

139

Every angle of an equilateral triangle always has a measure of 60°.

In any triangle, the longest side is always opposite from the largest angle. Likewise, the shortest side is always opposite from the smallest angle. In a right triangle, the longest side is always opposite from the right angle, as the right angle is the largest angle in the triangle.

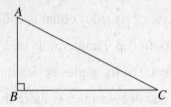

$\overline{AC}$ is the longest side of right $\triangle ABC$.

The sum of the lengths of any two sides of a triangle must be larger than the length of the third side.

In the diagram of $\triangle ABC$,

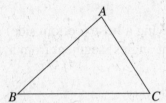

$\overline{AB} + \overline{BC} > \overline{AC}$

$\overline{AB} + \overline{AC} > \overline{BC}$

$\overline{AC} + \overline{BC} > \overline{AB}$

If one side of a triangle is extended, the exterior angle formed by that extension is equal to the sum of the other two interior angles.

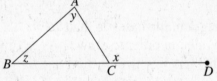

In the diagram of $\angle ABC$, side BC is extended to D.

$\angle ACD$ is the exterior angle formed.

$\angle x = \angle y + \angle z$

$x = 82° + 41°$

$\quad = 123°$

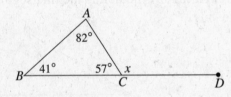

Pythagorean theorem

In any right triangle, the relationship between the lengths of the sides is stated by the **Pythagorean theorem.** The parts of a right triangle are as follows.

$\angle C$ is the right angle.

The side opposite the right angle is called the **hypotenuse** (side c). (The hypotenuse is always the longest side.)

The other two sides are called the **legs** (sides a and b).

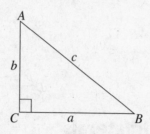

The three lengths a, b, and c are always numbers such that $a^2 + b^2 = c^2$

If $a = 3$, $b = 4$, and $c = 5$,

$$a^2 + b^2 = c^2$$
$$3^2 + 4^2 = 5^2$$
$$9 + 16 = 25$$
$$25 = 25$$

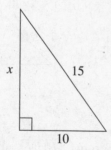

Therefore, 3-4-5 is called a **Pythagorean triple.** There are other values for a, b, and c that always work. Some are: 5-12-13 and 8-15-17. Any multiple of one of these triples also works. For example, using the 3-4-5 triple, 6-8-10, 9-12-15, and 15-20-25 are also Pythagorean triples.

If perfect squares are known, the lengths of these sides can be determined easily. A knowledge of the use of algebraic equations can also be used to determine the lengths of the sides.

$$a^2 + b^2 = c^2$$
$$x^2 + 10^2 = 15^2$$
$$x^2 + 100 = 225$$
$$x^2 = 125$$
$$x = \sqrt{125}$$
$$= \sqrt{25} \times \sqrt{5}$$
$$= 5\sqrt{5}$$

Quadrilaterals

A polygon having four sides is called a **quadrilateral.** There are four angles in its interior. The sum of these interior angles is always 360°. A quadrilateral is named by using the four letters of its vertices.

This is quadrilateral *ABCD*.

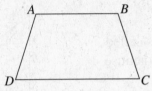

Types of quadrilaterals

The **square** has four equal sides and four right angles.

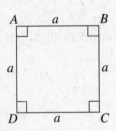

The rectangle has opposite sides equal and four right angles.

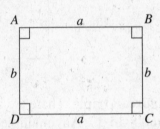

The parallelogram has opposite sides equal and parallel, opposite angles equal, and consecutive angles supplementary. Every parallelogram has a height.

$\angle A = \angle C$

$\angle B = \angle D$

$\angle A + \angle B = 180°$

$\angle A + \angle D = 180°$

$\angle B + \angle C = 180°$

$\angle C + \angle D = 180°$

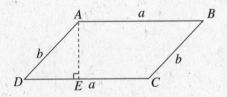

$\overline{AE}$ is a height of the parallelogram, $\overline{AB}\|\overline{DC}$, and $\overline{AD}\|\overline{BC}$.

The **rhombus** is a parallelogram with four equal sides. A rhombus has a height. $\overline{BE}$ is a height.

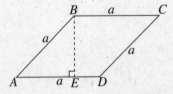

The **trapezoid** has only one pair
of parallel sides. A trapezoid has
a height. $\overline{AE}$ is the height. $\overline{AB} \| \overline{DC}$.

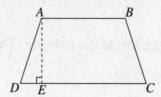

Other polygons

1. The **pentagon** is a five-sided polygon.

2. The **hexagon** is a six-sided polygon.

3. The **septagon** (or **heptogon**) is a seven-sided polygon.

4. The **octagon** is an eight-sided polygon.

5. The **nonagon** is a nine-sided polygon.

6. The **decagon** is a ten-sided polygon.

Facts about polygons

Regular polygons

Regular means all sides have the same length and all angles have the same measure. A regular three-sided polygon is the equilateral triangle. A regular four-sided polygon is the square. There are no other special names. Other polygons will simply be described as regular, if they are. For example, a regular five-sided polygon is called a regular pentagon. A regular six-sided polygon is called a regular hexagon.

Perimeter

Perimeter means the total distance all the way around the outside of any polygon. The perimeter of any polygon can be determined by adding up the lengths of all the sides. The total distance around will be the sum of all sides of the polygon. No special formulas are necessary.

Area

Area (A) means the amount of space inside the polygon. The formulas for each area are as follows:

Triangle: $A = \frac{1}{2}bh$

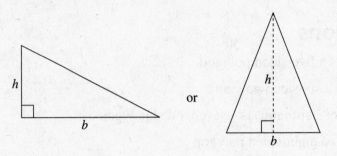

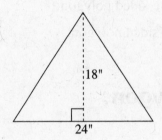

$$A = \frac{1}{2}bh$$
$$= \frac{1}{2}(24)(18)$$
$$= 216 \text{ sq in}$$

Square or rectangle: $A = lw$

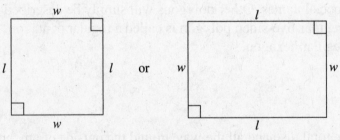

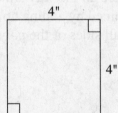

$A = l(w) = 4(4) = 16 \text{ sq in}$

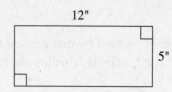

$A = l(w) = 12(5) = 60$ sq in

Parallelogram: $A = bh$

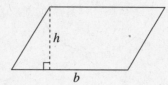

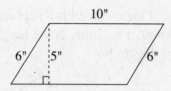

$A = b(h)$
$\quad = 10(5) = 50$ sq in

Trapezoid: $A = \frac{1}{2}(a + b)h$

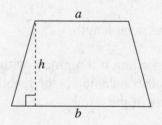

$A = \frac{1}{2}(a + b)h$
$\quad = \frac{1}{2}(8 + 12)7$
$\quad = \frac{1}{2}(20)7$
$\quad = 70$ sq in

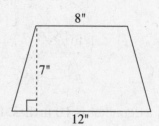

Circles

A closed shape whose side is formed by one curved line, all points of which are equidistant from the center point, is called a **circle.** Circles are named by the letter of their center point.

This is circle *M*.

M is the center point, since it is the same distance away from any point on the circle.

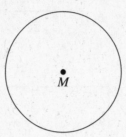

Parts of a circle

Radius has two meanings. One meaning is a segment that goes from the center of the circle to any point on the circle. Another meaning is the length of the segment that goes from the center of a circle to any point on the circle.

$\overline{MA}$ is a radius.

$\overline{MB}$ is a radius.

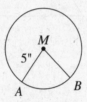

In any circle, all radii (plural) are the same length.

Diameter has two meanings. One meaning is a segment with endpoints on a circle that passes through the center of the circle. Another meaning is the length of the segment with endpoints on a circle passing through the center of the circle.

$\overline{AB}$ is a diameter.

$\overline{DC}$ is a diameter.

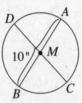

In this circle, the length of a diameter is 10 inches. In any circle, all diameters have the same length. The length of a diameter is two times the length of a radius.

A **chord** of a circle is a line segment whose endpoints lie on the circle.

$\overline{RS}$ is a chord.

$\overline{UV}$ is a chord.

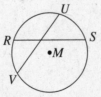

A diameter is the longest chord in any circle.

146

An **arc** of a circle is a portion of the circle between any two points on the circle. The symbol ⌢ is used to denote an arc. This symbol is written above the two endpoints that form the arc. Arcs are measured either in degrees or in some measure of length. A full rotation around a circle has a rotation measure of 360°. The rotation measure of an arc will then be a portion of the 360°. The distance around a circle is called **circumference**, which is discussed in the next section. The length of an arc is a portion of the circumference.

This is $\overset{\frown}{EF}$.

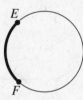

Minor $\overset{\frown}{EF}$ is the shorter distance between E and F.

Major $\overset{\frown}{EF}$ is the longer distance between E and F.

When $\overset{\frown}{EF}$ is written, the minor arc is assumed.

Area and circumference

Circumference is the distance around the circle. Since there are no sides to add up, a formula is needed. π (pi) is a Greek letter that represents a specific number. In fractional or decimal form, the commonly used approximations are $\pi \approx 3.14$ or $\pi \approx \frac{22}{7}$. The formula for circumference is $C = \pi d$ or $C = 2\pi r$.

In circle M, $d = 8$, since $r = 4$.

$C = \pi d$
$\quad = \pi(8)$
$\quad = 3.14(8)$
$\quad = 25.12$ in

The **area** of a circle can be determined by: $A = \pi\left(r^2\right)$

In circle M, $r = 5$, since $d = 10$.

$A = \pi\left(r^2\right)$
$\quad = \pi\left(5^2\right)$
$\quad = 3.14(25)$
$\quad = 78.5$ sq in

Volume

In three dimensions, there are different facts that can be determined about shapes. **Volume** is the capacity to hold. The formula for volume of each shape is different. The volume of any **prism** (a three-dimensional shape having many sides, but two bases) can be determined by: volume (V) = (area of base)(height of prism).

Specifically for a **rectangular solid,**

$V = (lw)(h)$

$\quad = lwh$

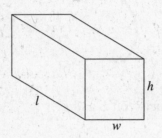

Specifically for a **cylinder** (circular bases),

$V = (\pi r^2)h$

$\quad = \pi r^2 h$

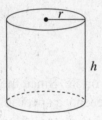

Volume is labeled "cubic" units.

Surface area

The **surface area** of a three-dimensional solid is the area of all of the surfaces that form the solid. Find the area of each surface, and then add up those areas. The surface area of a rectangular solid can be found by adding up the areas of all six surfaces.

The surface area of this prism is

top	$18 \times 6 = 108$
bottom	$18 \times 6 = 108$
left side	$18 \times 4 = 72$
right side	$18 \times 4 = 72$
front	$6 \times 4 = 24$
back	$6 \times 4 = \underline{24}$
	408 sq in

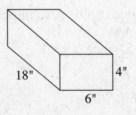

PART IV

SELECTIVE REVIEW OF GRAMMAR AND USAGE

The subjects in this section are arranged as follows:

Adjectives and Adverbs

Comparisons

Dangling Modifiers

Double Negatives

Either...Or and *Neither...Nor*

Exact Word Choice

Fewer and *Less*

Fragment Sentences

Idiom

Many and *Much*

Misplaced Modifiers

Parallelism

Pronouns

Punctuation: The Comma

Punctuation: The Semicolon

Punctuation: The Colon

Squinting Modifiers

Subject-Verb Agreement

Verb Tense

Wordiness

Selective Review of Grammar and Usage

PPST candidates should focus on understanding the basic knowledge of grammar, word choice (usage), sentence structure, punctuation, and spelling of standard written English. This selected review of grammar and usage is intended to familiarize you with common grammatical rules and conventions.

Adjectives and Adverbs

A common error is using an adjective when an adverb is required or vice versa. Adjectives describe things (nouns and pronouns), and adverbs describe actions (verbs).

Adjectives give additional information about nouns.

> The *coastal* region is known for its *foggy* nights.

Coastal gives additional information about *region,* and *foggy* gives additional information about *nights*.

Adverbs give additional information about verbs.

> Acting *quickly,* Superman prevented an earthquake from *completely* destroying the state of California.

Quickly gives additional information about *acting,* and *completely* gives additional information about *destroying*.

Comparisons

Sentence clarity suffers if the items being compared are not alike.

> His iridescent *jogging suit* was much more distracting than the other *athletes*.

In this case, a *jogging suit* is compared to *athletes*. These items are not alike. A clear and correct comparison compares the *jogging suit* to *other jogging suits*.

> His iridescent *jogging suit* was much more distracting than *those of* the other athletes.

The words as *and* than *are often part of the structure of comparison sentences. A clear and correct comparison structure may employ either an* as . . . as *phrase or an* as . . . as . . . than *phrase but never an* as . . . than *phrase.*

> *Correct:* Kurt is *as* talented *as* the other musicians.
>
> *Correct:* Kurt is *as* talented *as* but not more talented *than* the other musicians.
>
> *Incorrect:* Kurt is *as* talented *than* the other musicians.

Dangling Modifiers

A dangling modifier is an introductory phrase that does not refer clearly or logically to a subsequent modifier (usually the subject) in a sentence.

> Strolling along the beach, a wave suddenly drenched us.

This sentence seems to say that the *wave* is doing the *strolling*. A correct sentence clarifies the modifier as follows:

> While we were strolling along the beach, a wave suddenly drenched us.

In short, a dangling modifier is an introductory phrase that does not refer clearly or logically to a subsequent element (usually the subject) in a sentence.

Double Negatives

A double negative occurs when one negative word or phrase is used along with another.

> Fred could *not hardly* remember when he had enjoyed himself so much.

Not and *hardly* are both negative words, and when two negatives are used to modify the same term (in this case, *remember*), the result is a double negative. A correct expression requires only a single negative.

> Fred could *not* remember when he had enjoyed himself so much.

Either . . . Or and *Neither . . . Nor*

When comparing two items, you may use **either** *with* **or.**

> *Either* rain *or* snow is likely to spoil our vacation.

You may also use **neither** *with* **nor.**

> *Neither* rain *nor* snow will spoil our vacation.

Remember **never** *to use* **nor** *without* **neither,** *as in*

> *No* rain *nor* snow will spoil our vacation.

Exact Word Choice

Sometimes, words that sound alike are confused with one another. Checking their dictionary meanings will help you to avoid their misuse.

Commonly Confused Words	
adapt/adept	incite/insight
affect/effect	lay/lie
capital/capitol	persecute/prosecute
compile/comply	precede/proceed
detain/retain	raise/rise
elicit/illicit	set/sit
foreword/forward	their/there/they're
human/humane	weather/whether

Fewer and *Less*

When describing **countable** *items, use* **fewer.**

> There are *fewer teachers* in the job market this year.

When describing **uncountable** *items, use* **less.**

> Keeping one's car properly tuned means *less engine trouble* and *less gasoline consumption.*

Note that an uncountable item is not necessarily an immeasurable item. For example, *gasoline* may be measured but not counted.

Fragment Sentences

A fragment sentence is one that is incomplete, one in which crucial information is missing.

Here are some types of fragment sentences.

Fragment: After the movie is over.

Missing information: What happens after the movie is over.

Complete sentence: After the movie is over, *we will enjoy a late supper*.

Fragment: Central air conditioning, a heated pool, and a view of the valley.

Missing information: A subject and a verb.

Complete sentence: Their new *home featured* central air conditioning, a heated pool, and a view of the valley.

Fragment: Books with large, colorful pictures.

Missing information: A verb.

Complete sentence: Books with large, colorful pictures *are* rare.

Idiom

To native English speakers, certain expressions "sound right" because they are so commonly used. Such expressions are called "idiomatic" and are correct simply because they are so widely accepted.

Here is a list of examples.

Idiomatic	Unidiomatic
addicted *to*	addicted *from*
angry *with*	angry *at*
capable *of*	capable *to*
different *from*	different *than*
forbid *to*	forbid *from*
obedient *to*	obedient *in*
on *the* whole	on *a* whole

Remember that the standard of correctness is standard written English. Be alert to idiomatic expressions not acceptable in or characteristic of standard *written* English.

Many and *Much*

Many and *much* follow the same rules as do *fewer* and *less*.

Many *is used with* countable *items*.

> *Many trees* filled the landscape that now contains townhouses.

Much *is used with* uncountable *items*.

> *Much happiness* filled the house whenever the family gathered to celebrate.

Misplaced Modifiers

A misplaced modifier is one that is placed too close to a word that it could, but should not, modify.

> Ann prepared a roast for the family that was served burned.

In this case, because *that was served burned* is so close to *family*, the sentence seems to say that the *family* was *burned*. Here is a corrected version.

> Ann served a burned roast to the family.

Note that this correction also eliminates excess words.

Parallelism

Phrases in a sentence are parallel when they have the same grammatical structure.

Here are three examples of parallel phrases.

> to stay happy, to keep fit, and to prosper
> staying happy, keeping fit, and prospering
> happiness, fitness, and prosperity

Mixing structures in the following sentence results in *faulty* parallelism.

> *Faulty:* The young college graduate listed her goals as *staying happy, keeping fit,* and *prosperity.*
> *Correct:* The young college graduate listed her goals as *happiness, fitness,* and *prosperity.*

Sometimes, faulty parallelism occurs relative to only two items.

> *Faulty: Enjoying* the concert and *to meet* some of the performers delighted Fred.
> *Correct: Enjoying* the concert and *meeting* some of the performers delighted Fred.

155

Pronouns

A pronoun takes the place of a noun. Watch for correct pronoun references, and note whether the pronoun should be in the subjective or objective case.

Use I, he, she, we, **and** they *in place of the* **subject** *of a sentence. (The subject is the* **doer.***)*

Bill wrote a sentence.

He wrote a sentence.

I wrote a sentence.

Susan was late for work.

She was late for work.

My family always takes a summer vacation.

We always take a summer vacation.

Jerry's family always takes a summer vacation.

They always take a summer vacation.

Use me, him, her, us, **and** them *in place of the* **object** *of a sentence. (The object is the* **receiver.***)*

Bill greeted *Jerry*.

Bill greeted *him*.

Bill greeted *me*.

The boss fired *Susan*.

The boss fired *her*.

Camille helped *Christopher and me* pack our suitcases.

Camille helped *us* pack our suitcases.

The lifeguard saved *three people* from drowning.

The lifeguard saved *them* from drowning.

Use who *as a* **subject** *(a doer).*

Who knocked at the door?

Do you know *who knocked* at the door?

No doubt, it was a neighbor *who*, a few minutes ago, *knocked* at the door.

Use whom *as an* **object** *(a receiver).*

To *whom* were you *speaking*?

Your line was busy, and I wondered to *whom* you were *speaking*.

I'm the person *whom* you *telephoned* yesterday.

Personal Pronouns						
	Nominative (subject)		Objective (object)		Possessive (ownership)	
	singular	plural	singular	plural	singular	plural
First Person	I	we	me	us	my mine	our ours
Second Person	you	you	you	you	your yours	yours
Third Person	he she it	they	him her it	them	his her, hers its	their theirs

Relative Pronouns		
Nominative (subject)	Objective (object)	Possessive (ownership)
Who (persons)	whom	whose*
Which (things)	which	
That (things and persons)	that	

*The possessive *whose* is often used for animals and things, as in "That's the dog whose foot is often sore."

Punctuation: The Comma

Certain parts of sentences *cannot* be separated from one another. Therefore, commas should **not** be used in the following cases.

Do* not *use a comma to separate a subject from its verb.

The enclosed forms from our office, are to be filled out now.

(There should be no comma after *office*.)

Do* not *use a comma to separate a verb from its object.

Tell me before noon, if you are going to come.

(There should be no comma after *noon*.)

Do* not *use a comma to separate an adjective from its noun.

It was an old, rusty, car.

(There should be no comma after *rusty*.)

157

Do* not *use a comma to separate a preposition from its object.

It was a question of, what to do now.

(There should be no comma after *of*.)

Do* not *use a comma to separate a prepositional phrase from the word it modifies when it immediately follows the modified word.

The boat floated, in the lake.

(There should be no comma after *floated*.)

Do* not *use a comma to separate a coordinating conjunction from the word, phrase, or clause that it joins to the sentence.

Studying is easy for most, but, for me it is hard.

(There should be no comma after *but*.)

Do* not *use a comma to separate compound verbs from one another.

The cat played with the catnip mouse for hours, and then hid it under the sofa.

(There should be no comma after *hours*.)

The following sentences illustrate situations in which a comma **should** be used.

Use a comma before a coordinating conjunction in a compound sentence.

I felt happy about my new job, *but* the pay was not quite enough.

Use a comma to set off interrupting or introductory words or phrases.

Safe in the house, we watched the rain fall outside.
Tom, *after all*, is one of twelve children.

Use a comma to separate a series of words or word groups.

Diet, exercise, and *rest* all contribute to good health.
The threat of runaway inflation, the heightened tension regarding foreign affairs, and *the lack of quality education in many schools* are issues that will be addressed.

Use a comma to set off nonessential clauses and phrases that are descriptive but not needed to get across the basic meaning of the sentence. Such phrases are termed **nonrestrictive.**

Maria, *who dislikes school*, is failing English.

Remember, though, that a phrase necessary to the basic meaning of the sentence, a *restrictive* phrase, must *not* be set apart by commas.

The Maria *who dislikes school* is failing English.

The meaning here is that there are two or more Marias and that the one who dislikes school is the one who is failing English.

Use a comma to set off appositives (second noun or noun equivalents that give additional information about a preceding noun).

Mr. Johnson, *a teacher*, ran for chairman of the school board.

Use a comma to separate the elements of dates, places, addresses, degrees, and titles.

Dates: Tuesday, September 16, 2010, will be my twenty-ninth birthday.
Places: Stamford, Connecticut, is my home town.
Addresses: He has lived for years at *12345 Somewhere St., Anytown, Florida.*
Degrees: John Boswell, *M.A.,* is soon to become John Boswell, *Ph.D.*
Titles: Sam Owens, *Jr.,* owns a clothing store in the center of town.

Use a comma after introductory clauses or verb phrases.

Although I had six years of sewing experience, I still had difficulty making my first wool blazer.
By jogging two miles a day, Jack lost twenty pounds during the summer.

Punctuation: The Semicolon

The semicolon is like a balance. It always separates elements of equal power of meaning: two or more words, phrases, or sentences. *It should never separate a main clause from a subordinate clause or a word or phrase from a clause.*

Use a semicolon to separate main clauses when the separation is not done by a coordinating conjunction (and, but, or, nor, for).

Ask Joe for the book; he still has it.

Use a semicolon to separate main clauses joined by a coordinating conjunction when there are commas in any of the clauses.

Although it is dark, we should start now; for we must finish on time.

159

Use a semicolon to separate main clauses joined by a conjunctive adverb (therefore, however, moreover, nevertheless, etc.).

> We didn't have much time; nevertheless, we felt we should begin.

Use a semicolon to separate items in a series when there are commas within the items.

> Nora's dress was red, blue, and green; Lucy's was lilac and white; and Helen's was black, turquoise, and white.

Punctuation: The Colon

The colon is a formal introducer. It is usually translated to mean *as follows*. The colon should be employed sparingly and never after *is, are, was,* or *were* when presenting a series.

The major use of the colon is to introduce a formal appositive, list, summary, quotation, example, or other explanatory material whether or not the words **as follows** *or* **the following** *are used.*

> The following attended (*or,* Those who attended are as follows): Bob, Mary, Jack, and Sue.
>
> Patrick Henry's words were the rallying cry of the revolt: "Give me liberty or give me death!"

Squinting Modifiers

A squinting modifier is sometimes called an ambiguous modifier and consists of a modifier that could equally well modify **either** *of two words or phrases.*

> The executive entering the office *hurriedly* made the decision.

It is not clear whether *hurriedly* refers to the executive's entrance or the speed at which he or she made the decision. Here is a clearer version.

> Entering the office, the executive *hurriedly* made the decision.

Subject-Verb Agreement

A common error is subject-verb agreement. A plural subject goes with a plural verb; a singular subject goes with a singular verb.

The following sentence is *incorrect* because the subject is plural and the verb is singular.

> The *crate* of nails, bolts, and hinges *were* delivered to the factory on Tuesday.

The correct form of this sentence is

The *crate* of nails, bolts, and hinges *was* delivered to the factory on Tuesday.

The matter of subject-verb agreement becomes a bit more troublesome when the sentence begins with here or there.

The following sentence shows *incorrect* usage.

There *is* a *dusty old trunk* and *some boxes* in the attic.

Whenever a sentence begins with *here* or *there*, the subject *follows* the verb. In this case, the subject is plural, so the verb must also be plural, *are* instead of *is*.

Verb Tense

Another common error occurs when the verb tenses (past, present, future) are incongruent. Most verbs are regular. For these verbs, add –ed to talk about the past and will or shall to talk about the future.

Past: I *walked* yesterday.
Present: I *walk* today.
Future: I *will walk* tomorrow.

One way to practice the basic forms of regular verbs is to recite the *past tense* and *past participle* when you are given only the *present tense*. Here are some examples.

Present
I *talk* today.
I *help* you today.
I *close* shop early today.

Past (-ed)
I *talked* yesterday.
I *helped* you yesterday.
I *closed* shop early yesterday.

Past Participle (-ed)
I have *talked* to you on many occasions.
I have *helped* you often.
I have *closed* up shop early for a week.

161

Some verbs are **irregular** *and require special constructions to express the past and past participle.*

Here are some of the most troublesome irregular verbs.

Present	Past	Past Participle
begin	began	begun
burst	burst	burst
do	did	done
drown	drowned	drowned
go	went	gone
hang (to execute)	hanged	hanged
hang (to suspend)	hung	hung
lay (to put in place)	laid	laid
lie (to rest)	lay	lain
set (to place in position)	set	set
sit (to be seated)	sat	sat
shine (to provide light)	shone	shone
shine (to polish)	shined	shined
raise (to lift up)	raised	raised
rise (to get up)	rose	risen
swim	swam	swum
swing	swung	swung

Wordiness

For the PPST, the type of wordiness you should learn to recognize is repetition, *or* redundancy.

Here are some examples.

Several *new initiatives* were opposed by the panel, but the *final outcome* has not been announced.

Currently, there is *now* no doubt that the panel will *positively approve* the initiatives.

After *hearing* of the panel's decision, those *listening* to the announcement called it *important* and *significant.*

A Final Note

This review is intended to familiarize you with those common rules and conventions that seem most applicable to PPST questions. The explanations following each practice test provide further information about matters discussed here and some new information as well.

FOUR FULL-LENGTH PRACTICE TESTS

This section contains four full-length practice simulation PPSTs. Three practice tests model the format of the paper-based PPST, and Practice Test 4 models the format of the computer-based PPST. The practice tests are followed by complete answers, explanations, and analysis. The format, levels of difficulty, question structure, and number of questions are similar to those on the actual PPST. The actual PPST is copyrighted and may not be duplicated, and these questions are not taken directly from the actual tests.

When taking these tests, try to simulate the test conditions by following the time allotments carefully.

Answer Sheet for Practice Test 1

(Remove this sheet and use it to mark your answers.)

Reading Test

1 Ⓐ Ⓑ Ⓒ Ⓓ Ⓔ	21 Ⓐ Ⓑ Ⓒ Ⓓ Ⓔ		
2 Ⓐ Ⓑ Ⓒ Ⓓ Ⓔ	22 Ⓐ Ⓑ Ⓒ Ⓓ Ⓔ		
3 Ⓐ Ⓑ Ⓒ Ⓓ Ⓔ	23 Ⓐ Ⓑ Ⓒ Ⓓ Ⓔ		
4 Ⓐ Ⓑ Ⓒ Ⓓ Ⓔ	24 Ⓐ Ⓑ Ⓒ Ⓓ Ⓔ		
5 Ⓐ Ⓑ Ⓒ Ⓓ Ⓔ	25 Ⓐ Ⓑ Ⓒ Ⓓ Ⓔ		
6 Ⓐ Ⓑ Ⓒ Ⓓ Ⓔ	26 Ⓐ Ⓑ Ⓒ Ⓓ Ⓔ		
7 Ⓐ Ⓑ Ⓒ Ⓓ Ⓔ	27 Ⓐ Ⓑ Ⓒ Ⓓ Ⓔ		
8 Ⓐ Ⓑ Ⓒ Ⓓ Ⓔ	28 Ⓐ Ⓑ Ⓒ Ⓓ Ⓔ		
9 Ⓐ Ⓑ Ⓒ Ⓓ Ⓔ	29 Ⓐ Ⓑ Ⓒ Ⓓ Ⓔ		
10 Ⓐ Ⓑ Ⓒ Ⓓ Ⓔ	30 Ⓐ Ⓑ Ⓒ Ⓓ Ⓔ		
11 Ⓐ Ⓑ Ⓒ Ⓓ Ⓔ	31 Ⓐ Ⓑ Ⓒ Ⓓ Ⓔ		
12 Ⓐ Ⓑ Ⓒ Ⓓ Ⓔ	32 Ⓐ Ⓑ Ⓒ Ⓓ Ⓔ		
13 Ⓐ Ⓑ Ⓒ Ⓓ Ⓔ	33 Ⓐ Ⓑ Ⓒ Ⓓ Ⓔ		
14 Ⓐ Ⓑ Ⓒ Ⓓ Ⓔ	34 Ⓐ Ⓑ Ⓒ Ⓓ Ⓔ		
15 Ⓐ Ⓑ Ⓒ Ⓓ Ⓔ	35 Ⓐ Ⓑ Ⓒ Ⓓ Ⓔ		
16 Ⓐ Ⓑ Ⓒ Ⓓ Ⓔ	36 Ⓐ Ⓑ Ⓒ Ⓓ Ⓔ		
17 Ⓐ Ⓑ Ⓒ Ⓓ Ⓔ	37 Ⓐ Ⓑ Ⓒ Ⓓ Ⓔ		
18 Ⓐ Ⓑ Ⓒ Ⓓ Ⓔ	38 Ⓐ Ⓑ Ⓒ Ⓓ Ⓔ		
19 Ⓐ Ⓑ Ⓒ Ⓓ Ⓔ	39 Ⓐ Ⓑ Ⓒ Ⓓ Ⓔ		
20 Ⓐ Ⓑ Ⓒ Ⓓ Ⓔ	40 Ⓐ Ⓑ Ⓒ Ⓓ Ⓔ		

Mathematics Test

1 Ⓐ Ⓑ Ⓒ Ⓓ Ⓔ	21 Ⓐ Ⓑ Ⓒ Ⓓ Ⓔ
2 Ⓐ Ⓑ Ⓒ Ⓓ Ⓔ	22 Ⓐ Ⓑ Ⓒ Ⓓ Ⓔ
3 Ⓐ Ⓑ Ⓒ Ⓓ Ⓔ	23 Ⓐ Ⓑ Ⓒ Ⓓ Ⓔ
4 Ⓐ Ⓑ Ⓒ Ⓓ Ⓔ	24 Ⓐ Ⓑ Ⓒ Ⓓ Ⓔ
5 Ⓐ Ⓑ Ⓒ Ⓓ Ⓔ	25 Ⓐ Ⓑ Ⓒ Ⓓ Ⓔ
6 Ⓐ Ⓑ Ⓒ Ⓓ Ⓔ	26 Ⓐ Ⓑ Ⓒ Ⓓ Ⓔ
7 Ⓐ Ⓑ Ⓒ Ⓓ Ⓔ	27 Ⓐ Ⓑ Ⓒ Ⓓ Ⓔ
8 Ⓐ Ⓑ Ⓒ Ⓓ Ⓔ	28 Ⓐ Ⓑ Ⓒ Ⓓ Ⓔ
9 Ⓐ Ⓑ Ⓒ Ⓓ Ⓔ	29 Ⓐ Ⓑ Ⓒ Ⓓ Ⓔ
10 Ⓐ Ⓑ Ⓒ Ⓓ Ⓔ	30 Ⓐ Ⓑ Ⓒ Ⓓ Ⓔ
11 Ⓐ Ⓑ Ⓒ Ⓓ Ⓔ	31 Ⓐ Ⓑ Ⓒ Ⓓ Ⓔ
12 Ⓐ Ⓑ Ⓒ Ⓓ Ⓔ	32 Ⓐ Ⓑ Ⓒ Ⓓ Ⓔ
13 Ⓐ Ⓑ Ⓒ Ⓓ Ⓔ	33 Ⓐ Ⓑ Ⓒ Ⓓ Ⓔ
14 Ⓐ Ⓑ Ⓒ Ⓓ Ⓔ	34 Ⓐ Ⓑ Ⓒ Ⓓ Ⓔ
15 Ⓐ Ⓑ Ⓒ Ⓓ Ⓔ	35 Ⓐ Ⓑ Ⓒ Ⓓ Ⓔ
16 Ⓐ Ⓑ Ⓒ Ⓓ Ⓔ	36 Ⓐ Ⓑ Ⓒ Ⓓ Ⓔ
17 Ⓐ Ⓑ Ⓒ Ⓓ Ⓔ	37 Ⓐ Ⓑ Ⓒ Ⓓ Ⓔ
18 Ⓐ Ⓑ Ⓒ Ⓓ Ⓔ	38 Ⓐ Ⓑ Ⓒ Ⓓ Ⓔ
19 Ⓐ Ⓑ Ⓒ Ⓓ Ⓔ	39 Ⓐ Ⓑ Ⓒ Ⓓ Ⓔ
20 Ⓐ Ⓑ Ⓒ Ⓓ Ⓔ	40 Ⓐ Ⓑ Ⓒ Ⓓ Ⓔ

CUT HERE

Writing Test: Multiple Choice

Part A

```
 1 Ⓐ Ⓑ Ⓒ Ⓓ Ⓔ
 2 Ⓐ Ⓑ Ⓒ Ⓓ Ⓔ
 3 Ⓐ Ⓑ Ⓒ Ⓓ Ⓔ
 4 Ⓐ Ⓑ Ⓒ Ⓓ Ⓔ
 5 Ⓐ Ⓑ Ⓒ Ⓓ Ⓔ
 6 Ⓐ Ⓑ Ⓒ Ⓓ Ⓔ
 7 Ⓐ Ⓑ Ⓒ Ⓓ Ⓔ
 8 Ⓐ Ⓑ Ⓒ Ⓓ Ⓔ
 9 Ⓐ Ⓑ Ⓒ Ⓓ Ⓔ
10 Ⓐ Ⓑ Ⓒ Ⓓ Ⓔ
11 Ⓐ Ⓑ Ⓒ Ⓓ Ⓔ
12 Ⓐ Ⓑ Ⓒ Ⓓ Ⓔ
13 Ⓐ Ⓑ Ⓒ Ⓓ Ⓔ
14 Ⓐ Ⓑ Ⓒ Ⓓ Ⓔ
15 Ⓐ Ⓑ Ⓒ Ⓓ Ⓔ
16 Ⓐ Ⓑ Ⓒ Ⓓ Ⓔ
17 Ⓐ Ⓑ Ⓒ Ⓓ Ⓔ
18 Ⓐ Ⓑ Ⓒ Ⓓ Ⓔ
19 Ⓐ Ⓑ Ⓒ Ⓓ Ⓔ
20 Ⓐ Ⓑ Ⓒ Ⓓ Ⓔ
21 Ⓐ Ⓑ Ⓒ Ⓓ Ⓔ
```

Part B

```
22 Ⓐ Ⓑ Ⓒ Ⓓ Ⓔ
23 Ⓐ Ⓑ Ⓒ Ⓓ Ⓔ
24 Ⓐ Ⓑ Ⓒ Ⓓ Ⓔ
25 Ⓐ Ⓑ Ⓒ Ⓓ Ⓔ
26 Ⓐ Ⓑ Ⓒ Ⓓ Ⓔ
27 Ⓐ Ⓑ Ⓒ Ⓓ Ⓔ
28 Ⓐ Ⓑ Ⓒ Ⓓ Ⓔ
29 Ⓐ Ⓑ Ⓒ Ⓓ Ⓔ
30 Ⓐ Ⓑ Ⓒ Ⓓ Ⓔ
31 Ⓐ Ⓑ Ⓒ Ⓓ Ⓔ
32 Ⓐ Ⓑ Ⓒ Ⓓ Ⓔ
33 Ⓐ Ⓑ Ⓒ Ⓓ Ⓔ
34 Ⓐ Ⓑ Ⓒ Ⓓ Ⓔ
35 Ⓐ Ⓑ Ⓒ Ⓓ Ⓔ
36 Ⓐ Ⓑ Ⓒ Ⓓ Ⓔ
37 Ⓐ Ⓑ Ⓒ Ⓓ Ⓔ
38 Ⓐ Ⓑ Ⓒ Ⓓ Ⓔ
```

CUT HERE

Reading Test

TIME: 60 Minutes

40 Questions

Directions: A question or number of questions follows each of the statements or passages in this section. Using only the *stated* or *implied* information given in the statement or passage, answer the question or questions by choosing the *best* answer from among the five choices given.

1. The major function of social psychology as a behavioral science, and therefore as a discipline that can contribute to the solution of many social problems, is its investigation of the psychology of the individual in society. Thus, the scientist's main objective is to attempt to determine the influences of the social environment on the personal behavior of individuals.

   Which of the following best summarizes the passage?

   A. Social psychology is a science in which the behavior of the scientist in the social environment is a major function.

   B. The social environment influences the behavior of individuals.

   C. Social psychology studies the ways in which people in society are affected by their surroundings.

   D. Understanding human behavior, through the help of social psychology, leads to the eventual betterment of society.

   E. A minor objective of social psychology is the solution of social problems.

2. The quiet child is one of our concerns today. Our philosophy about children and speaking in the classroom has flip-flopped. Today we are interested in what Ruth Strickland implies when she refers to the idea of "freeing the child to talk."

   Which of the following is implied by this passage?

   A. Teachers in the past have preferred quiet and reticent students.

   B. The behavior of children in the classroom is a trivial concern that can change abruptly.

   C. Whether or not a child is quiet determines the quality of his or her education.

   D. Ruth Strickland never explicitly stated her opinions about children and speaking in the classroom.

   E. There are fewer quiet children today than in the past.

GO ON TO THE NEXT PAGE

Part V: Four Full-Length Practice Tests

3. For some, the term *creative writing* seems to imply precious writing, useless writing, imaginative writing, writing that is self-expressive rather than a necessity, something that is produced during leisure or as a hobby.

   By "precious," the author of this passage means

   A. immature

   B. costly

   C. dainty

   D. unfinished

   E. affected

4. No matter how significant the speaker's message, and no matter how strongly he or she feels about it, it will be lost unless the listeners attend to it. Attention and perception are key concepts in communication.

   The primary purpose of the statement is to

   A. imply that some speakers without strong feelings find an attentive audience

   B. note that some very important messages fall on deaf ears

   C. stress the critical role of listening in oral communication

   D. urge readers to listen more carefully to spoken language

   E. argue that attention and perception are unimportant concepts in communication

5. Many of today's secondary school students will retire (either voluntarily or by coercion) from their careers or professions between the ages of forty and fifty. Indeed, by 2035, the problems of today's elderly are going to be the problems of the middle-aged.

   If the above statement is true, then which of the following must also be true?

   A. People are beginning to age more quickly.

   B. There will be more leisure time available for more people in the future.

   C. Today's secondary school students will be entering careers that require youthful stamina.

   D. No one in the future will want to work during the second half of their lives.

   E. Retirement will become a more attractive possibility in the future.

Questions 6 and 7 refer to the following passage.

In future decades, what is actually required is the development of a new type of citizen—an individual who possesses confidence in his or her own potential, a person who is not intimidated by the prospect of actively pursuing a career after the age of forty-five, and an individual who comprehends that technology can produce an easier world but only humans can produce a better one.

170

6. Which of the following is an unstated assumption made by the author of this passage?

A. Technology is the unrecognized key to a better future.

B. Present citizens are intimidated by the prospect of ending their careers in middle age.

C. Present citizens do not have limitless potentials.

D. Many people in the future will pursue at least two careers in the course of a lifetime.

E. An easier world is not necessarily a safer one.

7. The author of the passage would disagree with which of the following statements?

A. The new type of citizen described in the passage does not presently exist.

B. Future decades may bring about a change in the existing types of citizens.

C. A new type of citizen will become necessary in future decades.

D. Technology should be regarded as a source of a better life.

E. Human potential is not limited, and we should be especially careful not to think of our potential as limited.

Questions 8, 9, and 10 refer to the following passage.

The arts have been dismissed by some legislators as mere entertainment. As we strive

not merely to amuse but to reveal the great truths of human nature, we must remember that some regard our performances as "sound and fury, signifying nothing."

8. The author of this passage is probably

A. a citizen writing to a legislator

B. an actor writing to other actors

C. an actor playing a part

D. a painter writing to other painters

E. a philosopher writing to political scientists

9. The passage supports a concept of art as

A. a political activity

B. more than entertainment

C. empty of entertainment value

D. generously subsidized by the government

E. of no use to a serious audience

10. The author repeats "some" in order to indicate that

A. the problem described is a relatively small one

B. the legislators may be in the same group that regards performances as signifying nothing

C. the actor will never meet with a wholly sympathetic audience

D. the "sound and fury" on stage is paralleled in the legislature

E. most members of the audience are merely amused

GO ON TO THE NEXT PAGE

Questions 11, 12, and 13 are based on the following passage.

If we must have evaluation, at least do it without grades. Grades are not good indicators of intellectual ability; we must abolish them. Then we will have students who are motivated by factors such as interest, factors more important than a letter on a transcript. And the abolition of grades will encourage us to concentrate less on evaluation and more on instruction.

11. In order to agree with this author's argument, we must presume that

  A. wherever grades exist, instruction is poor

  B. there are indicators of intellectual ability that are better than grades

  C. graded students are not good students

  D. intellectual ability can be measured only in a school situation

  E. grades are the remaining hindrance to effective education

12. A reader of this passage might conclude that the author feels that graded students are not motivated by

  A. the prospect of a high grade point average

  B. interest in the subject matter of their course

  C. the evaluation criteria established by their instructors

  D. a thoroughly prepared instructor

  E. the practicality of academic disciplines

13. This passage is most probably directed at which of the following audiences?

  A. Politicians

  B. Parents

  C. Students

  D. Teachers

  E. Civic leaders

Questions 14, 15, and 16 refer to the following passage.

We should spend more time enjoying life than preparing for its challenges, but sometimes we don't. For example, toward the end of every semester, all students at the university are tired and irritable because they have spent long nights preparing for final exams. Consequently, they rarely look back on college as a time spent enjoying good fellowship and extracurricular activities.

14. To agree with this author, we must accept which of the following implications of his or her argument?

  A. It is worthwhile to prepare only for enjoyment.

  B. School examinations do not require preparation.

  C. Preparation is inappropriate only toward the end of the semester.

  D. The result of preparation for exams is fatigue.

  E. College students study too much.

15. According to this writer, the most memorable characteristic of college life should be

A. social interaction

B. academic fastidiousness

C. the value of sleep

D. more efficient exam preparation

E. a pleasant attitude

16. The author might have strengthened the argument without abandoning it by

A. changing "all" to "some"

B. advancing arguments in favor of studying all night

C. acknowledging that being irritable is not necessarily related to fatigue

D. choosing a different example to illustrate the initial point

E. focusing the argument more explicitly on a particular audience

17. When asked by his students to comment on the value of steroids for increasing muscle size, the physical education teacher said, "Steroids can be very dangerous. Many bodybuilders use them for a short period before a contest. However, the long-term use of steroids might possibly cause severe damage to body organs, including the reproductive system, while it helps to build a muscular body."

In this statement, the teacher is

A. categorically against the use of steroids

B. an advocate of steroids but not of reproduction

C. recommending the short-term use of steroids

D. trying not to condemn steroid users

E. preferring muscle definition to muscle size

Questions 18 and 19 refer to the following passage.

In modern society, those who are most adaptable to both an inflating economy and the decreasing value of the individual will survive in comfort. It is these survivors who will have the most value in the future.

18. The kind of value that the survivors possess is

A. inflating

B. decreasing

C. individual

D. comfortable

E. unstated

GO ON TO THE NEXT PAGE

19. What conclusion can be drawn about value if we accept the author's statement?

    A. Value transcends the factors of time and place.

    B. Survival is priceless.

    C. Decreasing value must be tolerated.

    D. Socioeconomic factors affect the definition of value.

    E. Value is inversely proportional to the economy.

Questions 20 through 24 refer to the following passage.

Creative writing may serve many purposes for the writer. Above all, it is a means of self-expression. It is the individual's way of saying, "These are my
(5) thoughts, and they are uniquely experienced by me." But creative writing can also serve as a safety valve for dormant tensions. This implies that a period of time has evolved in which the child gave
(10) an idea some deep thought and that the message on paper is revealing of this deep, inner thought. Finally, a worthwhile by-product of creative writing is the stimulus it gives students to do
(15) further reading and experimentation in their areas of interest. A child might become an ardent reader of good literature in order to satisfy an appetite whetted by a creative writing endeavor.

20. The primary purpose of the author of this passage is to

    A. call attention to a widespread lack of self-expression

    B. address the increasing anxiety that plagues many individuals

    C. stress the value of good literature, both amateur and professional

    D. encourage the reader to try some creative writing

    E. discuss some positive purposes and effects of creative writing

21. The content of the passage indicates that the passage would be least likely to appear in which of the following?

    A. *Journal of English Teaching Techniques*

    B. *Psychology Today*

    C. *Journal of Technical Writing*

    D. *Teaching English Today*

    E. *The Creative Writer*

22. According to the passage, creative writing can help release dormant tensions because

    A. the writer will usually write something autobiographical

    B. understanding literature means understanding the tensions of the characters

    C. creative writing can express what the writer has long held within

    D. tensions are a by-product of writer's block

    E. self-expression is never tense

23. All of the following are probably important to the ability to write creatively EXCEPT

    A. deep thought

    B. time to think and ponder

    C. spelling

    D. reading

    E. good literature

24. According to the passage, creative writing is most of all a

    A. stimulus for further reading

    B. release valve for dormant tensions

    C. way of expressing one's feelings and thoughts

    D. chance to let off steam

    E. by-product of reading

Questions 25 through 30 are based on the following passage.

Throughout human history, predictions of future events have found receptive audiences: during the thirteenth century, the English scientist Roger
(5) Bacon discussed the development of such things as optical instruments and motor boats; in the fifteenth century, Leonardo da Vinci wrote about tanks and helicopters; in the nineteenth cen-
(10) tury, Jules Verne described trips to the moon. Humans have always been interested in where they are going. Since humanity's continued existence is dependent upon its making intelligent
(15) decisions about the future, such fascination has taken on a very practical dimension. Along with the changes in social mores and attitudes, greater numbers of

people are demanding a role in planning
(20) the future. The social studies curriculum must provide students with an understanding of how significant future challenges will be with regard to our national survival, social problems,
(25) religion, marriage and family life, and political processes.

It is vital that social studies teachers immerse themselves in the new field of futuristics—the study of future
(30) prospects and possibilities affecting the human condition. Futuristics, as an academic area, is already being taught at many major universities for the purpose of encouraging students to achieve an
(35) awareness that they can contribute to the development of a much better national and global society than they ever dreamed of. The perspective of futurism is very important for today's students,
(40) since they know they can do nothing about the past.

25. Which of the following is the intended audience for the passage?

    A. Students planning which courses to take in high school

    B. Teachers considering changing or enriching the curriculum

    C. Historians interested in the ways that the past reflects the future

    D. Politicians drafting future legislation that addresses present social problems

    E. Parents concerned about what their children should be learning

GO ON TO THE NEXT PAGE

26. In order to show that "humans have always been interested in where they are going," the author provides which of the following types of facts?

    A. Unfounded

    B. Extraterrestrial

    C. Political

    D. Historical

    E. Scientific

27. Which of the following is an assumption of the passage but is not explicitly stated?

    A. Futuristic studies should take precedence over all other social studies.

    B. Today's students know little about the past and less about the future.

    C. Many social studies curriculums do not adequately acknowledge the importance of futurism.

    D. Some figures in the past have been the equivalent of modern fortunetellers.

    E. Social studies gives little thought to the future.

28. In the passage, the intended meaning of "global society" is which of the following?

    A. A society well aware of the contributions of Bacon, da Vinci, and Verne

    B. A society whose students have had courses in international relations

    C. A society able to communicate with other societies around the globe

    D. A society including the globes of other solar systems

    E. A society including all the nations of the earth

29. Which of the following statements, if true, would most weaken the author's argument?

    A. Figures other than Bacon, da Vinci, and Verne might have been mentioned as well.

    B. Apart from Bacon, da Vinci, and Verne, many others who have tried to "see into" the future have voiced prospects and possibilities that did not come true.

    C. Those major universities not offering courses in futuristics are considering them.

    D. Futuristics has been the nonacademic interest of great numbers of people for many centuries.

    E. Futuristic predictions are the stock-in-trade of many sincere politicians trying to urge the passage of significant legislation.

30. The author of this passage is most likely

    A. a historian

    B. a traditionalist

    C. a scientist

    D. an educator

    E. a pacifist

Questions 31 through 35 refer to the following passage.

Possibly everyone at some point has been in a classroom where he or she didn't dare express an idea for fear that it would be chopped off. And if it was
(5) expressed, it was chopped off and no further ideas came forth. Perhaps everyone at some time has been in a student group where a participant started to express an insight but was nipped in the
(10) bud by a teacher who corrected the student's usage. Perhaps some have been in a classroom where a child was groping for just the right way to express a thought only to have the teacher or an-
(15) other child supply the words. And some have wondered why a certain child was so talkative at age five and so reticent at sixteen.

31. The author implies which of the following in the passage?

   A. Wondering about human inhibitions will do little to solve the problem.

   B. Only certain children are either uninhibited at age five or inhibited at age sixteen.

   C. Sixteen-year-olds should spend more time in the classroom with five-year-olds.

   D. Attending school may cause children to become inhibited.

   E. Inhibitions go along with maturity.

32. Which of the following terms is an appropriate substitute for "chopped off"?

   A. put out

   B. removed

   C. severely criticized

   D. misunderstood

   E. cut back

33. Which of the following techniques is the author using to make the point that classroom situations can be very undesirable?

   A. An appeal to the personal experiences of the readers

   B. Disguised references to recent educational theory

   C. Unsubstantiated and illogical anecdotes

   D. A story

   E. References to his or her own experiences as a teacher

34. The author's attitude may be described as being

   A. supportive

   B. critical

   C. skeptical

   D. favorable

   E. affected

GO ON TO THE NEXT PAGE

35. The author would probably most strongly agree with which of the following statements?

    A. Students should think carefully before expressing ideas in class.

    B. Teachers should be critical of students' expressions.

    C. Talkative students should be tactfully silenced.

    D. Teachers should be careful not to inhibit students' expressions.

    E. Teachers should assist students in completing their expressions.

36. In recent years, teachers in elementary schools have received modest pay raises regularly, but considering economic trends, their salaries have decreased twenty-three percent.

Which of the following best expresses the point of the statement above?

    A. Being a teacher means living at or below the poverty line.

    B. Many teachers must hold second jobs.

    C. The effects of the economy can negate the benefits of a pay raise.

    D. Teachers' salaries are not adequate.

    E. Those who teach in elementary schools can live on less than those who teach in high schools.

37. For preschool children, television cartoons could serve to stimulate them to create their own drawings if their parents provided them with the graphic materials and the indispensable encouragement.

The author of the statement would probably agree with which of the following?

    A. A decision to ban television cartoons as useless is not wise.

    B. Television cartoons are the preschooler's primary source of creative inspiration.

    C. For older children, cartoons have no educational value.

    D. Cartoons are a viable substitute for parents when they are not available.

    E. Cartoons accelerate a young child's learning of new words.

38. There are many people who, after experiencing severe failures and disappointments, lose every vestige of self-esteem. They view themselves as unworthy and incapable of success.

The author stresses which of the following responses to disappointment?

    A. Rehabilitation

    B. Hopelessness

    C. Optimism

    D. Humility

    E. Courage

39. It is clear that the first four or five years of a child's life are the period of most rapid change in physical and mental characteristics and greatest susceptibility to environmental influences. Attitudes are formed, values are learned, habits are developed, and innate abilities are fostered or retarded by conditions the child encounters during these early years.

Which of the following, if true, would most weaken the author's argument?

A. Many young children possess attitudes and habits similar to those of their peers.

B. There are significant, basic differences between a five-year-old from Samoa and one from New York.

C. "Midlife crisis" provokes many adults to change their entire personality structures within only a few months.

D. The environment continues to influence personal characteristics in adolescents.

E. Environmental influences can have either positive or negative effects on human development.

40. In order for an individual to judge whether two or more speech sounds are alike or different or to make more difficult judgments, the sounds must be kept in memory and retrieved for comparison.

The passage supports which of the following conclusions?

A. Most speech sounds are more different than they are alike.

B. Visual discrimination is easier than auditory discrimination.

C. A number of individuals cannot discriminate between different sounds.

D. People with good memories are also good listeners.

E. A person cannot compare two sounds at precisely the same time.

IF YOU FINISH BEFORE TIME IS CALLED, CHECK YOUR WORK ON THIS SECTION ONLY. DO NOT WORK ON ANY OTHER SECTION IN THE TEST.

Mathematics Test

TIME: 60 Minutes

40 Questions

Directions: Each of the questions or incomplete statements below is followed by five suggested answers or completions. Select the best answer or completion of the five choices given and fill in the corresponding lettered space on the answer sheet.

---

1. If 10 kilometers equal 6.2 miles, then how many miles are in 45 kilometers?

A. 4.5

B. 7.25

C. 27.9

D. 29.7

E. 62

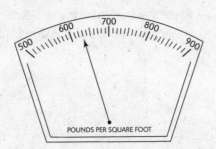

POUNDS PER SQUARE FOOT

2. A gauge, pictured above, measures pressure. The reading on the gauge in pounds per square foot is

A. 600.3

B. 603

C. 630

D. 730

E. 770

Bill for Purchases	
Science Textbooks	$840
Lab Equipment	460
Formaldehyde	320
Teacher's Manuals	120
TOTAL	$2220

3. Scholastic Supplies, Inc., sends the above bill to Eastside Middle School. Although the bill includes the cost of science lab workbooks, Scholastic Supplies forgot to list them on the bill. How much did the science lab workbooks cost Eastside Middle School?

A. $480

B. $500

C. $520

D. $560

E. $620

4. Springfield High School's average state testing scores over a five-year period were

	Math	Verbal
2005	520	540
2006	515	532
2007	518	528
2008	510	525
2009	507	510

What was the mean (average) of the verbal state testing scores for the five-year period 2005 through 2009?

A. 512

B. 514

C. 521

D. 527

E. 528

Sarah knows that a geometric figure is a rectangle and that it has sides of 18 and 22.

5. How can Sarah compute the area of a square that has the same *perimeter* as the rectangle discussed above?

A. Add 18 and 22, double this sum, divide by 4, then multiply by 2.

B. Add 18 and 22, double this sum, divide by 4, then multiply by 4.

C. Add 18 and 22, double this sum, divide by 4, then square the quotient.

D. Add 18 and 22, double this sum, then multiply by 4.

E. Add twice 18 to twice 22, divide by 2, then square the quotient.

6. Arnold purchases one pair of slacks, a dress shirt, a tie, and a sports coat. The shirt and slacks each cost three times what the tie cost. The sports coat cost twice what the shirt cost. If Arnold paid a total of $156 for all four items, what was the price of the pair of slacks?

A. $12

B. $36

C. $48

D. $78

E. $84

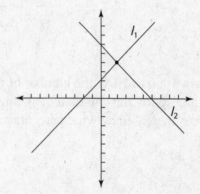

7. In the graph above, what is the solution of the equations of the two lines l_1 and l_2?

A. $x = 4, y = 2$

B. $x = 0, y = 2$

C. $x = 2, y = 0$

D. $x = 2, y = 4$

E. The solution cannot be determined from the information given.

GO ON TO THE NEXT PAGE

Questions 8 and 9 refer to the following graph.

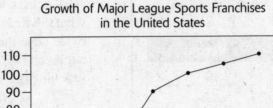

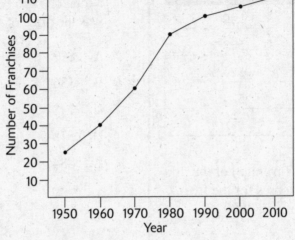

8. From 1960 to 1970, the number of major league sports franchises in the United States increased by what percentage?

   A. 20%

   B. 40%

   C. 50%

   D. 60%

   E. 100%

9. For which 10-year periods did the number of franchises increase by less than 10?

   I.   1950–1960

   II. 1970–1980

   III. 1990–2000

   IV. 2000–2010

   A. I and II only

   B. II and III only

   C. III and IV only

   D. I, III, and IV only

   E. I, II, III, and IV

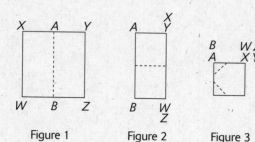

Figure 1   Figure 2   Figure 3

10. In Figure 1 above, a square piece of paper is folded along dotted line *AB* so that *X* is on top of *Y* and *W* is on top of *Z* (Figure 2). The paper is then folded again so that *B* is on top of *A* and *WZ* is on top of *XY* (Figure 3). Two small corners are cut out of the folded paper as shown in Figure 3. If the paper is unfolded, which of the following could be the result?

A.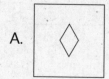

B.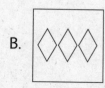

C.

D.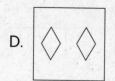

E.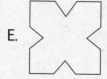

11. If CDs cost $2.98 for a package of two CDs, how much change will Roy receive from a twenty dollar bill if he purchases twelve CDs?

    A. $2.02

    B. $2.12

    C. $2.18

    D. $2.22

    E. $3.02

12. All of the following are equal to the equation $2x + 4 = 3x + 3$ EXCEPT

    A. $4 = x + 3$

    B. $-x + 4 = 3$

    C. $2x + 1 = 3x$

    D. $x = -1$

    E. $2x = 3x - 1$

13. Which of the following is the smallest?

    A. $\dfrac{3}{5}$

    B. $\dfrac{4}{9}$

    C. $\dfrac{7}{13}$

    D. $\dfrac{23}{44}$

    E. $\dfrac{2}{3}$

14. 210,000 equals

    A. $(2 \times 10^4) + (1 \times 10^3)$

    B. $(2 \times 10^5) + (1 \times 10^4)$

    C. $(2 \times 10^6) + (1 \times 10^5)$

    D. $(2 \times 10^7) + (1 \times 10^6)$

    E. $(2 \times 10^8) + (1 \times 10^7)$

Section **2** Mathematics Test

GO ON TO THE NEXT PAGE

183

Houses Sold in One Year	
Age	*Number*
1-2	1,200
3-4	1,570
5-6	1,630
7-8	1,440
9-10	1,720

15. According to the chart above, how many more houses from 5 to 10 years old were sold than those from 4 to 8 years old?

A. 2,455

B. 1,570

C. 150

D. 130

E. The number cannot be determined from the information given.

16. The product of two numbers is greater than 0 and equals one of the numbers. Which of the following must be one of the numbers?

A. −1

B. 0

C. 1

D. A prime number

E. A reciprocal

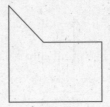

17. The best way to compute the area of the figure above would be to break it in which of the following ways?

A. 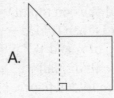   D.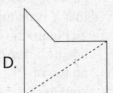

B. 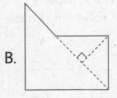   E.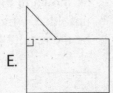

C.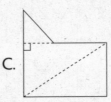

18. If $10m - 50 + 20p = 0$, what is the value of $m + 2p$?

A. 2

B. 5

C. 10

D. 20

E. 500

19. Round off 0.14739 to the nearest thousandth.

    A. 0.1473

    B. 0.1474

    C. 0.147

    D. 0.148

    E. 0.15

20. Given that $a \# b \# c = 2a - 3b + 5c$, what is the value of $3\#(-2)\#4$?

    A. 20

    B. 24

    C. 26

    D. 28

    E. 32

21. The large square above consists of squares and isosceles right triangles. If the large square has a side 4 cm, then the area of the shaded portion in square cm is

    A. 2

    B. 4

    C. 6

    D. 8

    E. 12

22. Juan approximated 35×45 as 40×50, but the answer was much too high. To get a better approximation, he should multiply

    A. 50×50

    B. 45×50

    C. 30×50

    D. 30×40

    E. 20×30

23. If 16 out of 400 dentists polled recommended Smile Bright toothpaste, what percent recommended Smile Bright?

    A. 4

    B. 8

    C. 16

    D. 25

    E. 40

24. Teachers will be assigned special camp duty one day of the week during a seven-day camping trip. If all the days of the week (Monday through Sunday) are tossed into a cap and each teacher chooses one day of the week, what is the probability that the first teacher will randomly select a weekday (Monday through Friday)?

    A. $\frac{1}{7}$

    B. $\frac{2}{7}$

    C. $\frac{1}{5}$

    D. $\frac{5}{7}$

    E. $\frac{5}{2}$

GO ON TO THE NEXT PAGE

Section **2** Mathematics Test

25. On the number line above, what is the point 15 units to the left of point Q?

   A.   10

   B.   5

   C.   0

   D.   −9

   E.   −10

26. If the product of two numbers is five more than the sum of the two numbers, which of the following equations could represent the relationship?

   A. $AB + 5 = A + B$

   B. $5AB = A + B$

   C. $AB = A + B + 5$

   D. $A/B = 5 + A + B$

   E. $A(B) + 5 = A + B + 5$

27. Which of the following is determined by division?

   I.   The price of car A if it costs six times the price of car B

   II.   The difference in temperature between two cities

   III.   The number of yards in 39 feet

   A.   I only

   B.   II only

   C.   III only

   D.   I and II only

   E.   I and III only

Hourly Snowfall Rate	
Temperature in degrees	*Average snowfall in inches*
−10	2
−15	2.5
−20	3
−25	3.5
−30	4

28. The chart above shows the temperature and snowfall during one day in Moose Jaw, Saskatchewan. Which of the following is true about the data published in the chart?

   A.   As the temperature increased, the amount of snowfall increased.

   B.   As the temperature decreased, the amount of snowfall decreased.

   C.   As the temperature increased, the amount of snowfall remained the same.

   D.   As the temperature decreased, the amount of snowfall increased.

   E.   As the temperature decreased, the amount of snowfall remained the same.

29. A Jet Ski is selling at a 30% discount off its sticker price. Its sticker price is $8,000. What is its new selling price?

   A. $2,400

   B. $5,600

   C. $6,600

   D. $7,970

   E. $7,976

30. Hector's new hybrid car averages 35 miles per each gallon of gasoline. Assuming Hector is able to maintain his average miles per gallon, how far can he drive on 12 gallons of gas?

    A.   Almost 3 miles

    B.   42 miles

    C.   350 miles

    D.   420 miles

    E.   700 miles

31. A parallelogram has two sides of dimensions 9 and 7. What would be the side of a square with the same perimeter?

    A.   32

    B.   18

    C.   14

    D.   8

    E.   4

32. It is estimated that at a picnic each adult will drink $\frac{1}{5}$ of a gallon of lemonade. How many gallons of lemonade should be brought to the picnic if 28 people, all adults, are expected to attend?

    A.   3

    B.   Between 3 and 4

    C.   5

    D.   Between 5 and 6

    E.   More than 6

33. If John can type twenty pages in four hours, how many hours will it take him to type fifty pages?

    A.   5

    B.   6

    C.   8

    D.   9

    E.   10

34. Tom purchased 20 goldfish at 85¢ each and then bought 8 bags of goldfish food, also at 85¢ each. What would be the simplest way to compute his total amount spent?

    A. $20 \times 85¢ + 4 \times 85¢ + 2 \times 85¢ + 2 \times 85¢$

    B. $28 \times 85¢$

    C. $8 \times 20 \times 85¢$

    D. $20 \times 85¢$

    E. $850¢ \times 2$

35. In Smallville's Little League, team A has twice as many victories as team B, team C has 5 fewer victories than team A, and team D has 4 more victories than team B. If total victories of all four teams equal 29, how many victories does team D have?

    A.   5

    B.   9

    C.   10

    D.   12

    E.   14

Section **2** Mathematics Test

GO ON TO THE NEXT PAGE

> All dogs are green.
> Bowser is a dog.

36. If the statements above are true, which of the following must also be true?

   A. Bowser can be blue.

   B. No cats are green.

   C. Some cats are green.

   D. Bowser is green.

   E. Bowser is not a dog.

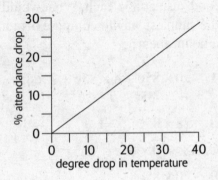

37. According to the graph above, if the temperature falls 30 degrees, what percentage will school attendance drop?

   A. 10

   B. 20

   C. 30

   D. 40

   E. 50

38. Maria needs to compute 30% of 50. To get a correct answer, all of the following will work EXCEPT

   A. 0.30×50

   B. 0.50×30

   C. $\frac{3}{10} \times 50$

   D. $50 \div \frac{10}{3}$

   E. $50 \div \frac{3}{10}$

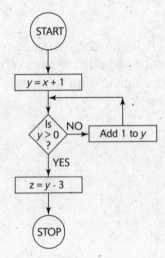

39. In the flow chart above, if $x = 3$, then what is the value of z?

   A. -1

   B. 0

   C. 1

   D. 3

   E. 6

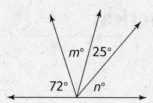

40. In the figure above, what is the number of degrees in the sum of $m + n$?

A. 83

B. 93

C. 97

D. 103

E. The number of degrees cannot be determined from the information given.

IF YOU FINISH BEFORE TIME IS CALLED, CHECK YOUR WORK ON THIS SECTION ONLY. DO NOT WORK ON ANY OTHER SECTION IN THE TEST.

Writing Test: Multiple-Choice Section

TIME: 30 Minutes

38 Questions

Part A

SUGGESTED TIME: 10 Minutes

21 Questions

Directions: Some of the following sentences are correct. Others contain problems in grammar, usage, idiom, diction, punctuation, and capitalization.

If there is an error, it will be underlined and lettered. Find the one underlined part that must be changed to make the sentence correct and choose the corresponding letter on your answer sheet. Mark **E** if the sentence contains no error.

1. <u>By dividing</u> the responsibility for the
      A
   project <u>between you and I</u>, <u>we</u> should
           B   C
   be able to complete <u>it</u> before Saturday.
                D
   <u>No error</u>
    E

2. The <u>witnesses'</u> testimony <u>does</u> not
       A   B
   differ significantly <u>to</u> the defense
               C
   lawyer's opening statement <u>about</u> the
                       D
   robbery. <u>No error</u>
          E

3. Though the two teams <u>scored only</u> one
                   A
   goal in the three games <u>they</u> played, the
                     B
   fine defensive play <u>seems satisfying</u> the
                  C
   large crowds <u>that</u> attended the matches.
              D
   <u>No error</u>
    E

4. Albertville, <u>nestling</u> on the northwest
            A
   fringe of the French Alps, <u>will be</u> the
                   B
   <u>site</u> of the meeting <u>in</u> 2010. <u>No error</u>
    C   D   E

5. After the first ten moves of the chess
   match, <u>it</u> <u>appeared</u> that the Hungarian
         A B
   champion <u>had fell</u> so far behind that she
             C
   <u>could not possibly recover</u>. <u>No error</u>
         D   E

6. Although you <u>have filled out</u> all the
              A
   forms and <u>paid</u> the fees, <u>one</u> still
          B   C
   must supply the consulate with a
   <u>recently taken</u> photograph. <u>No error</u>
      D   E

7. A number of conscripts, who
    A   B
would later join the Intelligence
        C
Service, were given intensive classes in
          D
Arabic and Chinese. No error
                      E

8. Hurrying to reach the bank before
    A
it closed, I left my attention wander and
    B   C
scraped the door of the car on the gate.
    D
No error
  E

9. Bellini's opera, a very forceful adaptation
                 A
of Shakespeare's play, does not provide
               B
hardly any of the rich characterization we
   B   C
find in the drama. No error
  D   E

10. In the interviews conducted by Mary
            A
Lee Johnson, an experienced journalist,
and her husband, men who would not
               B
answer her questions gladly replied
           C
to his. No error
 D   E

11. There is, according to today's *Times*,
   A   B
two races in the state Republican
      C
primary that are too close to predict.
          D
No error
  E

12. Given the rise in the number of
    A
propaganda broadcasts, it is no wonder
              B
that the public responds more skeptical
                C
to the latest claim by the opposition
D
party. No error
   E

13. Most of the runners finished before
noon with no ill effects from the smog,
            A   B
and a few were seriously unwell and
C   D
unable to complete the race. No error
                  E

14. The population of New Hampshire,
though increasing rapidly since 1990,
      A
are still far smaller than that of Rhode
B   C   D
Island or Connecticut. No error
              E

15. Plays like Ibsen's *Ghosts* or *St. Joan*,
     A
though often performed in London's
         B
West End, seen rarely in professional
       C   D
productions on Broadway. No error
              E

16. In regards to the sudden increase in the
    A   B
price of gasoline, six of the OPEC
nations have sent representatives
      C
to meet in Geneva. No error
 D   E

GO ON TO THE NEXT PAGE

17. In the early seventeenth century, young

boys <u>sung</u> the soprano <u>parts</u> that
     A   B

<u>are now sung</u> <u>by</u> women. <u>No error</u>
   C   D   E

18. The rising crime rate, in addition <u>to</u>
                              A

border control and drug smuggling, <u>are</u>
                                  B

to <u>be discussed</u> <u>on</u> the next broadcast of
    C   D

Meet the Press. <u>No error</u>
               E

19. If a person <u>concentrates</u> on getting <u>his</u>
              A   B

work done on time, <u>you</u> <u>will enjoy</u>
              C   D

recreational activities all the more.

<u>No error</u>
 E

20. <u>Ideas, that</u> <u>seemed</u> shocking to
    A   B

theatergoers in 1975 now <u>seem</u>
                     C

commonplace <u>to us</u>. <u>No error</u>
           D   E

21. <u>As</u> the two previous messages, the latest
   A

communication from the terrorists

<u>insists upon</u> a safe passage <u>out of</u> the
    B   C

country before any hostage <u>is released</u>.
                               D

<u>No error</u>
 E

Part B

SUGGESTED TIME: 20 Minutes

17 Questions

Directions: Some part of each sentence below is underlined; sometimes the whole sentence is underlined. Five choices for rephrasing the underlined part follow each sentence. The first choice, **A**, repeats the original, and the other four are different. If choice **A** seems better than the alternatives, choose answer **A**; if not, choose one of the others.

For each sentence, consider the requirements of standard written English. Your choice should be a correct, concise, and effective expression, not awkward or ambiguous. Focus on grammar, word choice, sentence construction, and punctuation. If a choice changes the meaning of the original sentence, do not select it.

22. Despite the dangers of the journey, all of the men selected for the expedition had an eagerness to set out at once.

    A. had an eagerness to set out

    B. were eager for setting out

    C. had eagerness for setting out

    D. wished eagerly for setting out

    E. were eager to set out

23. The state elections have not turned out as expected, there is no change in the number of Republican senators.

    A. as expected, there is

    B. as people expected, there is

    C. as expected; there is

    D. as expected, but there is

    E. as expected; there being

24. In modern Africa, some regimes which ignore the conventions on which modern diplomacy rests, Somalia or Darfur, for example.

    A. regimes which ignore

    B. regimes ignore

    C. regimes that ignore

    D. regimes, which ignore

    E. regimes ignoring

25. At midnight, the election results were uncertain, it was after three when they were conclusive.

    A. uncertain, it was after three when they were conclusive

    B. uncertain, it was after three when it was conclusive

    C. uncertain; it was after three when they were conclusive

    D. uncertain; it was after three when it was conclusive

    E. uncertain; being concluded after three

GO ON TO THE NEXT PAGE

Section **3** Writing Test

26. <u>Many songs were recorded by the rock group that</u> covertly encouraged drug use, according to the critics.

    A.   Many songs were recorded by the rock group that

    B.   Many songs were recorded by the rock group who

    C.   The rock group that recorded many songs

    D.   The recording of many songs by the rock group

    E.   The rock group recorded many songs that

27. The unexplained surcharge of eighty-five dollars <u>surprised and angered the customers</u>.

    A.   surprised and angered the customers

    B.   surprised the customers, and angered them

    C.   surprised the customers, angering them

    D.   was surprising to the customers, and it angered them

    E.   was a surprise and a source of anger to the customers

28. The position requires a worker who can <u>use the law library, the computer, and write fluently</u>.

    A.   use the law library, the computer, and write fluently

    B.   use the law library and the computer and write fluently

    C.   use the law library and use the computer and write fluently

    D.   use the law library, the computer, and fluent writing

    E.   use the law library and the computer; and write fluently

29. <u>Because the sales of cigarettes declined was why Joseph Cruz, the vice-president, believed the company lost money.</u>

    A.   Because the sales of cigarettes declined was why Joseph Cruz, the vice-president, believed the company lost money.

    B.   Because the sales of cigarettes declined, the vice-president, Joseph Cruz, believed was why the company lost money.

    C.   The vice-president, Joseph Cruz, believed why the company lost money was because the sales of cigarettes declined.

    D.   The vice-president, Joseph Cruz, believed the company lost money because the sales of cigarettes declined.

    E.   Joseph Cruz, the vice-president, believed the reason the company lost money was because the sales of cigarettes declining.

30. We ought to have two levels of diplomatic <u>immunity; one would allow</u> only favored nations to retain freedom from search.

    A. immunity; one would allow

    B. immunity, one would allow

    C. immunity, allowing

    D. immunity, one will allow

    E. immunity, which would allow

31. Some reptiles <u>living in the deserts</u> of New Mexico and Arizona were there centuries before the continent was discovered.

    A. living in the deserts

    B. which living in the deserts

    C. that are living in the deserts

    D. who live in the deserts

    E. who live in the desert

32. The president, as well as senators from four states, <u>have enthusiastically supported</u> the referendum.

    A. have enthusiastically supported

    B. enthusiastically support

    C. having enthusiastically supported

    D. has enthusiastically supported

    E. are enthusiastically supporting

33. Carefully watching the highway patrolman parked by the roadside, <u>my car nearly ran into</u> a slow-moving van.

    A. my car nearly ran into

    B. I nearly ran my car into

    C. my car was nearly run into

    D. my car nearly running into

    E. I ran my car nearly into

34. Gerrymandering <u>is when a voting area is unfairly divided</u> so that one political party gains advantage.

    A. is when a voting area is unfairly divided

    B. divides a voting area unfairly

    C. makes fair voting unfair

    D. occurs when a voting area is unfairly divided

    E. is when a voting area is divided unfairly

35. Steve Irwin was always portrayed on film as <u>fearless and having great skill with dangerous animals</u>.

    A. fearless and having great skill with dangerous animals

    B. fearless and skillful with dangerous animals

    C. having no fear and having great skill with dangerous animals

    D. fearless and with skill with dangerous animals

    E. facing dangerous animals with fear and with skill

36. <u>After having finished the marathon,</u> both the winner and the losers felt proud of their achievement.

    A. After having finished the marathon

    B. Having finished the marathon

    C. Having been finished after the marathon

    D. Finishing the marathon

    E. The marathon finished

GO ON TO THE NEXT PAGE

Section **3** Writing Test

37. <u>The actor, along with his butler, bodyguard, chauffeur, two maids, and four dogs, are on board</u> the train bound for Cannes.

   A. The actor, along with his butler, bodyguard, chauffeur, two maids, and four dogs, are on board

   B. The actor and his butler and also his chauffeur, together with two maids and including four dogs, are on board

   C. The actor, along with his butler, bodyguard, chauffeur, two maids, and four dogs, is on board

   D. The actor, along with his butler, bodyguard, chauffeur, two maids, and four dogs, are climbing onto

   E. The actor's butler, bodyguard, chauffeur, two maids, and four dogs are on board

38. <u>Neither the director nor the investors in the sequel predicts</u> that it will earn less money than the original film.

   A. Neither the director nor the investors in the sequel predicts

   B. Neither the investors in the sequel nor its director predicts

   C. The director of the sequel, along with its investors, predicts

   D. Neither the investors nor the directors of the sequel predicts

   E. About the sequel, neither the director nor the investors predict

IF YOU FINISH BEFORE TIME IS CALLED, CHECK YOUR WORK ON THIS SECTION ONLY. DO NOT WORK ON ANY OTHER SECTION IN THE TEST.

Writing Test: Essay Section

TIME: 30 Minutes

1 Essay

Directions: In this section, you will have 30 minutes to plan and write one essay on the topic given. You may use the paper provided to plan your essay before you begin writing. You should plan your time wisely. Read the topic carefully to make sure that you are properly addressing the issue or situation. **You must write on the given topic. An essay on another topic will not be acceptable.**

The essay question is designed to give you an opportunity to write clearly and effectively. Use specific examples whenever appropriate to aid in supporting your ideas. Keep in mind that the quality of your writing is much more important than the quantity.

Your essay is to be written in the space provided. No other paper may be used. Your writing should be neat and legible. Because you have only a limited amount of space in which to write, please do **not** skip lines, do **not** write excessively large, and do **not** leave wide margins.

Remember, use the bottom of this page for any organizational notes you may wish to make.

Topic

Different sports appeal to different people. Think of one sport that you enjoy, either as a spectator or as a participant. In the space provided, write an essay explaining why that particular sport appeals to you.

Answer Key for Practice Test 1

Reading Test		Mathematics Test		Writing Test Multiple-Choice	
1. C	21. C	1. C	21. D	1. B	21. A
2. A	22. C	2. C	22. C	2. C	22. E
3. E	23. C	3. A	23. A	3. C	23. C
4. C	24. C	4. D	24. D	4. E	24. B
5. B	25. B	5. C	25. E	5. C	25. C
6. B	26. D	6. B	26. C	6. C	26. E
7. D	27. C	7. D	27. C	7. E	27. A
8. B	28. E	8. C	28. D	8. C	28. B
9. B	29. B	9. C	29. B	9. B	29. D
10. B	30. D	10. C	30. D	10. E	30. A
11. B	31. D	11. B	31. D	11. A	31. A
12. B	32. C	12. D	32. D	12. C	32. D
13. D	33. A	13. B	33. E	13. C	33. B
14. E	34. B	14. B	34. B	14. B	34. B
15. A	35. D	15. E	35. B	15. C	35. B
16. D	36. C	16. C	36. D	16. A	36. B
17. D	37. A	17. E	37. B	17. A	37. C
18. E	38. B	18. B	38. E	18. B	38. B
19. D	39. C	19. C	39. C	19. C	
20. E	40. E	20. E	40. A	20. A	

Scoring Your PPST Practice Test 1

To score your PPST Practice Test 1, total the number of correct responses for each test. Do not subtract any points for questions attempted but missed, as there is no penalty for guessing. The scores for each section range from 150 to 190. Because the Writing Test contains multiple-choice questions and an essay, that score is a composite score adjusted to give approximately equal weight to the number right on the multiple-choice section and to the essay score. The essay is scored holistically (a single score for overall quality) from 1 (low) to 6 (high). Each of two readers gives a 1 to 6 score. The score that the essay receives is the sum of these two readers' scores.

Analyzing your test results

The following charts should be used to carefully analyze your results and spot your strengths and weaknesses. The complete process of analyzing each subject area and each individual question should be completed for this Practice Test. These results should be reexamined for trends in types of error (repeated errors) or poor results in specific subject areas. **This reexamination and analysis is of tremendous importance for effective test preparation.**

Practice Test 1: Subject area analysis sheet

	Possible	Completed	Right	Wrong
Reading Test	40			
Mathematics Test	40			
Writing Test	38			
TOTAL	118			

Analysis—tally sheet for questions missed

One of the most important parts of test preparation is analyzing why you missed a question so that you can reduce the number of mistakes. Now that you have taken Practice Test 1 and checked your answers, carefully tally your mistakes by marking each of them in the proper column.

	Total Missed	Simple Mistake	Misread Problem	Lack of Knowledge
Reading Test				
Mathematics Test				
Writing Test				
TOTAL				

Reviewing the data in the preceding chart should help you determine why you are missing certain questions. Now that you have pinpointed types of errors, focus on avoiding your most common type.

Score approximators

Reading Test

To approximate your reading score:

1. Count the number of questions you answered correctly.

2. Use the following table to match the number of correct answers and the corresponding approximate score range.

Number Right	Approximate Score Range
10–19	160–169
20–29	170–179
30–40	180–189

Remember, this is only an approximate score range. When you take the PPST, you will have questions that are similar to those in this book, however some questions may be slightly easier or more difficult.

Mathematics Test

To approximate your mathematics score:

1. Count the number of questions you answered correctly.

2. Use the following table to match the number of correct answers and the corresponding approximate score range.

Number Right	Approximate Score Range
0–10	150–160
11–20	161–170
21–30	171–180
31–40	181–190

Remember, this is an approximate score range.

Writing Test

These scores are difficult to approximate because the multiple-choice section score and the essay score are combined to give a total score.

Essay checklist

Use this checklist to evaluate your essay.

Diagnosis/prescription for timed writing exercise

A good essay will:

- ❏ Address the assignment

    Be well focused

- ❏ Be well organized

    Have smooth transitions between paragraphs

    Be coherent, unified

- ❏ Be well developed

    Contain specific examples to support points

- ❏ Be grammatically sound (only minor flaws)

    Use correct sentence structure

    Use correct punctuation

    Use standard written English

- ❏ Use language skillfully

    Use a variety of sentence types

    Use a variety of words

- ❏ Be legible

    Have clear handwriting

    Be neat

Reading Test

1. **C.** Choices **D** and **E** address subsidiary points only. Choice **A** mentions the behavior of the scientist rather than the behavior of individuals, and **B** does not even mention social psychology. Only **C** is both comprehensive and accurate.

2. **A.** The final sentence expresses an interest in and appreciation for *talking* children, thus implying that the *flip-flop* is a change from the past preference for quiet children.

3. **E.** Choices **A, B,** and **D** are terms with a negative connotation that suggest *creative writing* is "underdeveloped" or "incomplete." Choice **C** is ambiguous and irrelevant. Only **E** suggests the negative connotation of *precious,* which is the author's meaning in this passage.

4. **C.** Each of the other choices either describes a secondary rather than primary point or assigns a purpose (to urge) that is beyond the scope of the passage. And choice **E** is obviously incorrect.

5. **B.** The passage portrays early retirement as an unattractive, problematic occurrence that will affect many; **D** and **E** contradict the unattractive connotations of early retirement; and **A** and **C** state conclusions that are neither expressed nor implied in the passage.

6. **B.** By saying that the *new* type of citizen will not be intimidated by ending careers, the author assumes that *present* citizens *are* intimidated. Incorrect choices either state an implication rather than an assumption **D** or draw conclusions beyond the scope of the passage as in **A, C,** and **E.**

7. **D.** Toward the end of the passage, the author expresses a skeptical, qualified view of the value of technology. Each of the other choices is consistent with the author's views.

8. **B.** The *we* in the passage tells us that the author counts himself or herself among those who give performances.

9. **B.** As the author says, art is *not merely to amuse.*

10. **B.** The repeat of *some* recalls the earlier mention of *some legislators* and indicates that the legislators may be part of those who do not appreciate the full value of art.

11. **B.** In order to accept an argument abolishing grades, we must presume that there are viable alternatives. None of the other choices is a necessary condition for agreement with the argument.

12. **B.** By saying that the abolition of grades will increase student interest in subject matter, the author implies that graded students are less interested in and motivated by subject matter.

13. D. The words *we will have students* indicate that the author is a teacher talking to teachers; so does *us* in the third sentence.

14. E. Although choice **D** is part of the author's argument, acknowledging that exams cause fatigue will not make us accept the overall argument stressing fun over study. To accept that argument, we must accept the fact that students study too much.

15. A. The author stresses the value of *good fellowship and extracurricular activities,* both social characteristics.

16. D. Taking a negative view of studying, the author does not pick as strong and generally acceptable an example of enjoying life as might have been presented. Choices **A** and **C** would weaken rather than strengthen the argument. While changing *all* in choice **A** to *some* would seem to make the argument more believable, the use of the word *all* is much stronger, even though it is probably not true. **B** contradicts the argument. Choice **E** is too vague, not specifying *which* audience, so we cannot tell what effect such a change would have.

17. D. The teacher does not advocate, recommend, or prefer anything in particular; nor is the teacher categorically for or against steroids. Therefore, **A, B, C,** and **E** should be eliminated because they assign an *absolute* point of view that is not expressed.

18. E. The author says that survivors will be adaptable but does not specify the way in which adaptability will be a value.

19. D. Each of the other choices goes beyond the scope of the passage. Choice **D** is directly relevant to the author's assertion that the economy is a significant factor.

20. E. This is the most comprehensive choice, describing the overall purpose of the passage rather than secondary purposes and implications.

21. C. A discussion of creative writing is relevant to English and psychology but not to technical writing.

22. C. The passage states that dormant tensions may be released through the revealing of a *deep, inner thought.* Choice **C** refers to this idea.

23. C. Spelling is the one characteristic that the author neither expresses nor implies as relevant to creative writing.

24. C. The passage explicitly states that creative writing is, *above all, a means of self-expression.*

25. B. The passage stresses ways of changing the social studies curriculum, thus designating its audience as those who can effect such changes—teachers.

26. D. *Humans have always been interested in where they are going* is preceded by a series of historical facts, that is, facts about occurrences of the past.

27. C. By advocating the addition of futurism to the social studies curriculum, the author assumes that futurism is not adequately acknowledged. Without that assumption, the author would have no reason to make the argument.

28. E. By distinguishing *global* from *national* in the passage, the author suggests that a global society is larger and more inclusive than a national one but does not go so far as to suggest that such a society necessarily includes outer space.

29. B. Choices **C** and **D** would strengthen the argument of the value of futurism. Choices **A** and **E** are irrelevant to the strength or weakness of the argument. Choice **B** weakens the passage by calling into question those futurists of the past.

30. D. The overall stress on changes in education indicates that the author is an educator.

31. D. Through presenting a series of school situations in which students are discouraged from expressing themselves, the author implies that attending school may cause children to become inhibited.

32. C. The passage overall suggests that students are inhibited by being severely criticized or corrected. The meaning of *chopped off* given by **C** is consistent with this overall view.

33. A. The author repeatedly addresses the common experiences of *everyone*.

34. B. By citing a number of negative situations, the author leaves no question that he or she is critical of the practices described.

35. D. Choices **A, B,** and **C** contradict the implied argument of the passage, and **E** *may* contradict the implied argument because the meaning of *assist* is not made clear and possibly suggests that the teacher should supply words for the student. Choice **D** repeats the author's overall point.

36. C. Each of the other choices is beyond the scope of the passage.

37. A. Choices **C** and **E** make statements beyond the scope of the passage; **D** contradicts the passage (the parents' contribution is said to be *indispensable*); and **B** makes cartoons a *primary* source of inspiration. The author would agree that cartoons have some value and should not be banned.

38. B. The author stresses a severely negative response to disappointment, and only **B** supplies a negative term.

39. C. Choice **C** weakens the stress on early childhood as a time of rapid change by saying that midlife may be a time of rapid change as well.

40. E. By stressing the separateness of speech sounds in memory, the author supports the conclusion of **E.** Each of the other conclusions is beyond the scope of the passage.

Mathematics Test

1. C. One way to solve this problem is to set up a proportion: 10 kilometers is to 6.2 miles as 45 kilometers is to how many miles? This proportion is expressed in mathematical terms as

$$\frac{10\,\text{km}}{6.2\,\text{m}} = \frac{45\,\text{km}}{x}$$

Cross multiplying gives

$$10x = 6.2 \times 45$$
$$10x = 279$$

Dividing both sides by 10 gives

$$\frac{10x}{10} = \frac{279}{10}$$
$$x = 27.9$$

Another method is to realize that 45 kilometers is exactly $4\frac{1}{2}$ times 10 kilometers.

Therefore, the number of miles in 45 kilometers must be $4\frac{1}{2}$ times the number of miles in 10 kilometers, or $4\frac{1}{2}$ times 6.2. Thus, $4.5 \times 6.2 = 27.9$.

2. **C.** The gauge indicator is between 600 and 700, which eliminates choices **D** and **E,** each of which is over 700. The space between 600 and 700 is divided into 10 equal sections. Since the total between 600 and 700 is 100 pounds per square foot, each of these 10 sections equals 10 lbs/sq ft. The indicator is exactly three sections beyond 600, so $600 + 3(10) = 630$ lbs/sq ft.

3. **A.** The four listed items total $1,740. Therefore, by subtracting from the listed total of $2,220, we can see that the missing item must have cost $480. $2,220 - $1,740 = $480.

4. **D.** The total of the five verbal state test scores is 2,635. Dividing that total by 5 (the number of scores) gives 527 as the average.

5. **C.** Since the figure is a rectangle, its opposite sides are equal. To find its perimeter, first add the two touching sides, and then double the sum (or double each of the sides and add the results).

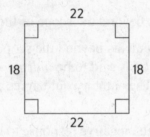

Now, to determine the side of a square with the same perimeter, simply divide the perimeter by 4, since the side of a square is $\frac{1}{4}$ its perimeter. Finally, to find the area of the square, multiply its side times itself (square it).

6. **B.** If we call the price of the tie x, then the price of the shirt is $3x$, the price of the slacks is $3x$, and the price of the coat is twice the shirt, or $6x$. Totaling the x's, we get $13x$. Since the total spent was $156, $13x = \$156$. Dividing both sides by 13 gives

$$\frac{13x}{13} = \frac{\$156}{13}$$
$$x = \$12$$

Therefore, the price of the pair of slacks, $3x$, is $3(\$12) = \$36$.

7. **D.** The solution of two lines can be determined by the coordinates of the point at which the lines intersect. Lines l_1 and l_2 intersect at (2,4). Therefore, $x = 2$ and $y = 4$.

8. **C.** In 1960, there were 40 sports franchises in the United States. By 1970, there were 60 sports franchises. So in 1970, there were "half again as many" as in 1960 ($40 + 20 = 60$). This is a 50% increase. Another way of computing percent change is by using the formula "change divided by starting point."

$$\frac{\text{change}}{\text{starting point}} = \frac{20}{40} = 0.50 = 50\%$$

9. C. For only two 10-year periods did the number of franchises increase by fewer than 10: from 1990 to 2000 (an increase of about 5) and from 2000 to 2010 (another increase of about 5). In each of the other 10-year periods shown on the chart, the number of sports franchises increased by more than 10.

10. C. Figure 3 shows that cuts are made through the original corners at A and B. This means that only choices **C** and **E** could be correct. Look at Figure 3 again and notice that the other cut was made at the original center, choice **C**.

11. B. To purchase twelve CDs, Roy must buy six packages. At $2.98 per package, he spends $17.88. His change from a twenty-dollar bill will be $20.00 − $17.88 = $2.12.

12. D. Solving the equation $2x + 4 = 3x + 3$, first subtract $2x$ from each side.

$$2x + 4 - 2x = 3x + 3 - 2x$$

$$4 = x + 3$$

Now, subtract 3 from both sides.

$$4 - 3 = x + 3 - 3$$

$$1 = x$$

By plugging in the above value of x (that is, 1) for each of the answer choices, we find that 1 satisfies all the equations except choice **D**.

$$\text{Does } x = -1? \text{ No.}$$

$$1 \neq -1$$

Therefore, **D** is the correct answer.

13. B. Note that all choices except **B** are larger than $\frac{1}{2}$. Choice **B**, $\frac{4}{9}$, is smaller than $\frac{1}{2}$.

14. B. 210,000 is equivalent to $(2 \times 10^5) + (1 \times 10^4)$. A fast way of figuring this is to count the number of places to the right of each digit that is not zero. For instance,

210,000   Note that there are 5 places to the right of the 2, thus 2×10^5.

210,000   There are 4 places to the right of the 1, thus 1×10^4.

So 210,000 may also be written $(2 \times 10^5) + (1 \times 10^4)$.

15. E. Since the chart does not distinguish how many houses are 3 years old or 4 years old, the answer cannot be determined.

16. C. If the product of two numbers equals one of the numbers, then $(x)(y) = x$. If this product is more than 0, neither of the numbers may be zero. Therefore, y must be 1: $(x)(1) = x$.

17. E. The best way to compute the area of the figure is to divide it into as few parts as possible, making each part a simple shape whose area is easily calculated (for instance, a triangle, rectangle, or square). Choice **E** divides the shape into a rectangle and a triangle.

18. B. This problem requires an algebraic solution. First add 50 to each side of the equation, changing its sign in the process:

$$10m - 50 + 20p = 0$$

$$10m + 20p = 50$$

You want to find $m + 2p$, so divide the left side of the equation by 10. However, to keep the equation balanced, you must do the same to the right side as well:

$$\frac{10m + 20p}{10} = \frac{50}{10}$$
$$m + 2p = 5$$

19. C. Rounding 0.14739 to the nearest thousandth means first looking at the digit one place to the right of the thousandths place: 0.147$\underline{3}$9. Since that digit is 4 or less, simply drop it. (There is no need to replace with zeros because they are not needed to the right of a decimal point.)

20. E. Following the formula, plug in 3 for a, -2 for b, and 4 for c. This gives:

$$a \# b \# c = 2a - 3b + 5c$$
$$3 \# (-2) \# 4 = 2(3) - 3(-2) + 5(4)$$
$$= 6 + 6 + 20$$
$$= 32$$

21. D. Since the large square has a side 4 cm, then its area must be 16. By careful grouping of areas, you will see that there are four unshaded smaller squares and four shaded smaller squares (match the shaded parts to form four squares). Therefore, half of the area is shaded, or 8 square cm.

22. C. Note that only choice **C** raises one of the numbers by 5 while it lowers the other number by 5. Choice **C** will give the best approximation of the five choices.

23. A. 16 out of 400 may be expressed as a percent as 16/400. Dividing 16 by 400 gives 0.04, or 4%.

24. D. Using the probability formula,

$$\text{probability} = \frac{\text{number of "lucky" chances}}{\text{total number of chances}},$$

the chance of choosing a weekday = 5 weekdays/7 total days = $\frac{5}{7}$.

25. E. Note that since there is a mark between +7 and +9, that mark must equal +8. Thus, each mark equals 1. Counting back, point Q is at +5. Therefore, 15 units to the left of +5 would be $+5 - 15 = -10$.

26. C. The *product of two numbers* indicates the numbers must be multiplied together. Their *sum* means "add." Therefore,

$$\underbrace{\text{the product of two numbers}}_{(A)(B)} \underbrace{\text{equals}}_{=} \underbrace{\text{five more than their sum}}_{A + B + 5}$$

27. C. Only III is determined by division ($39 \div 3$). The others are determined by multiplication ($6 \times B$) and subtraction, respectively.

28. D. Note that, for example, as the temperature decreased from −10° to −15°, the average amount of snowfall per hour increased from 2 to 2.5 inches. (Watch out for the minus sign, which means the temperature drops when it goes from −20° to −25°.) This relationship exists throughout the chart.

29. B. Thirty percent off the original price equals a discount of (0.30)($8,000) = $2,400. Therefore, the new selling price is $8,000 − $2,400 = $5,600.

30. D. Since Hector's hybrid car averages 35 miles for each gallon of gas, on 12 gallons he'll be able to drive 12×35, or 420 miles.

31. D. Remember that a parallelogram has equal opposite sides. Therefore, its sides are 9, 7, 9, and 7. Its perimeter, then, is 32. If a square has the same perimeter, one of its sides must be one-fourth of its perimeter (since the four sides of a square are equal). One-fourth of 32 is 8.

32. D. If each adult drinks $\frac{1}{5}$ of a gallon of lemonade, 1 gallon is consumed by each 5 adults. Since 28 adults attend the picnic, $\frac{28}{5} = 5\frac{3}{5}$, which is a number between 5 and 6.

33. E. There are several quick methods of solving this problem. As in question 1, a proportion can be set up.

$$\frac{20\,\text{pgs}}{4\,\text{hrs}} = \frac{50\,\text{pgs}}{x}$$

Cross multiplying will give $20x = 200$, or $x = 10$. This is done by dividing each side of the equation by 20. Or determining John's hourly rate (5 pages per hour) tells us he will need 10 hours to type 50 pages.

34. B. Note that a total of 28 items were purchased, each costing 85¢. Therefore, the simplest way to compute the total amount spent would be 28×85¢.

35. B. If team B's victories are called x, then team A must have $2x$ victories, team C must have $(2x − 5)$ victories, and team D must have $(x + 4)$ victories. All together these total $6x − 1$. We are told that the total equals 29 victories. Thus,

$$6x − 1 = 29$$
$$6x = 30$$
$$x = 5$$

Therefore, team D has $(x + 4)$ victories, or $(5 + 4) = 9$.

36. D. If all dogs are green, and Bowser is a dog, then it must logically follow that Bowser is green. Bowser might also have blue in his fur, but this does not have to be true. Nothing in the statements allows us to reach any conclusions about cats. Choice **E** contradicts the statements.

37. B. Note that on the graph a 30-degree drop in temperature on the line correlates with a 20% attendance drop (the fourth slash up the graph).

38. E. Note that 30% of 50 may be expressed as 0.30×50 or $\frac{3}{10} \times 50$. Whichever way it is expressed, it will still total 15. The only answer choice that does not total 15 is choice **E**, which totals $166\frac{2}{3}$.

39. C. Plug in 3 for *x*:

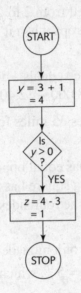

40. A. Since the sum of the angles is 180°, we have

$$m + n + 72 + 25 = 180$$
$$m + n + 97 = 180$$
$$m + n = 180 - 97$$
$$m + n = 83$$

Hence, the sum of $m + n$ is 83°.

Writing Test: Multiple-Choice Section

Part A

1. B. The pronoun *I* should be *me*, the objective case. It is the object of the preposition *between*.

2. C. The preposition *to* should be replaced by *from*. The idiom is to *differ from* not to *differ to*.

3. C. The verbal *seems satisfying* is incorrect. The first half of the sentence sets the action in the past (*scored*); to keep the tenses consistent, the verb should be *seems to have satisfied*.

4. E. The sentence is correct as written.

5. C. The correct verb form here is the past perfect *had fallen*. The past tense is *fell*; the past participle used to form the perfect tenses is *fallen*.

6. C. Since the sentence begins by using the second person subject (*you*), the subject of the main clause should also be the second person (*you*), not the third person (*one*).

7. E. The sentence is correct as written.

8. **C.** There is a diction error here, a confusion of the past tense of the verb *to leave* (*left*) with the past tense of the verb *to let* (*let*).

9. **B.** The sentence contains a double negative. It should omit either the *not* or the *hardly; provides hardly any* or *does not provide any*.

10. **E.** The sentence is correct as written.

11. **A.** Since the subject of the sentence is the plural *races,* the verb should be the plural *are.*

12. **C.** The adjective *skeptical* should be the adverb *skeptically,* modifying the verb *responds.*

13. **C.** Since the two parts of the sentence contrast *most* with *a few,* the use of *and* as the coordinating conjunction makes no sense. The better choice is *but.*

14. **B.** Since the subject of the sentence is the singular *population,* the verb should be the singular *is.*

15. **C.** As it stands, the sentence has no main verb. A correct version would be *are rarely seen.*

16. **A.** The problem is the phrase *in regards to.* The idioms the writer probably had in mind are *as regards* or *in regard to.* The sense of the sentence suggests that neither would fit as well as *in response to.*

17. **A.** The correct verb here is the past tense, *sang; sung* is the participle: *I sing; I sang; I have sung.*

18. **B.** The subject of the sentence is the singular *rate;* the verb should be the singular *is.*

19. **C.** Since the sentence begins by using the third person (*a person*) (*his*), the shift to the second person (*you*) should be corrected to *he.*

20. **A.** The comma after *Ideas* should be deleted.

21. **A.** The conjunction *As* should be replaced by the preposition *Like.* The opening words are a prepositional phrase, not a clause.

Part B

22. **E.** Choice E is grammatically correct, idiomatic, and more concise than choices **A, C,** and **D.** In most cases, an adjective followed by an infinitive is idiomatic and preferable to an adjective followed by *for* and a gerund.

23. **C.** Choices **A** and **B** join two complete sentences with a comma where a semicolon is needed. Given the meaning of the sentence, the conjunction *but* in choice **D** makes no sense. In **E,** there is no main verb in the second clause, so the sentence is a fragment.

24. **B.** Only choice **B** supplies the necessary main verb, *ignore.* In each of the other four versions, the sentence is a fragment lacking a main verb.

25. **C.** Choices **A** and **B** use a comma where a semicolon is needed to join two independent clauses without a conjunction. Since *results* is plural, the singular *it* in **D** is an agreement error. In **E,** there is no main verb after the semicolon.

26. E. The clause *that covertly encouraged drug use* modifies *songs* and should be placed as close to *songs* as possible. Additionally, choices **A** and **B** use the wordier passive voice. Choice **C** changes the meaning of the sentence.

27. A. Choice **A** is the most concise version of the sentence.

28. B. There are parallelism errors in choice **A** and an extra *and* in **C**. In **D,** *fluent writing* is the object of *use;* in **E,** the second clause is a fragment after the semicolon.

29. D. The clearest and most concise version of this sentence is **D**. The verbose *because . . . why* idiom should be avoided.

30. A. Choices **B** and **D** use a comma where a semicolon is needed. Choices **C** and **E,** by leaving out *one,* distort the meaning of the sentence.

31. A. Choice **A** is correct and concise. The pronoun *who,* used in **D** and **E,** should be used for people, not reptiles.

32. D. The subject of the sentence is the singular *president*. The phrase *as well as senators from four states* is parenthetical.

33. B. The participle (*watching*) at the beginning of the sentence modifies *I*, not *car*. To avoid a dangling participle, you must place the *I* after the comma. The adverb *nearly* should be next to the verb *ran*.

34. B. *Is when* is not acceptable because *gerrymandering* is not a time. Choice **E** repeats this error. **D** is not best because it leaves vague whether *gerrymandering* is synonymous with *unfair division*. **C** is very general and vague.

35. B. The original is flawed by faulty parallelism. *Fearless* is not parallel to *having great skill*. Choice **B** corrects this problem. *Fearless* is parallel to *skillful*. Choices **C** and **E** are both unnecessarily wordy.

36. B. *Having finished* expresses the past tense by itself, so *after* is repetitious (its meaning is already implied in *having finished*). None of the other choices expresses the past tense both economically and clearly.

37. C. The verb in this sentence should be *is* (not *are*) to agree with the singular subject, *actor*. A parenthetical phrase enclosed in commas and beginning with words such as *along with, including,* or *as well as* changes neither the subject nor the verb. Choice **B** correctly uses *are* because the subject in this sentence has been made plural; however, the construction is awkward and wordy. Choice **D** retains the incorrect *are* and changes the meaning of the sentence. **E** leaves out the fact that the actor is on the train.

38. B. When subjects are connected with *nor* or *or*, the verb is governed by the subject closest to it. In choices **A** and **D**, the closer subject does not agree with the verb. **E** is awkward. In **B**, the subject, *director*, agrees with the verb, *predicts*.

Answer Sheet for Practice Test 2

(Remove This Sheet and Use It to Mark Your Answers)

Reading Test

1 Ⓐ Ⓑ Ⓒ Ⓓ Ⓔ	21 Ⓐ Ⓑ Ⓒ Ⓓ Ⓔ
2 Ⓐ Ⓑ Ⓒ Ⓓ Ⓔ	22 Ⓐ Ⓑ Ⓒ Ⓓ Ⓔ
3 Ⓐ Ⓑ Ⓒ Ⓓ Ⓔ	23 Ⓐ Ⓑ Ⓒ Ⓓ Ⓔ
4 Ⓐ Ⓑ Ⓒ Ⓓ Ⓔ	24 Ⓐ Ⓑ Ⓒ Ⓓ Ⓔ
5 Ⓐ Ⓑ Ⓒ Ⓓ Ⓔ	25 Ⓐ Ⓑ Ⓒ Ⓓ Ⓔ
6 Ⓐ Ⓑ Ⓒ Ⓓ Ⓔ	26 Ⓐ Ⓑ Ⓒ Ⓓ Ⓔ
7 Ⓐ Ⓑ Ⓒ Ⓓ Ⓔ	27 Ⓐ Ⓑ Ⓒ Ⓓ Ⓔ
8 Ⓐ Ⓑ Ⓒ Ⓓ Ⓔ	28 Ⓐ Ⓑ Ⓒ Ⓓ Ⓔ
9 Ⓐ Ⓑ Ⓒ Ⓓ Ⓔ	29 Ⓐ Ⓑ Ⓒ Ⓓ Ⓔ
10 Ⓐ Ⓑ Ⓒ Ⓓ Ⓔ	30 Ⓐ Ⓑ Ⓒ Ⓓ Ⓔ
11 Ⓐ Ⓑ Ⓒ Ⓓ Ⓔ	31 Ⓐ Ⓑ Ⓒ Ⓓ Ⓔ
12 Ⓐ Ⓑ Ⓒ Ⓓ Ⓔ	32 Ⓐ Ⓑ Ⓒ Ⓓ Ⓔ
13 Ⓐ Ⓑ Ⓒ Ⓓ Ⓔ	33 Ⓐ Ⓑ Ⓒ Ⓓ Ⓔ
14 Ⓐ Ⓑ Ⓒ Ⓓ Ⓔ	34 Ⓐ Ⓑ Ⓒ Ⓓ Ⓔ
15 Ⓐ Ⓑ Ⓒ Ⓓ Ⓔ	35 Ⓐ Ⓑ Ⓒ Ⓓ Ⓔ
16 Ⓐ Ⓑ Ⓒ Ⓓ Ⓔ	36 Ⓐ Ⓑ Ⓒ Ⓓ Ⓔ
17 Ⓐ Ⓑ Ⓒ Ⓓ Ⓔ	37 Ⓐ Ⓑ Ⓒ Ⓓ Ⓔ
18 Ⓐ Ⓑ Ⓒ Ⓓ Ⓔ	38 Ⓐ Ⓑ Ⓒ Ⓓ Ⓔ
19 Ⓐ Ⓑ Ⓒ Ⓓ Ⓔ	39 Ⓐ Ⓑ Ⓒ Ⓓ Ⓔ
20 Ⓐ Ⓑ Ⓒ Ⓓ Ⓔ	40 Ⓐ Ⓑ Ⓒ Ⓓ Ⓔ

Mathematics Test

1 Ⓐ Ⓑ Ⓒ Ⓓ Ⓔ	21 Ⓐ Ⓑ Ⓒ Ⓓ Ⓔ
2 Ⓐ Ⓑ Ⓒ Ⓓ Ⓔ	22 Ⓐ Ⓑ Ⓒ Ⓓ Ⓔ
3 Ⓐ Ⓑ Ⓒ Ⓓ Ⓔ	23 Ⓐ Ⓑ Ⓒ Ⓓ Ⓔ
4 Ⓐ Ⓑ Ⓒ Ⓓ Ⓔ	24 Ⓐ Ⓑ Ⓒ Ⓓ Ⓔ
5 Ⓐ Ⓑ Ⓒ Ⓓ Ⓔ	25 Ⓐ Ⓑ Ⓒ Ⓓ Ⓔ
6 Ⓐ Ⓑ Ⓒ Ⓓ Ⓔ	26 Ⓐ Ⓑ Ⓒ Ⓓ Ⓔ
7 Ⓐ Ⓑ Ⓒ Ⓓ Ⓔ	27 Ⓐ Ⓑ Ⓒ Ⓓ Ⓔ
8 Ⓐ Ⓑ Ⓒ Ⓓ Ⓔ	28 Ⓐ Ⓑ Ⓒ Ⓓ Ⓔ
9 Ⓐ Ⓑ Ⓒ Ⓓ Ⓔ	29 Ⓐ Ⓑ Ⓒ Ⓓ Ⓔ
10 Ⓐ Ⓑ Ⓒ Ⓓ Ⓔ	30 Ⓐ Ⓑ Ⓒ Ⓓ Ⓔ
11 Ⓐ Ⓑ Ⓒ Ⓓ Ⓔ	31 Ⓐ Ⓑ Ⓒ Ⓓ Ⓔ
12 Ⓐ Ⓑ Ⓒ Ⓓ Ⓔ	32 Ⓐ Ⓑ Ⓒ Ⓓ Ⓔ
13 Ⓐ Ⓑ Ⓒ Ⓓ Ⓔ	33 Ⓐ Ⓑ Ⓒ Ⓓ Ⓔ
14 Ⓐ Ⓑ Ⓒ Ⓓ Ⓔ	34 Ⓐ Ⓑ Ⓒ Ⓓ Ⓔ
15 Ⓐ Ⓑ Ⓒ Ⓓ Ⓔ	35 Ⓐ Ⓑ Ⓒ Ⓓ Ⓔ
16 Ⓐ Ⓑ Ⓒ Ⓓ Ⓔ	36 Ⓐ Ⓑ Ⓒ Ⓓ Ⓔ
17 Ⓐ Ⓑ Ⓒ Ⓓ Ⓔ	37 Ⓐ Ⓑ Ⓒ Ⓓ Ⓔ
18 Ⓐ Ⓑ Ⓒ Ⓓ Ⓔ	38 Ⓐ Ⓑ Ⓒ Ⓓ Ⓔ
19 Ⓐ Ⓑ Ⓒ Ⓓ Ⓔ	39 Ⓐ Ⓑ Ⓒ Ⓓ Ⓔ
20 Ⓐ Ⓑ Ⓒ Ⓓ Ⓔ	40 Ⓐ Ⓑ Ⓒ Ⓓ Ⓔ

CUT HERE

Writing Test: Multiple Choice

Part A

1 Ⓐ Ⓑ Ⓒ Ⓓ Ⓔ
2 Ⓐ Ⓑ Ⓒ Ⓓ Ⓔ
3 Ⓐ Ⓑ Ⓒ Ⓓ Ⓔ
4 Ⓐ Ⓑ Ⓒ Ⓓ Ⓔ
5 Ⓐ Ⓑ Ⓒ Ⓓ Ⓔ
6 Ⓐ Ⓑ Ⓒ Ⓓ Ⓔ
7 Ⓐ Ⓑ Ⓒ Ⓓ Ⓔ
8 Ⓐ Ⓑ Ⓒ Ⓓ Ⓔ
9 Ⓐ Ⓑ Ⓒ Ⓓ Ⓔ
10 Ⓐ Ⓑ Ⓒ Ⓓ Ⓔ
11 Ⓐ Ⓑ Ⓒ Ⓓ Ⓔ
12 Ⓐ Ⓑ Ⓒ Ⓓ Ⓔ
13 Ⓐ Ⓑ Ⓒ Ⓓ Ⓔ
14 Ⓐ Ⓑ Ⓒ Ⓓ Ⓔ
15 Ⓐ Ⓑ Ⓒ Ⓓ Ⓔ
16 Ⓐ Ⓑ Ⓒ Ⓓ Ⓔ
17 Ⓐ Ⓑ Ⓒ Ⓓ Ⓔ
18 Ⓐ Ⓑ Ⓒ Ⓓ Ⓔ
19 Ⓐ Ⓑ Ⓒ Ⓓ Ⓔ
20 Ⓐ Ⓑ Ⓒ Ⓓ Ⓔ
21 Ⓐ Ⓑ Ⓒ Ⓓ Ⓔ

Part B

22 Ⓐ Ⓑ Ⓒ Ⓓ Ⓔ
23 Ⓐ Ⓑ Ⓒ Ⓓ Ⓔ
24 Ⓐ Ⓑ Ⓒ Ⓓ Ⓔ
25 Ⓐ Ⓑ Ⓒ Ⓓ Ⓔ
26 Ⓐ Ⓑ Ⓒ Ⓓ Ⓔ
27 Ⓐ Ⓑ Ⓒ Ⓓ Ⓔ
28 Ⓐ Ⓑ Ⓒ Ⓓ Ⓔ
29 Ⓐ Ⓑ Ⓒ Ⓓ Ⓔ
30 Ⓐ Ⓑ Ⓒ Ⓓ Ⓔ
31 Ⓐ Ⓑ Ⓒ Ⓓ Ⓔ
32 Ⓐ Ⓑ Ⓒ Ⓓ Ⓔ
33 Ⓐ Ⓑ Ⓒ Ⓓ Ⓔ
34 Ⓐ Ⓑ Ⓒ Ⓓ Ⓔ
35 Ⓐ Ⓑ Ⓒ Ⓓ Ⓔ
36 Ⓐ Ⓑ Ⓒ Ⓓ Ⓔ
37 Ⓐ Ⓑ Ⓒ Ⓓ Ⓔ
38 Ⓐ Ⓑ Ⓒ Ⓓ Ⓔ

CUT HERE

Reading Test

TIME: 60 Minutes

40 Questions

Directions: A question or number of questions follows each of the statements or passages in this section. Using only the stated or implied information given in the statement or passage, answer the question or questions by choosing the best answer from among the five choices given.

1. Recent studies show that aptitude test scores are declining because of lack of family stability and students' preoccupation with out-of-school activities. Therefore, not only the student's attitude but his or her home environment must be changed to stop this downward trend.

   Which of the following is one assumption of the above argument?

   A. Recent studies have refuted previous studies.

   B. Heredity is more important than environment.

   C. Aptitude test scores should stop declining soon.

   D. The accuracy of the recent studies cited is not an issue.

   E. More out-of-school activities are available than ever before.

2. Once again, our city council has shown all the firmness of a bowl of oatmeal in deciding to seek a "compromise" on sheep grazing in the city. As it is inclined to do more often than not, the council overturned a planning commission recommendation, this time to ban sheep grazing in the city.

   The passage above uses the phrase "bowl of oatmeal" in order to

   A. condemn the actions taken by the city council

   B. add levity to the otherwise tragic situation

   C. imply that grazing sheep would prefer oats

   D. praise the city council for its recent vote

   E. urge the city council to overturn the planning commission

Questions 3, 4, and 5 refer to the following passage.

Recent studies indicate that at the present rate of increase, within two years a single-family dwelling will be unaffordable by the average family. Therefore, apartment living will increase noticeably in the near future.

3. Which of the following statements is deducible from the argument?

   A. The recent studies were for a five-year period.

   B. Condominiums are expensive but plentiful.

   C. The average family income will decrease in the next two years.

   D. Home costs are increasing more rapidly than average family incomes.

   E. The average family will increase within the next two years.

4. The argument would be weakened by the fact(s) that

   I.   many inexpensive single-family dwellings are presently being built

   II. bank loan interest rates have increased

   III. apartment living is also becoming very expensive

   A. I only

   B. II only

   C. III only

   D. I and III only

   E. II and III only

5. The argument presented assumes that

   I.   the present rate of price increase will continue

   II. families will turn to renting apartments instead of buying homes

   III. construction of apartments will double within the next two years

   A. I only

   B. II only

   C. III only

   D. I and II only

   E. II and III only

Questions 6 through 9 refer to the following passage.

From the U.S. Supreme Court now comes an extraordinary decision permitting inquiries into the "state of mind" of journalists and the editorial process of
(5) news organizations. This is perhaps the most alarming evidence so far of a determination by the nation's highest court to weaken the protection of the First Amendment for those who gather and
(10) report the news.

The Court last year upheld the right of police to invade newspaper offices in search of evidence, and reporters in other cases have gone to jail to protect
(15) the confidentiality of their notebooks. Under the recent 6-3 ruling in a libel case, they now face a challenge to the privacy of their minds.

Few would argue that the First
(20) Amendment guarantees absolute freedom of speech or freedom of the press. Slander and libel laws stand to the contrary as a protection of an individual's

(25) reputation against the irresponsible dissemination of falsehoods. The effect of this latest decision, however, is to make the libel suit, or the threat of one, a clear invasion by the courts into the private decision-making that constitutes news (30) and editorial judgment.

In landmark decisions of 1964 and 1967, the Supreme Court established that public officials or public figures bringing libel actions must prove that a (35) damaging falsehood was published with "actual malice"—that is, with knowledge that the statements were false, or with reckless disregard of whether they were true or not.

(40) Justice Byron R. White, writing for the new majority in the new ruling, says it is not enough to examine all the circumstances of publication that would indicate whether there was malicious (45) intent or not. It is proper and constitutional, he says, for "state-of-mind evidence" to be introduced. The court is thus ordering a CBS television producer to answer questions about the thought (50) processes that went into the preparation and airing of a segment of *60 Minutes*.

That six justices of the Supreme Court fail to see this as a breach of the First Amendment is frightening. The (55) novelist George Orwell may have been mistaken only in the timing of his vision of a Big Brother government practicing mind-control.

6. This article deals principally with

   A. the U.S. Supreme Court's decisions

   B. explaining the First Amendment to the Constitution

   C. an attack on the freedom of the press

   D. slander and libel laws

   E. Big Brother in government

7. How many justices would have to change their minds to reverse this decision?

   A. one

   B. two

   C. three

   D. four

   E. five

8. This writer feels the Supreme Court is wrong in this case because

   A. newspapers were unsophisticated when the First Amendment was written

   B. reporters are entitled to special rights

   C. it challenges the privacy of a journalist's mind

   D. Judge White has himself been accused of slander and libel

   E. the Supreme Court is capable of malicious intent

9. What does "actual malice" (line 36) mean?

   A. Knowledge that the statements were false

   B. Reckless disregard of whether the statements were true or not

   C. Either **A** or **B**

   D. Libel

   E. None of these

GO ON TO THE NEXT PAGE

219

Questions 10 and 11 refer to the following passage.

Sometimes the U.S. government goes out of its way to prove it can be an absolute nuisance. Take the case of Southern Clay, Inc., which has a factory
(5) at Paris, Tennessee, putting out a clay product for cat boxes best known as "Kitty Litter."

It's a simple enough process, but the federal Mine Safety and Health
(10) Administration insists that since clay comes from the ground—an excavation half a mile from the Kitty Litter plant— the company actually is engaged in mining and milling. Therefore, says MSHA,
(15) Southern Clay is subject to all the rules that govern, say, coal mines working in shafts several hundred feet down.

The company has been told to devise an escape system and fire-fighting pro-
(20) cedure in case there is a fire in its "mine." Southern Clay estimates it will lose 6,000 man-hours in production time giving its 250 factory workers special training in how to escape from a mine
(25) disaster.

One thing that has always impressed us about cats, in addition to their tidiness, is that they seem to watch the human world with a sense of wise and
(30) detached superiority, as though they wondered what the hustle and bustle is all about. If they grin from time to time, as some people insist, it's no wonder.

10. The author's purpose in writing this article is to

A. explain how Kitty Litter is produced

B. describe the Mine Safety and Health Administration

C. show how tidy cats are

D. show that the government can sometimes be a nuisance

E. describe how to prevent fires in mines

11. What does the author mean by the article's last sentence?

A. Cats sometimes laugh at their own tidiness.

B. Cats sometimes seem to be amused by human antics.

C. People sometimes appear to be laughing at the antics of cats.

D. Some people think cats are laughing at the Kitty Litter plant.

E. Some people think cats are laughing at the futility of fire-fighting procedures.

12. The Jesuit Antonio Vieira, missionary, diplomat, and voluminous writer, repeated the triumphs he had gained in Bahia and Lisbon in Rome, which proclaimed him the prince of Catholic orators. His two hundred sermons are a mine of learning and experience, and they stand out from all others by their imaginative power, originality of view, variety of treatment, and audacity of expression.

The author's attitude toward Vieira may be described as

A. spiritual

B. idolatrous

C. indifferent

D. admiring

E. critical

13. While the 65-mile-per-hour speed limit was in effect, it not only lowered the number of accidents, it also saved many lives. Yet, auto insurance rates did not reflect this decrease. Therefore, insurance companies made profits rather than lowering premiums.

This argument implies that

A. the 65-mile-per-hour limit was unfair

B. auto manufacturers agreed with insurance companies' policies

C. insurance companies were taking advantage of drivers

D. saving lives was of more importance than lowering premiums

E. driving skills improved greatly while the 65-mile-per-hour limit was in effect

14. We all know life originated in the ocean. Science tells us so. Perhaps a bolt of lightning struck through the ammonia and methane gases of a volcanic planet, igniting some form of life in the primordial soup of the storm-tormented sea. But no scientific theory is sacrosanct. And now a group of scientists says we have it all wrong: Life originated in clay.

The passage above

A. suggests that the earth began as clay, not water

B. argues that science has been wrong about a certain theory

C. implies that scientists are usually proven wrong

D. presents an alternative theory about the creation of life

E. denies the existence of life in the primordial ocean

15. What history teaches is this: that people and governments have never learned anything from history.

The statement above may be best described as a(n)

A. ironic contradiction

B. historical truism

C. effective anagram

D. derisive condemnation

E. pragmatic condolence

GO ON TO THE NEXT PAGE

Questions 16 and 17 refer to the following passage.

California once prided itself on being the state with the finest roads in the nation. That is no longer true. Our gas taxes took care of California's highway
(5) needs for years, but they no longer are adequate. One reason the present tax no longer covers the bill is that modern cars are using less fuel. The main factor, though, is that the cost of building and
(10) maintaining highways has gone way up while the tax has remained fixed.

Certainly, California streets, roads, and highways need help. Two-thirds of city streets and 77 percent of country
(15) roads are substandard. Ruts and potholes can be found almost everywhere, and the longer they go without repair, the more they will cost.

16. Which of the following best summarizes the passage?

  A. Deterioration of California's roads has resulted from increased costs and decreased funds.

  B. The quality of California roads is now second in the nation.

  C. Fuel-efficient cars cause more wear and tear on the roads than did cars of the past.

  D. Every road in the state is marred with potholes.

  E. Over three-quarters of California's roads are substandard.

17. Which of the following is NOT a problem stated by the passage?

  A. Inadequate tax revenue

  B. Ruts and potholes

  C. Increased cost of building highways

  D. A fixed gas-tax rate

  E. Demand for new highways

Questions 18 and 19 refer to the following passage.

At the outset of the Civil War, the North possessed a large population, a superior rail system, a greater industrial capacity, greater capital assets, and a
(5) larger food-production capability than did the South. Despite the North's apparent economic superiority, the South did possess a few military advantages. Among them were fighting a defensive
(10) war on their home ground and an established military tradition. Most of the leaders of the pre-war army were from the South, while the North had to train a new military leadership.

18. The final sentence of this passage functions in which of the following ways?

  A. To support the general contention that most of the talent in the United States is concentrated in the South

  B. To hint that the North found many of its military leaders in the South

  C. To argue that the North entered the war without leaders

  D. To further explain the South's "established military tradition"

  E. To show that the South probably should have won the war

19. The author implies which of the following points in the passage?

    A. The North did not have an economic advantage at the end of the war.

    B. Previous to the beginning of the war, the South was already fighting another war and seasoning its leaders.

    C. Almost all the banks in the United States were located in the North.

    D. Military advantages are much more important than economic advantages.

    E. The North had a greater capacity for enduring a prolonged conflict.

20. Few opticians have recognized the value of target practice for stimulating the eyes and improving vision. The value of a day on the rifle range surpasses that of a whole crop of fresh carrots.

    The writer assumes that his or her readers are already convinced that

    A. poor eyesight is a widespread problem

    B. target practice is enjoyable and useful

    C. carrots are good for the eyes

    D. most people should own guns

    E. the "day" mentioned is an eight-hour day

Questions 21 through 26 refer to the following passage.

(1) The Morrill Act (1862) extended the principle of federal support for public education, the earliest attempt being the Northwest Ordinance of 1787. (2)
(5) The Morrill Act established land-grant colleges in each state and specified a curriculum based on agriculture and mechanical arts. (3) Land-grant colleges often were a state's first institution of
(10) public higher education. (4) Public support and public control strengthened the concept of the state-university system. (5) The Civil Rights Act of 1875 was the first federal attempt to provide equal
(15) educational opportunity. (6) The progressive theories of John Dewey also had a profound effect on public education. (7) Dewey believed that education included the home, shop, neighborhood,
(20) church, and school. (8) However, industrialization was destroying the educational functions of these institutions. (9) Dewey believed that the public schools must be society's instrument for "shap-
(25) ing its own destiny." (10) To do this the schools had to be transformed in order to serve the interests of democracy.

21. If this passage were divided into two paragraphs, the second paragraph would begin with

    A. sentence 3

    B. sentence 5

    C. sentence 6

    D. sentence 7

    E. sentence 8

GO ON TO THE NEXT PAGE

22. The passage implies that one significant contrast between the Morrill Act and Dewey's theories was

    A. Dewey's lack of faith in land-grant colleges

    B. the fact that the Morrill Act was not a democratic law

    C. the neglect in the Morrill Act of education's relationship to society

    D. Dewey's lack of knowledge about the Morrill Act

    E. the Morrill Act's stress on a heavily agricultural and mechanical curriculum

23. The word "also" in sentence 6 does which of the following?

    A. Opens the question concerning whether Dewey himself would have supported certain government acts concerning education

    B. Makes clear that Dewey's theories were innovative and inconsistent with government policy

    C. Makes the point that Dewey's theories were somewhat identical to material in the Morrill Act

    D. Suggests that the Morrill Act, Northwest Ordinance, and Civil Rights Act had a profound influence on public education

    E. Suggests that Dewey's theories did more than affect public education

24. Which of the following statements, if true, would best support sentences 7 and 8?

    A. Home, shop, neighborhood, church, and school each played an ever-increasing role in the world of learning.

    B. Learning was equated exclusively with industrial progress, while moral, social, and artistic growth was undervalued.

    C. Industry was shaping the destiny of the citizens, and Dewey was a strong industrial supporter.

    D. Industry was transforming the schools so that they could serve the interests of democracy.

    E. Sentence 3

25. This passage would be LEAST likely to appear in which of the following?

    A. An encyclopedia article summarizing the major legislation of the nineteenth century

    B. A brief survey of legislation and theories that significantly affected education

    C. An introduction to the theories of John Dewey

    D. An argument about the benefits of both progressive legislation and progressive educational theory

    E. A discussion of the relationship between social needs and school curriculum

26. The passage allows us to conclude which of the following?

A. Beyond the legislation discussed in the passage, no other government acts addressed the issue of public education.

B. Theorists always have a more significant effect on education than legislators do.

C. The framers of the Morrill Act did not appreciate the value of moral education.

D. Dewey succeeded to some extent in transforming public education.

E. The state-university system was a concept long before it became a reality.

27. It is an important guideline to avoid discussing other students during a parent-teacher conference. Such comments often result in an emotional reaction by the parent and can interfere with the purpose of the conference.

Which of the following facts, if true, would most strengthen the argument of the passage above?

A. The discussion of other students gives many parents a comfortable sense that the teacher understands the whole classroom "scene."

B. Most parents avoid taking the trouble to attend a conference.

C. The child's relationship with other students is most often the cause of problems that necessitate a conference.

D. Researchers witnessing parent-teacher conferences have verified that parents become angry in ninety percent of the conferences in which other students are discussed.

E. Emotional reactions by parents must be understood as the parents' legitimate expression of deeply felt concerns.

GO ON TO THE NEXT PAGE

28. A test is valid if it measures what it is intended to measure. A test is reliable if it is consistent. Therefore, a test may be consistent even though it does not measure what it is intended to measure.

The author's primary purpose in this passage is to

A. contribute to recent research in testing validity and reliability

B. question whether we should use the terms "valid" and "reliable" to describe tests

C. insist that all tests must be both valid and reliable

D. call for the abolition of invalid tests

E. explain the difference between validity and reliability

29. "Open houses" should be offered, as they enable a school district to present the school programs to the community. Effective open-house activities can further community participation in the educational process.

Which of the following is an unstated assumption of the author of this passage?

A. Most participants in open-house activities do not take a whole-hearted interest in the enterprise.

B. Without an open house, no members of the community would be aware of the available school programs.

C. Open-house activities are very rarely effective.

D. Community participation has a positive effect on the educational process.

E. Many school districts never hold an open house.

30. The failure of the progressive movement to adjust to the transformation of the American society spelled its ultimate collapse. The progressive educational theories of the early 1900s did not take into consideration the technological expertise of the nuclear age.

Which of the following best expresses the point of this passage?

A. At one time, the progressive movement served well the needs of American education.

B. The progressive theories were not adaptable to late-twentieth-century progress.

C. The progressive movement collapsed soon after its heyday in the early 1900s.

D. The progressive movement was motivated by theories too conservative to be useful.

E. No American student these days could possibly benefit from progressive educational theory.

Questions 31, 32, and 33 refer to the following passage.

The doctrine of association had been the basis for explaining memories and how one idea leads to another. Aristotle provided the basic law, association by
(5) contiguity. We remember something be-cause in the past we have experienced that something together with something else. Seeing a shotgun may remind you of a murder, or it may remind you of
(10) a hunting experience in Wyoming, de-pending on your history. When you hear the word "table," you are likely to think of "chair." "Carrots" makes you think of "peas"; "bread" makes you think

(15) "butter"; and so on. In each case the two items have been experienced contiguously—in the same place or at the same time or both. Today the terms *stimulus* and *response* are used to (20) describe the two units that are associated by contiguity.

31. The author of the passage would agree with which of the following statements?

A. Many of the associations which Aristotle posited have become part of modern experience.

B. There are a number of adults who have had no experiences and who therefore have no memories.

C. When one smells coffee, one is not likely to think of eating a donut.

D. No one thing is necessarily associated with any other thing in particular.

E. Guns always remind people of an experience in which someone or something was killed.

32. Which of the following statements, if true, would most weaken the argument of the passage?

A. Many people tend to become depressed when the weather is rainy.

B. Only a very few researchers question the doctrine of association.

C. More recent studies show that word-association responses are random and not determined by experience.

D. Of 100 people tested, 96 of those given the word "bread" responded with the word "butter."

E. Psychologists have found that we have many common associations.

33. The argument of the passage is best strengthened by which of the following statements?

A. It is certainly possible to experience more than two items contiguously.

B. The terms *stimulus* and *response* were never used by Aristotle.

C. Those Londoners who endured the German "bombings" of World War II still become fearful when they hear a loud noise.

D. Some people think of "butter" when they hear "carrots."

E. Aristotle's own writing is full of very uncommon and unexplained associations.

Questions 34 through 38 refer to the following passage.

The question might be asked: how can we know what is "really" real? Defined phenomenologically, "reality" becomes purely a hypothetical concept which ac-
(5) counts for the totality of all conditions imposed by the external world upon an individual. But since other individuals are included in each of our fields of experi-ence, it does become possible as we make
(10) identification of similarly perceived phe-nomena to form consensus groups. In fact, we often tend to ignore and even push out of awareness those persons and their assumptions regarding what is real
(15) which do not correspond to our own. However, such a lack of consensus also affords us the opportunity of checking our hypothesis about reality. We may change our concepts about reality and
(20) thus in doing so facilitate changes in our phenomenal world of experience. Scientists, for instance, deliberately set

GO ON TO THE NEXT PAGE

out to get a consensus of both their procedures and their conclusions. If they are
(25) successful in this quest, their conclusions
are considered by the consensus group as
constituting an addition to a factual body
of sharable knowledge. This process is
somewhat in contrast, for example, to
(30) those religious experiences considered to
be mystical. By their nature they are not
always available for communication to
others. However, even the scientific re-
searcher must finally evaluate the conse-
(35) quences of his research in his own,
personal phenomenological field. To use
a cliché: truth as beauty exists in the eyes
of the beholder.

34. Which of the following is a specific
example supporting the point of the
passage?

   A. Certain established scientific facts
      have not changed for hundreds of
      years.

   B. Part of the phrase in the last
      sentence is from a poem by Keats.

   C. Reality is a given, unique
      experience in an individual's
      phenomenal world.

   D. We think of our enemies in war as
      cruel and regard our own soldiers
      as virtuous.

   E. The fans at baseball games often
      see things exactly as the umpire
      sees them.

35. Applying the argument of the passage,
we might define a political party as

   A. a political group to which few
      scientists belong

   B. a consensus group whose
      individuals share a similar view of
      political reality

   C. a consensus group whose members
      are deluded about what is really
      "real" politically

   D. in touch with reality if it is a
      majority party and out of touch
      with reality if it is a minority party

   E. a collection of individuals who are
      each fundamentally unsure about
      what political reality is

36. When the author says that "reality" is a
"hypothetical concept" (lines 3–4), he
or she means that

   A. as for reality, there is none

   B. we can think about reality but
      never really experience it

   C. "reality" is not objective

   D. "reality" is a figment of your
      imagination

   E. "reality" is known only by
      scientists

37. According to the passage, one difference between a scientist and a mystic is that

   A. the scientist sees truth as facts; the mystic sees truth as beauty

   B. scientists are unwilling and unable to lend importance to religious experiences

   C. the work of the mystic does not have consequences that affect individuals

   D. the scientist is concerned with sharable knowledge, and the mystic may not be

   E. the scientist cannot believe in anything mystical

38. To the question "how can we know what is 'really' real?" (lines 1–2), this author would probably answer in which of the following ways?

   A. If no one sees things our way, we are detached from reality.

   B. Whatever we are aware of can legitimately be called real.

   C. What is really real is whatever a group of individuals believes.

   D. We can, if we use the scientific method.

   E. We cannot know what is "really" real because reality varies with individual perspective.

Questions 39 and 40 refer to the following passage.

A lesson plan is basically a tool for effective teaching. Its primary importance is to present objectives and content in a logical and systematic manner; as such, it is an integral part of the instructional process.

39. Which of the following is an unstated assumption made by the author of this passage?

   A. All features of the instructional process should have the same logical, systematic qualities as the lesson plan.

   B. Students learn best when material is not presented in a disorganized or unplanned manner.

   C. A teacher who is not a logical, systematic thinker has no place in the instructional process.

   D. The lesson plan is by far the most important tool for effective teaching.

   E. Teachers should not deviate from the lesson plan in any case.

40. The author uses the word "integral" (line 4) to mean

   A. original

   B. whole

   C. essential

   D. not segregated

   E. modern

IF YOU FINISH BEFORE TIME IS CALLED, CHECK YOUR WORK ON THIS SECTION ONLY. DO NOT WORK ON ANY OTHER SECTION IN THE TEST.

Mathematics Test

TIME: 60 Minutes

40 Questions

Directions: Each of the questions or incomplete statements below is followed by five suggested answers or completions. Select the best answer or completion of the five choices given and fill in the corresponding lettered space on the answer sheet.

1. Which of the following fractions is the largest?

   A. $\frac{25}{52}$

   B. $\frac{31}{60}$

   C. $\frac{19}{40}$

   D. $\frac{51}{103}$

   E. $\frac{43}{90}$

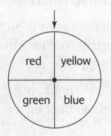

2. From the diagram of the spinner above, in spinning the spinner only once, what is the probability of spinning red, yellow, or blue?

   A. $\frac{1}{4}$

   B. $\frac{1}{3}$

   C. $\frac{1}{2}$

   D. $\frac{3}{4}$

   E. $\frac{3}{2}$

3. If $16\frac{1}{2}$ feet equal 1 rod, how many inches are there in 4 rods?

   A. $5\frac{1}{2}$

   B. 22

   C. 66

   D. 792

   E. 2,376

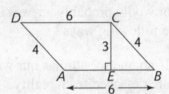

4. To compute the area of this figure, one would use

   A. 6×4

   B. 12×3

   C. 6×3

   D. $6 + 3$

   E. $4 \times (6 + 3)$

5. All of the following ratios are equal EXCEPT

    A. 1 to 4

    B. 3 to 8

    C. 2 to 8

    D. 3 to 12

    E. 4 to 16

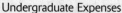

Undergraduate Expenses

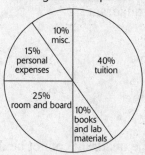

6. The chart above displays the costs in percentages associated with the average college undergraduate. If tuition for a given year is $19,200, how much is spent on books and lab materials?

    A. $1,920

    B. $4,000

    C. $4,800

    D. $5,600

    E. $6,400

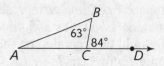

7. Given $\triangle ABC$ with $\angle BCD = 84°$ and $\angle B = 63°$, find the measure of $\angle A$ in degrees.

    A. 21

    B. 27

    C. 84

    D. 96

    E. 116

8. If Juan works 8 hours and receives $9.75 per hour and Mary works 24 hours and receives a total of $130, which of the following CANNOT be derived from the above statement?

    A. Juan's total

    B. Mary's wage per hour

    C. The difference between what Juan received and Mary received

    D. The average total received by Juan and Mary

    E. The hours Mary worked each day

9. If $3c = d$, then $c =$

    A. $3 + d$

    B. $3d$

    C. $\dfrac{d}{3}$

    D. $\dfrac{1}{3d}$

    E. $\dfrac{1+d}{3}$

Section **2** Mathematics Test

GO ON TO THE NEXT PAGE

10. On a map, 1 centimeter represents 35 kilometers. Two cities 245 kilometers apart would be separated on the map by how any centimeters?

   A.   5

   B.   7

   C.   9

   D.   210

   E.   280

11. Round off to the nearest tenth: 4316.136

   A.   4,320

   B.   4,216.14

   C.   4,316.13

   D.   4,316.106

   E.   4,316.1

12. Which of the following is a prime number?

   A.   9

   B.   13

   C.   15

   D.   21

   E.   24

13. The fraction $\frac{1}{8}$ is between the numbers listed in which of the following pairs?

   A. $\frac{1}{10}$ and $\frac{2}{17}$

   B.   0.1 and 0.12

   C.   0.08 and 0.1

   D.   1 and 2

   E. $\frac{1}{9}$ and $\frac{2}{15}$

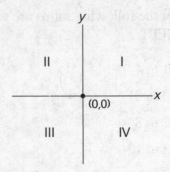

14. In the coordinate graph above, the point represented by (−3,4) would be found in which quadrant?

   A.   I

   B.   II

   C.   III

   D.   IV

   E.   The quadrant cannot be determined from the information given.

15. A class of 30 students all together have 60 pencils. Which of the following must be true?

   A.   Each student has 2 pencils.

   B.   Every student has a pencil.

   C.   Some students have only 1 pencil.

   D.   Some students have more pencils than do other students.

   E.   The class averages 2 pencils per student.

16. A man purchased 4 pounds of round steak priced at $3.89 per pound. How much change did he receive from a twenty-dollar bill?

   A. $4.34

   B. $4.44

   C. $4.46

   D. $15.56

   E. $44.66

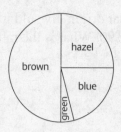

17. Sam tries to construct a pie graph representing eye color of his classmates. In his class of 24 students, 6 students have blue eyes, 12 students have brown eyes, 5 students have hazel eyes, and 1 student has green eyes. His teacher tells him that his graph (shown above) is not correct. In order to fix the graph, Sam should

   A. increase the amount of green and decrease the amount of blue

   B. increase the amount of blue and decrease the amount of hazel

   C. decrease the amount of blue and increase the amount of brown

   D. decrease the amount of hazel and increase the amount of brown

   E. increase the amount of hazel and increase the amount of blue

18. If D is between A and B on $\overleftrightarrow{AB}$, which of the following must be true?

   A. $AD = DB$

   B. $DB = AB - AD$

   C. $AD = AB + DB$

   D. $DB = AD + AB$

   E. None of the above

Questions 19 and 20 are based on the following graphs.

A COLLEGE STUDENT'S EXPENSES

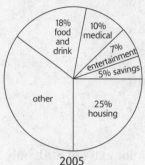

2005
Total Expenditure $30,000

2010
Total Expenditure $34,000

19. How much more money did this college student spend on medical expenses in 2010 than in 2005?

   A. $800–$900

   B. $900–$1,000

   C. $1,000–$1,100

   D. $1,100–$1,200

   E. $1,200–$1,300

GO ON TO THE NEXT PAGE

20. What was the approximate increase from 2005 to 2010 in the percentage spent on food and drink?

    A.   4%

    B.   18%

    C.   22%

    D.   40%

    E.   50%

21. In a senior class of 800, only 240 decide to attend the senior prom. What percentage of the senior class attended the senior prom?

    A.   8%

    B.   24%

    C.   30%

    D.   33%

    E.   80%

22. What is the probability of tossing a penny twice so that both times it lands heads up?

    A.   1/8

    B.   1/4

    C.   1/3

    D.   1/2

    E.   2/3

23. 0.0074 is how many times smaller than 740,000?

    A.   1,000,000

    B.   10,000,000

    C.   100,000,000

    D.   1,000,000,000

    E.   10,000,000,000

24. A suit that originally sold for $120 is on sale for $90. What is the rate of discount?

    A.   20%

    B.   25%

    C.   30%

    D. $33\frac{1}{3}\%$

    E.   75%

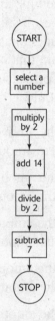

25. In the flow chart above, regardless of the number you select, the number at the end is always

    A. 5

    B. less than 14

    C. the same as the original number

    D. twice the original number

    E. an odd number

26. To change 3 miles to inches, you should

A. multiply 3 times 5,280

B. multiply 3 times 5,280 and then divide by 12

C. multiply 3 times 5,280 and then multiply by 12

D. divide 3 into 5,280 and then multiply by 12

E. divide 3 into 12 and then multiply by 5,280

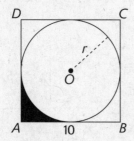

27. Circle *O* is inscribed in square *ABCD* as shown above. The area of the shaded region is closest to

A. 10

B. 25

C. 30

D. 50

E. 75

28. Today is Lucy's fourteenth birthday. Last year, she was three years older than twice Charlie's age at that time. Using *C* for Charlie's age now, which of the following can be used to determine Charlie's age now?

A. $13 - 3 = 2(C - 1)$

B. $14 - 3 = 2C$

C. $13 - 3 = 2C$

D. $13 + 3 = 2C$

E. $13 + 3 = 2(C - 1)$

29. Angela has nickels and dimes in her pocket. She has twice as many dimes as nickels. What is the best expression of the amount of money she has in cents if *x* equals the number of nickels she has?

A. $25x$

B. $10x + 5(2x)$

C. $x + 2x$

D. $5(3x)$

E. $20(x + 5)$

30. Four construction workers build a house containing 16 rooms. If the house has 4 floors and they take exactly 4 months (without stopping) to build it, then which of the following must be true?

I. They build 4 rooms each month.

II. Each floor has 4 rooms.

III. They build an average of 1 floor per month.

IV. The house averages 4 rooms per floor.

A. I and II only

B. II and III only

C. III and IV only

D. I, II, and III only

E. I, II, III, and IV

GO ON TO THE NEXT PAGE

Annual Number of Calls
to Emergency Services

Fire   Medical   Police

31. The annual number of calls to police emergency services exceeds the number of calls to medical emergency services by 200. Using the chart above, how many calls are made annually to emergency fire services?

    A.   4

    B.   200

    C.   400

    D.   600

    E.   800

32. A square 4 inches on a side is cut up into smaller squares 1 inch on a side. What is the maximum number of such squares that can be formed?

    A.   4

    B.   8

    C.   16

    D.   36

    E.   64

33. A 27-inch flat screen television set is marked down 20% to $320. Which of the following equations could be used to determine its original price, P?

    A. $\$320 - 0.20 = P$

    B. $0.20P = \$320$

    C. $P = \$320 + 0.20$

    D. $0.80P + 0.20P = \$320$

    E. $0.80P = \$320$

34. The areas of which of the following are equal?

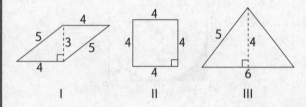

    I   II   III

    A.   I and II only

    B.   I and III only

    C.   II and III only

    D.   I, II, and III

    E.   None of them are equal.

35. Which of the following coordinate graphs displays a curved line passing through point (3,−2)?

A.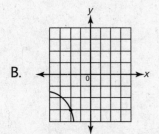

B.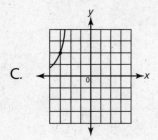

C.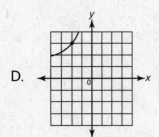

D.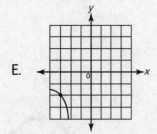

E.

Questions 36 and 37 refer to the following graph.

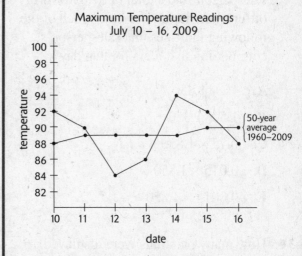

36. Of the seven days shown, about what percent of the days did the maximum temperature exceed the average temperature?

A. 3%

B. 4%

C. 43%

D. 57%

E. 93%

37. Between which two dates shown was the greatest increase in maximum temperature?

A. July 11–12

B. July 12–13

C. July 13–14

D. July 14–15

E. July 15–16

GO ON TO THE NEXT PAGE

38. A furniture salesperson earns a 15% commission on each sale. If the salesperson sold a total of $1,850 worth of furniture during one day, which of the following indicates that salesperson's commission in dollars for that day?

A. $15 \times 1,850$

B. $1.5 \times 1,850$

C. $0.15 \times 1,850$

D. $0.015 \times 1,850$

E. $0.0015 \times 1,850$

39. How many paintings were displayed at the County Museum of Art if 30% of them were by Monet and Monet was represented by 24 paintings?

A. 48

B. 50

C. 60

D. 76

E. 80

> The sum of two numbers equals one of the numbers.

40. If the above statement is true, which of the following best represents the relationship?

A. $x + y = y + x$

B. $(x)(y) = 1$

C. $x + y = 1$

D. $x + y = y$

E. $x + y = x + 1$

IF YOU FINISH BEFORE TIME IS CALLED, CHECK YOUR WORK ON THIS SECTION ONLY. DO NOT WORK ON ANY OTHER SECTION IN THE TEST.

Writing Test: Multiple-Choice Section

TIME: 30 Minutes

38 Questions

Part A

SUGGESTED TIME: 10 Minutes

21 Questions

Directions: Some of the following sentences are correct. Others contain problems in grammar, usage, idiom, diction, punctuation, and capitalization.

If there is an error, it will be underlined and lettered. Find the one underlined part that must be changed to make the sentence correct and choose the corresponding letter on your answer sheet. Mark **E** if the sentence contains no error.

1. The box of <u>nuts and bolts</u> <u>were</u> too
          A   B
   heavy for the little boy to carry <u>by</u>
                           C
   <u>himself</u>, so he asked <u>his</u> mother for
      C   D
   some help. <u>No error</u>
             E

2. <u>Not</u> able to keep a secret, <u>he announced</u>
    A   B
   the stupidity <u>of his friend</u> to the <u>whole</u>
               C   D
   class. <u>No error</u>
          E

3. <u>When</u> one wishes to be polite, <u>they</u>
      A   B
   must <u>refrain</u> from eating food with his
        C
   hands <u>when a knife</u> and fork have been
           D
   provided. <u>No error</u>
           E

4. During the examination, <u>two of the</u>
                     A
   <u>three hours</u> will be <u>allotted</u> for <u>writing</u>;
    A   B   C
   the third hour <u>would be</u> for editing your
               D
   work. <u>No error</u>
          E

5. The only <u>people</u> in the movie <u>theater</u> on
           A   B
   that stormy Monday night <u>were</u> the
                         C
   usher and <u>me</u>. <u>No error</u>
           D   E

6. Students who are <u>not</u> somewhat nervous
                A
   about taking an exam <u>tend to subvert</u>
                     B
   their ability by <u>their</u> very <u>nonchalance</u>.
               C   D
   <u>No error</u>
    E

GO ON TO THE NEXT PAGE

Section **3** Writing Test

7. The Japanese haiku form, <u>brief and</u>
A
<u>simple</u>, <u>lays somewhere</u> between the
A   B
<u>plainness</u> of a wish and the <u>elegance of</u>
C   D
a prayer. <u>No error</u>
E

8. The <u>anger of</u> the opposing candidates
A
<u>was obvious but</u> <u>neither</u> <u>of them</u>
B   C   D
insulted the other. <u>No error</u>
E

9. <u>Describing the auto accident</u> to a police
A
officer, Tim <u>hopped</u> onto a bus and <u>rode</u>
B   C
<u>away</u> from the wreck that <u>had once</u> been
C   D
his sleek, flawless Ferrari. <u>No error</u>
E

10. Everything that you, the voter, <u>needs</u> to
A
know about the candidates and <u>their</u>
B
opinions is contained in the <u>newly</u>
C
<u>published</u> voter information pamphlet
C
written by the <u>Secretary of State</u>.
D
<u>No error</u>
E

11. In opposition <u>to</u> President Bush's
A
foreign policy <u>were</u> the <u>house</u> Majority
B   C
Leader and the Chairman of the <u>Ways</u>
D
<u>and Means Committee</u>. <u>No error</u>
D   E

12. <u>Neither</u> my uncle <u>nor</u> my brother ever
A   B
refused to share <u>their</u> leisure time with
C
<u>me</u>, and so I was never short of
D
companions. <u>No error</u>
E

13. <u>By</u> speaking to millions about the high
A
incidence of heart attacks suffered by
unconditioned joggers, <u>Michael Rand</u>
B
persuades <u>one</u> to build speed and
C
endurance gradually and monitor their
<u>progress continually</u>. <u>No error</u>
D   E

14. Few scientists today expect <u>their</u>
A
discoveries to be compared with
<u>Einstein</u>, yet many work <u>hard</u> to advance
B   C
knowledge by <u>questioning and clarifying</u>
D
the major discoveries of the past.
<u>No error</u>
E

15. A strict and <u>highly disciplined</u>
A
upbringing had its <u>effect</u> on my cousin's
B
later life; he treated his own children
roughly and unfairly, intensifying <u>the</u>
C
<u>strictness</u> that he <u>had</u> experienced.
C   D
<u>No error</u>
E

16. Colin Powell, the former <u>Secretary</u>
    _A
    <u>of State</u>, once called for <u>bipartisan</u>
    _A   _B
    agreement <u>among</u> the members of
              _C
    Congress <u>whom</u>, he declared, were
             _D
    slowing his efforts toward peace.

    <u>No error</u>
    _E

17. Standing <u>alongside</u> my friend and <u>me</u> in
             _A   _B
    the hallway <u>were</u> Brad Pitt and
               _C
    Leonardo DiCaprio, but we <u>were</u> too
                              _D
    shy to step up and say hello. <u>No error</u>
                                  _E

18. By <u>understanding</u> what modern
       _A
    technology <u>would have lost</u> if the steam
               _B
    engine <u>would not have been</u> invented,
           _C
    we become certain that the Industrial

    Revolution <u>was</u> not an isolated and
               _D
    inconsequential event. <u>No error</u>
                           _E

19. Both opinions are <u>respectable, but</u> the
                      _A
    <u>one which</u> is supported by a specific
    _B
    plan <u>should</u> impress everyone as the
         _C
    <u>most</u> admirable. <u>No error</u>
    _D   _E

20. Only one <u>of the dozen</u> apartment <u>units</u> I
             _A   _B
    inspected <u>show</u> any neglect <u>on the part</u>
              _C   _D
    of the manager. <u>No error</u>
                    _E

21. At 6 a.m. <u>in the morning</u>, we trudged
             _A
    up the hill, <u>groggily</u> <u>looking</u> forward to
                 _B   _C
    a <u>fifteen-mile</u> hike. <u>No error</u>
      _D   _E

GO ON TO THE NEXT PAGE

Part B

SUGGESTED TIME: 20 Minutes

17 Questions

Directions: Some part of each sentence below is underlined; sometimes the whole sentence is underlined. Five choices for rephrasing the underlined part follow each sentence. The first choice, **A,** repeats the original, and the other four are different. If choice **A** seems better than the alternatives, choose answer **A;** if not, choose one of the others.

For each sentence, consider the requirements of standard written English. Your choice should be a correct, concise, and effective expression, not awkward or ambiguous. Focus on grammar, word choice, sentence construction, and punctuation. If a choice changes the meaning of the original sentence, do not select it.

22. Neither Barbara nor her friends is invited to pledge the local sorority.

    A. is invited to pledge the local sorority

    B. are invited to pledge the local sorority

    C. is pledging the local sorority

    D. are pledging the local sorority

    E. will pledge the local sorority

23. As the shrill, piercing sound of the sirens approached, several of my neighbors' dogs start to howl.

    A. approached, several of my neighbors' dogs start

    B. approached, several of my neighbors' dogs started

    C. approach, several of my neighbors' dogs starts

    D. approach, several of my neighbors' dogs start

    E. approach, several dogs of my neighbor started

24. On arriving at Los Angeles International Airport, his friends met him and took him immediately to his speaking engagement.

    A. On arriving at Los Angeles International Airport, his friends met him and took him immediately to his speaking engagement.

    B. Arriving at Los Angeles International Airport, his friends who met him immediately took him to his speaking engagement.

    C. When he arrived at Los Angeles International Airport, his friends met him and took him immediately to his speaking engagement.

    D. When he arrived at Los Angeles International Airport, he was taken immediately to his speaking engagement.

    E. After arriving at Los Angeles International Airport, he was immediately taken to his speaking engagement.

25. Among the members of the legal profession, there are <u>many who try to keep their clients out of court</u> and save them money.

  A. many who try to keep their clients out of court

  B. ones who try to keep their clients out of court

  C. they who try to keep their clients out of court

  D. many of whom try to keep their clients out of court

  E. a few who try to keep their clients out of court

26. <u>Whatever he aspired to achieve, they</u> were thwarted by his jealous older brothers.

  A. Whatever he aspired to achieve, they

  B. Whatever he had any aspirations to, they

  C. Whatever aspirations he had

  D. Whatever be his aspirations, they

  E. Many of his aspirations and goals

27. <u>Neither the scientists nor the ecologists knows</u> how to deal with the lethal effects of nuclear power plant explosions.

  A. Neither the scientists nor the ecologists knows

  B. Neither the scientists nor the ecologists know

  C. Neither the scientists or the ecologists know

  D. Neither the scientists together with the ecologists knows

  E. Not the scientists or the ecologists know

28. The job application did not state <u>to whom to be sent the personal references</u>.

  A. to whom to be sent the personal references

  B. to who the personal references should be sent

  C. to whom to send the personal references

  D. to whom the personal references will be sent

  E. to whom to send the personal references to

GO ON TO THE NEXT PAGE

Section 3 Writing Test

29. After battling hypertension for years, Paul Nguyen was relieved by the results of <u>his doctor's annual physical examination, which</u> indicated his blood pressure was normal.

    A. his doctor's annual physical examination, which

    B. his annual physical examination, that

    C. his annual physical examination, which

    D. an annual physical examination by his doctor, which

    E. his doctor's annual physical examination that

30. When the Democratic Party was the minority party, <u>its ability to win a presidential election was determined by the number of Republican and independent voters it attracts</u>.

    A. its ability to win a presidential election was determined by the number of Republican and independent voters it attracts

    B. its ability to win a presidential election is determined by the number of Republican and independent voters it attracts

    C. its ability to win a presidential election has been determined by the number of Republican and independent voters it attracts

    D. the number of Republican and independent voters it attracts determines its ability to win a presidential election

    E. the number of Republican and independent voters it attracted determined its ability to win a presidential election

31. Because she worked the night shift, <u>arriving at 10 p.m. and leaving at 6 a.m.</u>

    A. arriving at 10 p.m. and leaving at 6 a.m.

    B. having arrived at 10 p.m. and leaving at 6 a.m.

    C. she arrived at 10 p.m. and left at 6 a.m.

    D. with an arrival at 6 and a departure at 10

    E. from 10 p.m. to 6 a.m.

32. <u>Laying low in the tall jungle grass was</u> a lion and his mate, both waiting for the opportunity to catch some food.

    A. Laying low in the tall jungle grass was

    B. The tall jungle grass concealing their low-lying bodies,

    C. In the tall jungle grass, laying low, were

    D. Lying low in the tall jungle grass,

    E. Lying low in the tall jungle grass were

33. <u>Planning a career in business is often easier than to pursue it.</u>

- **A.** Planning a career in business is often easier than to pursue it.
- **B.** To plan a career in business is often easier than pursuing it.
- **C.** Planning a business career is often easier than pursuing it.
- **D.** The planning of a business career is often easier than its pursuit.
- **E.** A business career plan is often easier than a business career.

34. A fight broke out when the foreign ambassador <u>took a joke serious and punched the jokester hardly</u>.

- **A.** took a joke serious and punched the jokester hardly
- **B.** took a joke seriously and hardly punched the jokester
- **C.** hardly took a joke and seriously punched the jokester
- **D.** took a joke seriously and punched the jokester hard
- **E.** gave a hard punch to a serious jokester

35. The public soon became outraged at <u>the Cabinet member whom betrayed the public trust</u>, and they demanded his ouster.

- **A.** the Cabinet member whom betrayed the public trust
- **B.** the untrustworthy Cabinet member
- **C.** the Cabinet member with whom they betrayed the public trust
- **D.** the Cabinet member who, after betraying the public trust
- **E.** the Cabinet member who betrayed the public trust

36. Opinions about the ballot issue, of course, <u>varies according with the ethnic and economic status</u> of each voter.

- **A.** varies according with the ethnic and economic status
- **B.** varies according to ethnic and economic status
- **C.** changes with ethnicity and the economy
- **D.** vary according to the ethnic and economic status
- **E.** vary according to ethnic and economical status

GO ON TO THE NEXT PAGE

37. While declaring his support for a nuclear weapons freeze, <u>a small bomb exploded some distance from the Cabinet minister, who was startled but unharmed</u>.

   A. a small bomb exploded some distance from the Cabinet minister, who was startled but unharmed

   B. a small bomb startled the Cabinet minister, but did not harm him

   C. a small bomb startled the Cabinet minister from a distance, but did not harm him

   D. the Cabinet minister was startled by a bomb that exploded some distance from him, but unharmed

   E. the Cabinet minister was startled but unharmed by a small bomb that exploded some distance from him

38. Several disgruntled visitors had left the board meeting <u>before it had considered the new municipal tax cut</u>.

   A. before it had considered the new municipal tax cut

   B. before it considered the new municipal tax cut

   C. before the members considered the new municipal tax cut

   D. with the consideration of the new municipal tax cut yet to come

   E. previous to the new municipal tax cut

IF YOU FINISH BEFORE TIME IS CALLED, CHECK YOUR WORK ON THIS SECTION ONLY. DO NOT WORK ON ANY OTHER SECTION IN THE TEST.

STOP

Writing Test: Essay Section

TIME: 30 Minutes

1 Essay

Directions: In this section, you will have 30 minutes to plan and write one essay on the topic given. You may use the paper provided to plan your essay before you begin writing. You should plan your time wisely. Read the topic carefully to make sure that you are properly addressing the issue or situation. **You must write on the given topic. An essay on another topic will not be acceptable.**

The essay question is designed to give you an opportunity to write clearly and effectively. Use specific examples whenever appropriate to aid in supporting your ideas. Keep in mind that the quality of your writing is much more important than the quantity.

Your essay is to be written in the space provided. No other paper may be used. Your writing should be neat and legible. Because you have only a limited amount of space in which to write, please do **not** skip lines, do **not** write excessively large, and do **not** leave wide margins.

Remember, use the bottom of this page for any organizational notes you may wish to make.

Topic

Think of a friendship that you've made anytime during your lifetime that you now realize was or is important to you. In the space provided, write an essay explaining why that friendship is or was so important to you.

GO ON TO THE NEXT PAGE

Answer Key for Practice Test 2

Reading Test

1. D	21. C
2. A	22. E
3. D	23. D
4. D	24. B
5. D	25. A
6. C	26. D
7. B	27. D
8. C	28. E
9. C	29. D
10. D	30. B
11. B	31. D
12. D	32. C
13. C	33. C
14. D	34. D
15. A	35. B
16. A	36. C
17. E	37. D
18. D	38. E
19. E	39. B
20. C	40. C

Mathematics Test

1. B	21. C
2. D	22. B
3. D	23. C
4. C	24. B
5. B	25. C
6. C	26. C
7. A	27. A
8. E	28. A
9. C	29. A
10. B	30. C
11. E	31. E
12. B	32. C
13. E	33. E
14. B	34. B
15. E	35. A
16. B	36. D
17. B	37. C
18. B	38. C
19. C	39. E
20. A	40. D

Writing Test Multiple-Choice

1. B	21. A
2. E	22. B
3. B	23. B
4. D	24. C
5. D	25. A
6. E	26. C
7. B	27. B
8. B	28. C
9. A	29. D
10. A	30. E
11. C	31. C
12. C	32. E
13. C	33. C
14. B	34. D
15. E	35. E
16. D	36. D
17. E	37. E
18. C	38. C
19. D	
20. C	

Scoring Your PPST Practice Test 2

To score your PPST Practice Test 2, total the number of correct responses for each test. Do not subtract any points for questions attempted but missed, as there is no penalty for guessing. The scores for each section range from 150 to 190. Because the Writing Test contains multiple-choice questions and an essay, that score is a composite score adjusted to give approximately equal weight to the number right on the multiple-choice section and to the essay score. The essay is scored holistically (a single score for overall quality) from 1 (low) to 6 (high). Each of two readers gives a 1 to 6 score. The score that the essay receives is the sum of these two readers' scores.

Analyzing your test results

The following charts should be used to carefully analyze your results and spot your strengths and weaknesses. The complete process of analyzing each subject area and each individual question should be completed for this Practice Test. These results should be reexamined for trends in types of error (repeated errors) or poor results in specific subject areas. **This reexamination and analysis is of tremendous importance for effective test preparation.**

Practice Test 2: Subject area analysis sheet

	Possible	Completed	Right	Wrong
Reading Test	40			
Mathematics Test	40			
Writing Test	38			
TOTAL	118			

Analysis—tally sheet for questions missed

One of the most important parts of test preparation is analyzing why you missed a question so that you can reduce the number of mistakes. Now that you have taken Practice Test 2 and checked all your answers, carefully tally your mistakes by marking each of them in the proper column.

	Total Missed	Simple Mistake	Misread Problem	Lack of Knowledge
Reading Test				
Mathematics Test				
Writing Test				
TOTAL				

Reviewing the data in the preceding chart should help you determine why you are missing certain questions. Now that you have pinpointed types of errors, focus on avoiding your most common type.

Score approximators

Reading Test

To approximate your reading score:

1. Count the number of questions you answered correctly.

2. Use the following table to match the number of correct answers and the corresponding approximate score range.

Number Right	Approximate Score Range
10–19	160–169
20–29	170–179
30–40	180–189

Remember, this is only an approximate score range. When you take the PPST, you will have questions that are similar to those in this book; however some questions may be slightly easier or more difficult.

Mathematics Test

To approximate your mathematics score:

1. Count the number of questions you answered correctly.

2. Use the following table to match the number of correct answers and the corresponding approximate score range.

Number Right	Approximate Score Range
0–10	150–160
11–20	161–170
21–30	171–180
31–40	181–190

Remember, this is an approximate score range.

Writing Test

These scores are difficult to approximate because the multiple-choice section score and the essay score are combined to give a total score.

Essay checklist

Use this checklist to evaluate your essay.

Diagnosis/prescription for timed writing exercise

A good essay will:

- ❑ Address the assignment

  Be well focused

- ❑ Be well organized

  Have smooth transitions between paragraphs

  Be coherent, unified

- ❑ Be well developed

  Contain specific examples to support points

- ❑ Be grammatically sound (only minor flaws)

  Use correct sentence structure

  Use correct punctuation

  Use standard written English

- ❑ Use language skillfully

  Use a variety of sentence types

  Use a variety of words

- ❑ Be legible

  Have clear handwriting

  Be neat

Answers and Explanations for Practice Test 2

Reading Test

1. **D.** The author's entire argument is based on the recent studies indicating a downward trend in aptitude test scores. By extension, the author must assume that such studies are accurate.

2. **A.** The phrase *bowl of oatmeal* is used sarcastically to condemn the actions of the city council. Choice **B** is not correct as the situation is certainly not *tragic*.

3. **D.** Trends showing that within two years a single-family dwelling will be unaffordable by the average family indicate that not only must housing costs be going up, but the average family income will not meet the increased cost of housing.

4. **D.** Both statements I and III weaken the author's argument. Statement I, if true, suggests that, in fact, there will be affordable single-family homes for the average family. Statement III suggests that average families may find it difficult to afford renting an apartment, thus weakening the author's final sentence.

5. **D.** Both statements I and II are assumed by the author. First, the present trend (rise in housing cost) will continue, and second, families will turn to renting apartments (instead of, say, buying mobile homes or condominiums).

6. **C.** In both the introductory and final paragraphs, the writer is concerned with attacks on the First Amendment and throughout the article emphasizes this concern with a detailed look at what he or she thinks is an attack on a particular group, the press, that is guaranteed a certain amount of freedom by that amendment. Therefore, choices **A** and **B** are much too broad, and choices **D** and **E** are supporting ideas rather than principal ideas; *slander and libel laws* and *Big Brother in government* are mentioned only briefly.

7. **B.** Line 16 says a *6-3 ruling*. So if two justices change their minds, we would have a 4-5 ruling for the other side.

8. **C.** Lines 17–18 say that reporters *now face a challenge to the privacy of their minds,* and the last sentence in the passage is a statement against *mind-control.* All other choices are not explicitly supported by material in the passage.

9. **C.** As is stated in lines 36–39, actual malice is *with knowledge that the statements were false, or with reckless disregard of whether they were true or not.*

10. **D.** As is often the case, the first sentence states the main idea of the passage. Choice **A** is incorrect, both because it is too narrow and because the passage tells the reader only that Kitty Litter is made from clay and does not tell how it is produced. Choice **B** is also too narrow. Choice **C** is incorrect because only one sentence mentions this fact. Choice **E** is incorrect because the article does not describe a method for preventing fires.

11. **B.** The *they* in this sentence refers to *cats* in the first sentence of the paragraph. That first sentence describes cats watching the *hustle and bustle* with a sense of *superiority*. Given this information, we may infer that the grin described in the last sentence comes from watching the *hustle and bustle* of human antics, in this case, the antics of the U.S. government making itself a nuisance. Notice that all choices except **B** may be eliminated, if only because each describes cats *laughing* instead of grinning.

12. **D.** The tone of the author concerning Vieira is certainly positive but not so much as to be idolatrous or spiritual. *Admiring* is the best choice.

13. **C.** Since fewer accidents did not result in lower premiums, one suggestion of the passage is that insurance companies pocketed the savings rather than passing them on to the consumer. Thus, the author implies that insurance companies took advantage of drivers.

14. **D.** The brief passage introduces the possibility that life may have begun in clay instead of in water as scientists have believed. Choices **B, C,** and **E** are much too strong to be supported by the passage, and choice **A** refers to the earth instead of to life.

15. **A.** The first part of the quotation begins, *What history teaches is this . . .* , implying that we have something to learn from history. The second part goes on to state that we *never learned anything from history*. This is a contradiction using irony.

16. **A.** Choice **A** best summarizes the passage, citing two supporting points for the main idea—that California's roads have deteriorated. Choice **E** is incomplete, and the *over three-quarters* is correct only in reference to the state's country roads.

17. **E.** All the other choices are mentioned in the passage except the demand for new highways.

18. **D.** The sentence explains that the established military tradition supplied the South with military leaders.

19. **E.** The Northern advantages are all long-term, especially food production. Each of the other choices draws a conclusion beyond any implications in the passage.

20. **C.** By mentioning carrots in connection with improved eyesight and not explaining that implied connection, the author is assuming that readers readily see the connection.

21. **C.** Sentence 6 introduces a new topic; it shifts from a discussion of education legislation in general to a discussion of John Dewey in particular.

22. **E.** Sentence 7 stresses Dewey's belief that education is concerned with many areas and experiences. This belief contrasts with the Morrill Act's stress on agricultural and mechanical arts as primary educational areas.

23. **D.** *Also* indicates that Dewey's theories are being discussed in addition to previous information and that reference to the previous information is included in the statement about Dewey.

24. **B.** Dewey's belief in a comprehensive education is inconsistent with a focus on industrialization, and choice **B** explains that inconsistency, thus supporting the statement that industrialization is destructive.

25. A. The passage is about education and some related legislation but not about legislation in general.

26. D. We are told that Dewey's theories *had a profound effect on public education*. Each of the other choices draws a conclusion beyond the scope of the passage.

27. D. The passage states that discussion of other students has a negative effect on parents and on the conference; the fact expressed in choice **D** directly validates this assertion.

28. E. Each of the other choices introduces information well beyond the scope of the passage.

29. D. The author favors community participation in education; therefore, he or she must assume that such participation has a positive effect.

30. B. If we replace *late-twentieth-century progress* in choice **B** with the synonymous term used in the passage, *technological expertise of the nuclear age,* we see that **B** clearly reiterates the point of the passage.

31. D. Choice **C** flatly contradicts the argument of the passage, and **A** and **B** present information not touched on in the passage. Choice **E** is weak because associations are not universal; they depend on each individual's personal experience. This point—that associations are personal rather than universal—is expressed by **D.**

32. C. Choice **C** directly contradicts the point of the passage, which is that associations are determined by experience.

33. C. Choices **D** and **E** neither weaken nor strengthen the passage, simply suggesting other examples of associations without explaining the stimulus that produced them; **A** and **B** are irrelevant issues. Choice **C** strengthens the argument of the passage by citing an example of experience reinforcing an association—or, in other words, stimulating a response.

34. D. The point of the passage is that "reality" varies according to who experiences it and what "consensus group" he or she is a member of. Along this line, a war is a conflict between two different consensus groups, and so the example given by **D** is appropriate.

35. B. Both choices **B** and **C** mention a consensus group, but **C** says that the members of the group are deluded about reality, which contradicts the author's argument that no view of reality is, strictly speaking, a delusion.

36. C. Once again, the point of the passage is that different people or groups acquire different versions of reality based on their differing experiences. Reality is therefore subjective but not a mere figment of imagination.

37. D. This choice is validated by sentences 8 and 9 (lines 24–31) of the passage.

38. E. This choice has been explained in the discussions of questions 34 and 36.

39. B. By citing the value of planning the presentation of material in an orderly way, the author must assume that such organized instruction is beneficial. Each of the other choices draws conclusions beyond the scope of the passage.

40. C. None of the other choices makes good sense when substituted for *integral,* and *essential* is one of the meanings of *integral.*

Mathematics Test

1. **B.** Only choice **B**, $\frac{31}{60}$, is greater than $\frac{1}{2}$. All the other choices are less than $\frac{1}{2}$.

2. **D.** There are 3 chances out of 4 of spinning either red, yellow, or blue. Thus, the correct answer is 3/4.

3. **D.** $4 \text{ rods} = (4)\left(16\frac{1}{2}\right) = 66 \text{ feet}$

   $66 \text{ feet} \times 12 = 792 \text{ inches}$

4. **C.** Figure $ABCD$ is a parallelogram. The formula for the area of a parallelogram is area equals base times height. Since the base is 6 and the height (a perpendicular drawn to the base) is 3, the area would be computed by 6×3, or answer **C**.

5. **B.** Ratios may be expressed as fractions. Thus choice **A,** 1 to 4, may be expressed as $\frac{1}{4}$. Notice that **C, D,** and **E** are all fractions that reduce to $\frac{1}{4}$.

$$\frac{2}{8} = \frac{1}{4}$$
$$\frac{3}{12} = \frac{1}{4}$$
$$\frac{4}{16} = \frac{1}{4}$$

   Only **B** does not equal $\frac{1}{4}$.

6. **C.** On the chart, tuition is 40% of total expenses. Books and lab materials represent 10%, so they are exactly one-quarter of tuition. Since tuition is \$19,200 for the year, books and lab materials are one-quarter of that, or \$19,200 divided by 4 = \$4,800.

7. **A.** $\angle BCD = \angle A + \angle B$ (exterior angle of a triangle equals the sum of the opposite two angles). Then $84 = \angle A + 63°$, and $\angle A = 21°$.

8. **E.** Mary worked a total of 24 hours, but we do not know in how many days. Therefore, we cannot derive the number of hours she worked each day. Each of the other choices can be derived from the statement.

9. **C.** $3c = d$

   $$\frac{3c}{3} = \frac{d}{3}$$
   $$c = \frac{d}{3}$$

10. **B.** This question requires that you use a proportion.

$$\frac{\text{map (cm)}}{\text{actual (km)}} : \frac{1}{35} = \frac{x}{245}$$
$$35x = 245$$
$$x = 7$$

11. **E.** The tenth place is the number immediately to the right of the decimal point. To round off to the nearest tenth, check the hundredth place (two places to the right of the decimal point). If the hundredth number is a 5 or higher, round the tenth up to the next number. For instance, 0.36 would round to 0.4. If the hundredth is a 4 or lower, simply drop any places after the tenth place. For instance, 0.74356 would round to 0.7. Thus, 4,316.136 rounded to the nearest tenth is 4,316.1, which is answer choice **E.**

12. **B.** A prime number is a number that can be divided evenly only by itself and the number 1. Choices **A, C, D,** and **E** can all be divided evenly by 3. Answer choice **B,** 13, can be divided evenly only by itself and 1.

13. **E.** The fraction $\frac{1}{8}$ equals 0.125.

$$8\overline{)1.000} \quad .125$$

Thus it would lie between $\frac{1}{9}$ (0.111) and $\frac{2}{15}$ (0.133).

14. **B.** Points plotted on a coordinate graph are expressed (x,y), where x indicates the distance right or left and y indicates the distance up or down. Thus $(-3,4)$ means 3 "steps" left and then 4 "steps" up. This will place the point in quadrant II.

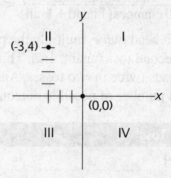

15. **E.** The only statement that *must* be true is **E,** "The class averages 2 pencils per student." Notice that 30 students could each have 2 pencils; so **C** and **D** may be false. Likewise, just one of the students could have all 60 pencils; therefore, **A** and **B** may be false. Only **E** *must* be true.

16. **B.** Four pounds of round steak at $3.89 per pound cost $15.56. Change from a twenty-dollar bill would therefore be $20.00 − $15.56, or $4.44.

17. **B.** In order to have the pie graph represent blue-eyed students as 6 out of 24, the piece of the "pie" representing blue-eyed students should be $\frac{6}{24}$, or $\frac{1}{4}$. So the blue piece needs to be increased. Likewise, for hazel to represent $\frac{5}{24}$, its piece of the pie should be slightly less than $\frac{6}{24}$, so its size should be decreased.

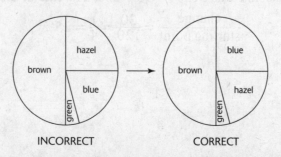

INCORRECT   CORRECT

18. B. Since D is between A and B on $\overleftrightarrow{AB}$, we know that the sum of the lengths of the smaller segments $\overline{AD}$ and $\overline{DB}$ is equal to the length of the larger segment $\overline{AB}$.

Hence,

$$AB = AD + DB$$

$$AB - AD = AD + DB - AD$$

$$AB - AD = DB$$

19. C. In 2005, 10% of $30,000, or $3,000, was spent on medical. In 2010, 12% of $34,000, or $4,080, was spent on medical. Thus, there was an increase of $1,080.

20. A. There was an increase from 18% to 22%, or 4%.

21. C. 240 out of 800 can be expressed $\frac{240}{800}$, which reduces to $\frac{3}{10}$, or 30%.

22. B. The probability of throwing a head in one throw is

$$\frac{\text{chance of a head}}{\text{total chances}(1\,\text{head} + 1\,\text{tail})} = \frac{1}{2}$$

Since you are trying to throw a head *twice*, multiply the probability for the first toss (1/2) times the probability for the second toss (again, 1/2). Thus, (1/2)(1/2) = (1/4), and 1/4 is the probability of throwing heads twice in two tosses. Another way of approaching this problem is looking at the total number of possible outcomes.

	First Toss	Second Toss
1.	H	H
2.	H	T
3.	T	H
4.	T	T

Thus there are four different possible outcomes. There is only one way to throw two heads in two tosses. Thus the probability of tossing two heads in two tosses is 1 out of 4 total outcomes, or 1/4.

23. C. Changing 740,000 to 0.0074 requires moving the decimal point 8 places to the left. This is the same as multiplying by 1/100,000,000. This is the same as saying it is 100,000,000 times smaller.

24. B. The amount of discount was $120 − $90 = $30. The rate of discount equals

$$\frac{\text{change}}{\text{starting point}} = \frac{30}{120} = \frac{1}{4} = 25\%$$

25. C. The final number is always the same as the number selected. For instance, try 10:

$$10 \times 2 = 20$$
$$20 + 14 = 34$$
$$34 \div 2 = 17$$
$$17 - 7 = 10$$

Or do it algebraically:

Select a number	x
Multiply by 2	$2x$
Add 14	$2x + 14$
Divide by 2	$x + 7$
Subtract 7	x

26. C. To change 3 miles to feet, simply multiply 3 times 5,280 (since 5,280 is the number of feet in a mile). This computation will give the number of feet in 3 miles. Then multiply this product by 12, since there are 12 inches in each foot. The resulting product will be the number of inches in 3 miles.

27. A. There are several approaches to this problem. One solution is to first find the area of the square: $10 \times 10 = 100$. Then subtract the approximate area of the circle: $A = \pi(r)^2 \approx 3(5^2) = 3(25) = 75$. Therefore, the total area inside the square but outside the circle is approximately 25. One quarter of that area is shaded. Therefore $\frac{25}{4}$ is approximately the shaded area. The closest answer is **A, 10.**

A more efficient method is to first find the area of the square: $10 \times 10 = 100$. Then divide the square into four equal sections as follows.

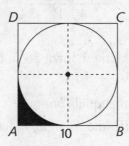

Since a quarter of the square is 25, the only possible answer choice for the shaded area is **A, 10.**

28. A. If today Lucy is 14, then last year she was 13. Likewise, if Charlie's age now is C, then last year he was $C - 1$. Now, put these into an equation.

$$\underbrace{\text{Lucy's age last year}}_{13} \underset{=}{\overset{\downarrow}{\text{ is }}} \underbrace{\text{three years older than Charlie's age last year}}_{2(C-1)+3}$$

Transposing, $13 - 3 = 2(C - 1)$.

29. A. The number of nickels that Angela has is x. Thus, the total value of those nickels (in cents) is $5x$. Angela also has twice as many dimes as nickels, or $2x$. The total value in cents of those dimes is $2x(10)$, or $20x$. Adding together the value of the nickels and dimes gives $5x + 20x$, or $25x$.

30. C. Only statements III and IV *must* be true. If the house has 4 floors and it takes exactly 4 months to build the house, the workers average 1 floor per month. And since the house has 16 rooms on 4 floors, the house averages 4 rooms per floor $\left(\frac{16}{4} = 4\right)$. However, I and II may not necessarily be true. To build 16 rooms in 4 months' time, the workers may not necessarily work at a steady pace, building 4 each month. They may, for example, build 5 rooms one month and 3 the next. Although they *average* 4 rooms per month, they don't have to build exactly 4 rooms each month. Likewise in II, just because a house *averages* 4 rooms on each floor does not mean the house necessarily has exactly 4 rooms on each floor. For example, the house could be built to have 6 rooms on the first floor, 3 rooms on the second and third floors, and 4 rooms on the top floor, which gives a total of 16 rooms.

31. E. The question states that 200 more emergency police calls are made annually than emergency medical calls. Police calls are represented on the chart by 3 telephones, and medical calls are represented by 2 telephones. Since the difference between them is 1 telephone, each telephone represents 200 emergency calls. Thus, because calls for fires are represented by 4 telephones, $4 \times 200 = 800$ calls for emergency fire services.

32. C. The maximum number of squares 1 inch by 1 inch will be 16.

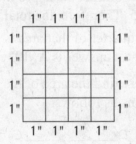

33. E. If the flat screen television is marked down 20%, then its current price is 80% of its original price. Thus, $0.80P = \$320$.

34. B. The area of I, the parallelogram, equals bh, or $4 \times 3 = 12$. The area of II, the square, equals s^2, or $4^2 = 16$. The area of III, the triangle, equals $\frac{1}{2}bh$, or $\frac{1}{2}(6)(4) = 12$. Thus, I and III are equal.

35. A. To locate the position of a point on a coordinate graph, you must know that the point's location is given in terms of (x,y). The first number is the x-coordinate, and it indicates the distance along the x-axis to the right or left of the origin (0). The second number is the y-coordinate, which indicates the distance up or down along the y-axis. Thus, the point $(3,-2)$ is 3 units to the right of the origin and 2 units down. The only curve that passes through that point is the curve in choice **A.**

36. D. There were 4 days (July 10, 11, 14, and 15) on which the maximum temperature exceeded the average; thus, $\frac{4}{7}$ is approximately 57%.

37. C. The maximum temperature rose from 86° to 94° from July 13 to July 14. This increase was the greatest.

38. C. To determine the salesperson's commission for that day, multiply 15% times $1,850. Fifteen percent is expressed in decimal form by 0.15, so the answer is 0.15×1850.

39. E. To solve this problem use a proportion:

Actual Paintings   % Numbers

$$\frac{\text{Part}}{\text{Whole}} \quad : \quad \frac{24}{x} = \frac{30}{100}$$

Cross multiply $30x = 2{,}400$
Divide each side by 30 $x = 80$
You could have also used

$$\frac{\text{"is"}}{\text{"of"}} = \frac{\% \text{ number}}{100}$$

The problem can be restated as 24 is 30% of what?

Therefore, 24 is the "is," 30 is the percent number, and "what" (the unknown) is the "of." Plugging into the equation, we get

$$\frac{24}{x} = \frac{30}{100}$$

and proceed as before.

40. D. The word *sum* indicates addition. The sum of two numbers is therefore $x + y$. If this sum equals one of the numbers, then the equation will be either $x + y = x$ or $x + y = y$.

Writing Test: Multiple-Choice Section

Part A

1. B. The subject is singular, *box*, so the verb must be singular, *was* instead of *were*.

2. E. This sentence contains no error.

3. B. *They* is meant to refer back to *one;* since *one* is singular, *they* (a plural) is incorrect. The correct pronoun is *one* or *he*.

4. D. The second verb, *would be,* must be the same tense as the first verb, *will be*. So *would be* must be changed to *will be*.

5. D. *Me* should be changed to *I*.

6. E. This sentence contains no error.

7. B. *Lays* should be changed to *lies,* which is correct when there is no object of the verb.

8. B. A comma is needed after *obvious* separating the two parts of the compound sentence joined by the conjunction.

9. **A.** *Describing* should be changed to *having described* or *after describing*. Otherwise, the sentence seems to say that Tim was describing *while* he hopped on a bus.

10. **A.** *Needs* does not agree with its subject, *you*. *Needs* should be changed to *need*.

11. **C.** The first letter should be a capital *H* in *House*.

12. **C.** *Neither my uncle nor my brother* is a singular subject; a plural compound subject uses *and* instead of *or* or *nor*. Since the subject is singular, the pronoun that refers to it must be singular, *his* instead of *their*.

13. **C.** *One* (singular) does not agree with *millions* and *their* (plural). *One* should be changed to *them*.

14. **B.** You cannot compare *discoveries* (things) with *Einstein* (a person), but you can logically compare *discoveries* with *Einstein's discoveries* or with *Einstein's*.

15. **E.** This sentence contains no error.

16. **D.** This is a pronoun error. *Whom* should be changed to *who*.

17. **E.** This sentence contains no error.

18. **C.** *Would not have been* should be changed to *had not been* in order to show that the invention of the steam engine is an *earlier action* than the probable loss by modern technology.

19. **D.** Since only two opinions are being compared, *most admirable* (which correctly refers to more than two things) should be changed to *more admirable*.

20. **C.** Since the subject of the sentence is singular, *one,* the verb must be singular, *shows* instead of *show*.

21. **A.** *In the morning* is an unnecessary repetition of the meaning of *a.m.*

Part B

22. **B.** Choice **B** contains the correct form *are* for the *neither . . . nor* construction. The verb in this case should be plural to match *friends,* which is the closer of the two subjects to the verb. Choice **D** correctly uses *are* but changes the meaning of the original.

23. **B.** Choice **B** corrects the verb agreement problem in the original wording. The verbs must both be past tense or both be present tense. No other choice uses proper tense without introducing a subject-verb agreement error.

24. **C.** Choice **C** clarifies the ambiguous wording of the original sentence. It is clear in **C** who is arriving and who is doing the meeting.

25. **A.** The original wording is the best expression of this idea. Choice **E** changes the meaning. The other choices are either stylistically awkward or ungrammatical.

26. **C.** Choice **C** best expresses the idea without changing the intent of the sentence as **E** does. The original and choices **B** and **D** are awkward.

27. B. Choice **B** correctly supplies the plural *know*, which agrees with *ecologists*. The subject closer to the verb determines the number of the verb in this case. Choice **B** also retains the necessary *neither . . . nor*.

28. C. Choice **C** best corrects the awkward wording in the original sentence. Choice **D**, although grammatically correct, changes the meaning of the original.

29. D. Choice **D** clarifies whose physical examination is in question, Paul's or the doctor's. Choice **C** is straightforward and concise, also leaving no doubt as to whose examination it is; however, the *doctor* is not mentioned, and because one cannot assume that all physical examinations are administered by a doctor, this information must be included.

30. E. Choice **E** is the most direct, concise wording of the original sentence. The verbs in these answer choices are the problem areas. Choice **B**, for example, is incorrect because of the present tense *is* and *attracts*.

31. C. The original sentence is a fragment; so are choices **B, D,** and **E.**

32. E. The verb *lying* (resting) is correct here; also, *were* is the correct verb because the subject, *a lion and his mate,* is plural. Choices **B** and **D** would make the sentence a fragment.

33. C. The original is flawed by faulty parallelism. *Planning* is not parallel to *to pursue* (the former a gerund, the latter an infinitive). Choice **C** corrects this problem; *planning* is parallel to *pursuing*.

34. D. Both errors in the original result from a confusion of adjectives and adverbs. *Seriously,* an adverb, correctly modifies the verb *took,* and *hard,* used as an adverb meaning "with strength," correctly modifies *punched*. Choices **B, C,** and **E** significantly change the meaning of the original.

35. E. The correct pronoun in this case is *who,* the subject of *betrayed*.

36. D. The original contains two errors. *Varies* does not agree with the plural subject, *opinions,* and *according with* is not idiomatic. Choice **C** is a correct phrase but changes and obscures the meaning of the sentence.

37. E. The introductory phrase is a dangling modifier, corrected by following *freeze* with *the Cabinet minister* to make clear to whom the introductory phrase refers. Choice **D** is not best because *but unharmed* is left in an awkward position.

38. C. The original contains two errors. *It* suggests that the meeting, not the members, does the considering, and *had considered* is a verb tense simultaneous with *had left* and does not indicate that considering the tax cut occurred after the visitors had left. Choice **D** is unnecessarily wordy and leaves unsaid who did the considering.

Answer Sheet for Practice Test 3

(Remove this sheet and use it to mark your answers.)

Reading Test

1 Ⓐ Ⓑ Ⓒ Ⓓ Ⓔ	21 Ⓐ Ⓑ Ⓒ Ⓓ Ⓔ
2 Ⓐ Ⓑ Ⓒ Ⓓ Ⓔ	22 Ⓐ Ⓑ Ⓒ Ⓓ Ⓔ
3 Ⓐ Ⓑ Ⓒ Ⓓ Ⓔ	23 Ⓐ Ⓑ Ⓒ Ⓓ Ⓔ
4 Ⓐ Ⓑ Ⓒ Ⓓ Ⓔ	24 Ⓐ Ⓑ Ⓒ Ⓓ Ⓔ
5 Ⓐ Ⓑ Ⓒ Ⓓ Ⓔ	25 Ⓐ Ⓑ Ⓒ Ⓓ Ⓔ
6 Ⓐ Ⓑ Ⓒ Ⓓ Ⓔ	26 Ⓐ Ⓑ Ⓒ Ⓓ Ⓔ
7 Ⓐ Ⓑ Ⓒ Ⓓ Ⓔ	27 Ⓐ Ⓑ Ⓒ Ⓓ Ⓔ
8 Ⓐ Ⓑ Ⓒ Ⓓ Ⓔ	28 Ⓐ Ⓑ Ⓒ Ⓓ Ⓔ
9 Ⓐ Ⓑ Ⓒ Ⓓ Ⓔ	29 Ⓐ Ⓑ Ⓒ Ⓓ Ⓔ
10 Ⓐ Ⓑ Ⓒ Ⓓ Ⓔ	30 Ⓐ Ⓑ Ⓒ Ⓓ Ⓔ
11 Ⓐ Ⓑ Ⓒ Ⓓ Ⓔ	31 Ⓐ Ⓑ Ⓒ Ⓓ Ⓔ
12 Ⓐ Ⓑ Ⓒ Ⓓ Ⓔ	32 Ⓐ Ⓑ Ⓒ Ⓓ Ⓔ
13 Ⓐ Ⓑ Ⓒ Ⓓ Ⓔ	33 Ⓐ Ⓑ Ⓒ Ⓓ Ⓔ
14 Ⓐ Ⓑ Ⓒ Ⓓ Ⓔ	34 Ⓐ Ⓑ Ⓒ Ⓓ Ⓔ
15 Ⓐ Ⓑ Ⓒ Ⓓ Ⓔ	35 Ⓐ Ⓑ Ⓒ Ⓓ Ⓔ
16 Ⓐ Ⓑ Ⓒ Ⓓ Ⓔ	36 Ⓐ Ⓑ Ⓒ Ⓓ Ⓔ
17 Ⓐ Ⓑ Ⓒ Ⓓ Ⓔ	37 Ⓐ Ⓑ Ⓒ Ⓓ Ⓔ
18 Ⓐ Ⓑ Ⓒ Ⓓ Ⓔ	38 Ⓐ Ⓑ Ⓒ Ⓓ Ⓔ
19 Ⓐ Ⓑ Ⓒ Ⓓ Ⓔ	39 Ⓐ Ⓑ Ⓒ Ⓓ Ⓔ
20 Ⓐ Ⓑ Ⓒ Ⓓ Ⓔ	40 Ⓐ Ⓑ Ⓒ Ⓓ Ⓔ

Mathematics Test

1 Ⓐ Ⓑ Ⓒ Ⓓ Ⓔ	21 Ⓐ Ⓑ Ⓒ Ⓓ Ⓔ
2 Ⓐ Ⓑ Ⓒ Ⓓ Ⓔ	22 Ⓐ Ⓑ Ⓒ Ⓓ Ⓔ
3 Ⓐ Ⓑ Ⓒ Ⓓ Ⓔ	23 Ⓐ Ⓑ Ⓒ Ⓓ Ⓔ
4 Ⓐ Ⓑ Ⓒ Ⓓ Ⓔ	24 Ⓐ Ⓑ Ⓒ Ⓓ Ⓔ
5 Ⓐ Ⓑ Ⓒ Ⓓ Ⓔ	25 Ⓐ Ⓑ Ⓒ Ⓓ Ⓔ
6 Ⓐ Ⓑ Ⓒ Ⓓ Ⓔ	26 Ⓐ Ⓑ Ⓒ Ⓓ Ⓔ
7 Ⓐ Ⓑ Ⓒ Ⓓ Ⓔ	27 Ⓐ Ⓑ Ⓒ Ⓓ Ⓔ
8 Ⓐ Ⓑ Ⓒ Ⓓ Ⓔ	28 Ⓐ Ⓑ Ⓒ Ⓓ Ⓔ
9 Ⓐ Ⓑ Ⓒ Ⓓ Ⓔ	29 Ⓐ Ⓑ Ⓒ Ⓓ Ⓔ
10 Ⓐ Ⓑ Ⓒ Ⓓ Ⓔ	30 Ⓐ Ⓑ Ⓒ Ⓓ Ⓔ
11 Ⓐ Ⓑ Ⓒ Ⓓ Ⓔ	31 Ⓐ Ⓑ Ⓒ Ⓓ Ⓔ
12 Ⓐ Ⓑ Ⓒ Ⓓ Ⓔ	32 Ⓐ Ⓑ Ⓒ Ⓓ Ⓔ
13 Ⓐ Ⓑ Ⓒ Ⓓ Ⓔ	33 Ⓐ Ⓑ Ⓒ Ⓓ Ⓔ
14 Ⓐ Ⓑ Ⓒ Ⓓ Ⓔ	34 Ⓐ Ⓑ Ⓒ Ⓓ Ⓔ
15 Ⓐ Ⓑ Ⓒ Ⓓ Ⓔ	35 Ⓐ Ⓑ Ⓒ Ⓓ Ⓔ
16 Ⓐ Ⓑ Ⓒ Ⓓ Ⓔ	36 Ⓐ Ⓑ Ⓒ Ⓓ Ⓔ
17 Ⓐ Ⓑ Ⓒ Ⓓ Ⓔ	37 Ⓐ Ⓑ Ⓒ Ⓓ Ⓔ
18 Ⓐ Ⓑ Ⓒ Ⓓ Ⓔ	38 Ⓐ Ⓑ Ⓒ Ⓓ Ⓔ
19 Ⓐ Ⓑ Ⓒ Ⓓ Ⓔ	39 Ⓐ Ⓑ Ⓒ Ⓓ Ⓔ
20 Ⓐ Ⓑ Ⓒ Ⓓ Ⓔ	40 Ⓐ Ⓑ Ⓒ Ⓓ Ⓔ

CUT HERE

Writing Test: Multiple Choice

Part A

1. Ⓐ Ⓑ Ⓒ Ⓓ Ⓔ
2. Ⓐ Ⓑ Ⓒ Ⓓ Ⓔ
3. Ⓐ Ⓑ Ⓒ Ⓓ Ⓔ
4. Ⓐ Ⓑ Ⓒ Ⓓ Ⓔ
5. Ⓐ Ⓑ Ⓒ Ⓓ Ⓔ
6. Ⓐ Ⓑ Ⓒ Ⓓ Ⓔ
7. Ⓐ Ⓑ Ⓒ Ⓓ Ⓔ
8. Ⓐ Ⓑ Ⓒ Ⓓ Ⓔ
9. Ⓐ Ⓑ Ⓒ Ⓓ Ⓔ
10. Ⓐ Ⓑ Ⓒ Ⓓ Ⓔ
11. Ⓐ Ⓑ Ⓒ Ⓓ Ⓔ
12. Ⓐ Ⓑ Ⓒ Ⓓ Ⓔ
13. Ⓐ Ⓑ Ⓒ Ⓓ Ⓔ
14. Ⓐ Ⓑ Ⓒ Ⓓ Ⓔ
15. Ⓐ Ⓑ Ⓒ Ⓓ Ⓔ
16. Ⓐ Ⓑ Ⓒ Ⓓ Ⓔ
17. Ⓐ Ⓑ Ⓒ Ⓓ Ⓔ
18. Ⓐ Ⓑ Ⓒ Ⓓ Ⓔ
19. Ⓐ Ⓑ Ⓒ Ⓓ Ⓔ
20. Ⓐ Ⓑ Ⓒ Ⓓ Ⓔ
21. Ⓐ Ⓑ Ⓒ Ⓓ Ⓔ

Part B

22. Ⓐ Ⓑ Ⓒ Ⓓ Ⓔ
23. Ⓐ Ⓑ Ⓒ Ⓓ Ⓔ
24. Ⓐ Ⓑ Ⓒ Ⓓ Ⓔ
25. Ⓐ Ⓑ Ⓒ Ⓓ Ⓔ
26. Ⓐ Ⓑ Ⓒ Ⓓ Ⓔ
27. Ⓐ Ⓑ Ⓒ Ⓓ Ⓔ
28. Ⓐ Ⓑ Ⓒ Ⓓ Ⓔ
29. Ⓐ Ⓑ Ⓒ Ⓓ Ⓔ
30. Ⓐ Ⓑ Ⓒ Ⓓ Ⓔ
31. Ⓐ Ⓑ Ⓒ Ⓓ Ⓔ
32. Ⓐ Ⓑ Ⓒ Ⓓ Ⓔ
33. Ⓐ Ⓑ Ⓒ Ⓓ Ⓔ
34. Ⓐ Ⓑ Ⓒ Ⓓ Ⓔ
35. Ⓐ Ⓑ Ⓒ Ⓓ Ⓔ
36. Ⓐ Ⓑ Ⓒ Ⓓ Ⓔ
37. Ⓐ Ⓑ Ⓒ Ⓓ Ⓔ
38. Ⓐ Ⓑ Ⓒ Ⓓ Ⓔ

CUT HERE

Practice Test 3 (Paper-Based Format)

Reading Test

TIME: 60 Minutes

40 Questions

Directions: A question or number of questions follows each of the statements or passages in this section. Using only the *stated* or *implied* information given in the statement or passage, answer the question or questions by choosing the *best* answer from among the five choices given.

1. A two percent budget cut ordered by the governor will seriously hamper the operation of the state university system, but while education will be hurt, the state budget in general will remain relatively unaffected.

   The author's attitude toward the governor's order is most likely

   A. neutral

   B. antagonistic

   C. understanding

   D. supportive

   E. inconsistent

Questions 2 and 3 refer to the following passage.

Parallax is a range-finding technique used to measure the distance to some nearby stars from the annual angular displacement of a nearby star against the background of more distant, relatively fixed stars. Behold parallax by noting the apparent position of a vertical pencil in front of your face with only your right eye, then your left eye; the pencil shifts across the background.

2. In order to make this passage clear to a general audience, the author can do which of the following?

   A. Concede that parallax is not the only range-finding technique used by astronomers

   B. Define "angular displacement" in nontechnical terms

   C. Cite references in *Scientific American*

   D. Explain that stars are never even "relatively" fixed

   E. Eliminate the demonstration using a pencil

GO ON TO THE NEXT PAGE

3. In the second sentence, the author suggests which of the following?

A. Most people have never really considered the position of a pencil.

B. The perceived position of any object varies according to the point from which it is observed.

C. Parallax is also a technique used by nonscientists.

D. The right eye is a more reliable observer than the left eye.

E. A pencil is very similar to a star.

4. All experts on testing and learning admit that multiple-choice tests measure knowledge only within limits. And yet the fact remains that multiple-choice tests are used, both in school and out of school, as significant indicators of intellectual ability and the capacity for learning.

The passage implies which of the following statements?

A. The administration of tests is a more cost-effective measure than the exploration of other modes of measurement.

B. Tests are appropriate only when the students tested have limited knowledge.

C. One's capacity for learning cannot be measured by any sort of test.

D. Those who work first-hand with tests must know something that the experts do not.

E. Those who administer tests may not be experts on testing.

Questions 5 through 8 are based on the following passage.

Ostensibly punishment is used to reduce tendencies to behave in certain ways. We spank and scold children for misbehavior; we fine, lock up, or assign
(5) to hard labor adults who break laws; we threaten, censure, disapprove, ostracize, and coerce in our efforts to control social behavior. Does punishment, in fact, do what it is supposed to do?
(10) The effects of punishment, it has been found, are not the opposite of reward. It does not subtract responses where reinforcement adds them. Rather it appears to temporarily suppress a behavior, and
(15) when punishment is discontinued, eventually responses will reappear. But this is only one aspect of the topic. Let us look at it in further detail.

Skinner defines punishment in two
(20) ways: first as the withdrawal of a positive reinforcer and second as the presentation of a negative reinforcer or aversive stimulus. We take candy away from a child or we spank him. Note that
(25) the arrangement in punishment is the opposite of that in reinforcement, where a positive reinforcer is presented and a negative reinforcer is removed.

Since we remove positive reinforcers
(30) to extinguish a response and also to punish it, a distinction must be made. When a response is made and no reinforcement follows, when *nothing* happens, the response gradually extin-
(35) guishes. However, if we *withdraw* a reinforcer and the withdrawal of a reinforcer is contingent on a response, responding is suppressed more rapidly. The latter is punishment. Sometimes we
(40) withdraw a privilege from a child to control his behavior. A teacher might keep a child in the classroom during recess or cancel a field trip as a result of misbehavior. Turning off the television

(45) when a child puts his thumb in his mouth may effectively suppress his thumbsucking. Most punishments of this sort utilize conditioned or generalized reinforcers. Quite frequently one (50) sees adults withdraw attention or affection as punishment for misbehavior, sometimes in subtle ways.

5. The passage equates taking candy away from a child with

    A. only one of many categories of punishment

    B. the presentation of a negative reinforcer

    C. the presentation of an aversion stimulus

    D. withdrawal of negative reinforcement

    E. withdrawal of positive reinforcement

6. Which of the following may be concluded from the last paragraph of the passage?

    A. Most children regard the classroom as a prison.

    B. It is usually best to ignore whatever bothers us.

    C. The author considers recess and field trips to be privileges.

    D. The withdrawal of affection is an unconscious form of punishment.

    E. Children who do not like television are harder to punish.

7. The passage does NOT do which of the following?

    A. Give a definite answer to the question posed in the first paragraph

    B. Discuss generally some of the effects of punishment

    C. Provide examples of some common forms of punishment

    D. Distinguish punishment from reinforcement

    E. Mention the temporary suppression of behavior

8. Which of the following facts, if true, supports one of the author's contentions about punishment?

    A. Those who were spanked as children may not praise the benefits of such discipline.

    B. Imposing longer jail terms on criminals does not necessarily permanently reduce their tendency to return to crime.

    C. Any species or race that is consistently punished will eventually become extinct.

    D. The temporary suppression of a negative behavior is a fine accomplishment.

    E. People who are consistently rewarded are incapable of punishing others.

GO ON TO THE NEXT PAGE

Questions 9 through 13 refer to the following passage.

He who lets the world, or his own portion of it, choose his plan of life for him has no need of any other faculty than the ape-like one of imitation. He (5) who chooses his plan for himself employs all his faculties. He must use observation to see, reasoning and judgment to foresee, activity to gather materials for decision, discrimination to (10) decide, and when he has decided, firmness and self-control to hold to his decision. And these qualities he requires and exercises exactly in proportion as the part of his conduct which he determines (15) according to his own judgment and feelings is a large one. It is possible that he might be guided in some good path, and kept out of harm's way, without any of these things. But what will be his com-(20) parative worth as a human being? It really is of importance, not only what men do, but also what manner of men they are that do it. Among the works of man, which human life is rightly employed in (25) perfecting and beautifying, the first in importance surely is man himself. Supposing it were possible to get houses built, corn grown, battles fought, causes tried, and even churches erected and (30) prayers said, by machinery—by automatons in human form—it would be a considerable loss to exchange for these automatons even the men and women who at present inhabit the more civilized (35) parts of the world, and who assuredly are but starved specimens of what nature can and will produce. Human nature is not a machine to be built after a model, and set to do exactly the work prescribed for it, but a tree, which requires to grow (40) and develop itself on all sides, according to the tendency of the inward forces which make it a living thing.

9. One major distinction in this passage is between

A. automatons and machines
B. people and machines
C. beauty and perfection
D. apes and machines
E. growing food and fighting battles

10. Which of the following groups represents the type of person that the author calls an "automaton" (lines 30–31)?

A. Comedians
B. Botanists
C. Workers on an assembly line
D. A team of physicians in surgery
E. Students who consistently ask challenging questions

11. Which of the following is an unstated assumption of the passage?

A. Mankind will probably never improve.
B. The essence of people themselves is more important than what people do.
C. It is desirable to let modern technology do some of our more unpleasant tasks.
D. Some people in the world do not select their own life plans.
E. What man produces is really no different from man himself.

12. The author would agree that a major benefit of letting the world choose for you your plan of life is

   A. simplicity

   B. profit

   C. friendship

   D. progress

   E. happiness

13. The author would probably agree with each of the following statements EXCEPT

   A. to conform to custom, merely *as* custom, does not educate or develop one

   B. human beings should use and interpret experience in their own way

   C. more good may always be made of an energetic nature than of an indolent and impassive one

   D. persons whose desires and impulses are their own are said to have character

   E. it makes good sense to choose the easy life of conformity

Questions 14 and 15 are based on the following passage.

   Charles Darwin was both a naturalist and a scientist. Darwin's *The Origin of Species* (1859) was based on twenty-five years of research in testing and checking
(5) his theory of evolution. "Darwinism" had a profound effect on the natural sciences, the social sciences, and the humanities. Churchmen who feared for the survival of religious institutions rushed
(10) to attack him. However Darwin never attempted to apply his laws of evolution to human society. It was the social Darwinists who expanded the theory of evolution to include society as a whole.
(15) The social Darwinists viewed society as a "struggle for existence" with only the "fittest" members of society able to survive. They espoused basically a racist and elitist doctrine. Some people were
(20) naturally superior to others; it was in the "nature of things" for big business to take over "less fit," smaller concerns.

14. The final sentence of the passage beginning "Some people . . ." (line 19) is the author's attempt to

   A. discredit Charles Darwin's theory

   B. voice his or her own point of view

   C. summarize one point of view

   D. give social Darwinism a fair shake

   E. explain the modern prominence of big business

15. The author's primary purpose in this passage is to

   A. warn of the dangers of having one's ideas abused

   B. show that Darwin was unconcerned with human society

   C. defend Darwin against modern charges of racism and elitism

   D. explain how Darwin's theory was applied to society

   E. give an example of Darwinian evolution

GO ON TO THE NEXT PAGE

16. Current evidence suggests that there is a marked tendency for children with superior IQs to be more mature both socially and physically than children of average ability. Also, educational research shows that gifted children also appear superior in memory and visual perception tests to children of average IQ.

In the preceding passage, the author is using "gifted children" to mean children

    A. from a higher socio-economic background

    B. who are in no way average

    C. with superior IQs

    D. who have submitted to educational research

    E. who build social relationships earlier

17. Prior to the 1980s, educational psychologists were primarily concerned with specific social, motivational, and cognitive aspects of learning. Recent comprehensive studies of early classroom learning experiences have drawn attention to the importance of multiple approaches to learning. Classroom curriculum now emphasizes activities that are sensitive to the unique abilities of individual students.

One of the author's points in this passage is that

    A. prior to the 1980s, no one noticed that the concerns of educational psychologists were limited

    B. educational psychologists tend to frequently shift their interests as a group

    C. after 1980, psychologists lost interest in the social, motivational, and cognitive aspects of learning

    D. the academic significance of classroom activities themselves has not been the concern of educational psychologists until fairly recently

    E. the decades preceding the 1980s were marked by poorly thought out, poorly implemented classroom activities

18. Pestalozzi (1746–1827) was influenced by Rousseau in adopting an educational philosophy based on the needs of the child. Pestalozzi recognized the dependence of the child on society for the development of effective personal growth. His most famous work was *Leonard and Gertrude* (1781).

The passage is LEAST likely to appear in which of the following?

A. An introduction to Pestalozzi's *Leonard and Gertrude*

B. An article surveying the influence of society on the personal growth of children

C. An essay describing the influence of Rousseau's educational philosophy

D. A journal of the history of education

E. The history of seventeenth-century Italy

19. Rewards tend to be more effective than punishment in controlling student behavior. Negative reinforcement often is accompanied by emotional side effects that may cause continued learning disabilities.

The author implies which of the following?

A. The same student who is punished frequently may have difficulty learning.

B. In society at large, rewards are not given nearly as often as they should be.

C. Negative reinforcement is much more useful out of school than it is in school.

D. The most effective punishment is that which is followed by a reward.

E. Learning disabilities often lead to emotional problems.

GO ON TO THE NEXT PAGE

20. Teacher salaries account for approximately seventy percent of a school budget. Any major proposal designed to reduce educational expenditures will ultimately necessitate a cut in teaching staff.

Neighborhood High School is staffed by fifty teachers, and its administration has just ordered a reduction in educational expenditures. According to the previous passage, which of the following will be one result of the reduction?

A. A reduction in both administrative and teaching salaries

B. A teaching staff dependent on fewer educational materials

C. A teaching staff of fewer than fifty teachers

D. A teaching staff of only fifteen teachers

E. A substantial change in the quality of education

21. Psychology is often considered a science of the mind. As an applied science, it seeks to generate comprehensive theories to explain human emotions and behavior. Despite its status as a science, the "methods" of psychology sometimes seem more speculative rather than rational and analytical.

Which of the following functions does the second sentence of the preceding passage perform?

A. Provides a description

B. Provides more information

C. Denies the truth of the first sentence

D. Uses a metaphor

E. Adds an inconsistency

22. Fifty years ago, most television programs were shown in black and white. These days, the brightly colored clothes most of us wear signal that the medium has changed.

The author implies which of the following in the previous passage?

A. Fifty years ago, people wore only black and white clothes.

B. Most people no longer will tolerate black and white television.

C. There is only a slight relationship between our self-image and the images we see on television.

D. Color television is significantly responsible for our preference for brightly colored clothes.

E. Clothing technology, like television, was relatively primitive fifty years ago.

23. The political party is a voluntary association of voters whose purpose in a democracy is to control the policies of government by electing to public office persons of its membership.

The preceding passage would be most likely to appear in which of the following?

A. An introductory text on political science

B. A general interest magazine

C. A manual of rules for legislators

D. A piece of campaign literature

E. A brief essay discussing the president's most recent news conference

Questions 24 and 25 refer to the following passage.

It may be true that there are two sides to every question, but it is also true that there are two sides to a sheet of flypaper and it makes a big difference to the fly which side he chooses.

24. This statement suggests that

  A. every question has only one answer

  B. the choice of questions is very important

  C. flypaper is not useful

  D. every question may be interpreted in more than one way

  E. every question is answered

25. Which of the following is true?

  I. The statement uses an analogy to make a point.

  II. The statement emphasizes the importance of choice.

  III. The statement points out the ways of getting stuck on a question.

  A. I only

  B. II only

  C. III only

  D. I and II only

  E. I and III only

Questions 26 through 30 are based on the following passage.

Some parents, teachers, and educators have tried to spoil the centennial celebration of one of America's greatest novels, *The Adventures of Huckleberry*
(5) *Finn,* by claiming that it and author Mark Twain were racist.

Most readers over the years have viewed this masterpiece as anything but offensive to blacks. Beneath the surface
(10) of a darn good yarn, it is one of several major writings by Twain that condemn the brutality of slavery. For some who suddenly find the novel offensive, the misunderstanding may lie in Twain's un-
(15) matched use of irony and the crude vernacular of river folk to tell the story of the friendship between a runaway Negro slave and young Huck—through the eyes of the uneducated boy.

(20) Any doubts about Mr. Twain's views on slavery should have been dispelled by an even later work published in 1894, *Pudd'nhead Wilson.* The famous murder trial story also shows how slavery
(25) damages the human personality. But silly detractors apparently need more than the unspoiled and color-blind innocence of Huck or the eccentric but clever lawyer Wilson. For them, we have a
(30) letter from Mr. Twain himself, or rather Samuel L. Clemens, the writer's real name.

Written the same year as *The Adventures of Huckleberry Finn,* the let-
(35) ter details Twain's offer to pay the expenses of one of the first black students at Yale Law School. The student Twain befriended and financially assisted, Warner T. McGuinn, was the com-
(40) mencement orator at his graduation and went on to a distinguished legal and political career in Baltimore.

"I do not believe I would very cheerfully help a white student who would
(45) ask a benevolence of a stranger, but I do not feel so about the other color. We have ground the manhood out of them and the shame is ours, not theirs; and we should pay for it," Mr. Clemens wrote
(50) Francis Wayland, the law school dean.

GO ON TO THE NEXT PAGE

In addition to being a critic of slavery, Mark Twain was fascinated with the subject of transmogrification. On this 100th anniversary of his death, Twain (55) might find ironic delight in the timing of the publication of a letter vindicating his commitment to racial progress.

26. The previous passage was written

   A. to promote the sale of *The Adventures of Huckleberry Finn*

   B. one hundred years after Mark Twain's death

   C. to exonerate those who claim Twain's writing was racist

   D. to explain the misunderstandings in Twain's philosophy

   E. as a condemnation of the principle of transmogrification

27. Mark Twain offered to pay the expenses of a Yale Law School student because the student

   A. was commencement orator at his graduation

   B. would go on to a distinguished law career

   C. was rightfully owed the assistance of whites

   D. was very needy and couldn't afford the tuition

   E. was also a severe critic of slavery

28. The "irony" referred to in the second paragraph (line 15) appears to have

   A. confused some readers about Twain's intentions

   B. made the language of the river folk difficult to understand

   C. convinced most readers that Twain's work was actually racist

   D. provided detractors with valid reason to condemn *Pudd'nhead Wilson*

   E. appeased Twain's critics about the author's feelings regarding slavery

29. The term "centennial celebration" (lines 2–3) is used to indicate

   A. a party held in Mark Twain's honor

   B. an anniversary of Twain's *Pudd'nhead Wilson*

   C. the 100th anniversary of Mark Twain's birth

   D. the 100th publication of *The Adventures of Huckleberry Finn*

   E. the 100th anniversary of the publication of *The Adventures of Huckleberry Finn*

30. According to the passage, Pudd'nhead Wilson was

   A. the student Twain befriended and financially assisted

   B. a runaway slave in one of Twain's works

   C. the dean of the Yale Law School

   D. the runaway slave in *The Adventures of Huckleberry Finn*

   E. a clever but somewhat bizarre fictional character

Questions 31, 32, and 33 refer to the following passage.

Our planet Earth has a tail and, although the appendage is invisible, it must be somewhat similar to those of comets and other heavenly bodies.

(5) Earth's tail is an egg-shaped zone of electrically charged particles positioned about 400,000 miles from us—always on the side away from the sun.

(10) Physicist Lou Frank, of the University of Iowa, says researchers recently calculated the tail's existence and position by examining Explorer 1 satellite photos of the northern and southern lights. These natural displays—the aurora borealis

(15) and the aurora australis—glow and flicker in the night sky of the Northern and Southern hemispheres.

The auroras occur because the solar wind racing from the sun pushes against

(20) the Earth's magnetic field and creates an electric power supply in our planet's newly discovered tail. The displays are seen frequently at times of sunspot activity, in the months of March and April,

(25) September and October. Their colors are mostly green, sometimes red. They have been observed in the continental United States and in Mexico.

31. According to the passage, which of the following can be inferred about the aurora borealis and aurora australis?

A. They are unnatural phenomena caused by solar wind.

B. They are caused by sunspot activity in March, April, September, and October.

C. They are electrical phenomena caused by solar wind and magnetism.

D. They are egg-shaped and occur about 400,000 miles away.

E. They were first photographed by Lou Frank of the University of Iowa.

32. All of the following are true about Earth's tail EXCEPT that

A. it is egg shaped

B. it contains charged particles

C. it remains on the side always away from the sun

D. it is invisible

E. it occurs during March, April, September, and October

33. It can be inferred from the passage that probably

A. aurora borealis and aurora australis occur at the equator

B. the Earth's magnetic field will someday transform this planet into a comet

C. astronomers will now be observing Earth's tail through high-power telescopes

D. the tails of comets are composed of electrically charged particles

E. the auroras race from the sun and push against the Earth's magnetic field

Questions 34, 35, and 36 are based on the following passage.

No matter what we think of Warren Beatty or his film *Reds,* we cheer his victory for artistic purity in preventing ABC-TV from editing his movie for

(5) television. An arbitrator ruled that Mr. Beatty's contractual right of "final-cut" authority, which forbids editing he doesn't approve, prevented Paramount Pictures from granting that authority to

(10) ABC-TV. The network planned to cut

GO ON TO THE NEXT PAGE

279

six minutes from *Reds*, a 196-minute film, and air the truncated version next week.

(15) Most theatrical films (movies made for theaters) ultimately appear on network television, usually preceded by the brief message "Edited for Television." The popular perception, argues Mr. Beatty, is that this editing removes obscenity. Often
(20) it does. Yet, some editing is done purely in the interests of commercial and local programming. Advertisements traditionally hover near hourly and half-hourly intervals. And local affiliate stations zeal-
(25) ously protect their 11 p.m. time slot because it is commercially lucrative.

Mr. Beatty's case illustrates why studios contracting with directors for films rarely grant the coveted right of final
(30) cut. Televised theatrical movies receive wide exposure and are lucrative; Paramount had a $6.5 million contract with ABC-TV for *Reds*. True artistic control in filmmaking will come only
(35) when all directors receive final-cut guarantees, a right the Directors Guild of America hopes to obtain in future talks with movie producers. Mr. Beatty's victory is a step in the direction of protec-
(40) tion for film.

34. Which of the following best supports the argument presented in the passage?

   A. It would be artistically impermissible to delete 64 bars from a Beethoven symphony or to skip Act II from *Hamlet*.

   B. Warren Beatty would be well served if he planned his theatrical features with television commercials in mind.

   C. The Directors Guild of America will have a difficult time acquiring artistic control for film directors.

   D. The phrase "Edited for Television" (line 17) refers only to the removal of obscenities.

   E. The best time to run commercials for television stations is at 11 p.m.

35. Which of the following is implied by the passage?

   A. Artists should not yield to the pressures of a commercial industry.

   B. The enormous amount of money involved in commercial television should temper an artist's ideals.

   C. Film editing should be performed with commercial as well as artistic goals in mind.

   D. Lucrative contracts demand compromise by all film collaborators.

   E. Film studios should never allow artists to control final-cut rights on feature films.

36. Which of the following is the best title for the passage?

A. Warren Beatty and *Reds*

B. The Final Cut: Beatty vs. ABC

C. Edited for TV: Removing Obscenity

D. How Films Get Cut for Television

E. Directors Guild of America: A New Battle

37. Adam Smith, the founder of political economy, treated economic existence as the true human life, treated money-making as the meaning of history, and was wont to describe statesmen as dangerous animals; yet this very England became what it became—the foremost country, economically speaking, in the world.

The meaning of "wont" in this passage is

A. desired

B. did not

C. accustomed

D. unlikely

E. unable

Questions 38 and 39 refer to the following passage.

The $5 million in state funds earmarked for advertising California's attractiveness as a tourist destination is an investment well worth making. Perhaps because California has long taken it for granted that everyone wants to come here, and maybe because for many years Hollywood was California's most powerful publicist, the state has never spent a dime promoting itself to potential visitors. And that may be at least partly responsible for the decline in tourism, including a 10 percent drop in spending. Since tourism is a $28 billion industry employing 1.6 million Californians, perhaps this new advertising was too long in coming.

38. Which of the following is an assumption of the passage?

A. California will never spend funds to promote tourism.

B. A proposed advertising campaign will decrease the competition from other states.

C. California tax revenues are only a result of tourism.

D. Increased tourism will result in higher state and local tax revenues as well as added state income.

E. More Californians are visiting other states than ever before.

39. Which of the following is implied by the passage?

A. If the advertising campaign works, the $5 million price tag will be a bargain.

B. Advertising campaigns should be carefully and slowly monitored.

C. Few Californians oppose the proposed advertising campaign.

D. Hollywood should not continue to be a drawing card to attract tourists.

E. The $28 billion is not enough to employ 1.6 million Californians.

GO ON TO THE NEXT PAGE

40. It would be splendid if the states were willing to subscribe to treaties agreeing to submit all their disputes to arbitration. But even though great advances have been made in persuading nations to submit disputes to judicial determination, governments have always made an exception of matters that they deemed of major importance.

In the passage above, the terms "states" and "nations" are probably

- **A.** without a judiciary
- **B.** without decisive government
- **C.** analogies
- **D.** metaphors
- **E.** synonyms

IF YOU FINISH BEFORE TIME IS CALLED, CHECK YOUR WORK ON THIS SECTION ONLY. DO NOT WORK ON ANY OTHER SECTION IN THE TEST.

Mathematics Test

TIME: 60 Minutes

40 Questions

Directions: Each of the questions or incomplete statements below is followed by five suggested answers or completions. Select the best answer or completion of the five choices given and fill in the corresponding lettered space on the answer sheet.

1. Five washloads of clothes need to be laundered. If each load takes a total of 15 minutes to be washed, and the laundry person begins washing at 3:20 p.m. and washes continually, at what time will all the loads be finished?

   A. 1:15 p.m.

   B. 3:35 p.m.

   C. 4:35 p.m.

   D. 5:35 p.m.

   E. 6:15 p.m.

2. Which of the following most closely approximates $\frac{3}{8}$?

   A. 0.25

   B. 0.38

   C. 0.46

   D. 0.50

   E. 0.83

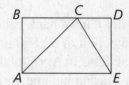

3. If triangle *ACE* is drawn inside rectangle *ABDE,* as above, which one of the following would be helpful in determining the area of triangle *ACE*?

   A. Length of *AC*

   B. Length of *CE*

   C. Length of *CD*

   D. Length of *DE*

   E. Midpoint of *BD*

Suzanne worked 47 hours at $9.10 per hour. How much did Suzanne earn?

---

4. Which of the following is the most appropriate way to estimate Suzanne's total earnings for the time worked?

   A. 40×9

   B. $50 \div 9$

   C. 50×9

   D. 91×47

   E. $40 \div 9$

GO ON TO THE NEXT PAGE

Section 2 Mathematics Test

5. If Tina was born on December 4, 1967, then how old could she be in 2015?

    A. 40

    B. 44

    C. 46 or 47

    D. 47 or 48

    E. 49 or 50

6. The Faculty Club's bank balance showed a deficit of $2,800 in March. If additional debts in April totaled $1,300, and there was no income during that month, what did the Faculty Club's balance book show?

    A. −$4,100

    B. −$1,500

    C. −$1,300

    D. $1,500

    E. $4,100

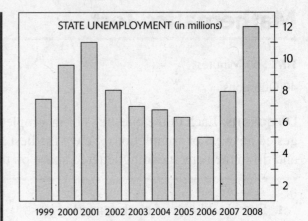

STATE UNEMPLOYMENT (in millions)

1999 2000 2001 2002 2003 2004 2005 2006 2007 2008

7. According to the graph above, approximately how many more people were unemployed in 2001 than in 2006?

    A. 10.5 million

    B. 8 million

    C. 6 million

    D. 4.5 million

    E. 4 million

8. Rounded to the nearest hundredth, 294.3549 would be expressed

    A. 0.35

    B. 0.36

    C. 294.35

    D. 294.36

    E. 300.00

On six tests, Zach averaged 85%.
Although he failed to achieve
a passing score on just one test (on
which he received a 56%),
he also scored 100% twice.

Pressure Gauge

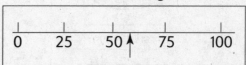

9. Which of the following can be
determined from the information
above?

   A. His two lowest percentage scores

   B. His three highest percentage scores

   C. The sum of all six percentage scores

   D. The sum of the three lowest
percentage scores

   E. The average of the three highest
percentage scores

11. The reading on the pressure gauge
above is approximately

   A. 35

   B. 50

   C. 60

   D. 70

   E. 75

12. Ashley purchased three times as many
carnations as roses. If roses cost $1
each, and carnations cost 50¢ each, and
she spent a total of $7.50 for the
flowers, how many roses did she
purchase?

   A. 2

   B. 3

   C. 4

   D. 5

   E. 6

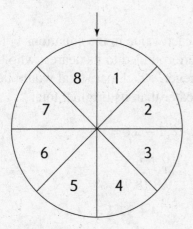

10. Using the spinner above, what is the
probability of getting 2 or 3 on the first
spin?

   A. $\dfrac{1}{8}$

   B. $\dfrac{1}{4}$

   C. $\dfrac{1}{3}$

   D. $\dfrac{3}{8}$

   E. $\dfrac{1}{2}$

13. If $\dfrac{3}{10}$ of a person's gross earnings is
paid to taxes, and last year Joshua paid
$15,000 in taxes, what were Joshua's
gross earnings last year?

   A. $45,000

   B. $50,000

   C. $65,000

   D. $70,000

   E. $105,000

Section **2** Mathematics Test

GO ON TO THE NEXT PAGE

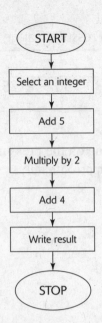

14. Regardless of the integer you select in the process shown above, the outcome must be

A. an even number

B. an odd number

C. a number greater than 18

D. a prime number

E. a multiple of 8 .

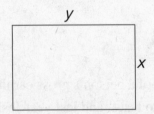

15. If the length of the rectangle above is tripled and the width is doubled, then the formula for the area of the new rectangle is

A. $A = \left(\dfrac{1}{2}\right)xy$

B. $A = xy$

C. $A = 2xy$

D. $A = 3xy$

E. $A = 6xy$

16. If $\begin{array}{|cc|} a & b \\ d & c \end{array} = \dfrac{a+b}{c+d}$ then $\begin{array}{|cc|} -2 & -4 \\ 1 & 5 \end{array} =$

A. 2

B. 1

C. 0

D. −1

E. −2

17. Which of the following expressions is NOT equivalent to the others?

A. $3^3 \times 4 \times 5$

B. $2^2 \times 5 \times 27$

C. $3^2 \times 7 \times 12$

D. $2^2 \times 15 \times 9$

E. $3^2 \times 6 \times 10$

18. If each value in the equations below were rounded to its nearest whole integer, which new total would be greater than its original total?

A. $8.2 - 5.6 =$

B. $10.4/9.8 =$

C. $(9.8)(8.7) =$

D. $25.4 + 97.3 =$

E. $980.3 - 452.6 =$

19. If points $P\,(1,1)$ and $Q\,(1,0)$ lie on the same coordinate graph, which must be true?

   I. P and Q are equidistant from the origin.

   II. P is farther from the origin than P is from Q.

   III. Q is farther from the origin than Q is from P.

   A. I only

   B. II only

   C. III only

   D. I and II only

   E. I and III only

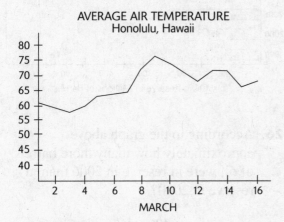

AVERAGE AIR TEMPERATURE
Honolulu, Hawaii

MARCH

20. Approximately how much greater was the highest average daily air temperature than the lowest average daily air temperature during the dates shown on the chart above?

   A. 75°

   B. 58°

   C. 28°

   D. 18°

   E.   6°

21. Maria plans to make sandwiches for a picnic. She has three types of bread from which to choose (rye, sourdough, and white), four types of meat from which to choose (salami, turkey, ham, and pastrami), and three types of cheese from which to choose (Swiss, cheddar, and jack). If Maria will only use one type of bread, one type of meat, and one type of cheese on each sandwich, how many different kinds of sandwiches can Maria make?

   A.   3

   B.   4

   C. 10

   D. 17

   E. 36

22. If the perimeter of a square is 20 inches, what is its area in square inches?

   A. 50

   B. 49

   C. 36

   D. 25

   E.   9

Section **2** Mathematics Test

GO ON TO THE NEXT PAGE

23. Theo walked $6\frac{1}{4}$ miles on Wednesday. Sasha walked $4\frac{3}{4}$ miles on Thursday. What is the difference between the distance Theo walked on Wednesday and the distance Sasha walked on Thursday?

   A. 11 miles

   B. $2\frac{1}{2}$ miles

   C. $2\frac{1}{4}$ miles

   D. $1\frac{3}{4}$ miles

   E. $1\frac{1}{2}$ miles

A painting crew painted 3 rooms on Monday, 5 rooms on Tuesday, 2 rooms on Wednesday, and 4 rooms on Thursday.

How many gallons of paint did the crew use?

---

24. What other information must be provided to solve the above problem?

   A. The average number of rooms in the house

   B. The average number of rooms painted per day

   C. The cost per gallon of paint

   D. The total number of rooms painted in the house

   E. The average number of gallons used per room

25. If $2x - 4y = 20$, then what is the value of $x - 2y$?

   A. 2

   B. 4

   C. 5

   D. 8

   E. 10

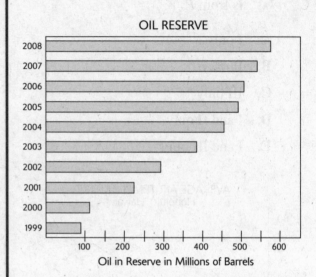

OIL RESERVE

Oil in Reserve in Millions of Barrels

26. According to the graph above, approximately how many more barrels of oil were in reserve in 2006 than in reserve in 2000?

   A. 400

   B. 500

   C. 300,000,000

   D. 400,000,000

   E. 500,000,000

27. If the volume of the above cube is 125, then the total surface area of the cube is

- **A.** 5
- **B.** 25
- **C.** 100
- **D.** 125
- **E.** 150

28. A fair spinner at a bazaar has 12 equal sections, numbered 1 through 12. If the spinner is spun twice, what is the probability that the second spin will come up an odd number?

- **A.** $\frac{1}{12}$
- **B.** $\frac{1}{6}$
- **C.** $\frac{1}{2}$
- **D.** $\frac{1}{1}$
- **E.** $\frac{2}{1}$

29. If a square carpet, 8 feet on a side, is cut up into smaller squares each 2 feet on a side, what is the largest number of smaller squares that can be formed?

- **A.** 8
- **B.** 16
- **C.** 32
- **D.** 64
- **E.** 128

30. What is $\frac{3}{5}$ of $\frac{30}{7}$?

- **A.** $\frac{33}{12}$
- **B.** $\frac{18}{7}$
- **C.** $\frac{29}{12}$
- **D.** $\frac{7}{50}$
- **E.** $\frac{1}{65}$

6"	2"	10"	2"	5"

31. Above are the measures of rainfall for five consecutive days during the winter. For the measure of those five days, which of the following is true?

- I. The median equals the mode.
- II. The median equals the arithmetic mean.
- III. The range equals the median.

- **A.** I only
- **B.** II only
- **C.** III only
- **D.** I and II only
- **E.** I and III only

GO ON TO THE NEXT PAGE

32. Which of the following polygons appears to contain two pairs of parallel sides?

A.

B.

C.

D.

E.

Tom is shorter than Lebron.

Lebron is taller than Tony.

Jordan is taller than Tom but shorter than Luke.

Luke is shorter than Tony.

33. Of the five people mentioned above, who is the shortest?

A. Tom

B. Lebron

C. Tony

D. Jordan

E. Luke

34. If 12 cups of flour are needed to make 5 cakes, how many cakes can be made with 30 cups of flour?

A. 2.5

B. 6

C. 10

D. 12.5

E. 60

35. Mrs. Solis purchased a refrigerator at a 30% discount off the retail price. If the retail price was $800, how much did Mrs. Solis pay for the refrigerator?

A. $2,400

B. $770

C. $660

D. $560

E. $240

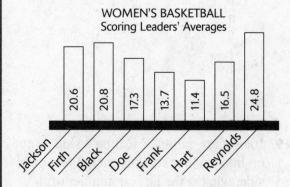

36. According to the bar graph above, Reynolds's average score exceeds Doe's average score by how many points?

A. 13.4

B. 11.1

C. 8.3

D. 7.4

E. 2.3

37. If 240 miles can be driven using 9 gallons of gasoline, how many miles can be driven using 12 gallons of gasoline?

 A. 80

 B. 270

 C. 320

 D. 370

 E. 480

38. Which of the following is a possible answer for $2x + 6 > 9$?

 A. -2

 B. $-1\frac{1}{2}$

 C. 1

 D. $1\frac{1}{2}$

 E. 2

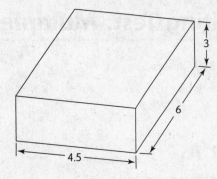

39. The dimensions of a rectangular sandbox are shown in the diagram above. Which one of the following expressions represents the area needed for a piece of plastic to cover the top?

 A. $4.5(6)(3)$

 B. $(4.5)(6)$

 C. $(4.5)(3)$

 D. $2(4.5) + 2(6) + (3)$

 E. $2(4.5) + 2(6)$

Net Films	Prices
New releases	$3.99
Educational releases	$1.99
All other releases	$2.99

40. Mark rented 3 DVDs from Net Films. Disregarding sales tax, what type(s) of DVDs did he rent if his total bill was $11.97?

 A. 3 educational releases

 B. 3 new releases

 C. 1 new, 1 educational, and 1 other release

 D. 2 new and 1 other release

 E. 2 other and 1 new release

IF YOU FINISH BEFORE TIME IS CALLED, CHECK YOUR WORK ON THIS SECTION ONLY. DO NOT WORK ON ANY OTHER SECTION IN THE TEST.

STOP

Writing Test: Multiple-Choice Section

TIME: 30 Minutes

38 Questions

Part A

SUGGESTED TIME: 10 Minutes

21 Questions

Directions: Some of the following sentences are correct. Others contain problems in grammar, usage, idiom, diction, punctuation, and capitalization.

If there is an error, it will be underlined and lettered. Find the one underlined part that must be changed to make the sentence correct and choose the corresponding letter on your answer sheet. Mark **E** if the sentence contains no error.

1. The <u>invitation asked</u> that I come <u>to</u>
        A   B

   the birthday party <u>at</u> the restaurant
                 C

   <u>in formal dress</u>. <u>No error</u>
      D   E

2. People <u>who</u> write <u>letters frequently</u>
         A   B

   <u>recount</u> the <u>same</u> experience to
     B   C

   <u>different</u> people. <u>No error</u>
      D   E

3. The effect of the <u>libraries</u> campaign to
                A

   encourage <u>children's</u> reading <u>has been</u>
            B   C

   overwhelmingly successful, according to

   the <u>fact-finding team</u>. <u>No error</u>
           D   E

4. The <u>welfare</u> of labor <u>is</u> conditioned by
        A   B

   <u>several</u> factors unique to the United
     C

   States <u>and occurring only in this</u>
            D

   <u>country</u>. <u>No error</u>
     D   E

5. Huong and <u>yourself</u> will attend the
           A

   conference <u>on behalf</u> of the entire
           B

   company <u>and report</u> the latest
           C

   technological advances to <u>us</u> next week.
                D

   <u>No error</u>
    E

6. To <u>help</u> students understand and use the
      A

   concepts of <u>science</u>, science educators
           B

   <u>place</u> much emphasis on observation,
    C

   discovery, and <u>the inquiry method</u>.
            D

   <u>No error</u>
    E

7. The music <u>had scarcely</u> begun <u>than</u> the
         A   B

   guests <u>started to fill</u> the dance floor,
        C

   most of them gyrating <u>out of time</u> with
               D

   the music. <u>No error</u>
         E

8. The policeman spoke <u>calmly</u> and firmly
   A
   to <u>we</u> <u>spectators</u> as he <u>directed</u> the
   B   C   D
   crowd out of the football stadium.

   <u>No error</u>
   E

9. The theme of the works <u>demonstrated</u> a
   A
   <u>recognition</u> yet a <u>departure from</u> the
   B   C
   past masters of epic poetry, <u>whose</u>
   D
   characters were greater than life.

   <u>No error</u>
   E

10. <u>Either this afternoon</u> or tomorrow
    A
    morning the state legislature <u>must</u>
    B
    decide <u>whether</u> or not <u>to enact</u> a new
    C   D
    tax cut. <u>No error</u>
    E

11. The <u>scope</u> of the community-
    A
    redevelopment project <u>has been</u>
    B
    enlarged and <u>will</u> require a minimum of
    C
    twenty-three new workers, <u>more or less</u>.
    D

    <u>No error</u>
    E

12. <u>Yesterday</u> several members of the class
    A
    <u>presented</u> opinion papers <u>based</u> on their
    B   C
    research <u>and respective points of view</u>.
    D

    <u>No error</u>
    E

13. <u>Students who</u> write <u>formal</u> term papers,
    A   B
    <u>even the most hardworking</u>, sometimes
    C
    have difficulty <u>with</u> placement and
    D
    order of footnotes. <u>No error</u>
    E

14. The <u>arguments for rent control</u> and the
    A
    arguments against rent control
    <u>expressed by those in opposition to it</u>
    B
    did not <u>convince</u> the city council
    C
    <u>one way or another</u>. <u>No error</u>
    D   E

15. When the home team <u>players</u> scored
    A
    three baskets in the final two minutes of
    the <u>game and</u> allowed no offsetting
    B
    points to the <u>visiting team</u>, <u>they literally</u>
    C   D
    broke the back of the opposition.

    <u>No error</u>
    E

16. The movie <u>received</u> an Oscar,
    A
    <u>a coveted award</u>, <u>for its</u> extraordinary
    B   C
    achievement in <u>special affects</u>. <u>No error</u>
    D   E

17. The <u>cause</u> of the accident <u>being</u> that
    A   B
    the intoxicated driver lost <u>control of the</u>
    C
    <u>wheel</u> and <u>veered</u> into an oncoming
    C   D
    truck. <u>No error</u>
    E

GO ON TO THE NEXT PAGE

Section **3** Writing Test

293

18. The typical plantation mansion <u>had</u>
                                    A
a high-columned <u>porch that</u> not
                    B
<u>only shaded</u> the first-floor rooms but
      C
gave the mansion an appearance of

<u>grandeur</u>. <u>No error</u>
   D   E

19. Rachel <u>Carson, a great American</u>
                        A
writer and marine biologist, produced

a series of books <u>that tells</u> what
                       B
people are doing to the delicate

balance of the <u>earth's life forms</u> on the
                        C
land <u>and in and near</u> the sea. <u>No error</u>
          D   E

20. Charles hated to play <u>chess with</u> anyone
                                    A
<u>who</u> was <u>better</u> than <u>he</u>. <u>No error</u>
  B   C   D   E

21. To keep <u>calm, to think</u> clearly, and
                    A
<u>answering</u> all the <u>questions that</u> are easy
    B   C
for <u>him or her are</u> three goals of any
        D
effective and well-prepared test taker.

<u>No error</u>
   E

Part B

SUGGESTED TIME: 20 Minutes

17 Questions

Directions: Some part of each sentence below is underlined; sometimes the whole sentence is underlined. Five choices for rephrasing the underlined part follow each sentence. The first choice, **A,** repeats the original, and the other four are different. If choice **A** seems better than the alternatives, choose answer **A;** if not, choose one of the others.

For each sentence, consider the requirements of standard written English. Your choice should be a correct, concise, and effective expression, not awkward or ambiguous. Focus on grammar, word choice, sentence construction, and punctuation. If a choice changes the meaning of the original sentence, do not select it.

---

22. The school-age child faces a formidable task when during the first few years of classroom experiences <u>he or she is expected to master the printed form of language</u>.

   A. he or she is expected to master the printed form of language

   B. he or she expects to master the printed form of language

   C. he or she faces expectations of mastering the printed form of language

   D. mastery of the printed form of language is expected of him or her

   E. mastery of print is expected by his or her teacher

23. He came to the United States as a young <u>man, he found</u> a job as a coal miner.

   A. man, he found

   B. man and found

   C. man and there he was able to find

   D. man and then finding

   E. man and had found

24. To a large degree, <u>poetry, along with all the other arts, is</u> a form of imitation.

   A. poetry, along with all the other arts, is

   B. poetry along with all the other arts is

   C. poetry, along with all the other arts, are

   D. poetry, and other arts, is

   E. poetry and art are

25. Delegates to the political convention found <u>difficulty to choose</u> a candidate from among the few nominated.

   A. difficulty to choose

   B. it difficult in making the choice of

   C. it difficult to choose

   D. choosing difficult when selecting

   E. making a choice difficult in selecting

GO ON TO THE NEXT PAGE

Section **3** Writing Test

26. Reading in any language can be viewed as a developmental task much the same as learning to walk, to cross the street independently, to care for one's possessions, or <u>accepting responsibility for one's own decisions</u>.

   A. accepting responsibility for one's own decisions

   B. accepting one's own decisions responsibly

   C. to accept responsibility for one's own decisions

   D. accepting responsibility and making one's own decisions

   E. to make one's own decisions

27. Sea forests of giant kelp, which fringe only one coastline in the Northern Hemisphere, <u>is native to shores</u> throughout the Southern Hemisphere.

   A. is native to shores

   B. is native to most shores

   C. are native only in shores

   D. are native

   E. are native to shores

28. A <u>university's board of regents and alumni association are two separate entities</u>, each having specialized areas of responsibility and kinds of authority.

   A. university's board of regents and alumni association are two separate entities

   B. universitys board of regents and alumni association are separate entities

   C. university's board of Regents and alumni Association are two separate entities

   D. university's board of regents and alumni association is separate entities

   E. university's board of regents and alumni association are entities

29. Like so many characters in Russian fiction, *Crime and Punishment* exhibits a behavior so foreign to the American temperament that many readers find the story rather incredible.

   A. *Crime and Punishment* exhibits

   B. those in *Crime and Punishment* exhibit

   C. those in *Crime and Punishment* exhibits

   D. often exhibiting

   E. characterized by

30. *Don Quixote* provides a cross section of Spanish life and thought and <u>portrays the feelings of many Spaniards</u> at the end of the chivalric age.

A. portrays the feelings of many Spaniards

B. portrayal of the feelings of many Spaniards

C. feelings portrayed by Spaniards

D. feelings

E. Spanish feelings

31. An infant, <u>whether lying alone in the crib or enjoying the company of adults, is consistently fascinated at</u> the movement of toes and fingers.

A. whether lying alone in the crib or enjoying the company of adults, is consistently fascinated at

B. alone or in company, is consistently fascinated at

C. whether lying alone in the crib or enjoying the company of adults, is constantly fascinated at

D. whether lying alone in the crib or enjoying the company of adults, is consistently fascinated by

E. lonely in the crib and enjoying the company of adults is consistently fascinated at

32. A policeman of proven valor, <u>the city council designated him</u> the "Outstanding Law Enforcement Officer of the Year."

A. the city council designated him

B. the city council's designating him

C. the city council will designate him

D. he designated the city council

E. he was designated by the city council

33. <u>If the room would have been brighter</u>, I would have been more successful in my search for the lost earrings.

A. If the room would have been brighter

B. If the room was brighter

C. If rooms were brighter

D. If the room could have been brighter

E. If the room had been brighter

34. After announcing that no notes could be used during the final exam, the instructor was compelled to fail <u>two students because they used notes anyway</u>.

A. two students because they used notes anyway

B. two students because of their notes

C. two students because of them using notes

D. two students whose notes were used

E. two students due to the use of their notes

Section **3** Writing Test

GO ON TO THE NEXT PAGE

297

35. The respiratory membranes, <u>through which exchange of gases occurs</u>, are the linings of the lungs.

   A. through which exchange of gases occurs

   B. through which exchange of gas occurs

   C. after gases are exchanged

   D. occurs through the exchange of gases

   E. through which gas is exchanged

36. Jeff is one of those <u>who tends to resist any attempt at</u> classification or regulation.

   A. who tends to resist any attempt at

   B. whose tendency to resist any attempt at

   C. who tend to resist any attempt at

   D. who tends to resist any attempt to

   E. who tends to resistance of any attempt at

37. <u>The amount of water in living cells vary</u>, but it is usually 65 percent and in some organisms may be as high as 96 percent or more of the total substance.

   A. The amount of water in living cells vary

   B. The amount of water varies

   C. The amount of water in cells vary

   D. The amount of water in living cells varies

   E. The amounts of water varies in living cells

38. <u>The belief of ancient scientists was</u> that maggots are generated from decaying bodies and filth and are not formed by reproduction.

   A. The belief of ancient scientists was

   B. The ancient scientists beliefs were

   C. The ancient scientists believe

   D. The belief of ancient scientists were

   E. The ancient belief of scientists was

IF YOU FINISH BEFORE TIME IS CALLED, CHECK YOUR WORK ON THIS SECTION ONLY. DO NOT WORK ON ANY OTHER SECTION IN THE TEST.

Writing Test: Essay Section

TIME: 30 Minutes

1 Essay

Directions: In this section, you will have 30 minutes to plan and write one essay on the topic given. You may use the paper provided to plan your essay before you begin writing. You should plan your time wisely. Read the topic carefully to make sure that you are properly addressing the issue or situation. **You must write on the given topic. An essay on another topic will not be acceptable.**

The essay question is designed to give you an opportunity to write clearly and effectively. Use specific examples whenever appropriate to aid in supporting your ideas. Keep in mind that the quality of your writing is much more important than the quantity.

Your essay is to be written in the space provided. No other paper may be used. Your writing should be neat and legible. Because you have only a limited amount of space in which to write, please do **not** skip lines, do **not** write excessively large, and do **not** leave wide margins.

Remember, use the bottom of this page for any organizational notes you may wish to make.

Topic

If you had to save two possessions from your burning house, what would you save? Explain why you selected them.

GO ON TO THE NEXT PAGE

Answer Key for Practice Test 3

Reading Test

1. B	21. B
2. B	22. D
3. B	23. A
4. E	24. D
5. E	25. D
6. C	26. B
7. A	27. C
8. B	28. A
9. B	29. E
10. C	30. E
11. D	31. C
12. A	32. E
13. E	33. D
14. C	34. A
15. D	35. A
16. C	36. B
17. D	37. C
18. E	38. D
19. A	39. A
20. C	40. E

Mathematics Test

1. C	21. E
2. B	22. D
3. D	23. E
4. C	24. E
5. D	25. E
6. A	26. D
7. C	27. E
8. C	28. C
9. C	29. B
10. B	30. B
11. C	31. B
12. B	32. D
13. B	33. A
14. A	34. D
15. E	35. D
16. D	36. B
17. C	37. C
18. C	38. E
19. B	39. B
20. D	40. B

Writing Test Multiple-Choice

1. D	21. B
2. B	22. A
3. A	23. B
4. D	24. A
5. A	25. C
6. E	26. C
7. B	27. E
8. B	28. E
9. B	29. B
10. E	30. D
11. D	31. D
12. D	32. E
13. C	33. E
14. B	34. A
15. D	35. A
16. D	36. C
17. B	37. D
18. E	38. A
19. E	
20. E	

Scoring Your PPST Practice Test 3

To score your PPST Practice Test 3, total the number of correct responses for each test. Do not subtract any points for questions attempted but missed, as there is no penalty for guessing. The scores for each section range from 150 to 190. Because the Writing Test contains multiple-choice questions and an essay, that score is a composite score adjusted to give approximately equal weight to the number right on the multiple-choice section and to the essay score. The essay is scored holistically (a single score for overall quality) from 1 (low) to 6 (high). Each of two readers gives a 1 to 6 score. The score that the essay receives is the sum of these two readers' scores.

Analyzing your test results

The following charts should be used to carefully analyze your results and spot your strengths and weaknesses. The complete process of analyzing each subject area and each individual question should be completed for this Practice Test. These results should be reexamined for trends in types of error (repeated errors) or poor results in specific subject areas. **This reexamination and analysis is of tremendous importance for effective test preparation.**

Practice Test 3: Subject area analysis sheet

	Possible	Completed	Right	Wrong
Reading Test	40			
Mathematics Test	40			
Writing Test	38			
TOTAL	118			

Analysis—tally sheet for questions missed

One of the most important parts of test preparation is analyzing why you missed a question so that you can reduce the number of mistakes. Now that you have taken Practice Test 3 and checked your answers, carefully tally your mistakes by marking each of them in the proper column.

	Total Missed	Simple Mistake	Misread Problem	Lack of Knowledge
Reading Test				
Mathematics Test				
Writing Test				
TOTAL				

Reviewing the data in the preceding chart should help you determine why you are missing certain questions. Now that you have pinpointed types of errors, focus on avoiding your most common type.

Score approximators

Reading Test

To approximate your reading score:

1. Count the number of questions you answered correctly.

2. Use the following table to match the number of correct answers and the corresponding approximate score range.

Number Right	Approximate Score Range
10–19	160–169
20–29	170–179
30–40	180–189

Remember, this is only an approximate score range. When you take the PPST, you will have questions that are similar to those in this book; however some questions may be slightly easier or more difficult.

Mathematics Test

To approximate your mathematics score:

1. Count the number of questions you answered correctly.

2. Use the following table to match the number of correct answers and the corresponding approximate score range.

Number Right	Approximate Score Range
0–10	150–160
11–20	161–170
21–30	171–180
31–40	181–190

Remember, this is an approximate score range.

Writing Test

These scores are difficult to approximate because the multiple-choice section score and the essay score are combined to give a total score.

Essay checklist

Use this checklist to evaluate your essay.

Diagnosis/prescription for timed writing exercise

A good essay will:

- ❑ Address the assignment

    Be well focused

- ❑ Be well organized

    Have smooth transitions between paragraphs

    Be coherent, unified

- ❑ Be well developed

    Contain specific examples to support points

- ❑ Be grammatically sound (only minor flaws)

    Use correct sentence structure

    Use correct punctuation

    Use standard written English

- ❑ Use language skillfully

    Use a variety of sentence types

    Use a variety of words

- ❑ Be legible

    Have clear handwriting

    Be neat

Answers and Explanations for Practice Test 3

Reading Test

1. **B.** The author's negative assessment suggests a negative attitude, and **B** offers the only negative choice.

2. **B.** Clarifying the confusing term *angular displacement* would help make the passage clearer.

3. **B.** The position of the pencil seemingly shifts according to which eye is seeing it—that is, according to the point from which it is observed.

4. **E.** The passage implies that those who administer the tests are different from experts on testing because the administrators do not see that the tests are limited measurements.

5. **E.** According to the third paragraph, taking candy away is the withdrawal of a positive reinforcer, and spanking is the presentation of a negative reinforcer.

6. **C.** The mention of recess and field trips follows this sentence: *Sometimes we withdraw a privilege from a child to control his behavior*. Therefore, we can conclude that the author is using recess and field trips as *examples* of such privileges.

7. **A.** The question posed in the first paragraph—"Does punishment, in fact, do what it is supposed to do?"—is not answered in a definite way. The first sentence of the passage says that *punishment is used to reduce tendencies to behave in certain ways*. The second paragraph goes on to state that punishment *seems to temporarily suppress a behavior*. This is a less-than-definite answer to the question.

8. **B.** Each of the other choices draws conclusions beyond the scope of the passage. The author suggests in the second paragraph that imposing punishment does not seem to have any *permanent* effect.

9. **B.** The author says that *human nature is not a machine* and stresses this point throughout the passage.

10. **C.** One way in which the author describes an automaton is a human machine *set to do exactly the work prescribed for it*. This description corresponds most closely to workers on an assembly line.

11. **D.** The author develops arguments in favor of *he who chooses his plan for himself;* therefore, the author must assume that there are those who need to hear this argument—namely, those who do not select their own life plans.

12. **A.** Early in the passage, the author shows that those who choose their own life plans must have complex skills, whereas those whose plan of life is chosen may live simply, with *no need of any other faculty than the ape-like one of imitation*.

13. E. The passage is an extended argument *against* the easy life of conformity.

14. C. The final sentence summarizes the *racist and elitist doctrine* mentioned in the sentence that precedes it.

15. D. The fourth sentence of the passage focuses on the relevance of Darwin's theory to human society, and the bulk of the passage develops this connection.

16. C. The second sentence distinguishes gifted children from children of average IQ and thereby equates gifted children with the *children with superior IQs* mentioned in the first sentence.

17. D. The author contrasts an early concern with social, motivational, and aptitudinal aspects of learning with the more recent interest in class activities. None of the other choices is an explicit point of the passage.

18. E. Since the passage describes the life and work of a man living in the eighteenth and nineteenth centuries, it would not be likely to appear in a seventeenth-century history.

19. A. Understanding punishment to be a type of negative reinforcement, we may infer that punishment may cause *continued learning disabilities*.

20. C. The passage says that budget cuts result in teaching staff cuts; choices **C** and **D** mention a staff cut, but **D** is a weak answer because it is overly specific and not necessarily true.

21. B. The second sentence adds more information about the *methods* of psychology.

22. D. The author sketches parallel changes in television and clothes, implying that the medium (TV) is responsible for changing taste in clothes.

23. A. The definition of a political party belongs in a text that explains such organizations and systems—namely, an introductory text on political science.

24. D. The statement initially assumes that *it is true there are two sides to every question*, but the passage says *it may be true*. Every question may be interpreted in more than one way.

25. D. Both statements I and II are true. Using the example of flypaper is an analogy; that it makes a big difference which side the fly chooses indicates the importance of choice. The statement does not, however, point out the ways of getting stuck on a question.

26. B. "On this 100th anniversary of his death, Twain . . ."

27. C. "We have ground the manhood out of them and the shame is ours, not theirs; and we should pay for it."

28. A. The irony and vernacular in *The Adventures of Huckleberry Finn* may have confused some readers and led to a *misunderstanding* of Twain's feelings about slavery and issues of race.

29. E. Choice **C** is incorrect because this is the 100th anniversary of his death according to the passage.

30. E. According to the passage, Pudd'nhead Wilson was *eccentric but clever*.

31. C. According to the passage, the auroras occur because of solar wind pushing against Earth's magnetic field, causing an electric power supply. In choice **B,** *caused by* makes the choice incorrect.

32. E. The auroras occur during these months; Earth's tail is always present.

33. D. Since Earth's tail is *similar to those of comets,* they are probably also composed of electrically charged particles.

34. A. Beatty argues that cutting even six minutes from his film destroys its artistic integrity. A similar and supporting line of argument would say that deleting parts of Beethoven's music or Shakespeare's plays would do the same.

35. A. The final sentence of the passage indicates that the author supports Beatty's demands. Only choice **A** reflects this point of view.

36. B. The thrust of the passage is the battle between Beatty and ABC for the final cut of the film *Reds.*

37. C. The passage suggests that Adam Smith considered statesmen in a negative way; thus, you can determine from context that *wont* is probably used to mean *accustomed.*

38. D. In promoting the spending of state funds to advertise California's tourist attractions, the author assumes such tourism will result in more income for the state. Choice **B** is incorrect because, while increased tourism may increase revenue, it cannot be assumed that such an increase will decrease the competition from other states.

39. A. Implied by the passage is the belief that the campaign, if effective, will bring in many times in tourist revenue what the advertising initially cost.

40. E. *States* and *nations* are used in the passage synonymously as *countries* or independently governed territories.

Mathematics Test

1. C. Five washloads at 15 minutes per load equals 1 hour and 15 minutes. If the washing commences at 3:20 p.m., adding 1:15 results in the work being finished at 4:35 p.m.

2. B. The decimal equivalent of the fraction $\frac{3}{8}$ may be found by dividing the numerator by the denominator, or 3 divided by 8.

$$
\begin{array}{r}
0.375 \\
8\overline{)3.000} \\
\underline{24} \\
60 \\
\underline{56} \\
40 \\
\underline{40}
\end{array}
$$

The closest answer choice is 0.38.

3. D. To find the area of a triangle, one needs to know its base and height. Line segment *DE* is the height of not only the rectangle, but also the triangle, and therefore would be helpful in determining the triangle's area.

4. C. Round 47 up to 50, round 9.10 down to 9, and then multiply the two values.

5. D. Depending on the date in 2015, Tina could be 47 or 48. If the date is before December 4, she is 47; if it is past her birthday, then she is 48.

6. A. Combining debts of $1,300 with a deficit of $2,800 gives a much bigger deficit: −$2,800 combined with −$1,300 = −$4,100.

7. C. In 2001, approximately 11 million people were unemployed. In 2006, approximately 5 million people were unemployed. So 11 million − 5 million = 6 million.

8. C. Evaluate the digit that is one place to the right of the hundredth place. Since that digit (thousandth place) is less than 5, that digit and all digits to its right are dropped.

$$294.3\underline{5}49 \text{ becomes } 294.35$$
$$\nearrow$$
$$\text{hundredth place}$$

9. C. If six tests average 85%, then their total must be 6 × 85, or 510 total percentage points. None of the other choices can be determined from the information given.

10. B. Since there are 2 favorable outcomes (2 or 3) and since there are 8 possible outcomes, the probability is $\frac{2}{8}$, or $\frac{1}{4}$.

11. C. A close look at the gauge shows that the arrow is between 50 and 75, but it is not past the halfway point, so it is approximately 60.

12. B. Algebraically: Let *x* equal number of roses; then 3*x* equals number of carnations.

$$(x)(1.00)+(3x)(0.50)=7.50$$
$$x + 1.5x = 7.50$$
$$2.5x = 7.50$$
$$x = 3 \text{ roses}$$

Working up from the answer choices might have been easier. Notice that only answer choice **B,** 3 roses, will give a total of $7.50, since 3 roses purchased means 9 carnations purchased (triple the number of roses). Three roses at $1 each plus 9 carnations at $0.50 each equals $3 + $4.50 = $7.50. Only choice **B** will result in $7.50 spent on all the flowers.

13. B. Set up an equation

$$\frac{3}{10} \text{ of gross is } 15,000$$

$$\frac{3}{10}x = 15,000$$

Multiply both sides by $\left(\frac{10}{3}\right)$:

$$\left(\frac{10}{3}\right) \times \left(\frac{3}{10}\right)x = \frac{\overset{5,000}{\cancel{15,000}}}{1}\left(\frac{10}{\cancel{3}_1}\right)$$
$$x = 5,000(10)$$
$$x = 50,000$$

Or realizing that $\frac{3}{10}x = 15{,}000$, then $\frac{1}{10}x = 5{,}000$, and $5{,}000 \times 10 = \$50{,}000$

14. A. You may notice that any integer multiplied by 2 leaves an even number. Adding 4 to an even number will always give an even number. Or you could try some values.

Let $x = 1$.

> 1 plus 5 equals 6, times 2 equals 12, plus 4 equals 16.

Let $x = 2$.

> 2 plus 5 equals 7, times 2 equals 14, plus 4 equals 18.

15. E. Tripling the length gives $3y$, and doubling the width gives $2x$. The area would then be $2x$ times $3y$, or $6xy$.

16. D. Substituting -2 for a, -4 for b, 5 for c, and 1 for d gives

$$\frac{-2 + -4}{5 + 1} = \frac{-6}{6} = -1$$

17. C. Working out each choice is probably the simplest method.

A. $27 \times 4 \times 5 = 108 \times 5 = 540$

B. $4 \times 5 \times 27 = 20 \times 27 = 540$

C. $9 \times 7 \times 12 = 63 \times 12 = 756$

The answer must be **C** because choices **A** and **B** are 540 and only one answer is *not* equivalent. You don't need to work further.

18. C. Rounding each value in choice **C** results in $(10)(9)$, which totals 90. The original total is $(9.8)(8.7) = 85.26$, or less than 90.

19. B. Plot the points on a coordinate graph.

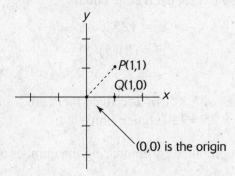

Only II is true. P is farther from the origin than P is from Q.

20. D. The highest average daily temperature during the dates shown was approximately $76°$. The lowest was approximately $58°$. Therefore, $76° - 58° = 18°$.

21. E. Total number of different combinations ("how many different kinds") is found by multiplying the number of ways for each item. Therefore, 3 different breads times 4 different meats times 3 different cheeses $= 3 \times 4 \times 3 = 36$.

22. D. For the perimeter of a square to be 20, each side must be 5 because all sides are the same. So the area is 5×5, or 25 square inches.

23. E. To answer this question, subtract the distance Sasha walked from the distance Theo walked.

$$
\begin{array}{rcl}
6\frac{1}{4} = & 5\frac{5}{4} \\
-4\frac{3}{4} = & -4\frac{3}{4} \\
\hline
& 1\frac{2}{4} = 1\frac{1}{2}
\end{array}
$$

Another way to approach this is to change each mixed fraction to an improper fraction and then subtract and reduce your answer.

$$
\begin{array}{rcl}
6\frac{1}{4} = & \frac{25}{4} \\
-4\frac{3}{4} = & -\frac{19}{4} \\
\hline
\frac{6}{4} = & 1\frac{2}{4} = 1\frac{1}{2}
\end{array}
$$

24. E. To determine the amount of paint used, one needs to know the number of rooms painted and how many gallons were used in each room. Since the question itself provides the number of rooms painted, choice **E** provides the necessary information.

25. E. Since $x - 2y$ is half of $2x - 4y$, then $x - 2y$ must be 10.

26. D. In 2006, approximately 500 million barrels were in reserve. In 2000, approximately 100 million barrels were in reserve. Therefore, there were approximately 400 million, or 400,000,000, more barrels in reserve in 2006 than in 2000.

27. E. If the volume of a cube is 125, each edge equals 5.

$$e^3 = 125$$
$$e^3 = (5)(5)(5)$$
$$e = 5$$

Each side will have an area of 5×5, or 25. Since there are 6 sides to a cube, the total surface area of the cube is $6 \times 25 = 150$ square units.

28. C. Simple probability is computed by comparing the number of favorable outcomes versus the number of total outcomes. Since there are 6 odd numbers from 1 to 12 (1, 3, 5, 7, 9, 11), out of a total of 12 numbers, the probability of getting an odd number is $\frac{6}{12}$, or $\frac{1}{2}$. In this problem, the result of the first spin has no effect on the result of the second spin.

29. B. The large carpet 8' by 8', equals 64 square feet. A small square, 2' by 2', equals 4 square feet. Dividing the large area of 64 by 4 equals 16 small squares.

30. B. $\frac{3}{5} \times \frac{30}{7} =$

Canceling gives $\frac{3}{\cancel{5}_1} \times \frac{\cancel{30}^6}{7} = \frac{18}{7}$

31. B. II only.

The arithmetic mean is the average (sum divided by number of items), or $6 + 2 + 10 + 2 + 5 = 25$ divided by $5 = 5$.

The median is the middle number after the numbers have been ordered: 2, 2, 5, 6, 10. The median is 5.

The mode is the most frequently appearing number: 2.

The range is the highest minus the lowest, or $10 - 2 = 8$.

Therefore, only II is true: the median (5) equals the mean (5).

32. D. Parallel lines are always the same distance apart. Only the figure in choice **D** appears to contain two pairs of parallel lines.

33. A. Since Tom is shorter than Lebron and Jordan, and Jordan is shorter than Luke, who is shorter than Tony, Tom is the shortest.

34. D. Since 30 cups is $2\frac{1}{2}$ times 12 cups, multiply 5 cakes by 2.5.

$$5 \times 2.5 = 12.5$$
$$\text{or}$$
$$\frac{12}{5} = \frac{30}{x}$$

Cross multiplying gives

$$12x = 150$$

Dividing by 12:

$$x = \frac{150}{12} = 12.5$$

35. D. Since Mrs. Solis received a 30% discount, she paid 70% of the retail price: $(0.70)(\$800) = \$560$. Mrs. Solis paid \$560.

36. B. Reynolds's average score was 24.8, and Doe's average was 13.7. Therefore, $24.8 - 13.7 = 11.1$.

37. C. Twelve gallons is one-third more than 9 gallons. Therefore, the number of miles will be one-third more than 240, or $240 + 80 = 320$. You could have used a proportion.

$$\frac{\text{miles}}{\text{gallons}} \cdot \frac{240}{9} = \frac{x}{12}$$

Cross multiplying gives

$$9x = 2{,}880$$

Dividing by 9:

$$x = \frac{2880}{9} = 320$$

38. E. Solving the inequality gives

Subtract 6.

$$
\begin{array}{r}
2x + 6 > 9 \\
-6 -6 \\
\hline
2x > 3
\end{array}
$$

Divide by 2.

$$\frac{2x}{2} > 3$$

$$x > \frac{3}{2}$$

or

$$x > 1\frac{1}{2}$$

Only choice **E** is a value greater than $1\frac{1}{2}$. You could also simply plug in the choices and eliminiate the ones that do not make the statement true.

39. B. You need to find the *area* of the top. Area = length $\times$ width. Length = 6 and width = 4.5. Therefore, area = $(6)(4.5)$.

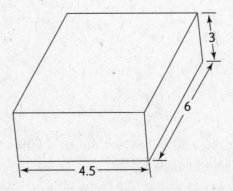

40. B. A careful look tells you that the only answer choice possible is

$$3 \times \$3.99 = \$11.97.$$

A quick way to approach this is to round prices up one cent

$$3 \times \$4.00 = \$12.00.$$

Writing Test: Multiple-Choice Section

Part A

1. **D.** *In formal dress* is a misplaced modifier that should be positioned near *come,* the word it modifies. Otherwise, the sentence seems to say that the restaurant is wearing formal dress.

2. **B.** Because of the placement of the word *frequently* in this sentence, it is unclear whether the people *wrote letters* frequently or *recount* frequently. To solve the problem, the word *frequently* could be placed preceding the word *write.* Using a comma between *letters* and *frequently* or between *frequently* and *recount* would be inappropriate because it would set off the subject from its verb.

3. **A.** *Libraries* should be either *libraries'* (the plural possessive) or *library's* (the singular possessive), depending on the intent of the writer. *Children's* **B** is the correct formation of an irregular plural possessive (*woman's/women's—man's/men's—mouse's/mice's*) where the root word changes to form the plural. *Fact-finding* correctly hyphenates two words used as a single adjective *preceding* a noun (*She was a well-known author* but *The author was well known*).

4. **D.** *And occurring only in this country* repeats the meaning of *unique* and is therefore unnecessary.

5. **A.** *You* is the correct pronoun in this sentence instead of *yourself. Yourself* is the reflexive form of the pronoun and is correct only in such structures as *You, yourself, must be there* (subject repeated for emphasis) and *You hurt yourself* (subject repeated as object).

6. **E.** This sentence contains no error. *The inquiry method* **D** is parallel to *observation* and *discovery* (all nouns). Adding the article *the* and the adjective *inquiry* to the noun does not change the fact that it is parallel.

7. **B.** *Than* is ungrammatical. *When* is correct after *had . . . begun,* introducing the adverb clause describing when the music began.

8. **B.** *We* is the subjective form of the pronoun and is incorrect. *Us* is the correct pronoun in this case. By mentally removing the word *spectators* and rereading the sentence, you can "hear" this error.

9. **B.** The correct idioms are *recognition of* and *departure from;* choice **C** is correct, but **B** must be completed with a preposition—*recognition of yet a departure from . . . Demonstrated* is correct, as it refers to *theme,* not to *works. Whose* is correct—not *who's* (the contraction for *who is*).

10. **E.** This is the correct spelling of *whether* as opposed to *weather.*

11. **D.** *More or less* contradicts the idea of *minimum* and should be eliminated for the sake of clarity.

12. **D.** *Respective points of view* repeats the idea expressed earlier in the sentence by *opinion* and should be omitted to correct the redundancy error.

13. **C.** The placement of *even the most hardworking* makes it seem that the phrase refers to *term papers* rather than to *students* (which it correctly modifies). The problem may be solved by moving the phrase to the beginning of the sentence. There should be no comma between *students* and *who* **A** because *who write formal term papers* is restrictive (not all students are discussed here). *Have difficulty with* **D** is the correct idiom.

14. **B.** *Expressed by those in opposition to it* is redundant when used with *arguments against.* In this context it might even be construed as referring to both *arguments for* and *arguments against,* which would make the sentence nonsensical. The phrase should be eliminated.

15. **D.** The word *literally* means "according to fact, free from exaggeration." The home team did not actually break the backs of the opposing players. The word that is wanted in this context is *figuratively,* meaning in a manner of speaking, characterized by a figure of speech. There should be no comma between *game* and *and.* The comma after *team* correctly sets off the subordinate clause from the main clause.

16. **D.** *Special affects* should be *special effects. Affect* is a verb, meaning "to act upon or influence." *Effect* is a noun, meaning a distinct impression (as in this example) or a verb meaning to bring about.

17. **B.** *Being* is ungrammatical and creates a sentence fragment. The word should be *was.*

18. **E.** This sentence contains no error.

19. **E.** The present tense is always used when referring to books; therefore, *tells* is correct. As *tells* refers to *a series* (singular) not to *books* (plural), the singular form of the verb is correct.

20. **E.** There is no error in the sentence. The pronouns *I, he, she,* and *they* are correct following *than.*

21. **B.** *To answer* instead of *answering* is correct parallel structure in this sentence.

Part B

22. **A.** None of the choices improves on the original wording.

23. **B.** Choice **B** corrects the run-on sentence. Two independent clauses cannot be connected with only a comma. Choice **B** adds *and* and eliminates *he,* correcting the structural error in the original. Choice **C** changes the meaning by emphasizing where he got a job and lacks a necessary comma before *and.*

24. **A.** Choice **A** is correct. *Along with all the other arts* should be set off by commas, and *is* is the correct verb form to agree with *poetry,* a singular subject. Choice **E** changes the meaning of the original sentence.

25. **C.** The phrase *difficulty to choose* is idiomatically incorrect. Choices **B** and **E** are wordy and awkward options, and choice **D** slightly changes the emphasis in the original sentence from *difficulty* to *choosing.* Choice **C** is the most direct wording. *Difficulty in choosing* would also be correct, but that is not given as an option.

26. C. The original sentence lacks parallel structure. Choices **B** and **D** do not change *accepting* to the parallel verb form *to accept*. Choice **E** changes the meaning of the sentence. Choice **C** is correct and parallel to the three other verb phrases *to walk, to cross the street independently,* and *to care for one's possessions.*

27. E. The singular verb *is* needs to be plural to agree with *sea forests.* Choice **B** is singular. Although *are* is used in choices **C** and **D**, **C** is idiomatically wrong, and **D** does not make sense. Choice **E** corrects the verb error and structurally fits with the rest of the original sentence.

28. E. *Entities* means "independent, separate, or self-contained units." To use *separate entities* is redundant. To use *two separate entities* is doubly redundant; it is obvious from the beginning of the sentence that there are two. All choices except **E** contain one or both of these errors. In addition, choice **B** drops a necessary apostrophe in *university's;* choice **C** capitalizes *regents* and *association* (these are not the names of specific groups and need not be capitalized; however, if capitals were used, *board* and *alumni* would have to be included); and **D** introduces a verb error in the singular *is* referring to the plural subject.

29. B. Characters cannot be compared to the novel *Crime and Punishment.* Choice **B** inserts *those,* which correctly words the comparison. Choices **D** and **E** create an incomplete sentence and leave out necessary information. *Exhibits* in choice **C** is singular and incorrect.

30. D. Choices **A** and **B** are not parallel and contain the redundant phrase *of many Spaniards.* Choices **C** and **E** are also redundant because they include the words *Spaniards* and *Spanish.* Choice **D** is parallel and concise.

31. D. *Fascinated by* or *fascinated with* is idiomatic. *Fascinated at* is not. All choices except **D** retain this error. Choices **B** and **E** also unnecessarily change the meaning of the sentence, as does **C** in substituting *constantly* for *consistently.*

32. E. The misplaced-modifier error is corrected in choice **E** by placing *he* close to the phrase *a policeman of proven valor.* Choice **D** changes the meaning of the original sentence.

33. E. This is a verb-tense error; *would have* should be changed to *had.*

34. A. The original sentence is correct. Choices **B, D,** and **E** are ambiguous; it is not clear *who* was using the notes. Choice **C** contains a grammar error; it uses *them* instead of *their.*

35. A. The sentence is correct as it stands. Choices **B** and **E** imply that there is only one type of gas, choice **C** implies that the membranes become linings only after the exchange of gases, and choice **D** implies that the membranes are caused by the exchange.

36. C. Following the construction *one of those who,* the verb must be plural, *tend* instead of *tends,* because the verb refers to *those* (plural), not to *one.* Only choice **C** supplies the verb *tend.* Choice **B** creates a sentence fragment; and choice **D** introduces an idiomatic error—*attempt to classification.*

37. D. The subject *amount* does not agree with the verb *vary.* Choice **D** corrects this error without changing the meaning of the original sentence.

38. A. The sentence is correct. Choices **B, C,** and **E** are grammatically correct but change the meaning slightly. Choice **D** contains a subject-verb error.

Answer Sheet for Practice Test 4

(Remove this sheet and use it to mark your answers.)

Reading Test

1 Ⓐ Ⓑ Ⓒ Ⓓ Ⓔ	26 Ⓐ Ⓑ Ⓒ Ⓓ Ⓔ
2 Ⓐ Ⓑ Ⓒ Ⓓ Ⓔ	27 Ⓐ Ⓑ Ⓒ Ⓓ Ⓔ
3 Ⓐ Ⓑ Ⓒ Ⓓ Ⓔ	28 Ⓐ Ⓑ Ⓒ Ⓓ Ⓔ
4 Ⓐ Ⓑ Ⓒ Ⓓ Ⓔ	29 Ⓐ Ⓑ Ⓒ Ⓓ Ⓔ
5 Ⓐ Ⓑ Ⓒ Ⓓ Ⓔ	30 Ⓐ Ⓑ Ⓒ Ⓓ Ⓔ
6 Ⓐ Ⓑ Ⓒ Ⓓ Ⓔ	31 Ⓐ Ⓑ Ⓒ Ⓓ Ⓔ
7 Ⓐ Ⓑ Ⓒ Ⓓ Ⓔ	32 Ⓐ Ⓑ Ⓒ Ⓓ Ⓔ
8 Ⓐ Ⓑ Ⓒ Ⓓ Ⓔ	33 Ⓐ Ⓑ Ⓒ Ⓓ Ⓔ
9 Ⓐ Ⓑ Ⓒ Ⓓ Ⓔ	34 Ⓐ Ⓑ Ⓒ Ⓓ Ⓔ
10 Ⓐ Ⓑ Ⓒ Ⓓ Ⓔ	35 Ⓐ Ⓑ Ⓒ Ⓓ Ⓔ
11 Ⓐ Ⓑ Ⓒ Ⓓ Ⓔ	36 Ⓐ Ⓑ Ⓒ Ⓓ Ⓔ
12 Ⓐ Ⓑ Ⓒ Ⓓ Ⓔ	37 Ⓐ Ⓑ Ⓒ Ⓓ Ⓔ
13 Ⓐ Ⓑ Ⓒ Ⓓ Ⓔ	38 Ⓐ Ⓑ Ⓒ Ⓓ Ⓔ
14 Ⓐ Ⓑ Ⓒ Ⓓ Ⓔ	39 Ⓐ Ⓑ Ⓒ Ⓓ Ⓔ
15 Ⓐ Ⓑ Ⓒ Ⓓ Ⓔ	40 Ⓐ Ⓑ Ⓒ Ⓓ Ⓔ
16 Ⓐ Ⓑ Ⓒ Ⓓ Ⓔ	41 Ⓐ Ⓑ Ⓒ Ⓓ Ⓔ
17 Ⓐ Ⓑ Ⓒ Ⓓ Ⓔ	42 Ⓐ Ⓑ Ⓒ Ⓓ Ⓔ
18 Ⓐ Ⓑ Ⓒ Ⓓ Ⓔ	43 Ⓐ Ⓑ Ⓒ Ⓓ Ⓔ
19 Ⓐ Ⓑ Ⓒ Ⓓ Ⓔ	44 Ⓐ Ⓑ Ⓒ Ⓓ Ⓔ
20 Ⓐ Ⓑ Ⓒ Ⓓ Ⓔ	45 Ⓐ Ⓑ Ⓒ Ⓓ Ⓔ
21 Ⓐ Ⓑ Ⓒ Ⓓ Ⓔ	46 Ⓐ Ⓑ Ⓒ Ⓓ Ⓔ
22 Ⓐ Ⓑ Ⓒ Ⓓ Ⓔ	
23 Ⓐ Ⓑ Ⓒ Ⓓ Ⓔ	
24 Ⓐ Ⓑ Ⓒ Ⓓ Ⓔ	
25 Ⓐ Ⓑ Ⓒ Ⓓ Ⓔ	

Mathematics Test

1 Ⓐ Ⓑ Ⓒ Ⓓ Ⓔ	26 Ⓐ Ⓑ Ⓒ Ⓓ Ⓔ
2 Ⓐ Ⓑ Ⓒ Ⓓ Ⓔ	27 Ⓐ Ⓑ Ⓒ Ⓓ Ⓔ
3 Ⓐ Ⓑ Ⓒ Ⓓ Ⓔ	28 Ⓐ Ⓑ Ⓒ Ⓓ Ⓔ
4 Ⓐ Ⓑ Ⓒ Ⓓ Ⓔ	29 Ⓐ Ⓑ Ⓒ Ⓓ Ⓔ
5 Ⓐ Ⓑ Ⓒ Ⓓ Ⓔ	30 Ⓐ Ⓑ Ⓒ Ⓓ Ⓔ
6 Ⓐ Ⓑ Ⓒ Ⓓ Ⓔ	31 Ⓐ Ⓑ Ⓒ Ⓓ Ⓔ
7 Ⓐ Ⓑ Ⓒ Ⓓ Ⓔ	32 Ⓐ Ⓑ Ⓒ Ⓓ Ⓔ
8 Ⓐ Ⓑ Ⓒ Ⓓ Ⓔ	33 Ⓐ Ⓑ Ⓒ Ⓓ Ⓔ
9 Ⓐ Ⓑ Ⓒ Ⓓ Ⓔ	34 Ⓐ Ⓑ Ⓒ Ⓓ Ⓔ
10 Ⓐ Ⓑ Ⓒ Ⓓ Ⓔ	35 Ⓐ Ⓑ Ⓒ Ⓓ Ⓔ
11 Ⓐ Ⓑ Ⓒ Ⓓ Ⓔ	36 Ⓐ Ⓑ Ⓒ Ⓓ Ⓔ
12 Ⓐ Ⓑ Ⓒ Ⓓ Ⓔ	37 Ⓐ Ⓑ Ⓒ Ⓓ Ⓔ
13 Ⓐ Ⓑ Ⓒ Ⓓ Ⓔ	38 Ⓐ Ⓑ Ⓒ Ⓓ Ⓔ
14 Ⓐ Ⓑ Ⓒ Ⓓ Ⓔ	39 Ⓐ Ⓑ Ⓒ Ⓓ Ⓔ
15 Ⓐ Ⓑ Ⓒ Ⓓ Ⓔ	40 Ⓐ Ⓑ Ⓒ Ⓓ Ⓔ
16 Ⓐ Ⓑ Ⓒ Ⓓ Ⓔ	41 Ⓐ Ⓑ Ⓒ Ⓓ Ⓔ
17 Ⓐ Ⓑ Ⓒ Ⓓ Ⓔ	42 Ⓐ Ⓑ Ⓒ Ⓓ Ⓔ
18 Ⓐ Ⓑ Ⓒ Ⓓ Ⓔ	43 Ⓐ Ⓑ Ⓒ Ⓓ Ⓔ
19 Ⓐ Ⓑ Ⓒ Ⓓ Ⓔ	44 Ⓐ Ⓑ Ⓒ Ⓓ Ⓔ
20 Ⓐ Ⓑ Ⓒ Ⓓ Ⓔ	45 Ⓐ Ⓑ Ⓒ Ⓓ Ⓔ
21 Ⓐ Ⓑ Ⓒ Ⓓ Ⓔ	46 Ⓐ Ⓑ Ⓒ Ⓓ Ⓔ
22 Ⓐ Ⓑ Ⓒ Ⓓ Ⓔ	
23 Ⓐ Ⓑ Ⓒ Ⓓ Ⓔ	
24 Ⓐ Ⓑ Ⓒ Ⓓ Ⓔ	
25 Ⓐ Ⓑ Ⓒ Ⓓ Ⓔ	

CUT HERE

Writing Test: Multiple Choice

Part A

1 Ⓐ Ⓑ Ⓒ Ⓓ Ⓔ
2 Ⓐ Ⓑ Ⓒ Ⓓ Ⓔ
3 Ⓐ Ⓑ Ⓒ Ⓓ Ⓔ
4 Ⓐ Ⓑ Ⓒ Ⓓ Ⓔ
5 Ⓐ Ⓑ Ⓒ Ⓓ Ⓔ

6 Ⓐ Ⓑ Ⓒ Ⓓ Ⓔ
7 Ⓐ Ⓑ Ⓒ Ⓓ Ⓔ
8 Ⓐ Ⓑ Ⓒ Ⓓ Ⓔ
9 Ⓐ Ⓑ Ⓒ Ⓓ Ⓔ
10 Ⓐ Ⓑ Ⓒ Ⓓ Ⓔ

11 Ⓐ Ⓑ Ⓒ Ⓓ Ⓔ
12 Ⓐ Ⓑ Ⓒ Ⓓ Ⓔ
13 Ⓐ Ⓑ Ⓒ Ⓓ Ⓔ
14 Ⓐ Ⓑ Ⓒ Ⓓ Ⓔ
15 Ⓐ Ⓑ Ⓒ Ⓓ Ⓔ

16 Ⓐ Ⓑ Ⓒ Ⓓ Ⓔ
17 Ⓐ Ⓑ Ⓒ Ⓓ Ⓔ
18 Ⓐ Ⓑ Ⓒ Ⓓ Ⓔ
19 Ⓐ Ⓑ Ⓒ Ⓓ Ⓔ
20 Ⓐ Ⓑ Ⓒ Ⓓ Ⓔ

21 Ⓐ Ⓑ Ⓒ Ⓓ Ⓔ
22 Ⓐ Ⓑ Ⓒ Ⓓ Ⓔ
23 Ⓐ Ⓑ Ⓒ Ⓓ Ⓔ
24 Ⓐ Ⓑ Ⓒ Ⓓ Ⓔ

Part B

25 Ⓐ Ⓑ Ⓒ Ⓓ Ⓔ
26 Ⓐ Ⓑ Ⓒ Ⓓ Ⓔ
27 Ⓐ Ⓑ Ⓒ Ⓓ Ⓔ
28 Ⓐ Ⓑ Ⓒ Ⓓ Ⓔ
29 Ⓐ Ⓑ Ⓒ Ⓓ Ⓔ
30 Ⓐ Ⓑ Ⓒ Ⓓ Ⓔ

31 Ⓐ Ⓑ Ⓒ Ⓓ Ⓔ
32 Ⓐ Ⓑ Ⓒ Ⓓ Ⓔ
33 Ⓐ Ⓑ Ⓒ Ⓓ Ⓔ
34 Ⓐ Ⓑ Ⓒ Ⓓ Ⓔ
35 Ⓐ Ⓑ Ⓒ Ⓓ Ⓔ

36 Ⓐ Ⓑ Ⓒ Ⓓ Ⓔ
37 Ⓐ Ⓑ Ⓒ Ⓓ Ⓔ
38 Ⓐ Ⓑ Ⓒ Ⓓ Ⓔ
39 Ⓐ Ⓑ Ⓒ Ⓓ Ⓔ
40 Ⓐ Ⓑ Ⓒ Ⓓ Ⓔ

41 Ⓐ Ⓑ Ⓒ Ⓓ Ⓔ
42 Ⓐ Ⓑ Ⓒ Ⓓ Ⓔ
43 Ⓐ Ⓑ Ⓒ Ⓓ Ⓔ
44 Ⓐ Ⓑ Ⓒ Ⓓ Ⓔ

Practice Test 4 (Computer-Based Format)

Reading Test

TIME: 75 Minutes

46 Questions

Directions: A question or number of questions follows each of the statements or passages in this section. Using only the *stated* or *implied* information given in the statement or passage, answer the question or questions by choosing the *best* answer from among the five choices given. No previous knowledge of the topic is necessary to answer the questions.

Questions 1 and 2 refer to the following passage.

Although some purists argue that the 1906 games in Athens shouldn't really be considered Olympic games because an Olympiad is four years and the correct
(5) interval would be from 1904 (the games in St. Louis) to 1908 (the games in London), the 1906 Athens games are written into the record as Olympic games. For Americans especially, this is
(10) important, because the 1906 games were the first time the United States had a real Olympic team: thirty-five athletes, financed by nationwide donations. The participating athletes were selected by an
(15) American Olympic committee, headed by its honorary chairman President Theodore Roosevelt, who had always enthusiastically supported all athletics.

1. The primary purpose of the passage is to

   A. explain why the 1906 games in Athens are not officially considered Olympic games.

   B. show the importance of Theodore Roosevelt to the development of an American team.

   C. describe the selection process for Olympic athletes.

   D. document the first time the United States had a real Olympic team.

   E. criticize those who don't accept the 1906 contest as true Olympic games.

GO ON TO THE NEXT PAGE

2. The term "purists" in the first sentence refers to

  A. inexperienced historians.

  B. people of limited imagination.

  C. people who adhere strictly to a definition.

  D. people who are not corrupted by popular opinion.

  E. uninformed amateurs.

Questions 3 through 6 refer to the following passage.

Urban legends are a form of modern folklore—a combination of fairy tales, parables, and information from the grapevine. Unlike fairy tales, however,
(5) urban legends are intended to be taken as truth, stories of real events happening to real people, even when the events seem not only unlikely but also bizarre or farcical. Usually urban legends are
(10) passed on in the form of "I heard it from a friend of a friend." The audience assumes that while the story isn't firsthand information, it comes from a source close enough to be verified, if one chose
(15) to verify it, which one seldom does. While some urban legends are elaborate stories filled with gruesome details, others are succinct. For example, the story that Mrs. O'Leary's cow caused The
(20) Great Chicago Fire by knocking over an oil lamp is an urban legend captured in a single line.

With the advent of the Internet, cyber-legends are born every day and cover
(25) subjects ranging from massive governmental conspiracies to animals performing incredible feats to medical mishaps and miracles to tear-jerking stories of redemption. Some contain warnings about
(30) products (deodorant causes cancer, for example) or the end of the world. The Internet has become the backyard fence of the good old days, when gossip and stories were exchanged without the filter
(35) of facts and hardcore information.

Like every form of mythology and folklore, urban legends reveal aspects of human nature. A quick look at urban legends in today's world reveals both
(40) our fears and suspicions and our need to believe in miracles, both our taste for shocking details and our need for a good cry.

3. Which of the following is an unstated assumption of the author expressed in the passage?

  A. Urban legends are part of an oral tradition.

  B. If a story is particularly bizarre, it is untrue.

  C. People will try to verify a story that is passed on to them by a friend.

  D. Urban legends are dangerous and cause serious misunderstandings.

  E. The story of Mrs. O'Leary's cow and The Great Chicago Fire is unlikely but true.

4. According to the passage, the difference between fairy tales and urban legends is that

A. fairy tales have individual authors, whereas urban legends do not.

B. urban legends are produced for adults, whereas fairy tales are for children.

C. fairy tales don't deal with grotesque behavior, whereas urban legends often relish in bizarre details.

D. the intention of urban legends is to cause people to change behavior, whereas the intention of fairy tales is to entertain.

E. fairy tales are intended to be seen as fiction, whereas urban legends are intended to be seen as fact.

5. The author's intention in the last sentence of the passage is to

A. contrast the modern world with an earlier age.

B. summarize some of the main themes of modern urban legends.

C. criticize the quality of urban legends passed on through the Internet.

D. show that urban legends lack the charm of earlier legends and fairy tales.

E. ridicule people's need to pass on stories that are not true.

6. In the second paragraph, the author uses the metaphor of the backyard fence to describe the Internet for which of the following reasons?

A. Both can be sources of uncensored tales and information.

B. Both are means by which uneducated people can communicate with each other.

C. A backyard fence, like the Internet, has a definite purpose.

D. The Internet, like the backyard fence, encourages casual friendships.

E. Both are the result of urban existence.

Question 7 refers to the following passage.

The products of Cro-Magnons, who lived more than 50,000 years ago, include tools of diverse shapes and multipiece modern weapons. However, of all the Cro-Magnon products that have been unearthed, the best known are their works of art. Anyone who has seen the life-sized paintings of bulls and horses in the Lascaux Cave in southwestern France will acknowledge that their creators were ancestors of modern man.

GO ON TO THE NEXT PAGE

7. According to the statement, it can be inferred that

   A. the images painted in the Lascaux Cave by the Cro-Magnons are clearly recognizable today.

   B. the weapons created during the Cro-Magnon era differ from those created by Neanderthals.

   C. art was one of the Cro-Magnons' primary interests.

   D. the production of art is more significant than the production of tools in a civilization.

   E. the Cro-Magnons are the oldest representative of the human species.

Questions 8 and 9 refer to the following passage.

Charles Darwin's early life doesn't suggest the importance of his place in history. Darwin was a mediocre student and showed no signs of academic preco-
(5) ciousness. He hated the regimentation of the school curriculum, which was at that time centered on the classics. Because of his father's wishes, Darwin entered medical school, but he wasn't successful
(10) there either. In fact, he was so repulsed by cutting up a human cadaver that he never finished his studies. At the end of his rope, Darwin's father ordered Charles to apply to Cambridge
(15) University to obtain a degree that would allow him to join the clergy. Ironically, Charles Darwin's monumental adult work—the theory of evolution—not only changed the world but also threw
(20) into question many religious beliefs.
Like Darwin, Albert Einstein can per-haps be described as a "late bloomer." Born in southern Germany in 1879, Einstein didn't learn to speak until he

(25) was three years old, failed his college entrance exams on the first try, was not an outstanding student at the Zurich Polytechnic Institute, and worked for seven years in the Swiss patent office.
(30) This is the man who in 1905 produced three papers that have been judged "among the greatest in the history of physics." The first won its author the Nobel Prize, the second provided proof
(35) that atoms exist, and the third changed the world.

8. Which of the following would be the best concluding statement for this passage?

   A. Both Charles Darwin and Albert Einstein endured unhappy childhoods and were not understood by their families.

   B. Darwin and Einstein are both examples of men who thought "outside the box."

   C. Problems early in life don't necessarily determine a person's later achievements, as the lives of these two men illustrate.

   D. Scientific breakthroughs are often the result of "happy accidents."

   E. Darwin and Einstein are the two most important scientists born in the nineteenth century.

9. The author of the passage uses all of the following in presenting his subject EXCEPT

   A. understatement

   B. irony

   C. comparison

   D. specific detail

   E. transitions

Section 1 Reading Test

Questions 10 through 12 refer to the following passage.

The ancient Greeks discovered that the earth was a sphere, though this view wasn't generally accepted for centuries. By the fifteenth century, however, most educated people believed that the world was round. The notion that it was Christopher Columbus who convinced King Ferdinand and Queen Isabella of the earth's spherical shape is simply wrong. It was the measurement of the earth's circumference, not the shape of the earth, that was in question. In fact, whereas most scholars of his time thought the circumference was 25,000 miles, Columbus chose an estimate of 18,000 miles to present his case to the king and queen. The smaller estimate, made by Posidonius, was less accurate and less accepted—but it also made the trip appear shorter and more achievable. And, of course, a shorter, more achievable distance meant the cost would be more reasonable. It appears that even in the fifteenth century, monetary concerns sometimes determined how a project was presented to those who held the purse strings.

10. The main idea of the passage is that

- **A.** the actual circumference of the earth is 25,000 miles.
- **B.** by the fifteenth century most people believed the earth was a sphere.
- **C.** it took centuries for people to accept the Greeks' discovery that the earth was a sphere.
- **D.** the circumference of the earth, not its shape, was an issue for Columbus.
- **E.** Columbus was mistaken in his estimate of the earth's circumference.

11. It can be inferred from the passage that

- **A.** the monarchs of Spain doubted whether Columbus could be successful in his voyage.
- **B.** Posidonius was viewed as a doubtful source of information.
- **C.** Columbus purposely chose Posidonius's estimate rather than the more accepted estimates of the circumference of the earth.
- **D.** Although the ancient Greeks discovered the earth was round, it wasn't until Columbus's voyage that this was confirmed.
- **E.** Uneducated people in the fifteenth century refused to believe the earth was a sphere.

12. The last sentence in the passage can best be described as

- **A.** mildly cynical.
- **B.** detached.
- **C.** informative.
- **D.** objective.
- **E.** harshly critical.

Questions 13 through 16 refer to the following passage.

Michael Shermer, author of the book *How We Believe,* uses the word "patternicity" to describe people's tendency to find meaningful patterns in what they
(5) see, or think they see, in nature. Our brains, Shermer says, are "pattern recognition machines." Sometimes the patterns or connections we see are real. When they are, we learn things about
(10) our environment that are useful in survival. As Shermer says, "We are the

GO ON TO THE NEXT PAGE

ancestors of those most successful at finding patterns."

But, according to Shermer, our brains (15) don't always distinguish between true and false patterns. We did not, as Shermer says, evolve a "Baloney Detection Network." Therefore, we need science with its "self-correcting mecha- (20) nisms of replication and peer review" to help us separate false patterns from real ones.

If Shermer is correct, why didn't we, through natural selection, develop a (25) "Baloney Detection Network"? Harvard University biologist Kevin R. Foster and University of Helsinki biologist Hanna Kokko tested Shermer's theory. Through evolutionary modeling and a series of (30) complex formulas, Foster and Kokko concluded that "the inability of individ- uals, human or otherwise, to assign causal probabilities to all sets of events that occur around them will often force (35) them to lump causal associations with noncausal ones. . . . Natural selection will favor strategies that make incorrect causal associations in order to establish those associations that are essential for (40) survival and reproduction." For exam- ple, predators avoid nonpoisonous snakes that mimic poisonous species in areas where the poisonous species is common. If they didn't employ this (45) "false patterning," they would be in dan- ger from the snakes that are actually poi- sonous. Natural selection, therefore, has perhaps rewarded patternicity, even when the patterns are false.

13. According to the passage, "patternicity" can best be described as

A. the tendency to see connections and patterns in nature.

B. a uniquely human trait that causes the mind to make erroneous connections.

C. the mind's ability to separate false patterns from real ones.

D. a series of causal probabilities that are subject to interpretation.

E. the willingness to create false meanings for connected events.

14. Shermer uses the term "Baloney Detection Network" to describe which of the following?

A. The function of science in detecting false patterning

B. A natural ability to separate false patterns from real ones

C. The replication of experimental results

D. Nonscientific methodologies employed by scientists

E. A characteristic of humankind developed through natural selection

15. According to Foster and Kokko's experimentation

   A. false causal associations are a result of the failure of the "Baloney Detection Network."

   B. natural selection has eliminated the tendency of the human brain to make false connections.

   C. the ability to see both false and true causal relationships can lead to survival.

   D. natural selection favors predators who can discriminate between poisonous and nonpoisonous snakes.

   E. instinct is the key factor in a predator's ability to sense danger.

16. Foster and Kokko's conclusions assume that

   A. what Shermer calls patternicity is actually instinct.

   B. nonpoisonous snakes can purposely mimic poisonous ones.

   C. nonhuman species share with humans the tendency to recognize patterns.

   D. patternicity is a negative phenomenon in humans.

   E. Shermer's referring to the brain as a "pattern recognition machine" is misleading.

Question 17 refers to the following passage.

   According to a recent Harris Poll of 2,600 respondents, 72 percent of Americans believe their actions have a significant effect on the environment. Twenty-five percent say they haven't taken any steps to reduce their environmental footprint. What the poll shows is that enthusiasm for "living green" is growing, but at the same time many respondents are uncertain what steps to take in their daily lives.

17. It can be inferred from the passage that the author believes

   A. the sampling in the polls was too small to be of any significance.

   B. people are unwilling to change their habits or their lifestyles.

   C. the failure to "live green" is based on a lack of information.

   D. the media doesn't cover environmental problems sufficiently.

   E. many people answered the poll questions dishonestly.

Questions 18 and 19 refer to the following passage.

   While Chinese history is not the oldest in the world, Chinese civilization has remained recognizably the same in the essentials, making it the oldest homogeneous major culture in the world. The Chinese people, their language, and the essence of their culture, in spite of innovative and sometimes violent changes, have maintained certain constant characteristics. The country is so large and the regional differences so great that in the course of its history China might have broken up into separate nations, as Europe did after the fall of the Roman empire, but it didn't. The reason may be that it was ruled by a very powerful and stable bureaucracy.

GO ON TO THE NEXT PAGE

18. The passage is primarily concerned with the

    A. differences between China and Europe after the fall of the Roman empire.

    B. relative insignificance of China's regional differences.

    C. the stability of Chinese culture and civilization.

    D. effects of internal conflict on Chinese civilization.

    E. effect of China's size on its culture.

19. According to the passage, China may have remained intact as a country because

    A. the Chinese people believed in the same religion.

    B. a powerful bureaucracy ruled the country.

    C. the Chinese people spoke the same language.

    D. the country was isolated from outside influences.

    E. violence and change were not part of the national character.

Questions 20 through 23 refer to the following passage.

Homework overload has always been a complaint of school children, especially but not exclusively, during the teenage years. Today, parents are be-
(5) coming increasingly concerned about their children's burden, complaining that the children need more sleep and more free time and that families need more time to spend together.

(10) The fact is that homework has been controversial in the United States since the beginning of the twentieth century. In a *Ladies Home Journal* article of 1900, editor Edward Bok referred to
(15) night study as a "fearful evil," and just a year later the California Legislature banned homework for students under age fifteen and for older children limited the time for homework to thirty minutes.
(20) In 1997, however, that law was taken off the books.

When the Soviets launched Sputnik in 1957, there was a scramble in American education to "get us back on top," and
(25) more homework in schools was a by-product. Then again in the 1980s, Japan's growing power in the business world spurred another resurgence of homework assignments. In recent years,
(30) children of very young ages have been assigned school work to take home.

Some parents are now yelling "Enough!" Some school districts are responding to their concerns by limiting
(35) the amount of homework teachers can assign. Parents and others point out that in addition to kids needing free time, many colleges require that a student be "well rounded," which encourages stu-
(40) dents to participate more in sports, clubs, and other activities.

But along with that argument comes another that is significant. Too many times, according to its critics, homework
(45) isn't meaningful but rather "busywork" that accomplishes little other than taking up a young person's valuable time. Among teachers, however, there is disagreement about what constitutes busy-
(50) work and what constitutes practice. According to one mathematics teacher, "Even if a student gets three problems correct in class, he needs to do forty more at home so that the concept be-
(55) comes second nature to him."

20. Which of the following would be the best title for this passage?

   A. "A Crisis in the Classroom"

   B. "Modern Theories of the Value of Homework"

   C. "Teachers versus Students: The Homework Wars"

   D. "Too Much Homework?"

   E. "The History of Homework in America"

21. According to the passage, homework assignments increased in the 1980s because

   A. Japanese success in business increased interest in improving U.S. education.

   B. students had begun slipping in academic achievement tests.

   C. parents wanted their children to get into better colleges.

   D. the United States wanted to model public schools after Japanese schools.

   E. U.S. productivity was in decline and schools were blamed.

22. The last sentence of paragraph 2 implies that

   A. the homework law was deemed unconstitutional.

   B. school districts and teachers opposed the law.

   C. attitudes toward homework had undergone changes since 1901.

   D. the homework law was seen as frivolous and completely unnecessary.

   E. most school districts did not conform to the requirements of the law.

23. The function of the last sentence of the passage is to

   A. criticize parents who object to homework.

   B. suggest that teachers have a selfish interest in assigning homework.

   C. note that there is a different side to the argument that homework is "busywork."

   D. summarize the points made in the passage.

   E. draw a conclusion from the arguments made against homework.

Questions 24 and 25 refer to the following passage.

Amphibians are becoming extinct faster than any other group of organisms. Because they are dependent on both land and water, if either habitat suffers, they also suffer. Their thin skins
(5) make it easy for them to take in air and water but also make them vulnerable to pollutants. The most immediate threat to amphibians is a parasitic fungus called
(10) *amphibian chytrid,* which was probably accidentally spread by African clawed frogs that were shipped worldwide for lab studies and pregnancy tests before the 1950s. But an even greater threat is
(15) loss of habitat. Critical breeding ponds have been lost to construction and development. Zoos are the best bet for saving amphibians and later returning them into the wild, but currently the number of
(20) zoos around the world can support at best about fifty species. Although there

GO ON TO THE NEXT PAGE

are cases in which species raised in captivity have been reintroduced to the wild, the project would be monumental (25) for amphibians.

24. According to the passage, amphibians are most at risk of extinction because of

   A. their thin skins.

   B. their dependency on air and water.

   C. their use as experimental animals.

   D. a parasitic fungus.

   E. a continuing loss of habitat.

25. The author of the passage makes all of the following assumptions EXCEPT

   A. there is value in protecting all species of amphibians.

   B. the loss of breeding grounds for amphibians will continue.

   C. releasing amphibians raised in captivity into the wild would be impossible.

   D. the availability of more zoos would increase the number of species that could be saved.

   E. scientists have not yet eradicated *amphibian chytrid* in the wild.

Questions 26 and 27 refer to the following passage.

     Why do hotels and restaurants throw away more than a million and a half tons of perfectly good food every year, even during times when unemployment is ris-
(5) ing and record numbers of people are in need? A 1996 federal law shields people from liability for sickness from food donations, so the reason isn't a legal problem. More disturbingly, it is logistics.
(10) Caterers and hotels find it "too much hassle" to arrange for leftover food to be

distributed to homeless shelters or soup kitchens. It is outrageous to think that the main reason for depriving needy (15) people of food is that distributing it requires a little extra work.

26. In context, the word "logistics" means

   A. handling of the details.

   B. motivation for the action.

   C. attitude toward the poor.

   D. selfishness.

   E. illogical behavior.

27. With which of the following statements is the author LEAST likely to agree?

   A. The failure to distribute leftover food is not because of legal liability.

   B. Homeless shelters and soup kitchens could contact local hotels and restaurants and arrange to pick up leftover food.

   C. The 1996 federal law should be repealed.

   D. A database of shelters and soup kitchens should be made available to caterers.

   E. The amount of food that could be distributed is significant.

Questions 28 and 29 refer to the following passage.

     Two important factors for a manufacturing company to consider before deciding to enter the global market are "Can we produce enough inventory to
(5) fill foreign orders?" and "Does our product meet local standards and regulations?" If enough product can't be produced to fill foreign orders efficiently, or if the product doesn't meet the local

(10) requirements and cannot be modified to meet these requirements, the result could be "channel frustration," which is defined as a situation in which the foreign market wants a product but can't
(15) buy it because of inadequate supply or because the product fails to meet local regulations. "Channel - frustration" breeds unhappy customers and could lead to an exporter's retreat from the
(20) market.

28. The passage is most likely to appear in

A. a magazine article profiling multinational corporations.

B. a how-to book for new managers.

C. a newspaper editorial on foreign trade barriers.

D. a news article on standards for products marketed in the European Union.

E. a general guide to companies interested in global marketing.

29. From the passage it can be inferred that

A. entering foreign markets is an important way to increase profit.

B. modification of an existing product may be necessary if the product is going to be marketed in other countries.

C. "channel frustration" is the most common problem for companies that want to enter foreign markets.

D. elimination of foreign tariffs would be a positive step for successful global marketing.

E. in general, small companies should not consider entering foreign markets.

Questions 30 and 31 refer to the following passage.

In experiments, Friederike Range of the University of Vienna has shown that dogs have a sense of fair play. According to Range's findings, dogs are the first
(5) animals outside primates that passed a test for reacting negatively to inequity. They became increasingly fidgety and finally stopped shaking hands altogether when, although they themselves weren't
(10) rewarded, they saw fellow dogs being given a treat for the same trick. Interestingly, the dogs cooperated longer if their fellow dogs didn't get a snack either. Biologists suggest that an
(15) aversion to inequity is critical for cooperative behavior, because it keeps slackers from overwhelming the system. The sense of fairness could also show up in other animals that exhibit cooperative
(20) behavior, says Frans de Waal of Emory University's Yerkes National Primate Research Center in Atlanta. "You'd expect it in canines, but perhaps not in domestic cats, which are solitary hunters."

30. The main point of the passage is that

A. dogs are more advanced than cats because they believe in fair play.

B. everyone should be rewarded equally.

C. being treated equally may foster cooperation in dogs.

D. most dogs will not perform tricks unless they receive an immediate reward.

E. the intelligence of dogs is proved by Range's experiment.

GO ON TO THE NEXT PAGE

31. From the passage it can be inferred that cats wouldn't pass the inequity aversion test because

   A. cooperation is not required among cats.

   B. cats cannot be trained as effectively as dogs.

   C. dogs mimic humans in their behavior while cats do not.

   D. cats are not as intelligent as dogs.

   E. cats are uninterested in rewards.

Questions 32 and 33 refer to the following passage.

     Businesses don't have many privacy rights, nor should they. While they do have a right to record their transactions with customers, and transactions done
(5) on credit usually do require that the customer provides personal data to prove creditworthiness, businesses must disclose what they are doing with a person's information. Businesses usually
(10) provide customers with copies of their privacy policy, and if a customer doesn't like the policy, he or she can move on. (But in fact many people don't actually read privacy policy disclosures or under-
(15) stand the implications.) What the law needs to do is ensure that companies actually follow the practices they disclose.

32. The purpose of the parenthetical sentence in the passage is to

   A. criticize businesses for providing detailed privacy policies.

   B. indicate that businesses mislead the public in the privacy policies.

   C. advocate for tougher privacy policies.

   D. indicate that consumers are to blame for violations of their privacy.

   E. state a fact about a common response to published privacy policies.

33. The implication of the last sentence in the passage is that

   A. privacy policies are useless.

   B. companies do not always adhere to their own privacy policies.

   C. the consumer should be more vigilant about privacy rights

   D. many businesses don't issue privacy policies.

   E. lawsuits are common when businesses ignore privacy rights.

Questions 34 and 35 refer to the following passage.

Anthropologists and molecular biologists are working on a project to find forgotten human migration routes by searching for genetic footprints. They
(5) have run into some problems because many indigenous groups—for example, in the Americas and Australia—are reluctant to submit DNA samples. The reasons are varied. One is that pharma-
(10) ceutical companies will exploit useful details in the genetic makeup of these groups, profit largely from it, and pay them nothing. Another reason not related to a financial issue is that informa-
(15) tion about the migration routes of their ancestors might contradict a group's own cultural traditions about its origins. For example, Native Americans who believe they have always occupied certain
(20) lands don't want to be told that it is likely their ancestors arrived from Siberia 13,000 years ago. The desire for genetic privacy among some of these native peoples is understandable, consider-
(25) ing a history of oppression and mistreatment.

34. It can be inferred from the passage that

A. some indigenous groups do not believe in the validity of genetics.

B. reluctance to submit DNA samples may be due to past injustices.

C. indigenous people who won't submit DNA samples may prevent discovery of lifesaving pharmaceuticals.

D. in spite of overwhelming evidence, Native Americans do not accept Siberia as their country of origin.

E. the researchers probably have ulterior motives in their tracking of migrations.

35. According to the passage, many indigenous groups

A. refuse to be part of the modern world.

B. are uneducated.

C. do not respect scientific inquiry.

D. want to preserve cultural traditions about their origins.

E. would be willing to submit DNA if they were paid for it.

Question 36 refers to the following passage.

At the beginning of Queen Victoria's reign (1837), women in England had few rights over their bodies, their property, and their children. Largely because
(5) of the suffrage movement, which came to the public's attention thirty years later, things began to change. John Stuart Mill presented Parliament with the first petition for female suffrage in
(10) 1866. The single most important reform passed after this was the Married Women's Property Act of 1882, which gave women some degree of financial independence. As the writer Virginia
(15) Woolf wrote later, financial independence was crucial for all other kinds of independence.

36. The Married Women's Property Act of 1882 was most important because it

A. gave women full rights over their bodies, property, and children.

B. was a necessary first step toward independence.

C. resulted from women's protesting the status quo.

D. was passed because of John Stuart Mill's petition.

E. made it possible for women to own businesses.

GO ON TO THE NEXT PAGE

Question 37 refers to the following passage.

     An entire field of science, called ethnobiology, studies peoples' knowledge of the wild plants and animals in their environment. Most of the studies have
(5) focused on surviving hunting-gathering peoples who still rely heavily on natural products and wild foods. The studies show that these people are walking encyclopedias of natural history, with
(10) names (in their local languages) for thousands of animal and plant species, and a detailed knowledge of these species' characteristics, distribution, and potential use. Obviously, as people in
(15) creasingly depend on domesticated plants and animals, this traditional knowledge is lost. In a city, for example, most people wouldn't be able to distinguish a poisonous mushroom from one
(20) that is safe to eat. Members of a tribe in New Guinea, however, know twenty-nine types of edible mushroom species, have different words in their language for each of them, and know where in the
(25) forest to look for them.

37. The purpose of the passage is to

  A. describe hunting-gathering peoples' knowledge of plants and animals in their environment.

  B. contrast hunting-gathering people with modern urban dwellers.

  C. criticize the tendency of modern man to rely heavily on domesticated plants and animals.

  D. emphasize the importance of recording and preserving the knowledge possessed by tribes who rely on natural products and wild foods.

  E. define the term ethnobiology.

Questions 38 through 40 are based on the following passage.

     David Hume's main work appeared originally under the title *A Treatise of Human Nature,* but the book was not received very enthusiastically by the pub
(5) lic. Hume rewrote it, polishing its style, improving its structure, and adding three new chapters. It was then published in 1748 as *An Enquiry Concerning Human Understanding.* The work's clarity,
(10) spiced with sarcasm and tongue-in-cheek remarks, is somewhat deceitful. It conceals cunning perplexities. Also, the book occasionally shows some vacillation on the author's part. For example,
(15) Hume, who was a skeptic and agnostic, unexpectedly in section 12 of the *Enquiry* turns into a dogmatist critical of skepticism.

38. The word "cunning" as it is used in the passage means

  A. attractive.

  B. puzzling, mysterious.

  C. subtle, crafty.

  D. unnecessary, redundant.

  E. deceitful.

39. The passage suggests that Hume's 1748 work

  A. is not useful because of Hume's inconsistency about his beliefs.

  B. isn't as straightforward as it seems to be.

  C. was not received well by the public.

  D. is sarcastic about skepticism.

  E. is an important work in the defense of agnosticism.

40. The passage implies that Hume revised his book

   A. because it was not well received by the public.

   B. to expand on its general premises.

   C. because he wanted to improve its structure.

   D. to clarify what appeared to be his inconsistencies.

   E. because his philosophical beliefs had changed.

Question 41 refers to the following passage.

    Louise Erdrich is an American writer descended from the first Americans. Her mother was part Chippewa and part French, and her grandmother was a
(5) tribal chairwoman. Although Erdrich chronicles Native American ways in her fiction, her novels and short stories include many other sorts of Americans, from a reclusive sculptor in New
(10) Hampshire to a small-minded German sister-in-law to a Eurasian doctor. Erdrich is also thought of as a teller of folk tales and parables, but much of her writing is outside of that category.
(15) Erdrich probes emotions between parent and child, man and woman, brother and sister, man and beast.

41. The main idea of the passage is that Erdrich

   A. successfully uses her Native American heritage in novels and short stories.

   B. should be considered a master of modern American fiction.

   C. uses well-known legends throughout her works.

   D. is an author with themes and concerns beyond Native American culture.

   E. is a minor but worthwhile author.

Question 42 is based on the following passage.

    Humpback whales assemble in subtropical or tropical waters to mate and to calve. Researchers don't understand why the whales migrate to these winter-
(5) ing grounds, but it appears to be more for physical than biological reasons. Most breeding grounds are warmer, shallower, and more protected than summer feeding areas, and these factors may
(10) offer more protection for mothers and their newborn calves. The dense congregation of whales in these wintering grounds also brings together males and females, who may feed in different areas
(15) during the summer.

GO ON TO THE NEXT PAGE

42. The reason that humpback whales migrate to warmer waters to mate is probably

   A. because a number of whales from different areas congregate in these waters.

   B. similar to the reason birds migrate in winter.

   C. because the physical characteristics of these waters are more conducive to breeding.

   D. because whales possess a genetic predilection for tropical and subtropical waters.

   E. because food becomes less available in colder waters.

Questions 43 and 44 refer to the following passage.

(5)

Respiration and breathing are sometimes used synonymously, but it is necessary to understand clearly the distinction between them. All living cells respire, whereas breathing is a function of many multicellular animals. Respiration is a chemical process within the cells, whereas breathing is a renewal of air or water on a surface through which an exchange of oxygen and carbon dioxide can take place. Respiration is a process of releasing energy from food, whereas breathing is a method of providing oxygen for absorption and of removing carbon dioxide after respiration is complete.

(10)

(15)

43. Respiration is a process within cells that

   A. provides oxygen.

   B. removes carbon dioxide.

   C. absorbs oxygen.

   D. provides carbon dioxide.

   E. releases energy.

44. It can be inferred from the passage that

   A. respiration is more important than breathing.

   B. not all multicellular animals breathe.

   C. respiration takes place on the surface whereas breathing is cellular.

   D. without breathing, respiration could not take place.

   E. breathing and respiration are different types of chemical reactions in the cells.

Questions 45 and 46 refer to the following passage.

(5)

An epidemic of "germaphobia" is loose in the United States. The upside of spending time, effort, and money on personal hygiene and home cleanliness is obvious. But there is a downside too. First, sanitizing everything we can lay our carefully washed hands on and trying to eliminate any possibility that our children will come in contact with germs, can undermine our immune systems and possibly prevent them from working when we really need them. Second, too many cleaning products can expose us to toxic chemicals, and it is possible that such products could promote the rise of more resistant germs, just as an overuse of antibiotics can lead to "superbugs."

(10)

(15)

(20)

Microbiologist Lynn Bry says that many germs are essential, providing vital functions to our bodies such as breaking down food and securing nutrients, and protecting us from those germs (a minority) that cause disease. "If you were germ free, you'd be dead within two weeks," Bry says. She adds that we have an "irrational fear of germs and dirt." Bry advocates appropriate hygiene

(25)

and cleanliness—not sucking your fin-
(30) gers after you touch a raw chicken, for
example—and washing your hands with
hot water and soap. But, she adds, "You
don't need to scrub yourself until you're
sore."

(35)   On the surface, our germaphobic tendencies are growing because of our desire to promote health. But underneath,
according to many psychologists, lies
the need to exercise control over an en-
(40) vironment we perceive as hostile.
Cleaning can temporarily allay anxi-
eties, the extreme being obsessive-com-
pulsive behaviors such as constant
hand-washing. Anxiety can lead people
(45) to misperceive risks and distort probabilities. For example, the chances of dying from a case of salmonella are lower
than the chances of dying from obesity-
related causes.

45. To determine whether germ-resistant
products and cleaning products are
beneficial to public health, it would be
most helpful to

   A. know the exact manufacturing
      processes and chemical ingredients
      of the products.

   B. conduct controlled testing with
      groups of people using the
      products and groups not using the
      products.

   C. conduct a nationwide survey of
      people who use the products.

   D. gather anecdotal evidence from
      people in all parts of the country.

   E. compare communicable disease
      statistics in the United States with
      communicable disease statistics in
      another country.

46. According to the passage,
microbiologist Lynn Bry would be
LEAST likely to agree with which of
the following statements?

   A. People should be more informed
      about safe cleaning products.

   B. Children should be taught to wash
      their hands before and after meals.

   C. A spotless house could indicate an
      anxious resident.

   D. Covering your mouth when you
      cough or sneeze serves no purpose.

   E. Riding on a motorcycle without a
      helmet is probably more dangerous
      than eating an unwashed apple.

IF YOU FINISH BEFORE TIME IS CALLED, CHECK YOUR WORK ON THIS
SECTION ONLY. DO NOT WORK ON ANY OTHER SECTION IN THE TEST.

Mathematics Test

TIME: 75 Minutes

46 Questions

Directions: Each of the questions or incomplete statements below is followed by five suggested answers or completions. Select the best answer or completion of the five choices given and fill in the corresponding answer choice.

This is a sample of what will appear on your computer screen when you take the computerized test with the correct answer checked.

Example:

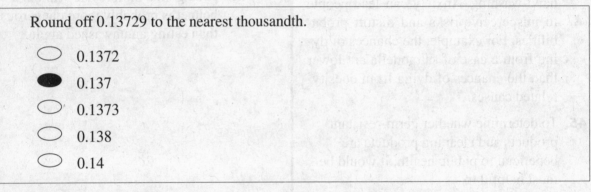

Round off 0.13729 to the nearest thousandth.

- ⬭ 0.1372
- ⬤ 0.137
- ⬭ 0.1373
- ⬭ 0.138
- ⬭ 0.14

Click on your choice.

1. When the value 7,500 is written in prime factored form, it becomes $2^x 3^y 5^z$. What is the value of xyz?

   A. 6

   B. 8

   C. 10

   D. 12

   E. 30

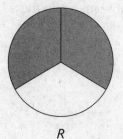 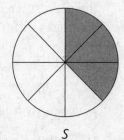

R   S

2. What is the sum of the shaded area of figure R and the shaded area of figure S, above, if each circle represents a unit circle divided into equal parts?

   A. $\dfrac{9}{16}$

   B. $1\dfrac{7}{9}$

   C. $\dfrac{7}{24}$

   D. $1\dfrac{1}{24}$

   E. $\dfrac{1}{4}$

3. Hot dogs are packaged with h hot dogs in each package. Hot dog buns are packaged with b buns in each package. If you were to buy an equal number of hot dogs and buns so that each hot dog gets a bun, what would be the *least* number of each you would need to buy?

   Which of the following methods could be used to find the solution to this problem?

   A. Add h and b

   B. Find the greatest common factor of h and b

   C. Find the least common multiple of h and b

   D. Divide h by b

   E. Multiply h and b

4. Which of the following directions when followed would correctly express the value 24.7×10^3 in scientific notation?

   A. Add three zeros to the right of the 7

   B. Move the decimal point to the left one position and increase the exponent by 1

   C. It already is currently expressed in scientific notation

   D. Move the decimal point to the left one position and decrease the exponent by 1

   E. Move the exponent to the right one position and decrease the exponent by 1

GO ON TO THE NEXT PAGE

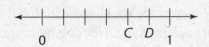

5. Assuming the spaces in the number line above are equal in length, which of the following expressions produces a value that lies between C and D on the number line?

A. $\frac{1}{3} \times \frac{1}{5}$

B. $\frac{2}{3} - \frac{1}{5}$

C. $\frac{1}{3} + \frac{2}{5}$

D. $\frac{1}{3} \div \frac{2}{5}$

E. $\frac{2}{5} \div \frac{1}{3}$

6. In a senior citizens home with a population of 250 people, everyone is from 75 to 90 years old and 12% of this population is age 80 or younger. If the remaining population is evenly distributed, how many people in this home are age 85?

A. 22

B. 24

C. 25

D. 27

E. 30

7. The price of gasoline went from $2.25 per gallon to $2.50 per gallon. What was the percent increase in the cost of gasoline?

A. 9%

B. 10%

C. $11\frac{1}{9}\%$

D. $12\frac{1}{2}\%$

E. 25%

8. The annual salaries of three people are listed below.

Person 1: $45,256
Person 2: $57,254
Person 3: $72,978

Jim estimated the sum of these salaries by first rounding each to the nearest thousand. Bob estimated the sum of these salaries by first rounding each to the nearest ten. By how much do these estimates differ?

A. $110

B. $490

C. $530

D. $600

E. $3,490

9. 24 is x less than half of y. Which of the following expresses this relationship?

A. $x = 24 - \frac{y}{2}$

B. $24 = \frac{y}{2} - x$

C. $24 = \frac{2}{y} - x$

D. $x = \frac{y}{2} + 24$

E. $24 < x - \frac{1}{2}y$

10. A snail moves $4\frac{1}{3}$ inches every $\frac{1}{4}$ hour. At this pace, how long will it take the snail to move 26 inches?

A. $\frac{1}{2}$ hour

B. $1\frac{1}{12}$ hours

C. $1\frac{1}{2}$ hours

D. 6 hours

E. $450\frac{2}{3}$ hours

11. The problem below shows the steps for finding the product of a two-digit number with a three-digit number using the standard multiplication algorithm. The missing digits are represented with the letters x, y, and z.

$$
\begin{array}{r}
2x4 \\
\times \quad 5y \\
\hline
1404 \\
+ \quad 11z00 \\
\hline
13104
\end{array}
$$

What is the result of $x + yz$?

A. 136

B. 126

C. 63

D. 45

E. 16

hours worked	money earned
0	0
2	15
4	30
6	45
8	60
10	75

12. The table above gives the amount of money earned for different amounts of time worked. Which of the following graphs best represents the data in the table?

A.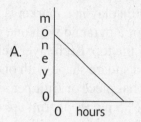

B.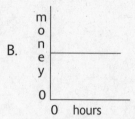

C.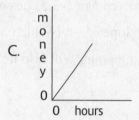

D.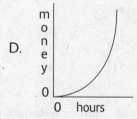

E.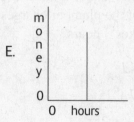

GO ON TO THE NEXT PAGE

13. A fruit display in a market is in the shape of a pyramid with one piece of fruit at the top. Each layer below the top forms a square shape with one additional piece of fruit per side. If a total of 55 pieces of fruit are used, how many layers of fruit will there be?

A. 4

B. 5

C. 6

D. 7

E. 8

14. The ordered pair $(-3,5)$ lies on a line with a slope of $-\frac{2}{3}$. Which of the following points will also lie on this line?

A. $(1,7)$

B. $(-1,8)$

C. $(-1,5)$

D. $(-6,7)$

E. $(-6,3)$

15. A plumber charges d dollars per minute he works plus $25.00 for driving time to get to the job. What will be the total amount the plumber charges for a job that takes 3 hours?

A. $28d$

B. $3d + 25$

C. $3(d + 25)$

D. $120d + 25$

E. $180d + 25$

$$7x + 3(x + 5) = 2x - 7$$

16. Which of the following equations could occur as a step in solving the above equation for x?

A. $8x = -22$

B. $8x = -12$

C. $8x = -15$

D. $12x = 8$

E. $12x = -22$

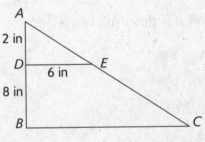

$AD = 2$ in $BD = 8$ in $DE = 6$ in $\overline{DE} \parallel \overline{BC}$

17. What is the length of BC in the figure above?

A. 12 in

B. 16 in

C. 18 in

D. 24 in

E. 30 in

18. Triangle ABC is obtuse. Angle A has a measure of $45°$. Which of the following could be the measure of one of the other angles?

A. 35°

B. 45°

C. 55°

D. 65°

E. None of the above could be the measure of one of the other angles

19. A right triangle has legs with lengths of 9 inches and 12 inches. What is the perimeter of this triangle?

A. 15 in

B. 21 in

C. 36 in

D. 42 in

E. 54 in

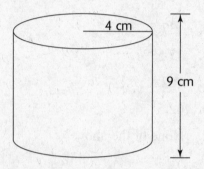

20. The right cylinder above has a base with a radius of 4 centimeters and a height of 9 centimeters. Between the surface area and the volume of this cylinder, which measurement will have the greater numerical value and by how much?

A. Volume, 36π

B. Surface area, 40π

C. Volume, 40π

D. Surface area, 72π

E. Volume, 72π

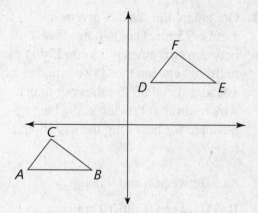

21. In the figure above, $\triangle ABC$ is congruent to $\triangle DEF$. The coordinates of points A, B, C, and D are $A\,(-7,-5)$, $B\,(-2,-5)$, $C\,(-4,-1)$, and $D\,(1,6)$. What are the coordinates at point F?

A. $(4,10)$

B. $(6,10)$

C. $(6,6)$

D. $(8,15)$

E. $(6,11)$

22. If the quadratic expression $x^2 - 13x - 48$ is correctly written in factored form, then what must be one of the factors?

A. $(x-3)$

B. $(x+3)$

C. $(x-6)$

D. $(x+4)$

E. $(x-8)$

Section **2** Mathematics Test

GO ON TO THE NEXT PAGE

23. On a map, the scale is given as 1 cm = 25 mi. The map distance between two cities is 15 cm. If you plan to drive between these two cities at an average speed of 35 miles per hour, which of the following is the best estimate for how long the trip should take?

A. Between 8 and 9 hours

B. Between 9 and 10 hours

C. Between 10 and 11 hours

D. Between 11 and 12 hours

E. Between 12 and 13 hours

24. How many square feet are in 2 square yards?

A. 6

B. 9

C. 12

D. 18

E. 27

1	2	3	4	5	6	7	8	9	10
65	49	32	65	65	82	50	75	60	57

25. The table above gives John's test results for the 10 tests given in his mathematics class. Find the mean, median, mode, and range for these values. Use them to calculate the following:

(mean − median) × (mode − range)

A. −37.5

B. 37.5

C. −62.5

D. 62.5

E. None of the above

26. Two dice with number representations from 1 to 6 are tossed. What is the probability that the product of the two numbers shown on the dice is less than 20?

A. $\dfrac{7}{36}$

B. $\dfrac{3}{4}$

C. $\dfrac{2}{9}$

D. $\dfrac{7}{9}$

E. $\dfrac{29}{36}$

27. Frank spent $100 for a cell phone and accessories. If the accessories cost $20 more than the cell phone, how much did he pay for the accessories?

A. $20

B. $30

C. $40

D. $50

E. $60

28. Put the following number values in order from greatest to least:

$A = -5.15$, $B = -\dfrac{26}{5}$,

$C = -5\dfrac{1}{2}$, $D = -5$

A. A, B, C, D

B. D, C, B, A

C. C, B, A, D

D. D, A, B, C

E. B, A, C, D

Married men	25
Married women	35
Single men	15
Single women	45

29. The chart above shows the number of men and women in a club and their marital status. If one individual was randomly selected from this club, what is the probability the individual would be male?

A. $\dfrac{1}{8}$

B. $\dfrac{5}{24}$

C. $\dfrac{1}{3}$

D. $\dfrac{1}{2}$

E. $\dfrac{2}{3}$

30. If $4P + 20 = Q$, then $P + 12 =$

A. $Q - 8$

B. $\dfrac{Q}{4} - 8$

C. $\dfrac{Q}{4} + 7$

D. $4Q + 7$

E. $\dfrac{Q}{4} + 17$

Section **2** Mathematics Test

GO ON TO THE NEXT PAGE

31. Which of the following procedures could correctly be used to put the fraction $\frac{a}{b}$ into percent form?

    A. Divide a into b, move the decimal point two places to the left, and add a percent sign.

    B. Divide a into b, move the decimal point two places to the right, and add a percent sign.

    C. Multiply the fraction $\frac{a}{b}$ by 100%.

    D. Solve the proportion $\frac{a}{b} = \frac{100}{x}$ and add a percent sign to the value of x.

    E. Divide b into a, move the decimal point two places to the left, and add a percent sign.

Number	Frequency
3	4
4	8
6	2
7	4
8	2

32. Use frequency table above to determine the mean for the set of data.

    A. 3.5

    B. 4

    C. 5

    D. 5.6

    E. 6

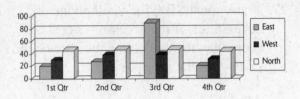

33. According to the chart above, approximately how much greater were the second quarter earnings for West than the fourth quarter earnings for East?

    A. 5

    B. 10

    C. 20

    D. 30

    E. 35

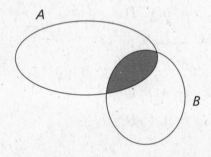

34. In the Venn diagram above, oval A represents all shapes that are rectangles, and oval B represents all shapes that are rhombuses. What shapes does the shaded region represent?

    A. all trapezoids

    B. all parallelograms

    C. all kites

    D. all squares

    E. all quadrilaterals

35. Triangle *ABC* is drawn on a coordinate plane. Its vertices are at *A*(2,3), *B*(6,3), and *C*(6,8). Which of the following is the best approximation of its perimeter?

   A. Between 6 and 7

   B. 9

   C. 10

   D. Between 15 and 16

   E. 20

36. What should be the next two numbers be in the following sequence?

   1, 4, 9, 16, 25, . . .

   A. 35, 45

   B. 35, 46

   C. 36, 47

   D. 36, 49

   E. 37, 50

37. Which of the following is a representation of the value 4?

   A. $12 - 6 + 2$

   B. $32 \div 4 \times 2$

   C. $16 \div 8 \times 2$

   D. $8 \div \frac{1}{2}$

   E. None of the above represents the value 4

38. A container weighs 220 pounds. Which of the following is the best approximation of this weight in kilograms? (1 kilogram weighs approximately 2.2 pounds)

   A. 484

   B. 220

   C. 110

   D. 100

   E. 48.4

39. A collection of writing instruments consists of 24 pens, 12 pencils, 6 markers, and 2 highlighters. Which of the following statements about this collection is false?

   A. The ratio of pens to pencils is 2 to 1.

   B. The ratio of pens to markers is 8 to 2.

   C. The ratio of highlighters to pencils is 6 to 1.

   D. Pens make up more than 50% of the collection.

   E. All of the above statements are true.

Section **2** Mathematics Test

GO ON TO THE NEXT PAGE

symbols	value
@ + # + # + #	20
@ + # + # + & + & + & + &	42
@ + @ + @ + @	8

40. In the table above, all the symbols represent number values. All the arithmetic is addition. What is the value of &?

A. 2

B. 6

C. 7

D. 28

E. Cannot be determined with the given information

41. If three yards of material cost $2.97, what is the price per foot?

A. $0.33

B. $0.99

C. $2.94

D. $3.00

E. $8.91

42. Which of the following is NOT a correct way to find x if $x = 25\%$ of 40?

A. $0.25 \times 40 = x$

B. $\frac{25}{100} = \frac{40}{x}$

C. $\frac{x}{25} = \frac{40}{100}$

D. $40 \times \frac{1}{4} = x$

E. All of the above are correct

43. If the statement "3 and 4 are factors of a number N" is true, then which of the following statements *must* also be true?

A. 3 is a multiple of N and 4 is a multiple of N.

B. The only factors of N are 3 and 4.

C. 12 is a multiple of N.

D. 7 is a factor of N.

E. 12 is a divisor of N.

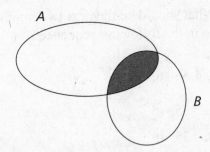

44. In the Venn diagram above, if oval A represents all the positive multiples of 4 that are less than 100, and oval B represents all the positive multiples of 6 that are less than 100, then how many numbers are in the shaded portion?

A. 4

B. 8

C. 10

D. 12

E. 24

Family Budget

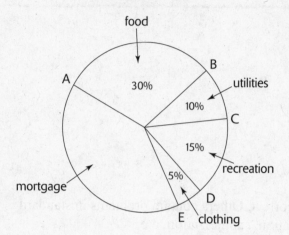

45. The pie chart above shows the allocation of money for a family budget. If this family plans to spend $3,600 on clothing, how much will the family spend on the mortgage?

   A. $3,600

   B. $7,200

   C. $14,400

   D. $28,800

   E. Insufficient information

46. If the natural numbers from 21 to 50 are written individually on index cards and put into a box, and one of the cards is randomly selected, what is the probability that it would be a prime number?

   A. $\dfrac{1}{5}$

   B. $\dfrac{4}{15}$

   C. $\dfrac{7}{29}$

   D. $\dfrac{7}{30}$

   E. $\dfrac{8}{29}$

Section **2** Mathematics Test

IF YOU FINISH BEFORE TIME IS CALLED, CHECK YOUR WORK ON THIS SECTION ONLY. DO NOT WORK ON ANY OTHER SECTION IN THE TEST.

Writing Test: Multiple-Choice Section

TIME: 38 Minutes

44 Questions

Part A: Usage

SUGGESTED TIME: 13 Minutes

24 Questions

Directions: Some of the following sentences are correct. Others contain problems in standard written English—grammar, usage, diction, punctuation, capitalization, etc.

If there is an error, it will be underlined and lettered. Find the *one* underlined part that must be changed to make the sentence correct and fill in the corresponding answer choice. Mark **E** if the sentence contains no error. *No sentence has more than one error.*

This is a sample of what will appear on your computer screen if you take the computer-based test. To select your answer, just click on any part of your underlined choice as illustrated below in choice **C**.

Example:

A flock of <u>pigeons</u> <u>is</u> unexpected this time of year, and <u>its</u> especially surprising
        A   B   C

to see the birds winging through the city <u>amidst</u> a snowstorm. <u>No error</u>.
                                    D   E

Click on your choice.

1. The man <u>who took the pictures of the</u>
   <u>party</u> was <u>later arrested, and he</u>
   $\;\;\;\;\;\;$A$\;\;\;\;\;\;\;\;\;\;$B$\;\;\;\;\;\;$C
   complained that the police <u>had broke</u>
   $\;$D
   his camera in the scuffle. <u>No error</u>
   $\;$E

2. When in front of an audience, a person
   should be sure to project <u>their</u> voice
   $\;$A
   <u>so that</u> even the people sitting in the
   $\;$B
   back row <u>can hear</u> what is <u>being said</u>.
   $\;\;\;\;\;\;\;\;\;$C$\;\;\;\;\;\;\;\;\;\;\;\;\;\;\;$D
   <u>No error</u>
   $\;$E

3. The counselor was <u>speaking angrily</u> to
   $\;\;\;\;\;\;\;\;\;\;\;\;\;\;\;\;\;\;$A
   Dave, <u>whom</u> he had <u>seen sleeping</u>
   $\;\;\;\;\;\;$B$\;\;\;\;\;\;\;\;\;$C
   during the <u>whole entire</u> meeting.
   $\;\;\;\;\;\;\;\;\;\;\;\;$D
   <u>No error</u>
   $\;$E

4. Although Mrs. Williams <u>insists that</u> she
   $\;$A
   likes <u>working in the bagel shop</u>, she
   $\;\;\;\;\;\;$B
   never eats <u>them</u> <u>herself</u>. <u>No error</u>
   $\;\;\;\;\;\;\;\;\;\;$C$\;\;\;\;$D$\;\;\;\;\;\;$E

5. Even though the dog <u>smelled badly</u>, the
   $\;\;\;\;\;\;\;\;\;\;\;\;\;\;\;\;\;\;\;$A
   family insisted <u>it</u> wanted to adopt <u>him</u>,
   $\;\;\;\;\;\;\;\;\;\;$B$\;\;\;\;\;\;\;\;\;\;\;\;$C
   and the manager of the shelter <u>drew up</u>
   $\;$D
   the adoption papers. <u>No error</u>
   $\;\;\;\;\;\;\;\;\;\;\;\;\;\;\;\;\;$E

6. Without the <u>captain</u> and <u>I</u>, the
   $\;\;\;\;\;\;\;\;\;$A$\;\;\;\;\;\;$B
   passengers would have panicked and
   perhaps caused a <u>worse</u> situation than
   $\;\;\;\;\;\;\;\;\;\;\;\;\;\;\;$C
   the one <u>we were faced</u> with now.
   $\;\;\;\;\;\;\;\;\;$D
   <u>No error</u>
   $\;$E

7. <u>Waiting in front of the railroad station</u>,
   $\;\;\;\;\;\;\;\;\;\;\;\;\;\;\;\;$A
   evening turned into night, and I realized
   $\;$B
   that my friend Paul, <u>who had promised</u>
   $\;$C
   <u>to pick me up</u>, was <u>letting me down</u>
   $\;\;$C$\;\;\;\;\;\;\;\;\;\;\;\;\;\;\;\;$D
   again. <u>No error</u>
   $\;\;\;\;\;$E

8. Those <u>who had entered the race</u>
   $\;\;\;\;\;\;\;\;\;\;\;\;$A
   <u>were asked to meet</u> at the <u>fairgrounds</u>
   $\;\;\;\;$B$\;\;\;\;\;\;\;\;\;\;\;\;\;\;\;$C
   an hour before the event <u>was scheduled</u>
   $\;$D
   to begin. <u>No error</u>
   $\;\;\;\;\;\;\;\;$E

9. The members of the <u>school board</u>
   $\;\;\;\;\;\;\;\;\;\;\;\;\;\;\;\;\;$A
   agreed to take a <u>vote; but only</u> after
   $\;\;\;\;\;\;\;\;\;\;\;\;\;\;\;$B
   <u>they discussed</u> in detail the financial
   $\;$C
   implications of allowing students from
   out of the district to register for the
   <u>advanced mathematics</u> classes. <u>No error</u>
   $\;\;\;\;\;$D$\;$E

10. <u>We</u> and the neighbors <u>couldn't hardly</u>
    $\;$A$\;\;\;\;\;\;\;\;\;\;\;\;\;\;$B
    believe the number of robberies
    <u>that had been reported</u> since the
    $\;\;\;\;\;\;$C
    streetlights <u>had been removed</u>. <u>No error</u>
    $\;\;\;\;\;\;\;\;\;\;$D$\;\;\;\;\;\;\;\;\;\;\;$E

GO ON TO THE NEXT PAGE

Section **3** Writing Test

11. She was <u>fired off of</u> her job because she
    A
    <u>had been absent</u> for a week without
    B
    <u>having called</u> in to let <u>anyone</u> know.
    CD
    <u>No error</u>
    E

12. The <u>r</u>evolutionary movement<u>,</u> that had
    AB
    been so <u>well documented</u> in
    C
    Gunderson's articles ended almost
    before it <u>began</u>. <u>No error</u>
    DE

13. The councilman succeeded in telling
    us what was going on in the
    <u>community, but,</u> in spite of <u>us</u> seniors in
    AB
    the group wanting to take action, he
    <u>attempted to</u> convince us that nothing
    C
    we could do would <u>effect</u> the council's
    D
    policy. <u>No error</u>
    E

14. If the head of the department
    <u>would have notified</u> the employees <u>who</u>
    AB
    needed to update their tax forms, the
    misunderstanding between the vice
    president and <u>him</u> could have been
    C
    avoided, and valuable time
    <u>could have been saved</u>. <u>No error</u>
    DE

15. <u>Except</u> for a few regions in Ireland, the
    A
    Welsh <u>stand apart</u> in retaining their
    B
    <u>very unique</u> place names, especially in
    C
    the <u>north</u>. <u>No error</u>
    DE

16. <u>With a major storm approaching</u>, the
    A
    inhabitants of the small village were
    told to <u>pack up</u> their most important
    B
    possessions, lock the windows and
    doors, and <u>to move</u> as fast as they could
    C
    to <u>higher</u> ground. <u>No error</u>
    DE

17. He had arrived in <u>Washington, D.C.</u>,
    A
    taken a taxi to the <u>Lincoln Memorial</u>,
    B
    and <u>went</u> from there directly to
    C
    his hotel, which was near the
    <u>Potomac River</u>. <u>No error</u>
    DE

18. After the phone <u>call that</u> announced
    A
    they had won the sweepstakes, they
    finished the meeting <u>quick</u> and rushed
    B
    to the <u>office where</u> the winnings were to
    C
    be distributed by <u>closing time</u> that day.
    D
    <u>No error</u>
    E

19. After the airplane had landed and all the passengers <u>had disembarked</u>, the
$$\overset{}{\underset{A}{}}$$
<u>men who</u> were responsible for
$$\overset{}{\underset{B}{}}$$
removing the baggage <u>arrived and</u>
$$\overset{}{\underset{C}{}}$$
began loading a large <u>amount</u> of
$$\overset{}{\underset{D}{}}$$
suitcases and boxes in record time.

<u>No error</u>
$$\overset{}{\underset{E}{}}$$

20. It is important that when a guest requests that <u>their</u> room <u>be cleaned</u>
$$\overset{}{\underset{A}{}}\quad\overset{}{\underset{B}{}}$$
immediately, the <u>staff sends</u> the maids
$$\overset{}{\underset{C}{}}$$
right away and instructs them to work
<u>as fast and efficiently</u> as possible.
$$\overset{}{\underset{D}{}}$$
<u>No error</u>
$$\overset{}{\underset{E}{}}$$

21. The <u>present incumbent</u> had promised to
$$\overset{}{\underset{A}{}}$$
reduce congestion in the downtown
area, increase revenues from city
parking <u>lots,</u> and prohibit delivery
$$\overset{}{\underset{B}{}}$$
trucks from double parking, but he has
not accomplished any of <u>these</u> things,
$$\overset{}{\underset{C}{}}$$
and <u>therefore</u> we should not return him
$$\overset{}{\underset{D}{}}$$
to office. <u>No error</u>
$$\overset{}{\underset{E}{}}$$

22. For Mrs. Burton, the most <u>rewarding</u>
$$\overset{}{\underset{A}{}}$$
part of her existence was her home and
family<u>,</u> and she wasn't willing to lose <u>it</u>
$$\overset{}{\underset{B}{}}\qquad\overset{}{\underset{C}{}}$$
because of her <u>brother's</u> financial woes.
$$\overset{}{\underset{D}{}}$$
<u>No error</u>
$$\overset{}{\underset{E}{}}$$

23. The documents were <u>delivered by</u> the
$$\overset{}{\underset{A}{}}$$
messenger service after Mr. Weber and
Mr. Lincoln <u>had left</u> for the day, which
$$\overset{}{\underset{B}{}}$$
meant that <u>they</u> were unavailable for the
$$\overset{}{\underset{C}{}}$$
trial the next <u>day, and therefore</u> the
$$\overset{}{\underset{D}{}}$$
lawyer asked the judge for a
continuance. <u>No error</u>
$$\overset{}{\underset{E}{}}$$

24. <u>Irregardless</u> of how many times the
$$\overset{}{\underset{A}{}}$$
<u>French</u> restaurant had been <u>cited</u> by the
$$\overset{}{\underset{B}{}}\qquad\overset{}{\underset{C}{}}$$
<u>city's</u> health department, customers
$$\overset{}{\underset{D}{}}$$
continued to come in for dinner,
particularly on the evenings when the
owner offered free wine. <u>No error</u>
$$\overset{}{\underset{E}{}}$$

GO ON TO THE NEXT PAGE

Part B: Sentence Correction

SUGGESTED TIME: 25 Minutes

20 Questions

Directions: Some part of each sentence below is underlined; sometimes the whole sentence is underlined. Five choices for rephrasing the underlined part follow each sentence. The first choice, **A,** repeats the original, and the other four are different. If choice **A** seems better than the alternatives, choose **A**; if not, choose one of the others.

For each sentence, consider the requirements of standard written English. Your choice should be a correct, concise, and effective expression, not awkward or ambiguous. Focus on grammar, word choice, sentence construction, and punctuation. If a choice changes the meaning of the original sentence, do not select it.

This is a sample of what will appear on your computer screen when you take the computerized test with the correct answer checked.

Example:

The forecaster predicted <u>rain and the sky was clear</u>.

- ⬭ rain and the sky was clear
- ⬭ rain but the sky was clear
- ⬭ rain the sky was clear
- ⬤ rain, but the sky was clear

Click on your choice.

25. Folic acid seems to <u>offer protection, for example one study showed</u> that it cut the rate of neural tube defects in infants.

   A. offer protection, for example one study showed

   B. offer protection, for example one study will show

   C. offers protection, for example one study will have shown

   D. offer protection. For example, one study showed

   E. have offered protection, for example, one study showed

26. <u>After receiving the estimate from the insurance company, the car was delivered</u> to Mack's Body Shop to be repaired.

   A. After receiving the estimate from the insurance company, the car was delivered

   B. After I received the estimate from the insurance company, I delivered the car

   C. The car was delivered, after I received the estimate from the insurance company,

   D. After having received the estimate from the insurance company, the car was delivered

   E. The car was to be delivered, after having received the estimate from the insurance company,

27. <u>The volcano was erupting after twenty dormant years and it spews fountains of lava into the air.</u>

   A. The volcano was erupting after twenty dormant years and it spews fountains of lava into the air.

   B. The volcano was erupting after twenty dormant years, and it spewed fountains of lava into the air.

   C. The volcano is erupting, after twenty dormant years, and spews fountains of lava into the air.

   D. The volcano was erupting and it spewed fountains of lava into the air after twenty dormant years.

   E. After twenty dormant years, the volcano was erupting, spewing fountains of lava into the air.

28. <u>The schools in the inner city are more in need of funding than the suburbs.</u>

   A. The schools in the inner city are more in need of funding than the suburbs.

   B. The schools in the inner city need more funding than the suburbs.

   C. The schools in the inner city are more in need of funding than those schools that are in the suburbs.

   D. The schools in the inner city, unlike the suburbs, are more in need of funding.

   E. Inner city schools need more funding than suburban schools.

GO ON TO THE NEXT PAGE

Section **3** Writing Test

355

29. He discovered that riding a bicycle to work, which he had begun doing in the summer when the weather was warm, was a good way to get exercise, and therefore he decided to give up his membership at the gym.

    A. He discovered that riding a bicycle to work, which he had begun doing in the summer when the weather was warm, was a good way to get exercise, and therefore

    B. Riding a bicycle to work, he discovered, which he had begun doing in the summer when the weather was warm, was a good way to get exercise, and therefore

    C. In the summer when he began doing it, he discovered, that riding a bicycle to work was a good way to get exercise and therefore

    D. He discovered that riding a bicycle to work which he had begun doing in the summer when the weather was warm was a good way to get exercise

    E. Riding a bicycle to work which he had begun doing in the summer, he discovered, when the weather was warm, was a good way to get exercise, and therefore

30. After living for several years in Seattle, he decided to move to a place where the sun would shine, the surfing would be good, and to meet the woman of his dreams.

    A. where the sun would shine, the surfing would be good, and to meet the woman of his dreams

    B. where the sun shines, the surfing is good, and to possibly meet the woman of his dreams

    C. where the sun would shine, where the surfing would be good, and where he might meet the woman of his dreams

    D. where the sun shines and the surfing was good, and where he might meet the woman of his dreams

    E. where the sun would shine and the surfing would be good, and to meet the woman of his dreams

31. Because old-growth forests in the United States are fast disappearing and because not enough effort has been made by the government to limit logging operations; citizens must take action.

    A. operations; citizens must take action

    B. operations, citizens must take action

    C. operations. Citizens must take action

    D. operations, and citizens must take action

    E. operations, but citizens must take action

32. The members of the district council decided <u>to withhold approval for the amusement park until it submitted an environmental impact statement</u> and provided assurance that sufficient security could be provided.

   A. to withhold approval for the amusement park until it submitted an environmental impact statement

   B. that withholding approval for the amusement park until it submitted an environmental impact statement

   C. to withhold approval for the amusement park until its owners submitted an environmental impact statement

   D. to withhold approval for the amusement park until they submitted an environmental impact statement

   E. to withhold approval for the amusement park until was submitted to them an environmental impact statement

33. The police <u>have and will continue to patrol</u> the streets around the area where the robberies were committed last month.

   A. have and will continue to patrol

   B. had and had continued to patrol

   C. will be patrolling and will continue to be patrolling

   D. have patrolled and will continue to patrol

   E. had patrolled and will continue to have patrolled

34. <u>In spite of the fact that the people on the train were annoyed by the child screaming, not one of them had chose</u> to complain to the porter.

   A. In spite of the fact that the people on the train were annoyed by the child screaming, not one of them had chose

   B. Despite the fact that the people on the train were annoyed by the child screaming, not one of them had chose

   C. Although the people on the train were annoyed by the child's screaming, not one of them had chosen

   D. Although the people on the train were annoyed by the child's screaming, not one of them had chose

   E. Despite the fact of being annoyed by the child screaming, not one of the people had chosen

35. <u>Ms. Swanson, the head of the Geology Department, invited him and me</u> to accompany her on the trip to Tibet.

   A. Ms. Swanson, the head of the Geology Department, invited him and me

   B. Ms. Swanson, who was the head of the Geology Department, invited him and I

   C. Ms. Swanson the head of the Geology Department, invited he and I

   D. Ms. Swanson, the head of the Geology Department invited me and him

   E. Ms. Swanson, whom was the head of the Geology Department, invited he and I

36. Buying a house in Florida, they discovered after doing some research, <u>was more expensive than in New Jersey</u>.

    A. was more expensive than in New Jersey

    B. would be more expensive than in New Jersey

    C. was more expensive than to buy one in New Jersey

    D. was more expensive than buying one in New Jersey

    E. would be more expensive than New Jersey

37. He <u>had been laying in the sun for hours and his back was more red than</u> his swimming trunks.

    A. had been laying in the sun for hours and his back was more red than

    B. had been lying in the sun for hours, and his back was redder than

    C. had laid in the sun for hours; and his back was more red than

    D. had lied in the sun for hours, and his back was redder than

    E. had been laying in the sun for hours but his back was redder than

38. <u>The concert at Lincoln Center and the coverage of the concert in the newspapers was the impetus</u> that the soprano's career needed.

    A. The concert at Lincoln Center and the coverage of the concert in the newspapers was the impetus

    B. The Lincoln Center concert and its coverage in the newspapers were the impetus

    C. The concert at Lincoln Center as well as the coverage of it in the newspapers was the impetus

    D. The Lincoln Center concert and it's coverage in the newspapers were the impetus

    E. The concert at Lincoln Center, as well as its coverage in the newspapers, were the impetus

39. <u>To the university faculty, his coming to speak was considered</u> a victory for academic freedom.

    A. To the university faculty, his coming to speak was considered

    B. To the university faculty, him coming to speak was considered

    C. Him coming to speak was considered by the university faculty

    D. The fact that he was coming to speak was considered by the university faculty

    E. The university faculty considered his coming to speak

40. The group of foreign tourists <u>were suspected with inferring that</u> the guard at the border had threatened them.

    A. were suspected with inferring that

    B. were suspected of inferring that,

    C. was suspected with implying, that

    D. was suspected of implying that

    E. were suspected with implying, that

41. <u>The man who had ran for treasurer of the club had absconded with the groups' membership fees</u> and was nowhere to be found.

    A. The man who had ran for treasurer of the club had absconded with the groups' membership fees

    B. The man, who had ran for treasurer of the club, had absconded with the groups' membership fees

    C. The man, who had run for treasurer of the club, had absconded with the group's membership fees

    D. The man, who had run for treasurer of the club, had absconded with the groups membership fees

    E. The man who had ran for treasurer of the club, had absconded with the group's membership fees

42. <u>It was either Mr. McMullin or it was someone who looked like him that borrowed the tools, that Harold needed</u> to fix the faucet.

    A. It was either Mr. McMullin or it was someone who looked like him that borrowed the tools, that Harold needed

    B. Either Mr. McMullin or someone who looked like him had borrowed the tools Harold needed

    C. It was either Mr. McMullin or someone who looked like him that had borrowed the tools Harold needed

    D. Either Mr. McMullin or it was someone who looked like him that borrowed the tools, Harold needed

    E. It was either Mr. McMullin, or it was someone who looked like him, that borrowed the tools, that Harold needed

GO ON TO THE NEXT PAGE

43. <u>After the conclusion of the presentation, the whole entire audience burst into applause and agreed to cooperate together in order to clean up</u> the community park.

    A. After the conclusion of the presentation, the whole entire audience burst into applause and agreed to cooperate together in order to clean up

    B. At the conclusion of the presentation, the whole entire audience burst into applause and agreed to cooperate to clean up

    C. When the presentation had been concluded, the entire audience burst into applause and agreed to cooperate in order to clean up

    D. After the presentation, the entire audience burst into applause and agreed to cooperate to clean up

    E. After the end of the presentation, the whole entire audience burst into applause and agreed to cooperate together to clean up

44. The excavations at Ceren reveal <u>the prosperity of the rural Mayans, the staples of their diet, and</u> the architecture of their homes.

    A. the prosperity of the rural Mayans, the staples of their diet, and

    B. the prosperity of the rural Mayan; the staples of their diets; and

    C. the prosperity of the rural Mayans, and the staples of their diet, and

    D. the rural Mayans, the prosperity and the diet they ate, as well as

    E. how prosperous the rural Mayans were, what their diet was, and

IF YOU FINISH BEFORE TIME IS CALLED, CHECK YOUR WORK ON THIS SECTION ONLY. DO NOT WORK ON ANY OTHER SECTION IN THE TEST.

Writing Test: Essay Section

Time: 30 Minutes

1 Essay

Directions: You will have 30 minutes to plan and write an essay on the topic specified. Read the topic carefully. You will probably find it best to spend time considering the topic and organizing your thoughts before you begin writing. DO NOT WRITE ON A TOPIC OTHER THAN THE ONE SPECIFIED. IN ORDER FOR YOUR TEST TO BE SCORED, YOUR RESPONSE MUST BE IN ENGLISH.

Read the opinion stated below:

"An important issue facing us today is the preservation of our planet. Supporting efforts to improve the environment on a global scale is crucial. However, individual efforts to combat pollution, global warming, and the depletion of natural resources are not likely to make a difference."

Discuss the extent to which you agree or disagree with this opinion. Support your views with specific reasons and examples from your own experience, observations, or reading.

Answer Key for Practice Test 4

Reading Test

1. D	24. E
2. C	25. C
3. A	26. A
4. E	27. C
5. B	28. E
6. A	29. B
7. A	30. C
8. C	31. A
9. A	32. E
10. D	33. B
11. C	34. B
12. A	35. D
13. A	36. B
14. B	37. A
15. C	38. C
16. C	39. B
17. C	40. A
18. C	41. D
19. B	42. C
20. D	43. E
21. A	44. B
22. C	45. B
23. C	46. D

Mathematics Test

1. B	24. D
2. D	25. A
3. C	26. D
4. B	27. E
5. C	28. D
6. A	29. C
7. C	30. C
8. B	31. C
9. B	32. C
10. C	33. C
11. D	34. D
12. C	35. D
13. B	36. D
14. D	37. C
15. E	38. D
16. A	39. C
17. E	40. C
18. A	41. A
19. C	42. B
20. C	43. E
21. A	44. B
22. B	45. D
23. C	46. D

Writing Test Multiple-Choice

1. D	23. C
2. A	24. A
3. D	25. D
4. C	26. B
5. A	27. E
6. B	28. E
7. A	29. A
8. E	30. C
9. B	31. B
10. B	32. C
11. A	33. D
12. B	34. C
13. D	35. A
14. A	36. D
15. C	37. B
16. C	38. B
17. C	39. E
18. B	40. D
19. D	41. C
20. A	42. B
21. A	43. D
22. C	44. A

Scoring Your PPST Practice Test 4

To score your PPST Practice Test 4, total the number of correct responses for each test. Do not subtract any points for questions attempted but missed, as there is no penalty for guessing. The scores for each section range from 150 to 190. Because the Writing Test contains multiple-choice questions and an essay, that score is a composite score adjusted to give approximately equal weight to the number right on the multiple-choice section and to the essay score. The essay is scored holistically (a single score for overall quality) from 1 (low) to 6 (high). Each of two readers gives a 1 to 6 score. The score that the essay receives is the sum of these two readers' scores.

Analyzing your test results

The following charts should be used to carefully analyze your results and spot your strengths and weaknesses. The complete process of analyzing each subject area and each individual question should be completed for this Practice Test. These results should be reexamined for trends in types of error (repeated errors) or poor results in specific subject areas. **This reexamination and analysis is of tremendous importance for effective test preparation.**

Practice Test 4: Subject area analysis sheet

	Possible	Completed	Right	Wrong
Reading Test	46			
Mathematics Test	46			
Writing Test	44			
TOTAL	136			

Analysis—tally sheet for questions missed

One of the most important parts of test preparation is analyzing why you missed a question so that you can reduce the number of mistakes. Now that you have taken Practice Test 4 and checked your answers, carefully tally your mistakes by marking each of them in the proper column.

	Total Missed	Simple Mistake	Misread Problem	Lack of Knowledge
Reading Test				
Mathematics Test				
Writing Test				
TOTAL				

Reviewing the data in the preceding chart should help you determine why you are missing certain questions. Now that you have pinpointed types of errors, focus on avoiding your most common type.

Score approximators

Reading Test

To approximate your reading score:

1. Count the number of questions you answered correctly.

2. Use the following table to match the number of correct answers and the corresponding approximate score range.

Number Right	Approximate Score Range
0–11	150–160
12–23	161–170
24–34	171–180
35–46	181–190

Remember, this is only an approximate score range. When you take the PPST, you, will have questions that are similar to those in this book; however some questions may be slightly easier or more difficult.

Mathematics Test

To approximate your mathematics score:

1. Count the number of questions you answered correctly.

2. Use the following table to match the number of correct answers and the corresponding approximate score range.

Number Right	Approximate Score Range
0–11	150–160
12–23	161–170
24–34	171–180
35–46	181–190

Remember, this is an approximate score range. Some of the questions on the actual computer-based exam are experimental and will *not* count toward your score.

Writing Test

These scores are difficult to approximate because the multiple-choice section score and the essay score are combined to give a total score.

Essay checklist

Use this checklist to evaluate your essay.

Diagnosis/prescription for timed writing exercise

A good essay will:

- ❏ Address the assignment

    Be well focused

- ❏ Be well organized

    Have smooth transitions between paragraphs

    Be coherent, unified

- ❏ Be well developed

    Contain specific examples to support points

- ❏ Be grammatically sound (only minor flaws)

    Use correct sentence structure

    Use correct punctuation

    Use standard written English

- ❏ Use language skillfully

    Use a variety of sentence types

    Use a variety of words

Answers and Explanations for Practice Test 4

Reading Test

1. **D.** The second sentence makes the main point of the passage. **A, B,** and **C** are secondary points, and there is no criticism in the passage **E.**

2. **C.** From the context, it is clear that *purists* refers to those who insist that because an Olympiad is four years, the 1906 games in Athens cannot be considered Olympic games.

3. **A.** The third sentence of the passage indicates that the author sees urban legends as part of an oral tradition. **C** is directly contradicted in the passage, and although it is stated that urban legends are often bizarre, no assumption is made that *bizarre* is equal to *untrue* **B. E** is not indicated in the passage, nor does the passage make the judgment in **D.**

4. **E.** The second sentence makes this point. **A** and **B** are not supported, and **C** is not true; fairy tales sometimes deal with grotesque behavior. Nothing in the passage indicates that the intention of urban legends is to change behavior; in fact, no intention whatsoever is suggested **D.**

5. **B.** The last sentence briefly touches on the main themes of urban legends. It doesn't contrast modern legends with those of the past to make a point about changes in the world **A,** nor does it make judgments **C, D, E.**

6. **A.** According to the passage, both the backyard fence and the Internet are places where information is passed without the filter of facts. **D** may be true, but it isn't the reason the metaphor is used. **C** is vague, and **E** is untrue. Nothing in the passage suggests that people who use the Internet and talk over the backyard fence are uneducated **B.**

7. **A.** The first sentence makes it clear that the depictions on the cave walls can be easily identified. There isn't enough information to imply **C,** to draw the conclusion of **D,** or to suggest **E.** The Neanderthals aren't mentioned in the passage **B.**

8. **C.** Each paragraph deals with failures and problems in the early life of a scientist whose later work changed the world. **A** is not accurate; nothing indicates Einstein wasn't understood, only that he was slow in learning to speak and not academically successful. **B** is certainly true, but it is not the subject of the passage. **D** is irrelevant, and **E** doesn't logically conclude the content of the passage.

9. **A.** The author doesn't use understatement. Irony **B** is built into the passage, which deals with the world-changing work of two men who didn't show early promise. The two men are compared **C,** specific details are included about each man **D,** and the transition *Like Darwin,* opens the second paragraph **E.**

10. **D.** The main point of the passage is that it was not the earth's shape but its circumference that was important to Columbus. The actual circumference of the earth is not given; 25,000 miles was the opinion of scholars at the time, and not a main point **A. B, C,** and **E** are secondary points.

11. **C.** That Columbus chose an estimate of 18,000 miles rather than the generally accepted 25,000 miles indicates that he wanted the trip to be more palatable to the monarchs. The last sentence of the passage reinforces this point. Nothing suggests that **A** is true, and **B** is not implied but rather stated. There is no information to support **D** as a possible inference, nor is it suggested that uneducated people *refused to believe* the earth was a sphere **E.**

12. **A.** The last sentence is mildly cynical, not harshly critical **E.** This sentence does suggest a cynical opinion about the funding of projects, and therefore **B, C,** and **D** are not good answers.

13. **A.** **B** describes *patternicity* as *uniquely human*, but the passage refers to experiments showing that other animals also seem to have the trait. The passage also makes it clear that patternicity doesn't distinguish false from real patterns **C. D** is irrelevant to the passage, and although patternicity can involve false meanings, it isn't limited to them **E.**

14. **B.** Shermer refers to a "Baloney Detection Network" that would allow people to separate false patterns from real ones. Unfortunately, Shermer says, humans did not develop such a network. **E** is the opposite of the point Shermer makes, and **A, C,** and **D** are simply incorrect.

15. **C.** The results of the experiments indicated that predators avoided nonpoisonous snakes that mimicked poisonous ones and that this example of patternicity led to the predators' survival. Nothing suggests that instinct is the key factor **E.** The experiments are unrelated to Shermer's "Baloney Detection Network" **A,** and **B** and **D** are the opposite of the point made by the experiments.

16. **C.** The experiments dealt with nonhuman predators, which indicates that Foster and Kokko assumed that nonhuman species also find patterns in nature. **A** is not indicated, and the word *purposely* in **B** rules out that choice. Shermer makes a point in the passage that the ability to recognize patterns is a positive trait in humans and helps us understand our environment, although sometimes what we see as a pattern is false. This eliminates choice **D. E** is irrelevant to the experiments and not supported by any evidence in the passage.

17. **C.** In the last sentence, the passage states that respondents to the poll are *uncertain* what steps to take, even though they support *living green*. The suggestion here is that a lack of information is the problem. **D** is the second-best answer, but the passage does not single out the media as being at fault. The other choices are not implied.

18. **C.** It is the stability of the Chinese civilization that is emphasized in the passage. **A** is a secondary point, and **D** and **E,** though mentioned, are not the main point. The regional differences **B** are not described as *relatively insignificant,* even though they have not significantly destabilized China's civilization.

19. **B.** The last sentence suggests that the powerful bureaucracy may have been responsible for the country's stability. The other choices may or may not be true, but they are not given as the possible cause of China's stability.

20. **D.** Of the choices given, **D** is the one that best covers the subject of the passage. The passage refers to events that influenced the assigning of homework, but these are not the main idea **E**. The passage doesn't present theories **B** nor does it suggest that the problem is *teacher versus student* **C**. The word *crisis* in **A** is too strong, and, in addition, the passage concerns homework, not the classroom.

21. **A.** In paragraph 3, the Japanese success in business is given credit for the drive to improve U.S. education and a resulting resurgence in the amount of homework assigned. **B, C, D,** and **E,** while they may or may not be true, are not covered in the passage.

22. **C.** According to the passage, the law against homework was passed in 1901 and taken off the books in 1997. The implication is that attitudes toward homework changed. **B, D,** and **E** may be true, but none of them is specifically cited as the reason for repeal of the law. Constitutionality **A** is not an issue.

23. **C.** The last sentence is the only argument for *busywork* (homework) in the passage. It suggests no criticism of parents **A** nor does it suggest that teachers have a *selfish* interest **B**. The last sentence introduces a different point of view; it doesn't summarize or draw a conclusion **D, E.**

24. **E.** Although **A, B,** and **D** are all contributing factors, it is the loss of habitat that is cited as the biggest threat to amphibians. **C** is not indicated as a factor.

25. **C.** The passage states that such a release would be monumental but not impossible. In the preceding sentence, zoos are described as the best chance for amphibians, and the implication is that after being bred in captivity, the amphibians would be released into the wild.

26. **A.** In this passage, the problem with distributing food to the poor is seen as a matter of handling the details, which *logistics* means. None of the other definitions of logistics is correct.

27. **C.** The author would not favor repeal of a law that shields people from liability for their donations. The law makes it more likely, not less likely, that food will be donated. From information in the passage, the author is likely to agree with all the other statements.

28. **E.** This passage is most likely to appear in a general guide for companies. It is unlikely that it would be in a how-to book for new managers **B** or in a news article that specifically covered standards for the European Union **D**. It doesn't present an opinion and therefore would not appear in an editorial **C**, nor would it be appropriate in an article profiling multinational corporations **A.**

29. **B.** The only inference that can be made is that in order to meet the requirements of local standards, the company would be required to make modifications to the product. **A, C, D,** and **E** may or may not be true, but they cannot be inferred from information in the passage.

30. **C.** The primary point made in the passage is that dogs react badly to inequity and that by being treated equally, they are more likely to cooperate. This conclusion is reached not because they are more advanced than cats **A,** but because, unlike cats, they are related to animals that hunt in packs. The experiment doesn't prove intelligence **E**. **B** is too broad a conclusion, and nothing implies **D.**

369

31. A. Cats are solitary hunters and therefore, theoretically at least, they would not have a basic aversion to inequity. **B** and **C** may or may not be true, but the passage doesn't imply that these are the reasons they wouldn't pass the aversion test. Nothing in the passage indicates the truth of **D** or **E**.

32. E. The only purpose of the parenthetical sentence is to state a fact. It does not criticize businesses for providing privacy policies or for misleading the public **A, B.** It is also not *advocating* or *blaming* **C, D.**

33. B. The clear implication of the last sentence is that companies do not currently always follow the policies they disclose, and that the law should ensure that they do. **A** is definitely not implied, and **C,** while perhaps true, is not the point of the passage, which is not intended to criticize the consumer. **D** and **E** are perhaps true, but they aren't implied by the last sentence of the passage.

34. B. The last sentence of the passage suggests this point. **D** may seem a possible inference, but the passage doesn't indicate that the evidence is *overwhelming*. Also, nothing in the passage suggests **A** or **C,** which may or may not be true. The author does not indicate that the researchers have *ulterior motives* **E.**

35. D. According to the passage, information about migration routes might contradict a group's own legends and traditions about its origins. While the other choices may or may not be true, they do not apply to the point being made in the passage.

36. B. According to Virginia Woolf, financial independence was a crucial first step toward all other forms of independence for women. The Married Woman's Property Act gave women some degree of financial independence—but not full rights **A,** and nothing suggests that it was concerned with women's rights to own businesses **E. C** and **D,** while both true, are not why the Married Woman's Property Act was important.

37. A. This is the main purpose of the passage. **B** and **E** are secondary, and the passage neither emphasizes the importance of recording the knowledge of hunting-gathering people **D** nor does it *criticize* anyone **C.**

38. C. In this passage, the word *cunning* refers to the subtle perplexities in Hume's ideas, which are masked by the clarity of his style.

39. B. By using the word *cunning* and stating that the work's clarity is somewhat deceitful, the author of the passage indicates that Hume's writing is not as straightforward as it seems. Nothing suggests that Hume's second version of the *Treatise* was poorly received **C,** that Hume was sarcastic about skepticism (although he was critical) **D,** or that he defended agnosticism in the work **E.** Also, the author does not imply that the work isn't *useful* **A.**

40. A. No reason is given for the revision, and the only one implied is that the work was not well received. Although he did improve its structure, this is not given as a motivation for the revision **C.**

41. D. The passage describes Erdrich's Native American heritage and her use of it in her writing, but the main point is to describe her as an author who goes beyond the Native American culture for her characters and themes. The passage doesn't make a judgment about her place in American literature **A, B, E,** nor does it mention her use of well-known legends **C.**

42. C. The reason the humpback whales mate and calve in warmer waters is physical, not biological **D. A** is accurate, but it is not cited as the main reason for the whales' migration. No parallel is drawn between whale migration and bird migration **B,** nor is food supply in colder waters mentioned **E.** The primary assets of the tropical waters are that they are warmer, shallower, and provide more protection for mothers and calves.

43. E. The last sentence of the passage defines respiration in this way. The other sentences relate to breathing, not respiration.

44. B. The second sentence states that breathing is a function of many multicellular animals. From this it can be inferred that not all multicellular animals breathe. The passage doesn't imply that either respiration or breathing is more important than the other **A,** and **C, D,** and **E** are simply incorrect according to the information provided in the passage.

45. B. Although perhaps impractical, **B** would provide the most accurate information. Surveys and anecdotal evidence **C, D** would be more affected by the subjects' attitudes toward the subject, and **E** would have too many variables. **A,** while providing information about cleaning products, would not measure the benefits of these products.

46. D. Bry advocates appropriate hygiene and cleanliness, and covering one's mouth during a cough or sneeze would be considered an example. Bry would most likely agree with the other statements.

Mathematics Test

1. B. Factor 7,500 into the product of primes.

$$7,500 = 75 \times 100$$
$$= (3 \times 25) \times (4 \times 25)$$
$$= 3 \times 5 \times 5 \times 2 \times 2 \times 5 \times 5$$
$$= 2^2 \times 3^1 \times 5^4$$

Therefore, $x = 2$, $y = 1$, and $z = 4$. Then $xyz = (2)(1)(4) = 8$.

2. D. Circle R has 2 of 3 parts shaded, so it represents the fraction $\frac{2}{3}$. Circle S has 3 of 8 parts shaded so it represents the fraction $\frac{3}{8}$. *Sum* is the answer to addition; therefore,

$$\frac{2}{3} + \frac{3}{8} = \frac{16}{24} + \frac{9}{24} = \frac{25}{24} = 1\frac{1}{24}.$$

3. C. Use an example. Suppose hot dogs come 8 in a package and hot dog buns come 6 in a package. The least number of each you would need is 24 (the least common multiple of 6 and 8) so that each hot dog has a bun. If you were to multiply 6 and 8 and use 48, that also would make it so that each hot dog has a bun, but it would not be the *least* amount that makes this situation true.

4. B. If you were to expand the value 24.7×10^3, it would be 24,700 (move the decimal point to the right 3 positions). Now rewrite 24,700 in scientific notation. It is 2.47×10^4. Hence, the decimal point in the original expression is moved to the left one position, and the exponent is increased by 1.

5. C. Six equal spaces are marked from 0 to 1, which makes each space represent a length of $\frac{1}{6}$. This puts C at $\frac{4}{6}$ and D at $\frac{5}{6}$. One method to determine which of the expressions has a value between $\frac{4}{6}$ and $\frac{5}{6}$ is to use decimal approximations. $\frac{4}{6} \approx 0.6666$ and $\frac{5}{6} \approx 0.833$. $\frac{1}{3} \times \frac{1}{5}$ has the value $\frac{1}{15} \approx 0.6666$, which is not between the C and D values. $\frac{2}{3} - \frac{1}{5}$ has the value $\frac{7}{15} \approx 0.4666$, which also is not between the C and D values. $\frac{1}{3} + \frac{2}{5}$ has the value $\frac{11}{15} \approx 0.7333$, which *is* between the C and D values. $\frac{1}{3} \div \frac{2}{5}$ has the value $\frac{5}{6}$, which is the D value, but is not *between* the C and D values. $\frac{2}{5} \div \frac{1}{3}$ has the value $\frac{6}{5}$, which is not between the C and D values.

6. A. First find 12% of 250. $0.12 \times 250 = 30$, which means that 30 people are aged 75 to 80. The remaining people are aged 81 to 90, which represents 10 age groups. Since there are 250 people total, and 30 people are 80 years old and younger, then 220 people are 81 to 90 years old. Knowing that the remaining people are evenly distributed, divide the 220 by the 10 age groups remaining. $220 \div 10 = 22$.

7. C. $\text{Percent change} = \frac{\text{amount of change}}{\text{starting amount}} \times 100\%$

The change from $2.25 to $2.50 is $0.25. The starting amount was $2.25.

$$\frac{0.25}{2.25} = \frac{25}{225} = \frac{1}{9} \times 100\% = 11\frac{1}{9}\%$$

8. B. Jim rounds to the nearest thousand and then adds up the values.

Jim's estimates and sum are $45,000 + $57,000 + $73,000 = $175,000.

Bob rounds to the nearest ten and then adds up the values.

Bob's estimates and sum are $45,260 + $57,250 + $72,980 = $175,490.

The difference between these amounts is $175,490 - $175,000 = $490.

9. B. Make a literal translation of the English.

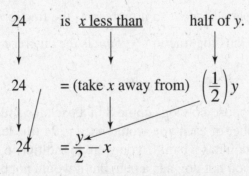

$$24 \quad \text{is} \quad \underline{x \text{ less than}} \quad \text{half of } y.$$

$$24 \quad = (\text{take } x \text{ away from}) \quad \frac{y}{2}$$

$$24 \quad = \frac{y}{2} - x$$

10. C.

Create a proportion.

$$\frac{\text{inches}}{\text{hours}} : \frac{4\frac{1}{3}}{\frac{1}{4}} = \frac{26}{x}$$

Cross multiply to clear the proportion.

$$4\frac{1}{3}x = \frac{1}{4} \times 26$$

Convert $4\frac{1}{3}$ into an improper fraction.

$$\frac{13}{3}x = \frac{13}{2}$$

Multiply each side of the equation by $\frac{3}{13}$.

$$x = \frac{3}{2} = 1\frac{1}{2}$$

11. D. Start with the "y."

$$
\begin{array}{r}
2x4 \\
\times 5y \\
\hline
1404 \\
+11z00 \\
\hline
13104
\end{array}
$$

Since $y \times 4$ produces a 4, y is either a 1 or a 6. ($1 \times 4 = 4$, $6 \times 4 = 24$) If y is a 1, then the first product line would have to be the repeat of $2x4$. Since this is not the case, the y must be 6.

So now the problem looks like this:

$$
\begin{array}{r}
2x4 \\
\times 56 \\
\hline
1404 \\
+11z00 \\
\hline
13104
\end{array}
$$

The "x" has to be a number that when it is multiplied by 6 (remember, $y = 6$) and 2 is added to that ($6 \times 4 = 24$, carry the 2) the result ends in a zero. Only the values 3 or 8 can work. If $x = 8$, then $284 \times 6 = 1,704$, but the problem says it will be 1,404, hence $x \neq 8$. Therefore $x = 3$ and $234 \times 6 = 1,404$, as expected. Finally, since 4 adds with z to make a number that ends in a 1, z must be 7.

Therefore, $x = 3$, $y = 6$, and $z = 7$

$$x + yz = 3 + (6)(7)$$

$$= 3 + 42 \text{ (recall order of operations)}$$

$$= 45$$

12. C. According to the table, as the hours increase, so does the money. Only the third and fourth choices show this. The table shows that $(0,0)$ belongs on the graph. Both the third and fourth choices also show this. According to the table, as hours increase by 2, money increases by 15. Since this rate of change is constant, the graph is linear, hence only choice **C** is correct.

13. B. The top of the pyramid has one piece of fruit. The layer below it is a square with 2 pieces of fruit per side. Hence, the second layer from the top contains 4 pieces of fruit. The layer below that forms a square with 3 pieces of fruit per side, so it contains 9 pieces of fruit. Keep adding these square numbers together until the total is 55. $1 + 4 + 9 + 16 + 25 = 55$. Hence, 5 layers of fruit make up the pyramid.

14. D. A slope of $-\frac{2}{3}$ means either $\frac{-2}{3}$ or $\frac{2}{-3}$. Slope means $\frac{\text{rise}}{\text{run}}$. Therefore, from one point to another point, you can either have a "rise" of –2 and a "run" of +3, or a "rise" of +2 and a "run" of –3. If you start at $(-3,5)$ on a graph, and do a "rise" of –2 and a "run" of +3, you would be at the point $(3,0)$, which is not one of the answer choices. If you start at $(-3,5)$ and do a "rise" of +2 and a "run" of –3, you would be at $(-6,7)$.

15. E. Notice that the plumber charges by the minute. There are 180 minutes in 3 hours. Since the plumber charges d dollars per minute, he will charge $180d$ dollars for 3 hours. He also charges \$25 for driving time, so the total charge will be $180d + 25$ dollars.

16. A. Notice that all the choices have the x on the left side of the equation and the constants on the right. Go through the solving process and stop when you recognize the answer.

$$7x + 3(x + 5) = 2x - 7 \quad \text{(distributive property)}$$

$$7x + 3x + 15 = 2x - 7 \quad \text{(combine like terms)}$$

$$10x + 15 = 2x - 7 \quad \text{(subtract } 2x \text{ from each side of the equation)}$$

$$8x + 15 = -7 \quad \text{(subtract 15 from each side of the equation)}$$

$$8x = -22$$

17. E. With segment DE parallel to segment BC, $\triangle ABC$ is similar to $\triangle ADE$. This makes corresponding sides (sides in the same relative position) proportional. That means $\frac{AD}{AB} = \frac{DE}{BC}$. $AD = 2$, $AB = 10$ ($AB = AD + DB$), and $DE = 6$. Substitute these values into the proportion and solve.

$$\frac{2}{10} = \frac{6}{BC} \quad \text{Cross multiply to clear the proportion}$$

$$2BC = 60 \quad \text{Divide both sides by 2}$$

$$BC = 30$$

18. A. Since triangle ABC is obtuse, one of its angles is more than 90°. Since the sum of the angles of any triangle is 180°, and one angle is already given as 45°, the remaining angle must be less than 45°.

$$(\text{more than 90}) + 45 + (\text{remaining angle}) = 180$$

$$(\text{more than 135}) + (\text{remaining angle}) = 180$$

$$(180 - \text{more than 135 leaves less than 45})$$

$$\text{remaining angle} < 45°$$

The only answer less than 45° is 35°.

19. C. To find the perimeter of a triangle, add together the lengths of its sides. The triangle given is a right triangle, which means you can use the Pythagorean theorem to find the missing side because the other two sides are given. The legs of a right triangle refer to the sides that form the right angle, hence the missing side is the hypotenuse, or the longest side.

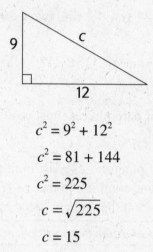

$$c^2 = 9^2 + 12^2$$

$$c^2 = 81 + 144$$

$$c^2 = 225$$

$$c = \sqrt{225}$$

$$c = 15$$

Remember, the question asked for the perimeter of the triangle, not how long the hypotenuse is. The perimeter is $9 + 12 + 15 = 36$.

20. C. To find the surface area of the right cylinder, picture the circular top and bottom removed and the shell rolled out to form a rectangle.

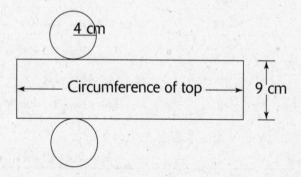

To find the surface area of the right cylinder, add together the areas of the two circles and the area of the rectangular shell. The area of a circle is found by using the formula $A = \pi r^2$. The radius of each circle is 4 cm, therefore the area of each circle is $(4)^2\pi$ or 16π cm^2. The rectangular shell has a length the same as the circumference of the top of the cylinder. The formula for the circumference of a circle is $C = \pi d$, where d is the diameter of the circle. Since the circle has a radius of 4 cm, its diameter is 8 cm. The rectangle has an area of $8\pi \times 9 = 72\pi$ cm^2. The total surface area is $2(16\pi) + 72\pi = 32\pi + 72\pi = 104\pi$ cm^2.

To find the volume of a right cylinder, use the formula $V =$ (area of base) $\times$ (height). The base of the cylinder is a circle of radius 4 cm and the height of this cylinder is 9 cm. The volume of this cylinder is $(16\pi$ cm$^2)(9$ cm$) = 144\pi$ cm^3.

Numerically, the volume had the greater value by 40π, $(144\pi - 104\pi = 40\pi)$.

21. A. Since $\triangle ABC$ is congruent to $\triangle DEF$, segment AC has the same length as segment DF. Point A is located at $(-7,-5)$ and point C is located at $(-4,-1)$. To get from point A to point C, move 3 units to the right and 4 units up. Then to get from point D to point F, do the same thing. Point D is located at $(1,6)$. Moving 3 units to the right and 4 units up brings you to $(4,10)$.

22. B. To factor the expression $x^2 - 13x - 48$, find two expressions that will multiply to become this expression.

$$x^2 - 13x - 48$$

$$(\qquad)(\qquad)$$

The first positions in each set of parentheses must multiply to make x^2, hence

$$(x\qquad)(x\qquad)$$

The last positions in each set of parentheses must multiply to make -48 in such a way that the remaining two multiplications combine to make $-13x$. All possibilities that multiply to make x^2 at the beginning and -48 at the end are listed in the following chart.

		Sum of other two multiplications	
1	−48	−47	$(x + 1)(x - 48) = x^2 - 47x - 48$
−1	48	+47	$(x - 1)(x + 48) = x^2 + 47x - 48$
2	−24	−22	$(x + 2)(x - 24) = x^2 - 22x - 48$
−2	24	+22	$(x + 2)(x - 24) = x^2 -+22x - 48$
3	**−16**	**−13**	$\mathbf{(x + 3)(x - 16) = x^2 - 13x - 48}$
−3	16	+13	$(x - 3)(x + 16) = x^2 + 13x - 48$
4	−12	−8	$(x + 4)(x - 12) = x^2 - 8x - 48$
−4	12	+8	$(x - 4)(x + 12) = x^2 - +8x - 48$
6	−8	−2	$(x + 6)(x - 8) = x^2 - 2x - 48$
−6	8	+2	$(x - 6)(x + 8) = x^2 - +2x - 48$

Notice that only the factors $(x + 3)$ and $(x - 16)$ produce the desired result. Only $(x + 3)$ is a correct choice.

23. C. First use proportions to find the actual distance to be traveled.

$$\frac{\text{map (cm)}}{\text{actual (miles)}}$$

$$\frac{1}{25} = \frac{15}{x}\qquad \text{Cross multiply to clear the proportion.}$$

$$x = 375$$

The distance traveled is 375 miles.

To find the amount of time it will take to travel this distance at 35 miles per hour, use the formula that says (rate) × (time) = (distance).

(35 mi/hr) × (t hr) = 375 mi   (divide each side of the equation by 35 mi/hr)

The resulting time is between 10 and 11 hours.

24. D. A square yard is a square that is 1 yard on each side. See the illustration below.

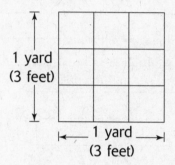

Each small square is one foot on an edge, which makes it a square foot. Notice that one square yard contains 9 square feet. Therefore 2 square yards will be 18 square feet.

25. A. The *mean* of a set of data is the sum of the data values divided by the number of data values.

$$\frac{65+49+32+65+65+82+50+75+60+57}{10} = \frac{600}{10} = 60$$

The *median* of a set of data values is the middle value when the data is listed from smallest to largest.

Smallest   Largest

32   49   50   57   60   65   65   65   75   82

Middle values

Because there is an even number of data values, there are two middle values.

The median becomes the mean of these two values.

$$\text{Median} = \frac{60+65}{2} = \frac{125}{2} = 62.5$$

The *mode* of a set of data values is the value repeated most often.

$$\text{Mode} = 65$$

The *range* of a set of data values is the difference between the largest and smallest values.

$$\text{Range} = 82 - 32 = 50$$

$$(\text{mean} - \text{median}) \times (\text{mode} - \text{range})$$

$$(60 - 62.5) \times (65 - 50) = (-2.5) \times (15) = -37.5$$

26. **D.** Probability is the comparison of the number of favorable outcomes in an event versus the total number of outcomes possible in the event.

$$\text{Probability} = \frac{\#\,\text{favorable}}{\#\,\text{total}}$$

The following table shows a setup for viewing all the possibilities. The top row contains the possibilities for one die, and the far left column contains the possibilities for the other die.

product	1	2	3	4	5	6
1	✓	✓	✓	✓	✓	✓
2	✓	✓	✓	✓	✓	✓
3	✓	✓	✓	✓	✓	✓
4	✓	✓	✓	✓		
5	✓	✓	✓			
6	✓	✓	✓			

Notice there are 36 total spaces within the table, indicating a total of 36 possible outcomes. In this table, check marks are placed where the product of the numbers on the two dice is less than 20. Recall that *product* is the answer to multiplication. The locations for 4×5 and 5×4 are blank because 20 is *not* less than 20. There are 28 favorable outcomes. Therefore, the probability is $\frac{28}{36} = \frac{7}{9}$.

27. **E.** Be sure you answer the question. The question is to find the cost of the cell phone, not the cost of the accessories. This problem can be worked algebraically or by trial and error.

To do the problem algebraically, start by either representing the cost of the cell phone or the cost of the accessories. Suppose x = the cost of the cell phone, and then $x + 20$ = the cost of the accessories, since the accessories cost $20 more than the cell phone. The combined cost is $100, so

$$x + x + 20 = 100$$

$$2x + 20 = 100$$

$$2x = 80$$

$$x = 40$$

But the "x" is the cost of the cell phone, and the question asks for the cost of the accessories. Because the accessories cost $20 more than the phone, the answer is $60. Suppose x = the cost of the accessories, and then $x - 20$ = cost of the cell phone. Then the new equation would have be

$$x + x - 20 = 100$$

$$2x - 20 = 100$$

$$2x = 120$$

$$x = 60$$

Since the "*x*" here represents the cost of the accessories, you have the desired answer.

The answer can also be found by trial and error. Remember, the answer choices represent the cost of the accessories.

cost of accessories + cost of cell phone = 100 (recall that the accessories are $20 more than the cell phone)

$20 + 0 = 100$ NO

$30 + 10 = 100$ NO

$40 + 20 = 100$ NO

$50 + 30 = 100$ NO

$60 + 40 = 100$ YES

28. D. Perhaps the easiest way to see this problem is to locate the values on a number line. The farther to the right a number falls on the number line, the greater its value. Since the order requested is from greatest to least, look for the number value farthest to the right first and then list them as you go to the left. Rewrite each of the values in decimal form. *A* is already in decimal form. When you divide –26 by 5 you get –5.2 (the same as –5.20) in decimal form, hence *B* = –5.20. When you rewrite $-5\frac{1}{2}$ in decimal form, you get –5.5 (the same as –5.50). When you rewrite –5 in decimal form, you get –5.0 (the same as –5.00). Now look at the number line from –4 to –6.

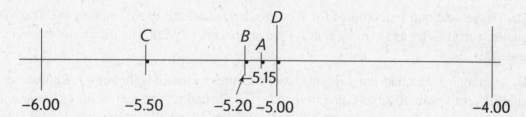

C. The club has 25 married men and 15 single men as members, so there are 40 males total. The total number of members in the club is 120. The probability of randomly selecting a male is $\frac{40}{120}$, which reduces to $\frac{1}{3}$.

0. C. Solve the original equation for *P*.

$$4P + 20 = Q \qquad \text{Subtract 20 from each side of the equation.}$$

$$4P = Q - 20 \qquad \text{Divide each side of the equation by 4.}$$

$$P = \frac{Q}{4} - \frac{20}{4}$$

$$P = \frac{Q}{4} - 5 \qquad \text{Add 12 to each side of the equation.}$$

$$P + 12 = \frac{Q}{4} - 5 + 12$$

$$P + 12 = \frac{Q}{4} + 7$$

31. C. To be correct, choices **A, B,** and **E** would need to have read "Divide b into a, move the decimal point two places to the right, and add a percent sign." Also, to be correct, choice **D** would have had to be "Solve the proportion $\frac{a}{b} = \frac{x}{100}$ and add a percent sign to the value of x."

Multiplying a number by 100 and adding a percent sign will not change its value but will express it as a percentage.

32. C. The mean of a set of data is the sum of all its values divided by the number of values. The frequency table indicates how often a value is repeated. This table shows that the number 3 occurs 4 times, the number 4 occurs 8 times, etc. Multiply the number with its frequency and then add these results to find the total of all the numbers. Then add up the numbers in the frequency column to find how many numbers there are.

Number	Frequency	Totals
3	4	12
4	8	32
6	2	12
7	4	28
8	2	16
	20	100

Then, 100 divided by 20 is 5.

33. C. The second quarter earnings for West (in dark gray) are approximately 40. The fourth quarter earnings for East (in light gray) are approximately 20. The difference between 40 and 20 is 20.

34. D. Rectangles are quadrilaterals (four-sided figures) with all right angles. Rhombuses are quadrilaterals with all sides equal in length. The shaded region represents quadrilaterals that have both of these properties. Quadrilaterals that have all right angles and all sides of equal length are called squares.

35. D. Look at the sketch below of triangle *ABC* in the coordinate plane.

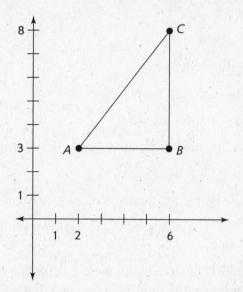

Notice that triangle *ABC* is a right triangle since segment *AB* is horizontal and segment *BC* is vertical. Perimeter means the distance around. The distance from *A* to *B* is 4 (6 – 2 = 4). The distance from *B* to *C* is 5 (8 – 3 = 5). The distance from *A* to *C* can be found using the Pythagorean theorem.

$$AC^2 = AB^2 + BC^2$$

$$AC^2 = (4)^2 + (5)^2$$

$$AC^2 = 16 + 25$$

$$AC^2 = 41$$

$$AC = \sqrt{41}$$

AC is between 6 and 7.

The perimeter of triangle *ABC* = 4 + 5 + (a number between 6 and 7)

$$= 9 + \text{(a number between 6 and 7)}$$

$$= \text{a number between 15 and 16}$$

36. D. One approach is to look for a pattern using the differences between the consecutive numbers.

> From 1 to 4, there is a difference of 3.
>
> From 4 to 9, there is difference of 5.
>
> From 9 to 16, there is a difference of 7.
>
> From 16 to 25, there is a difference of 9.
>
> Based on this pattern, the next difference should be 11 and then 13 after that.
>
> 25 + 11 = 36, and 36 + 13 = 49.

Another approach is to recognize the numbers as being special numbers.

> $1 = 1^2$, $4 = 2^2$, $9 = 3^2$, $16 = 4^2$, $25 = 5^2$, so the next two numbers should be 6^2 and 7^2, or 36 and 49.

37. C. The order of operations is involved with these calculations. Operations with parentheses are performed first, followed by multiplication and division in the order they occur from left to right, followed by addition and subtraction in the order they occur from left to right.

So, working through all the answer choices:

$$12 - 6 + 2 = 6 + 2 = 8$$

$$32 \div 4 \times 2 = 8 \times 2 = 16$$

$$8 \div \frac{1}{2} = 8 \times 2 = 16$$

$$16 \div 8 \times 2 = 2 \times 2 = 4$$

38. D. This problem can be easily solved using proportions.

$$\frac{\text{kilograms}}{\text{pounds}} : \frac{1}{2.2} = \frac{x}{220} \qquad \text{Clear the proportion by cross multiplying.}$$

$$2.2x = 220 \qquad \text{Divide each side of the equation by 2.2}$$

$$x = 100$$

9. C. Ratios can be expressed as fractions with the numerator being the first value expressed in the ratio and the denominator the second value expressed in the ratio. Ratios that reduce to the same value are equal ratios. The ratio of pens to pencils = $\frac{24}{12}$, which reduces to $\frac{2}{1}$. Therefore statement **A** is true. (Remember, you are looking for the statement that is false.) The ratio of pens to markers = $\frac{24}{6}$, which reduces to $\frac{4}{1}$. In statement **B,** the ratio of pens to markers is 8 to 2, which also reduces to $\frac{4}{1}$. Therefore statement **B** is true. The ratio of highlighters to pencils = $\frac{2}{12}$, which reduces to $\frac{1}{6}$. The statement **C** says the ratio of high-lighters to pencils is 6 to 1, which is expressed as $\frac{6}{1}$ and is not the same as $\frac{1}{6}$. Therefore statement **C** is false. Since the entire collection consists of 44 items ($24 + 12 + 6 + 2 = 44$) and there are 24 pens, more than half of the collection is made up of pens. Therefore statement **D,** which states that pens make up more than 50% of the collection is true. Only statement **C** is false.

40. C. Begin by looking for a relationship that involves only one symbol. The third row that shows @ + @ + @ + @ = 8 involves only the symbol @. This statement says that when four numbers of the same value are added together, the answer is 8. That is, $4(@) = 8$. From this we can conclude that @ has the value 2. The question is to find the value of &, so 2 is not the answer to the question. Now look for a row that involves only the @ and one other symbol. The first row shows that @ + # + # + # = 20. Since we know @ has the value 2, the first equation becomes

$$2 + \# + \# + \# = 20 \quad \text{which is the same as saying}$$

$$2 + 3(\#) = 20 \quad \text{Subtract 2 from each side of the equation.}$$

$$3(\#) = 18 \quad \text{Divide each side of the equation by 3.}$$

$$\# = 6$$

Now, go to the remaining row and replace @ with 2 and # with 6 to get

$$2 + 6 + 6 + \& + \& + \& + \& = 42$$

$$14 + 4(\&) = 42 \quad \text{Subtract 14 from each side of the equation.}$$

$$4(\&) = 28 \quad \text{Divide each side of the equation by 4.}$$

$$\& = 7$$

41. A. Notice that the information given is in *yards* and the question asks for the answer in *feet*. Since 1 yard is the same as 3 feet, buying 3 yards of material is the same as buying 9 feet of material. The question can be restated as, *if 9 feet of material cost \$2.97, what is the price per foot?* Dividing \$2.97 by 9 is \$0.33. You could also have noticed that if 9 feet of material cost \$2.97, each foot would have to cost less than a dollar. Choices **A** and **B** are the only two answer choices less than a dollar.

42. B. Twenty-five percent of 40 means to multiply 25% with 40. This can be done by changing 25% either into its decimal form or its fraction form.

$25\% = 0.25$ as a decimal or $= \frac{25}{100} = \frac{1}{4}$ as a fraction.

Therefore choice **A** and choice **D** are each correct ways for finding x.

Remember, though, you are looking for the way that is NOT correct.

Percentage problems can also be worked as a proportion: $\frac{\text{part}}{\text{whole}} = \frac{\%\text{-number}}{100}$.

In this case, x is the "part," "40" is the "whole," and the "%-number" is "25."

$\frac{x}{40} = \frac{25}{100}$ is one form of a correct proportion. Notice that neither the second nor the third choices look exactly like this. To see which proportion has the same meaning as $\frac{x}{40} = \frac{25}{100}$, cross multiply to see which produces the same next line.

When you cross multiply this equation, $\frac{x}{40} = \frac{25}{100}$, you get $100x = (25)(40)$.

With choice **C**, $\frac{x}{25} = \frac{40}{100}$, when you cross multiply, you also get $100x = (25)(40)$, which means choice **C** is also a correct method for finding x.

With choice **B**, $\frac{25}{100} = \frac{40}{x}$, when you cross multiply, you get $25x = (40)(100)$, which is not the same as what is the correct answer. Hence, only choice **B** is NOT a correct method for finding x.

43. E. Note that the question asked what *must* be true, not what could be true. If 3 and 4 are factors of N, then $N = 3 \times 4 \times$ (some natural number). If the "some natural number" is 1, then $N = 12$. If the "some natural number" is 2, then N is 24, and so on. This means that N must be a multiple of 12. Another way to say this is that 12 goes into N without a remainder. This is the same as saying 12 is a divisor of N.

Choice **A** says that 3 is a multiple of N. Since N is already greater than 3, 3 is not a multiple of N.

Choice **B** says the only factors of N are 3 and 4. This could be true, but is not necessarily true. It would be true if the "some number" was 1, but the "some number" did not have to be just 1. Remember that you are looking for what *must* be true.

Choice **C** says that N is a multiple of 12. N could be the value 12, and then 12 would be a multiple of N. But N could also be more than 12, say 24, which then means that 12 is not a multiple of N.

Since $N = 3 \times 4 \times$ (some natural number), it is not true that 7 had to be a factor of N, therefore choice **D** does not have to be true. Only the choice **E** *must* be true.

44. B. The shaded portion represents all the common multiples of 4 and 6 that are less than 100. The least common multiple of 4 and 6 is 12. The next common multiple of 4 and 6 is 24. Therefore the shaded portion has multiples of 12 and the question becomes "how many multiples of 12 are less than 100?" You can divide 100 by 12 to see how many 12s are in 100. 100 divided by 12 equals 8 plus a remainder. Therefore, 8 multiples of 12 are in 100. You could also simply list the multiples of 12 (12, 24, 36, 48, 60, 72, 84, 96) and then count how many are in the list. There are eight multiples of 12 that are less than 100.

D. One approach for solving this problem is to use a proportion.

$$\frac{\text{clothing money}}{\text{clothing percent number}} = \frac{\text{mortgage money}}{\text{mortgage percent number}}$$

First find the percentage of the budget that goes to the mortgage. Since the entire budget represents 100%, subtract the known percentages from 100% to get the percentage spent on the mortgage.

$$100\% - (30\% + 10\% + 15\% + 5\%) = 40\%$$

Now use the above proportion.

$$\frac{3600}{5} = \frac{x}{40}$$ Cross multiply to clear the proportion.

$$5x = 144{,}000$$ Divide each side of the equation by 5.

$$x = 28{,}800$$

Alternatively, if you had noticed that 40% is exactly 8 times as much as 5%, then you could have calculated that the mortgage is 8 times that of the clothing.

$$\$3{,}600 \times 8 = \$28{,}800$$

46. **D.** Probability compares favorable outcomes to total outcomes. To find total outcomes, you need to see how many natural numbers there are from 21 to 50. The most common error made is to simply subtract 21 from 50 to get 29. When you do this, you are forgetting to count the number 21. There are 30 natural numbers from 21 to 50. Next, you need to see how many of the numbers from 21 to 50 are prime numbers. The prime numbers from 21 to 50 are 23, 29, 31, 37, 41, 43, and 47. So, there are 7 prime numbers. Therefore, the probability is $\frac{7}{30}$.

Writing Test: Multiple-Choice Section

Part A

1. **D.** *Had broke* is not the correct past participle of *break*. The correct past participle is *had broken*.

2. **A.** The antecedent of the pronoun *their* is *person*, which is singular. The correct pronoun would be *his, her,* or *his or her*.

3. **D.** *Whole entire* is redundant. One of the words (e.g., *whole*) should be dropped.

4. **C.** There is no antecedent for the pronoun *them*. In the original sentence, it appears that Mrs. Williams never eats bagel shops. *Them* should be replaced with *bagels*.

5. **A.** Usually verbs are modified by adverbs (e.g., *badly*), but *smelled* in this sentence is a linking verb, and linking verbs are modified by adjectives (*bad*). If the meaning of the sentence were that something was wrong with the dog's nose, then *badly* would be correct. But clearly the meaning here is that the dog has an odor.

385

6. B. The object of the preposition *without* is *me,* not *I.* If you read the sentence without *captain,* the correct case of the pronoun will be obvious.

7. A. *Waiting in front of the railroad station* is a dangling, or misplaced, participial phrase. is not *the evening* that is waiting in front of the railroad station, but *I.* The participial phrase should be directly followed by the word it is modifying. The sentence could be cor rected in different ways: *As I waited in front of the railroad station ...* or *Waiting in front of the railroad station as evening turned into night, I realized ... .*

8. E. This sentence is correct. *Who had entered the race* is a restrictive clause, which means that no commas should be used to set it off. The verbs **B** and **D** are correct, and *fair-grounds* **C** is not a proper noun and therefore shouldn't be capitalized.

9. B. A semicolon is incorrect here and turns the clause that follows it into a fragment. A comma should be used instead.

10. B. *Couldn't hardly* is incorrect; the correct expression is *could hardly.* The subjective pro-noun *we* **A** is correct; it is part of the sentence's compound subject. The verb forms in the sentence are also correct.

11. A. The correct idiom is *fired from,* not *fired off of.*

12. B. No comma should be used before the modifying phrase beginning with *that. Revolutionary* **A** is not capitalized because no particular revolutionary movement is identi-fied. *Well documented* **C** is correct, and *began* **D** is the correct past tense of the verb.

13. D. The correct word here is the verb *affect. Effect* is usually a noun: *the effect of the policy.* When it is a verb, it means "to bring about, to accomplish." *Us* **B** is correct here as the object of the preposition *of.* The comma between *community* and *but* correctly sepa-rates two independent clauses **A** and *attempted to* **C** is the correct idiom.

14. A. A common error is to use the conditional *would have* in an *if* clause. Instead, the past perfect should be used here: *If the head of the department had notified. Who* **B** is the cor-rect pronoun because it is the subject of a verb (*needed to*), and *him* **C** is the correct pro-noun because it is the object of the preposition *between.* The conditional *could have been saved* **D** is correct because it appears in the clause that states the consequences of the *if* clause.

15. C. *Unique* is a word that cannot be compared; it means "one of a kind" and therefore, it cannot be "very one of a kind."

16. C. This is an error in parallel structure. *To pack up their most important possessions, lock the windows and doors, and move* (not *to move*) corrects the problem. The initial *to* covers the three items in the series and shouldn't be dropped from the second item and then be repeated with the third item. The sentence could also be corrected by adding *to* to the sec-ond item in the series: *To pack up ... to lock ... and to move.*

17. C. *Went* is the past tense of *go,* and to be consistent with the other verbs (*had arrived* and [*had*] *taken*), [*had*] *gone* is required here.

18. B. The adverb *quickly* should be used here. It modifies the verb *finished.* No comma is needed at **C**; the clause beginning with *where* is restrictive, and restrictive clauses should not be set off with commas.

9. D. *Amount* refers to a bulk or mass. The correct word here is *number,* which refers to individual countable items. No comma is needed to set off the *who* clause, which is restrictive.

0. A. *Person* is a singular noun; therefore, the pronoun should be singular. *His* or *her* (or *his or her*) would be correct. Although a plural pronoun with an indefinite noun or pronoun (*someone, anyone, person,* etc.) is becoming more common, it is still not standard. **C** is correct; *staff* is a collective noun (like *group, team, choir,* etc.) and as such can take a singular verb.

21. A. *Present incumbent* is a redundant phrase. *Incumbent* refers to the person currently in office. The comma after *lots* **B** is a series comma and is correct. The antecedent of the pronoun *these* **C** is the series that precedes it.

22. C. This is an agreement problem. *It* is a singular pronoun, but the antecedent is plural: *home and family. Them* would be the correct pronoun. The comma after *family* **B** is correct; it divides two independent clauses. *Brother's* **D** is a possessive noun, and the apostrophe is properly placed.

23. C. The antecedent of the pronoun *they* is not clear here. Does *they* refer to the documents or to Mr. Weber and Mr. Lincoln? The sentence should be rewritten to avoid this possible confusion, or the word *documents* should be repeated instead of using the pronoun.

24. A. *Irregardless* is not a word; it is often mistakenly used for *regardless. Cited* **C** is the correct word in this context, and *city's* **D** is the correct possessive of *city.*

Part B

25. D. The comma after *protection* creates a run-on sentence, or comma splice. *For example* begins an independent clause. It has both a subject and a predicate and can stand alone. Therefore, it should be separated from the first clause by a period or a semicolon. Also, a comma should follow the introductory phrase *For example* (as it does in choice **D**).

26. B. The original sentence begins with a dangling modifier; it appears that the car received the estimate. Choice **B** corrects that problem. Choice **B** also uses the active voice of the verb (*I delivered*), which is preferable to the passive voice (*car was delivered*). The other choices either do not remedy the basic problem or are awkwardly constructed.

27. E. This choice corrects the problem of inconsistent tenses in the original sentence and is also the most concise version. It uses subordination well. The comma after *erupting* is correct.

28. E. The original sentence parallels schools in the inner city with the suburbs rather than with schools in the suburbs. It is also wordy (*are more in need of*). Choice **E** corrects both problems.

29. A. This sentence is correct as it is.

30. C. Although this choice is wordier than the others, it is the only one that corrects the faulty parallel structure. Choices **A, B,** and **E** are all examples of faulty parallelism, while choice **D** uses inconsistent tenses.

31. B. The semicolon after *operations* in the original sentence is incorrect and makes the opening clause a sentence fragment. The comma in choice **B** corrects the problem.

32. C. In the original sentence, the amusement park is the antecedent of the pronoun *it*, which suggests that the park must submit an environmental impact report. It is the owners of the park that must submit the report. Choice **E** corrects the problem but awkwardly uses the passive voice of the verb.

33. D. *Will continue to patrol* is a correct construction, but *have ... patrol* is not. *Patrolled* must be added to complete the verb in the first part of the predicate.

34. C. This choice corrects all the problems in the sentence. First, *in spite of the fact* and *despite the fact* are wordy; *although* is a better choice. Second, the possessive case of a noun is used with a gerund (which is a participle that functions as a noun): *child's screaming*, not *child screaming*. Third, the correct verb form is *had chosen*, not *had chose*.

35. A. The sentence is correct. The objective case of the pronouns (*him* and *me*) is used because they are the objects of the verb *invited*.

36. D. *Buying one in New Jersey* is parallel to *Buying a house in Florida*. The other choices are not parallel.

37. B. The correct verb is *lie*, not *lay*. *Laying* takes an object: *laying the book down*, *laying the carpet*, etc. *Lying* does not: *I lie down for a nap*, *I lie in the sun*, etc. Also, the comparative of *red* is *redder*, not *more red*.

38. B. The main problem with the sentence is that the subject and verb don't agree. The subject is plural (*concert* and *coverage*) and the verb is singular (*was*). Choice **B** corrects the problem and also eliminates unnecessary words.

39. E. Although the original sentence is grammatically correct, the verb is in the passive voice. The active voice of the verb is preferred. The use of *his* with the gerund *coming* is correct.

40. D. First, *group* is singular and takes a singular verb (*was*). Second, the correct idiom is *suspected of*, not *suspected with*. Third, the correct verb is *imply*, not *infer*. *Imply* means "to suggest something indirectly." *Infer* means "to conclude from facts or indications": *I imply that you are unwelcome, and you infer that I don't like you*.

41. C. The past participle of *run* is *had run*, not *had ran*. The noun *group* is singular, and the possessive is *group's*, not *groups'*. Commas should be used around *who had run for treasurer of the club*; it adds information to *man*.

42. B. This choice maintains parallelism but is less wordy than the original sentence. Also, the comma after *tools* in the original sentence and in choices **D** and **E** is incorrect.

43. D. This choice eliminates unnecessary words (*After the conclusion of* = *After*; *in order to* = *to*) and redundancies (*whole entire*; *cooperate together*).

44. A. This sentence is a series; the original version here is the best of the five—parallel, correctly punctuated with commas, and concise. The semicolons of **B** are incorrect; **C** has an extra "and." **D** and **E** break up the parallel construction.

1. Make sure that you are familiar with the testing center location and nearby parking facilities.

2. The last week of preparation should be spent on a general review of key concepts, test-taking strategies, and techniques.

3. Don't cram the night before the exam. It's a waste of time!

4. Arrive at the testing center in plenty of time.

5. Remember to bring the proper materials: identification, three or four sharpened Number 2 pencils, an eraser, and a watch.

6. Start off crisply, working the questions you know first and then coming back and trying to answer the others.

7. Try to eliminate one or more choices before you guess, but make sure you fill in all of the answers. There is no penalty for guessing.

8. Mark in reading passages, underline key words, write out important information, and make notations on diagrams. Take advantage of being permitted to write in the test booklet (scratch paper or a dry-erase board are provided to those taking the computer-based test).

9. Make sure that you are answering "what is being asked" and that your answer is reasonable.

10. Cross out incorrect choices immediately. This strategy will keep you from reconsidering a choice that you've already eliminated.

11. Using the "Taking the PPST: Two Successful Overall Approaches" (pages 7–10) is the key to getting the questions right that you should get right, resulting in a good score on the PPST.

Wiley Publishing, Inc.
End-User License Agreement

READ THIS. You should carefully read these terms and conditions before opening the softwa
packet(s) included with this book "Book". This is a license agreement "Agreement" between y
and Wiley Publishing, Inc. "WPI". By opening the accompanying software packet(s), you ackı
edge that you have read and accept the following terms and conditions. If you do not agree and
not want to be bound by such terms and conditions, promptly return the Book and the unopene
software packet(s) to the place you obtained them for a full refund.

1. **License Grant.** WPI grants to you (either an individual or entity) a nonexclusive license t
   one copy of the enclosed software program(s) (collectively, the "Software") solely for you
   own personal or business purposes on a single computer (whether a standard computer or
   workstation component of a multi-user network). The Software is in use on a computer wl
   it is loaded into temporary memory (RAM) or installed into permanent memory (hard disk
   CD-ROM, or other storage device). WPI reserves all rights not expressly granted herein.

2. **Ownership.** WPI is the owner of all right, title, and interest, including copyright, in and to
   the compilation of the Software recorded on the physical packet included with this Book
   "Software Media". Copyright to the individual programs recorded on the Software Media i
   owned by the author or other authorized copyright owner of each program. Ownership of tl
   Software and all proprietary rights relating thereto remain with WPI and its licensers.

3. **Restrictions on Use and Transfer.**

   (a) You may only (i) make one copy of the Software for backup or archival purposes, or (ii)
   transfer the Software to a single hard disk, provided that you keep the original for backu
   or archival purposes. You may not (i) rent or lease the Software, (ii) copy or reproduce th
   Software through a LAN or other network system or through any computer subscriber sy
   tem or bulletin-board system, or (iii) modify, adapt, or create derivative works based on t
   Software.

   (b) You may not reverse engineer, decompile, or disassemble the Software. You may transfer
   the Software and user documentation on a permanent basis, provided that the transferee
   agrees to accept the terms and conditions of this Agreement and you retain no copies. If
   Software is an update or has been updated, any transfer must include the most recent upd
   and all prior versions.

4. **Restrictions on Use of Individual Programs.** You must follow the individual requirement
   and restrictions detailed for each individual program on the Software Media. These limitati
   are also contained in the individual license agreements recorded on the Software Media. Th
   limitations may include a requirement that after using the program for a specified period of
   time, the user must pay a registration fee or discontinue use. By opening the Software
   packet(s), you agree to abide by the licenses and restrictions for these individual programs
   are detailed on the Software Media. None of the material on this Software Media or listed i
   this Book may ever be redistributed, in original or modified form, for commercial purposes

5. **Limited Warranty.**

   (a) WPI warrants that the Software and Software Media are free from defects in materials ar
   workmanship under normal use for a period of sixty (60) days from the date of purchase
   this Book. If WPI receives notification within the warranty period of defects in materials
   workmanship, WPI will replace the defective Software Media.

WPI AND THE AUTHOR(S) OF THE BOOK DISCLAIM ALL OTHER WARRANTIES, EXPRESS OR IMPLIED, INCLUDING WITHOUT LIMITATION IMPLIED WARRANTIES OF MERCHANTABILITY AND FITNESS FOR A PARTICULAR PURPOSE, WITH RESPECT TO THE SOFTWARE, THE PROGRAMS, THE SOURCE CODE CONTAINED THEREIN, AND/OR THE TECHNIQUES DESCRIBED IN THIS BOOK. WPI DOES NOT WARRANT THAT THE FUNCTIONS CONTAINED IN THE SOFTWARE WILL MEET YOUR REQUIREMENTS OR THAT THE OPERATION OF THE SOFTWARE WILL BE ERROR FREE.

This limited warranty gives you specific legal rights, and you may have other rights that vary from jurisdiction to jurisdiction.

Remedies.

- WPI's entire liability and your exclusive remedy for defects in materials and workmanship shall be limited to replacement of the Software Media, which may be returned to WPI with a copy of your receipt at the following address: Software Media Fulfillment Department, Attn.: CliffsNotes® Praxis I®: PPST® with CD-ROM, 4th Edition, Wiley Publishing, Inc., 10475 Crosspoint Blvd., Indianapolis, IN 46256, or call 1-877-762-2974. Please allow four to six weeks for delivery. This Limited Warranty is void if failure of the Software Media has resulted from accident, abuse, or misapplication. Any replacement Software Media will be warranted for the remainder of the original warranty period or thirty (30) days, whichever is longer.

- In no event shall WPI or the author be liable for any damages whatsoever (including without limitation damages for loss of business profits, business interruption, loss of business information, or any other pecuniary loss) arising from the use of or inability to use the Book or the Software, even if WPI has been advised of the possibility of such damages.

- Because some jurisdictions do not allow the exclusion or limitation of liability for consequential or incidental damages, the above limitation or exclusion may not apply to you.

U.S. Government Restricted Rights. Use, duplication, or disclosure of the Software for or on behalf of the United States of America, its agencies and/or instrumentalities "U.S. Government" is subject to restrictions as stated in paragraph (c)(1)(ii) of the Rights in Technical Data and Computer Software clause of DFARS 252.227-7013, or subparagraphs (c) (1) and (2) of the Commercial Computer Software - Restricted Rights clause at FAR 52.227-19, and in similar clauses in the NASA FAR supplement, as applicable.

General. This Agreement constitutes the entire understanding of the parties and revokes and supersedes all prior agreements, oral or written, between them and may not be modified or amended except in a writing signed by both parties hereto that specifically refers to this Agreement. This Agreement shall take precedence over any other documents that may be in conflict herewith. If any one or more provisions contained in this Agreement are held by any court or tribunal to be invalid, illegal, or otherwise unenforceable, each and every other provision shall remain in full force and effect.

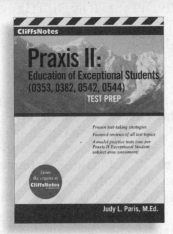
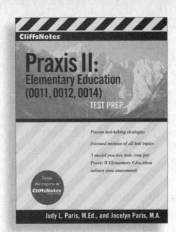

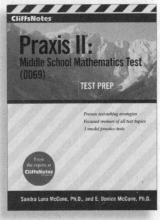

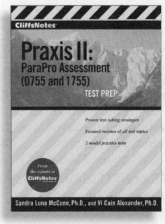